Contemporary Peacemaking

Contemporary Peacemaking

Conflict, Violence and Peace Processes

Edited by

John Darby
Professor of Comparative Ethnic Studies
University of Notre Dame

and

Roger Mac Ginty
Lecturer, Department of Politics
University of York

macmillan

Editorial matter and selection, Introduction and Conclusion © John Darby and
Roger Mac Ginty 2003
Chapter 20 © Roger Mac Ginty 2003
Chapter 21 © John Darby 2003
Remaining chapters © Palgrave Macmillan Ltd 2003

First published 2003 by
PALGRAVE MACMILLAN
Houndmills, Basingstoke, Hampshire RG21 6XS and
175 Fifth Avenue, New York, N.Y. 10010
Companies and representatives throughout the world

PALGRAVE MACMILLAN is the global academic imprint of the Palgrave
Macmillan division of St. Martin's Press, LLC and of Palgrave Macmillan Ltd.
Macmillan® is a registered trademark in the United States, United Kingdom
and other countries. Palgrave is a registered trademark in the European
Union and other countries.

ISBN 1–4039–0138–4 hardback
ISBN 0–4039–0139–2 paperback

This book is printed on paper suitable for recycling and made from fully
managed and sustained forest sources.

A catalogue record for this book is available from the British Library.

Library of Congress Cataloging-in-Publication Data

Contemporary Peacemaking: conflict, violence, and peace processes/edited by John
Darby, Roger Mac Ginty.
    p. cm.
Includes bibliographical references and index.
ISBN 1–4039–0138–4 (hardback: alk. paper) – ISBN 1–4039–0139–2 (pbk.: alk. paper)
    1. Pacific settlement of international disputes. 2. Peace. I. Darby, John (John P.)
II. Mac Ginty, Roger, 1970–

JZ6010.C665 2002
327.1'72–dc21   2002026760

10   9   8   7   6   5   4   3   2   1
12   11   10   09   08   07   06   05   04   03

Printed and bound in Great Britain by
Antony Rowe Ltd, Chippenham and Eastbourne

Contents

Notes on the Contributors

Cynthia J. Arnson is Deputy Director of the Latin American Program of the Woodrow Wilson International Center for Scholars. She is editor of *Comparative Peace Processes in Latin America*, author of *Crossroads: Congress, the President, and Central America, 1976–1993*.

Dinorah Azpuru is a PhD Candidate in Political Science at the University of Pittsburgh, USA. She has been Vice-Dean and Professor of the College of Political Science at University Rafael Landivar in Guatemala and has written extensively about democracy and peace in Central America. She is currently a political researcher at a Guatemalan research centre, ASIES.

Christine Bell is Professor of Public International Law at the University of Ulster. She is author of *Peace Agreements and Human Rights* and a member of the Northern Ireland Human Rights Commission.

Charles T. Call is Assistant Professor for Research at Brown University's Watson Institute for International Studies, and was a Guest Scholar at the US Institute of Peace in 2001–2. He has written on policing, human rights and post-conflict rule-of-law issues, most recently in *Comparative Politics, Global Governance* and *International Peacekeeping*.

John Darby is Professor of Comparative Ethnic Studies at the Kroc Institute in the University of Notre Dame, where he is Director of the Research Initiative on the Resolution of Ethnic Conflict. He was founding director of INCORE at the University of Ulster. His recent books include *The Management of Peace Processes* and *Guns and Government* (both with Roger Mac Ginty), and *The Effects of Violence on Peace Processes*.

Virginia Gamba is Director of Safer Africa. She specializes in global security issues with particular reference to arms management and disarmament, micro-development and security, civil–military integration and defence restructuring. She is the author of *Signals of War* (with L. Freedman), *Governing Arms, The Southern African Experience* and the UNIDIR collection on *The Management of Arms during Peace Processes*.

Yash Ghai is Professor of Law at the University of Hong Kong. He was Chair of the Constitution of Kenya Review Commission (2000–2) and is author of *Autonomy and Power: Negotiating Competing Claims in Multi-ethnic States* and *Hong Kong's New Constitutional Order: Resumption of Chinese Sovereignty and the Basic Law*.

Adrian Guelke is Professor of Comparative Politics and Director of the Centre for the Study of Ethnic Conflict at Queen's University, Belfast. His publications include *South Africa in Transition: the Misunderstood Miracle, The Age of Terrorism and the International Political System* and *Northern Ireland: the International Perspective*.

Brandon Hamber is an Associate of the Belfast-based think-tank, Democratic Dialogue, and an Honorary Fellow at the School of Psychology at the Queen's University in Belfast. He coordinated the Transition and Reconciliation Unit at the Centre for the Study of Violence and Reconciliation in South Africa. He edited *Past Imperfect: Dealing with the Past in Northern Ireland and Societies in Transition*.

John Paul Lederach is Professor of International Peacebuilding at the Joan B. Kroc Institute for International Peace Studies at the University of Notre Dame and a Distinguished Scholar at Eastern Mennonite University's Conflict Transformation Program. He works extensively as a practitioner in conciliation processes, active in Latin America, Africa and Central Asia.

John Loughlin is Professor of European Politics at Cardiff University. His recent publications include *Subnational Democracy in the European Union: Challenges and Opportunties, Autonomies Insulaires: vers une politique de différence pour la Corse* (edited with C. Olivesi) and *The Political Economy of Regionalism* (edited with M. Keating). In 2002, he will publish (with M. Keating and K. Deschouwer), *Culture, Institutions and Regional Development: a Comparative Analysis*.

Roger Mac Ginty is a Lecturer at the Postwar Reconstruction and Development Unit, Department of Politics, University of York. He is principal investigator of the Economic and Social Research Council's project 'Devolution and institutional change in Northern Ireland'. His recent publications include *The Management of Peace Processes* (2000) and *Guns and Government* (2002) (both with John Darby).

Christopher Mitchell currently holds the French-Cumbie Chair of Conflict Analysis at the Institute for Conflict Analysis and Resolution, George Mason University in Virginia. He is the author of the *Handbook of Conflict Resolution* and *Gestures of Conciliation* and has worked as a mediator and facilitator in Africa, Europe and the Middle East.

Ben Reilly is a Research Fellow in the National Centre for Development Studies at the Australian National University, Canberra. He was previously a Senior Programme Officer at the International Institute for Democracy and Electoral Assistance (IDEA) in Stockholm, Sweden. His books include *Democracy in Divided Societies: Electoral Engineering for Conflict Management, Electoral Systems and Conflict in Divided Societies, Democracy and Deep Rooted Conflict: Options for Negotiators* and *The International IDEA Handbook of Electoral System Design*.

Timothy D. Sisk is Associate Professor in the Graduate School of International Studies, University of Denver, where he also serves as faculty in the Master of Arts Program in Conflict Resolution. He is currently finishing a book titled *Beyond Bloody Sundays: Violence and Negotiation in Ethnic Conflict*. Sisk is the author of five books including *Democratization in South Africa* and *Power Sharing and International Mediation in Ethnic Conflicts*.

William Stanley teaches political science at the University of New Mexico and directs UNM's Latin American and Iberian Institute. He is author of *The Protection Racket State*. He has published widely on political violence and its prevention, particularly through reforms of judicial, police and military institutions.

Stephen John Stedman is Senior Research Scholar at the Center for International Security and Cooperation at Stanford University, where he teaches political science and directs the university's honors program in international security studies.

Pierre du Toit is Professor in the Department of Political Science at the University of Stellenbosch, South Africa. In 1992 he was awarded a Peace Fellowship from the Jennings Randolph Program for International Peace at the United States Institute of Peace in Washington. His latest book is *South Africa's Brittle Peace – the Problem of Post-Settlement Violence*.

Fernand de Varennes is a senior lecturer at the School of Law, Murdoch University, Perth, Australia. He was Director of the Asia-Pacific Centre for Human Rights and the Prevention of Ethnic Conflict.

Gadi Wolfsfeld holds a joint appointment in political science and communication at the Hebrew University of Jerusalem. His research deals with the role of the news media in political conflicts and peace processes. His most recent book was entitled *Media and Political Conflict: News from the Middle East*.

Crawford Young is Rupert Emerson and H. Edwin Young Professor of political science at the University of Wisconsin-Madison. His major books include *Politics in the Congo*, *The Politics of Cultural Pluralism*, *Ideology and Development in Africa*, *The Rise and Decline of the Zairian State* and *The African Colonial State in Comparative Perspective*. A former President of the African Studies Association, he is a fellow of the American Academy of Arts and Sciences.

Marie-Joëlle Zahar is an Assistant Professor of political science at the Université de Montreal. She specializes in the politics of non-state actors engaged in civil conflicts. She has published articles in *International Peacekeeping* and the *International Journal*, and has contributed chapters to several edited books on conflict resolution and peace implementation.

I. William Zartman is the Jacob Blaustein Professor of International Organizations and Conflict Resolution and Director of the Conflict Management Program at the Paul H. Nitze School of Advanced International Studies, Johns Hopkins University, Washington, DC. He has contributed to the development of the field of negotiation analysis, editing and coauthoring *Power and Negotiation* (with Jeffrey Z Rubin), *Peacemaking in International Conflict: Methods and Techniques* (with Lewis Rasmussen), *Preventive Negotiation: Avoiding Conflict Escalation, Elusive Peace: Negotiating an End to Civil War* and *Ripe for Resolution*.

Acknowledgements

The editors acknowledge with gratitude the research funding provided by the United Nations University, UNESCO's Culture of Peace Programme, the European Union and the Northern Ireland Community Relations Unit. During the period when this book was conceived and completed, John Darby was based at the Joan B. Kroc Institute for International Peace Studies at Notre Dame University, and is grateful for the interest and support of its director Scott Appleby, as well as Tristan Borer, Siobhan McEvoy-Levy, Raimo Väyrynen, Robert Johansen and other colleagues. Roger Mac Ginty is grateful to colleagues at the Postwar Reconstruction and Development Unit and the Department of Politics at the University of York, particularly Sultan Barakat, Mark Evans and Anna O'Connell. The authors are also grateful for administrative support from the Ethnic Studies Network, principally through Gillian Robinson and Lyn Moffett, in hosting a conference when early drafts of the chapters were delivered. We would like to acknowledge Alison Howson from Palgrave Macmillan. Our main thanks, of course, are due to the contributing authors.

List of Abbreviations

AG	Administrator-General
ANC	African National Congress
ARENA	National Republican Alliance
BiH	Bosnia-Hercegovina
BMATT	British Military Assistance Training Team
CDG	Chicken dilemma game
CEH	Historical Clarification Committee
CIVPOL	United Nations Civilian Police
CMF	Commonwealth Monitoring Force
CNRT	National Council for Timorese Resistance
CODESA	Congress for a Democratic South Africa
COPAZ	National Commission for the Consolidation of Peace
DPA	Dayton Peace Agreement
DTA	Democratic Turnhalle Alliance
DUP	Democratic Unionist Party
EC	European Community
ECOMOG	Economic Community of West African States Monitoring Group
ECOWAS	Economic Community of West African States
ETA	Euskadi ta Askatasuna/Basque Homeland and Freedom
EU	European Union
FLNC	Front de Libération Nationale de la Corse
FMLN	Farabundo Marti National Liberation Front
FRELIMO	Front for the Liberation of Mozambique
FRG	Guatemalan Republican Front
FUNCINPEC	Front for a Independent, Neutral, Peaceful and Cooperative Cambodia
GCE	Spanish Civil Guard
HB	Herri Batasuna
ICJ	International Court of Justice
IEC	Independent Electoral Commission
IFOR	Implementation Force
IFP	Inkatha Freedom Party
IRA	Irish Republican Army
KLA	Kosovo Liberation Army
LAPD	Los Angeles Police Department
LTTE	Liberation Tigers of Tamil Eelam
MEO	Mutually enticing opportunities
MHS	Mutually hurting stalemate
MINUGUA	United Nations Verification Mission in Guatemala
MONUA	United Nations Observer Mission in Angola

MPLA	Popular Movement for the Liberation of Angola
MPNP	Multi Party Negotiating Process
NATO	North Atlantic Treaty Organization
NCA	Norwegian Church Aid
NP	National Party
NYPD	New York Police Department
OAS	Organization of American States
OAU	Organization of African Unity
ONUCA	United Nations Observer Group in Central America
ONUMOZ	United Nations Operation in Mozambique
ONUSAL	United Nations Mission in El Salvador
OSCE	Organization for Security and Cooperation in Europe
PDG	Prisoners' dilemma game
PLO	Palestine Liberation Organization
PMA	Ambulatory Military Police
PNC	National Civilian Police
PNV	Partido Nacionalista Vasco
REMHI	Recovery of Historical Memory
RENAMO	Mozambique National Resistance
RUC	Royal Ulster Constabulary
RUF	Revolutionary United Front
SAG	South African government
SDLP	Social Democratic and Labour Party
SFOR	Stabilization Force
SOC	State of Cambodia
SWAPO	South West African Peoples' Party
TEC	Transitional Executive Council
TRC	Truth and Recovery Commission
UDA	Ulster Defence Association
UKUP	United Kingdom Unionist Party
UNAMSIL	United Nations Observer Mission in Sierra Leone
UNAVEM II	United Nations Angola Verification Mission II
UNDP	United Nations Development Programme
UNDPKO	United Nations Department of Peacekeeping Operations
UNITA	National Union for Total Independence of Angola
UNMIK	United Nations Interim Administration in Kosovo
UNOMIL	United Nations Observer Mission in Liberia
UNOSOM	United Nations Operation in Somalia
UNPROFOR	United Nations Protection Force
UNTAG	United Nations Transition Assistance Group
UNTAET	United Nations Transitional Administration in East Timor
URNG	Guatemalan National Revolutionary Unit
WCG	Western Contact Group

Introduction: What Peace? What Process?

John Darby and Roger Mac Ginty

While the years after the Cold War have been marked by an upsurge in so-called 'new wars' and shocking cases of mass and individual brutality, there have also been a significant number of conflict terminations.[1] Indeed, memorable scenes from the post-Cold War period include Nelson Mandela's inauguration as President of post-apartheid South Africa, the Rabin–Arafat handshake on the White House lawn, Slobadan Milošović in the dock for war crimes, and queues of patient voters waiting to exercise their franchise in East Timor and Kosovo. Wallensteen and Sollenberg record that 56 civil wars came to an end in the 1989–2000 period.[2] To a certain extent the high number of conflict terminations is merely a function of the high number of conflicts and the inability of antagonists to sustain their violent campaigns over extended time periods. Yet, such a mass of conflict settlements also presents a corpus of evidence and case studies from which to draw conclusions on how violent conflicts come to an end. Conclusions can also be drawn on the quality and longevity of any peace, and the possibility of transferring lessons from one peace process to another.

This volume seeks to explore and identify the essential components of contemporary peace processes. It deliberately steps back from the tradition of studies of a single peace process or peace initiatives in a particular region and instead adopts a thematic approach. The aim is to focus on key themes and stages in peace processes. The book is organized around five time phases in peace processes: preparing for peace, negotiations, violence, peace accords and peacebuilding. While it is hoped that all of the major aspects of peace processes can be encompassed within this framework, it is recognized that there is no such thing as a typical peace process that follows a linear progression from the first pre-negotiation soundings to the institutionalization of a post-peace accord political dispensation. Certain components of a peace process defy neat categorization or inclusion in particular phases of the process. The dismantling of a peace process into five themes or time phases aids conceptualization. The reality of peace processes is often a stop–start dynamic and a complex choreography whereby the sequencing of initiatives or concessions is timed to suit local circumstances.

In keeping with the five main themes or stages of peace processes, the book is divided into five sections. Each section contains chapters with a specific focus relevant to the theme or stage of the peace process. For example, the section on negotiations contains a chapter on the rules and procedures of peace negotiations and a chapter on the role of mediation in ending conflict. The book is deliberately comparative, drawing on a wide range of contemporary cases with the aim of illuminating the generalities and specifics of peace processes. The result is a 'state of the art' survey of contemporary peacemaking.

Peace processes are taken to mean persistent peace initiatives involving the main antagonists in a protracted conflict. They are likely to be more significant than an isolated peace initiative. Instead a peace process will have certain robust and systemic qualities enabling it to withstand some of the pressures hurled against it, and to develop beyond initial statements of intent made by the main actors. The extensive set of variables involved in peace processes greatly complicates the task of definition. Peace initiatives can be formal or informal, public or private, subject to popular endorsement or restricted to elite-level agreement. They can be sponsored by the United Nations or other external parties, or can spring from internal sources. All peace processes are fragile, and most fail sooner rather than later. The task of the implementation of any accord is highly dependent on the political will of the parties and on the international political and economic context.

We suggested in 2000 that five essential criteria are required for a successful peace accord: that the protagonists are willing to negotiate in good faith; that the key actors are included in the process; that the negotiations address the central issues in dispute; that force is not used to achieve objectives; and that the negotiators are committed to a sustained process. We continued:

> Outside these general principles, peace processes follow greatly varied directions. Pre-negotiation contacts may be used to test the ground, and may involve external or internal mediators. The official process usually begins with a public announcement and often with a ceasefire. Once started, the rules and sequence of negotiation are determined by negotiators who, by definition, have little experience of negotiation. It is not essential to start with a defined constitutional or political outcome for the process, but a peace process cannot be regarded as completed unless a political and constitutional framework has been agreed. Even if it is, the detailed implementation presents other opportunities for failure. Throughout, the process is likely to run into periods, sometimes extensive, of stalemate. The ultimate test of its durability is its ability to retain all of its key characteristics and to leave open the possibility of restoring momentum.[3]

As noted, many academic studies have concentrated on single cases, with the Oslo process between Israel and some Palestinian groups and the Northern Ireland peace process producing a particularly high volume of research and commentary. The transition to democracy in South Africa also received much attention in the peace process literature. Other peace initiatives, for example in Mindanao, Guinea-Bissau or Sudan received considerably less attention. As the 1990s progressed, comparative studies began to capitalize on the simultaneous existence of a number of peace processes. Studies of peace processes also became more sophisticated, mirroring the broadening of peace processes beyond security and constitutional issues to include social, cultural and economic concerns.

Subfields of specialist academic interest grew around the issue of spoiler groups in peace processes, truth recovery and attempts to deal with the past, and 'DDR' or demobilization, disarmament and reintegration. Other issues received relatively scant attention. For example, the differing impacts of peace processes on men and women are under-researched as are the long-term economic effects of peace initiatives. Most studies of peace processes though, took place within a framework of liberal optimism, informed by the view that peace processes were generally 'good things'. It is difficult to argue against such a view, particularly given the enormous potential of peace initiatives to arrest long-running conflicts and create frameworks in which antagonists can develop mechanisms to manage violent relationships.

Critiques of peace processes

Peace process critics may have a vested interest in the perpetuation of the conflict and may fear that a particular peace initiative will involve unsustainable costs for their position. Such critics are often brushed aside as being partisan, antediluvian wreckers of the peace for whom no option, other than total victory, would be acceptable. More fundamental criticisms lie in the fact that many contemporary peace processes fail to address the underlying causes of conflicts. Instead, they concentrate on the manifestations of conflicts and often deflect attention away from the real business of peacemaking. There is a danger that the protracted conflict gives way to the protracted peace process in which the original causes of the conflict persist and are joined by new grievances sparked by the peace process.

The sheer volume of activity associated with many peace processes may distort the true impact of any initiative, and give an overly optimistic view of progress. Political negotiations, resettlement programmes, donor's conferences, prisoner releases, security sector reform, truth recovery processes and democracy training will doubtless attract much attention. Indeed, each has the capacity to result in real and positive change. Yet despite micro-level changes, it is perfectly possible for the macro-level dynamics of the conflict to survive largely unchanged. For example, enormous effort may be invested in the establishment of an inclusive legal code or in reform of the judiciary. Yet such efforts can do little, in the short term at least, to counter ingrained perceptions that the law operates for one community and against another. Nor can the institution of a new political dispensation do much to alter patterns of land-ownership, trade and consumption, which may play a major role in the conflict.

Furthermore, contemporary peace processes have a strong tendency to entrench both the participants in the conflict and the conflict itself. In the case of the participants, a peace process risks reinforcing key actors in the roles they adopted during the conflict. Those who held the guns or the dominant position on the battlefield when a ceasefire was called become negotiating partners regardless of their ability to represent their community. Other voices, often those without firepower, tend to go unheard. This might help explain why many peace processes are overwhelmingly male. An entrenched peace process might serve to arrest the transition of protagonists to pragmatists rather than encourage the broadening of political representation.

At a wider level, the entrenchment of the entire process may see a peace process adopt semi-permanent forms without holding the capacity to deal with the true causes of the conflict. This is not to deny the potential benefits that accrue from a peace process reaching a developed stage. Instead it notes the danger of the peace process losing any momentum to effect genuine change. In a sense, the peace process may become a forum for conflict by other means. Mutually exclusive politico-religious blocs in Northern Ireland, Israel–Palestine and elsewhere have been able to retain their exclusive political perspectives notwithstanding the operation of a peace process. Indeed, in certain cases, peace processes have become so ingrained that they provide useful avenues for conflict protagonists to stall, prevaricate and deflect attention away from genuine peace initiatives. Under such circumstances, peace processes, once institutionalized, stymie opportunities for real political change, and instead channel energies in preordained directions that often reflect international rather than local opinion.

Some peace processes are largely creatures of the international community. They reflect the desired outcome of key states in the international community rather than the wishes of local communities. Bosnia-Hercegovina is a case in point. In many ways it is the product of planning in Western capitals rather than the result of local decisions. It is an artificial construct that leaves few of its inhabitants happy and risks storing up ethno-national tensions for the future. But, for the international community, the Bosnian 'solution' holds a number of advantages. Foremost among these is the impression that 'something has been done' about Bosnia. While an agreement may have been reached, a settlement remains far off.

Interventions by the international community have also been criticized as self-serving. Some peace processes have become the vehicles through which a number of regional organizations have jockeyed for position in the post-Cold War period of readjustment. The practice of international intervention – regardless of rhetoric and original motive – is invariably perceived as one-sided. The result is that the impartiality of subsequent interventions in the same conflict or region is seriously undermined. While NATO's actions against Serb forces in Kosovo and Serbia in 1999 can be explained by military and humanitarian expediency, their long-term political impact is manifest in strained relations with a sullen and resentful Serb population.

Serious problems arise from the lack of connection between peace processes driven by the international community and local interests that have little appetite for reconciliation. This is sometimes evidenced by the creation of an artificial civil society supported by the international community but has shallow roots at the local level.[4] Often the primary linkage between the nascent civil society and the international community is funding, rather than a shared philosophy of civic pluralism. Perceived international interference in civil society risks tainting the very notions of civil society and citizenship, and the persistence of ethnic voting patterns and allegiances (encouraged by the debates and choices structured by the peace process) provides a true indicator of the salience of partisan politics.

Despite the enormous sums invested by the international community, the protracted peace processes of the 1990s have failed to tackle many of the developmental problems that lie at the heart of many deeply divided societies. Issues such as rural unemployment, the need for the retraining of former combatants, and the need to staunch the brain drain constitute real threats to the peace. For the international community though, the chief aim is often to reconnect the conflict area with the global economy. Neo-liberal economic principles are the norm. The result is that the market economy is often strengthened, but long-term sustainable development is compromised. Although the former conflict area may be the recipient of large-scale aid, much of this reinforces its position as a consuming rather than a producing society. This failure to meet the economic needs of post-war populations is linked to a further problem associated with peace processes: their failure to fulfil public expectations. Local parties, and the international community, will often 'sell' a peace process or accord in terms of its economic benefits and positive potential in terms of standards of living. Yet there are few quick fixes, and local populations may quickly become disillusioned if they fail to see tangible benefits from the peace process. Indeed, local level reconciliation often relies on humdrum functional interaction between divided communities. It is the buying and selling of agricultural supplies, rather than the hubris of signing ceremonies in the corridors of power that will make or break a peace process. Without economic development, the opportunities for local interchange are limited and suspicion and distrust are likely to continue.

In short, contemporary peace processes run the risk of freezing conflicts into a negative peace that may minister to the manifestations of the conflict, but bypass the underlying causes. A situation of permanent impermanence may arise in which the peace process becomes protracted and produces a new set of grievances.

The continued need for peace processes

Despite the possible pitfalls, the promise held out by peace processes is enormous. There is a chance that a successful peace process will create the political space to enable the antagonists to enter into a serious dialogue that will address the underlying causes of the conflict. Moreover, the potential benefits stemming from the *process* of making peace are not to be underestimated. A peace process holds out the prospect of reducing the costs of an ongoing conflict, whether the costs are measured in terms of human lives, quality of life opportunities, or squandered economic potential. It is in the realm of humanitarian benefits that peace processes can have most impact. Seemingly prosaic details such as fewer checkpoints or easier access to markets and schools constitute the real peace dividend.

The need for peace processes remains strong. September 11 and the subsequent 'war on terror' are likely to be exceptions to the complex political emergencies that will dominate the first decades of the twenty-first century. Instead a series of familiar problems are likely to persist and will require serious inquiry:

- how to satisfy demands for, and resistance to, autonomy and separation;
- how to accommodate the needs of minorities, and the insecurities of the majorities, in deeply divided societies;

- how to identify, or cultivate, moments in which political rather than military initiatives might be fruitful;
- how to deal with violence deliberately targeted at derailing peace initiatives;
- how to deal with former combatants and their weapons;
- how to reconcile a society with its fraught past;
- how to realize a peace dividend in terms of jobs, housing and sustainable development.

Notes

1. The term 'new wars' is closely associated with Mary Kaldor. See her *New and Old Wars: Organized Violence in a Global Era* (Cambridge: Polity, 1999).
2. They note that 22 conflicts were ended by peace agreement and 34 by ceasefire or other methods. M. Sollenberg & P. Wallensteen, 'Armed Conflict 1989–2000', *Journal of Peace Research*, 38, 5 (November 2001), 629–44.
3. J. Darby & R. Mac Ginty, *The Management of Peace Processes* (London: Macmillan – now Palgrave Macmillan, 2000), p. 8.
4. Although not the result of a peace process, the *New York Times* reported that Afghanistan's caretaker Prime Minister, Hamid Karzai, was 'sustained entirely by his charisma and western cash' (26 March 2002).

Part I

Preparing for Peace

Peace processes do not emerge from a vacuum. They require conscious decisions, initial steps, fresh analyses and risk taking. Altered local and international circumstances, both contrived and fortuitous, can also play a role. What seems essential from the outset is a clear conflict analysis in which the causes, manifestations and costs of the conflict can be reviewed. The immediacy of violence and recrimination means that this is not always possible. The tendency of 'ethnic conflict' to adopt peculiar dynamics and forms of violence that demand tailored responses further complicates matters. But ethnic conflicts are not ancient, tribal or biologically determined. They are usually driven by modern, rational causes and their management requires equally modern, rational approaches.

Preparations for a peace process are necessarily delicate and often proceed against a backdrop of continuing violence and instability. Often it is easier to continue the conflict than to investigate the possibilities of peace and the accompanying accusations of treachery. Those moments that bear the possibility for positive engagement with antagonists are often fleeting and require 'cultivation'. Events beyond the control of any of the immediate participants in the conflict often have a decisive influence in tipping a conflict towards a more or less violent trajectory. System level change, in the form of changing economic, ideological or strategic fortunes, can have a major impact in creating the conditions whereby a sustainable peace process can develop.

Ultimately, the pre-negotiation phase of a peace process requires faith. It is nothing less than a high-risk gamble to ascertain the seriousness of other conflict participants. The chances of collapse in the early stages are high and are increased by the distrust, secrecy and involvement of third parties that characterize initial exchanges. Parties may offer or demand signals of good faith. Termed 'confidence-building measures', these vary from public statements of intent, to the release of prisoners or ceasefires. The aim of the initial phase of a peace process is to create the environment in which serious inter-party negotiations can start.

1
Explaining the Conflict Potential of Ethnicity

Crawford Young

Characteristics of ethnicity

Ethnicity, as collective phenomenon and form of identity, has in the contemporary world a singular capacity for social mobilization. Although it is not inherently conflictual, ethnicity has psychological properties and discursive resources which have the potential to decant into violence. No other form of social identity, in the early twenty-first century, has a comparable power, save for the closely related forms of collective affiliation, race and religion. Social class, however significant a political vector, lacks in most settings the clarity of boundaries, the primordial dimensions and affective resonance evident in ethnicity. Other forms of social categorization, such as occupation, gender, political affiliation, or the many other kinds one might list, although frequently a basis for competition and conflict, fall far short of the potential volatility of ethnic consciousness. The task of this chapter is to unravel the distinctive properties of ethnicity which explain this phenomenon.

Instances of conflict pitting human groups bearing different ethnonyms extend far back into the mists of the past in all parts of the world. Indeed, some authors assert that a prehistoric competence in recognizing and utilizing group solidarity was a key to survival in the early years of the species, embedding a genetic propensity to within-group kin-like altruism, and distrust tinged with fear towards the out-group 'other'.[1] Others trace 'ethnie' as a state-forming force back more than two millennia.[2] But the scale and salience of ethnic conflict have increased in recent decades. There is surely significance in the recent origins of the term 'ethnicity', which the linguistic custodians of the *Oxford English Dictionary* had yet to uncover in the 1933 edition, acknowledging its currency only in the 1972 supplement.[3]

Equally significant is the contemporary coinage (1944) of the term 'genocide', a word precipitated by the Holocaust. In its original usage, configured by the Nazi effort to exterminate Jews (and Roma), genocide meant the deliberate policy of a state to liquidate an entire people. By extension, genocide has come to include lethal assaults by one people upon another, with an intention of their physical elimination. Emblematic of the political force of ethnicity is the frequency of genocidal events and allegations in the 1990s: Bosnia, Rwanda, Burundi, Kosovo.

Once given lexical recognition, ethnicity has been defined in diverse ways, usually in terms of some of its attributes: mythical kinship, ancestry, language, shared values, common culture and the like. I prefer conceptualizing ethnicity in terms of three prime components. Firstly, ethnos is rooted in a variable array of shared properties. Language is often a core element, but not always (Hutu and Tutsi in Rwanda and Burundi share the same language; Serbian and Croatian are mainly distinguished by the script). The metaphor of fictive kinship is usually present, joined to a mythology of shared ancestry. Common cultural practices and symbols help define group identity. Sometimes the group is defined by a particular economic or social niche.

Equally important are the other two attributes. The shared culture becomes a visible ingredient in identity when it is joined to active collective consciousness. This in turn is contingent upon 'the other'. A group achieves consciousness not only in terms of the culture they share, but whom they are not. The boundary which demarcates 'we' and 'they' is critical in giving social meaning to the collective self.[4]

Ethnicity and nationalism

Grasping the conflict potential of ethnicity requires exploring its relationship to nationalism. Whether one traces its origin to sixteenth-century England (for example, Greenfeld) or the French Revolution (for example, Hobsbawm), nationalism is a distinctly modern ideology which links an assertion of collective identity, initially ethnic, to a particular set of political claims.[5] The nation achieves fulfilment through possession of its own state. This vocation rests upon two master precepts: popular sovereignty, and the doctrine of self-determination. The former locates the ultimate source of legitimation not in the institutions of rule, much less in a monarch, but in the citizenry collectivized as a 'people'. The latter asserts a right of a 'people', originally understood as an ethnic collectivity, to have their own state, or at least autonomous self-rule.

Nationalism as an ideology also elevates the mythologies associated with ethnicity to new levels of intensity. By joining the intrinsic solidarities of ethnicity to the institutional resources of a state, nationalism ratchets up the stakes of potential conflict any number of notches. Nationalism, runs the epigram, is ethnicity with an army and a navy. The most aggressive forms of nationalism, in the contemporary world, are those with an explicit ethnic content: ethnonationalism, a term given currency by Walker Connor.[6]

We need at once to underline that nationalism and ethnicity are not identical terms. The most crucial distinction between ethnicity and nationalism lies in the nature of the political claims advanced. Of the thousands of ethnic groups in the world, only a modest minority assert a demand for full sovereignty. There is, of course, always the possibility that ethnic consciousness may mutate into ethnonationalism, but there is no inevitable progression.

Conversely, not all nationalism is ethnic; it can be grounded in shared political values (civic nationalism), a given territory or a shared history of colonial oppression. However, the sharpness of the distinction between civic and ethnic nationalism drawn by some authors (for example, Greenfeld) has been subject to effective critique.[7] Even in the swathe of countries from the Atlantic to the Pacific, in Europe, the northern part of the Eurasian land mass, and parts of South-East Asia where the dominant ethnic group gives its name to the state, there is a discernible spectrum in the degree to which the discourse of nationalism is exclusively ethnic, or reflects shared political values (the republican virtues of liberty, equality and fraternity of the French Revolution, or the 'constitutional patriotism' of post-war Germany). Western hemisphere nationalisms originated in a territorialized rendition of the Creole or settler independence elites needing to demarcate their identity from that of the former colonial ruler.[8] Most African and Asian nationalisms imagined a community from culturally diverse populations whose shared historical experience was colonial oppression. To transform from ideology of anti-colonial revolt into doctrine of post-colonial state legitimation, such a nationalism was compelled to assert an exclusively territorial referent, and deny any ethnic attachments.

Thus ethnicity and nationalism are overlapping but distinct terms. But their area of intersection as well as the zones of differentiation assume in the nineteenth and especially the twentieth centuries a new importance for some other reasons. Here we need to note the marriage through hyphenation of state and nation. The great imperial multinational states (Austro-Hungarian, Ottoman and most recently the Soviet) shattered before the force of ethnonationalism in the wake of lost wars, hot or cold, and the overseas empires dissolved under the impact of anti-colonial nationalism and a newly hostile international environment. In the wake of this epic transformation of the world state system, the ideology of nationalism, however defined, silently permeated reason of state.[9] The imperative of legitimation compelled states to represent themselves at least as nations in formation, and to deploy the considerable didactic capacities of the state to 'nation-building'.

The nationalizing of the state posed the issue of inclusion with a novel intensity. In the substantial number of states where a 'titular nation' named the country, cultural communities who fell outside the reach of this dominant identity became 'national minorities', a category whose juridical personality first achieved international recognition after the First World War. Even when 'nation' was a more political or territorial idea than ethnic, patterns of exclusion were frequent (indigenous or African diaspora peoples in Western hemisphere states).

Further intensifying the conflict potential of cultural pluralism was the vast expansion in the role of the twentieth-century state. The fraction of total resources subject to allocation through the public domain rose sharply, through the emergence of the Welfare State, costly technological innovations in the military field and the enlargement of the administrative reach of the state. Despite the modest retrenchments associated with the rise of market liberalism in the 1980s, the group stakes in access to and control of state power are immensely greater than in previous centuries.

This leads to two basic premises regarding the contemporary political landscape. Firstly, the politics of cultural pluralism are framed by the state system. Conflict and competition between ethnic groups, virtually without exception, occur within the political arena enclosed by the territorial boundaries of a nation-state. Secondly, the overwhelming majority of the nearly 200 nation-state entities, defined by United Nations membership, are culturally plural. Even with an only moderately rigorous definition of homogeneity, one is hard pressed to identify more than a dozen countries devoid of cultural plurality.

The variable conflict potential of ethnicity

With the context of ethnicity thus described, we may now return to explaining its conflict potential. Critical to an understanding of its mobilizational force is a recognition that ethnicity is highly variable along two dimensions. Firstly, at a group level, ethnicity is not constantly activated. In any given social space there is likely to be some multiplicity of ethnic groups; most of the time, even though some consciousness of difference is present, interaction is civil and ethnicity quiescent. Social capital may accumulate primarily within groups, but everyday transactions involve no discernible tension.

The texture of group relationships varies widely. In some settings, such as that of the Swedish minority in Finland, cultural rights are well assured, political tensions are minimal and intermarriage frequent. In others, a long-standing pattern of everyday frictions, and endemic political competition, keep ethnicity foregrounded, as in the relationships between Flemings and Walloons in Belgium. In still others, an ineradicable memory of conquest and subordination continuously reinscribes difference in social and political life, as with francophone Quebec or Chechens in the Russian Federation. In yet other instances, the stigmatization and marginalization by dominant components of society force consciousness into a ghetto escapable only through identity denial or assertion (Ainu in Japan, Roma in Europe). Territorially concentrated groups, which have the possibility of a self-determination claim, are differently positioned from those who are geographically dispersed. The ethnic consciousness of those who have voluntarily migrated differs fundamentally from that of national minorities with a strong sense of territorial attachment and linguistic distinctiveness; these contrasts give rise to very different ethnic claims,[10] and makes intergenerational dilution a possible, even likely outcome. These enduring patternings of group relationships all shape the intensity of ethnicity.

Secondly, one must recollect that ultimately ethnicity is experienced and performed at an individual level. Here as well the range of possible variation is very wide. The daily life of a given individual may have a low level of interactions defined by ethnic content; equally variable is the degree to which the 'other' is encountered in situations evoking threat or antagonism. Ethnic consciousness is reinforced or attenuated by the frequency of identity performance, through participation in rituals or routines defined by ethnicity (a rite of passage, a religious ceremony, even a meal). The individual member of the Arab minority in Israel finds identity constantly imposed by the manifold differences in citizenship status, and the ebb and flow of confrontation and crisis between Israel, the nascent state of Palestine and the Arab world more broadly. It is frequently performed in diverse protest actions. However, ethnic Americans of European ancestry, as Mary Waters[11] engagingly shows, find ethnicity an option, to be ignored or employed dependent on context and situation; for many, ethnicity is a very weakly held identity, further attenuated for many by multiple ancestries. Where large numbers of ethnic subjects hold only a feeble level of communal consciousness, and participate only sporadically or not at all in rituals of identity, the mobilization potential of ethnicity is far less than for a group such as Palestinian Arabs in Israel or Palestine.

Analytical approaches to ethnicity

In recent years, ethnicity has frequently been analysed in terms of three dimensions: the primordial, the instrumental and the constructivist.[12] These three faces of cultural pluralism can provide a useful framework for illuminating the aspects of ethnicity which explain its exceptional potential for conflictual mobilization. The three are distinguishable only analytically; in real world social action they are interwoven.

The primordial dimension of ethnicity calls attention to its affective properties. For those whose ethnic moorings are robust, the consciousness of cultural identity is deeply embedded in the constitution of the self. The solitary individual bereft of anchorings in some web of cultural affinity and solidarity is unusual. Although ethnicity is not the only available such relationship, it enjoys an unusually broad array of discursive resources in framing identity: name, language, narratives of shared ancestry, cultural practices, common symbols. There is force to the primordialist arguments of Harold Isaacs that ethnic identity serves basic human needs for a safe place of ultimate belonging.[13]

The social psychology of identity provides important clues to the puzzle of the social force of ethnicity.[14] The child acquires early from the socializing influence of family, school and play group a cognitive capacity to recognize difference and to derive expectations of nurture from 'we' or danger from 'they'.[15] The perceptual representation of the ethnic 'we' is normally laden with positive symbols, and not infrequently with some sense of past harm rendered by some ethnic other. Ethnicity beyond the boundary of the collective self is often subject to negative stereotyping; the universal phenomenon of the ethnic joke could not subsist but for the widely shared attribution of particular characteristics to ethnic populations, usually at least mildly pejorative. The negative stereotype quickly mutates into apprehensions of hostile behaviour on the part of the ethnic other. Fear is a singularly powerful emotional field. Its nature and impact are well captured by the words of a Northern Nigerian delegate to constitutional talks on the eve of the Nigerian civil war:

> We all have our fears of one another. Some fear that the opportunities in their own areas are limited and they would therefore wish to expand and venture unhampered in other parts. Some fear the sheer weight of numbers of other parts which they feel could be used to the detriment of their own interests. Some fear the sheer weight of skills and the aggressive drive of other groups which

they feel has to be regulated if they are not to be left as the economic, social, and possibly political, under-dogs in their own areas of origin in the very near future. These fears may be real or imagined; they may be reasonable or petty. Whether they are genuine or not, they have to be taken account of because they influence to a considerable degree the actions of the groups towards one another and, more important perhaps, the daily actions of the individual in each group towards individuals from other groups.[16]

The emotive properties of ethnicity and the cognitive frames it provides lend themselves to the historicization of the collective self. Ethnicity frequently invokes the language and symbols of kinship.[17] By historical legerdemain, imagined kinship becomes shared ancestry. Identity in the process acquires a potent narrative.

The instrumental dimension of ethnicity captures its utilization as a weapon in social competition.[18] The ethnic politician is a familiar figure in contemporary politics, using the group as a vote bank in electoral competition. Particularly in urban settings, the social competition for scarce resources – employment, housing – readily translates into ethnic mobilization. Nigerian popular imagery expresses metaphorically the instrumental aspect of ethnicity; politics, runs the aphorism, is about cutting the national cake. The resources of the country, in this colourful portrait, are sweet to the taste, and divisible into slices. The relative size of the servings will be visible to all; elementary justice requires equal slices, but the ethnic partisanship of the power-holder who holds the knife makes likely unequal portions.

The instrumental use of ethnicity has feedback consequences. The more ethnic mobilization is deployed as a political weapon, the more the ethnic other is compelled to respond by counter-mobilization. This readily decants into a cycle of out-bidding, which deepens the politicization of identity and sharpens antagonisms, a possible dynamic identified long ago by Rabushka and Shepsle, armed with rational choice theory.[19] In turn, its repeated instrumental use tends to inscribe it more deeply in the popular consciousness.

Practitioners of rational choice theory such as Russell Hardin also persuasively argue that the prior existence of group consciousness means that 'self-interest can often successfully be matched with group interest'.[20] As well, mobilized ethnicity provides its leaders with effective resources for both summoning and enforcing solidarity. The large flow of funds from the Tamil diaspora to the insurgent 'Tigers' in Sri Lanka is assured not only by the dictates of ethnic solidarity, but by the capacity of Tiger representatives abroad to identify, monitor and discipline reluctant diasporic Tamils.

Finally, a full grasp of ethnicity requires attention to the processes by which identity is socially constructed. Ultimately all forms of identity are social constructs, products of human creativity. Examination of the dynamics of ethnogenesis in any given group illuminates the nature of the discursive resources of the group. Crucial is the role of cultural entrepreneurs who codify and standardize a language, equipping it with a written form, create an ethnos-centred historical narrative, populated with internal heroes and external villains, and build a literary tradition.

The constructivist focus reveals the uneven degree of mobilization potential among ethnic communities. Some have only a weak ideology of the collective self; absent such discursive capacity, activation is much more difficult. An extensively elaborated theorization of the group as speakers of a prestigious language, holders of a deep and heroic historical legend, and possessors of a rich cultural tradition constitutes ethnicity ripe for mobilization.

The dynamic of ethnic conflict

With ethnicity thus assembled, we can begin to appreciate its primal force in some conflict situations. When antagonism between groups, or state repressive action directed at an ethnic community, reaches a threshold of mutual threat, then the emotional dimensions of ethnic consciousness can take command. The other can come to pose a mortal threat to one's very existence; in the genocidal confrontations in Rwanda, Burundi and former Yugoslavia in the 1990s this clearly became the case. Along with fear came the longing for revenge. In polarized moments, selective perception is general. The atrocities committed towards the ethnic in-group are instantly perceived and indeed exaggerated in the rumours which flood an environment of violent confrontation. The harms which may have been inflicted upon the ethnic other recede into the remote recesses of awareness. Thus a passion for vengeance takes hold; this punitive impulse is entirely separated from any need to identify perpetrators. Any random members of the ethnic other are suitable victims for retribution.

In such situations, the ethnic other becomes dehumanized and demonized. As a source of boundless evil, and a mortal threat to the ethnic self, moral inhibitions dissolve and unspeakable violence can occur: the widespread use of machetes in the mass killings in Rwanda, or the large-scale rape accompanying these deadly episodes, whose purpose was much less sexual gratification than ritualized humiliation and moral destruction of the ethnic other. Indeed, the singular bestiality often associated with ethnic violence further escalates the fears and animosities. Such eruptions of inter-group hostility are inscribed in historical memory, and are not readily dissolved. Control of political power becomes a matter of life or death. Should power be the exclusive possession of one's ethnic adversaries, one is fated to unlimited insecurity (among several studies on Rwanda, see Prunier; on Burundi, Lemarchand).[21]

Comparative study of the deadly ethnic riot reveals a common set of patterns reflecting the pathologies described above.[22] The riot differs from the genocidal struggles in Rwanda, Burundi or Bosnia in its relatively brief duration and often greater spontaneity. However, in regions such as South Asia where communal violence has become an institutionalized part of the landscape, riots accumulate specialized personnel, readily available for participation, and what Brass[23] terms 'fire-tenders', who have an interest in sustaining communal tensions. In turn, individual episodes are easily converted into grand narratives of communal conflict, by the press or by the state authorities.

Our discussion has focused upon ethnicity. One may note that much of the analysis would also apply to the sometimes overlapping but analytically distinct forms of identity constituted by race and religion. Race is defined by a social definition of phenotype, a construction originating in the imposition of hierarchy upon differentiated populations coerced into unfree labour, and permeated with stigmatization of the subordinated as inferior. Thus, in contrast to ethnicity which is an asserted form of consciousness, race categories were assigned by the dominant.[24] Though racial solidarity comes to be asserted by the oppressed categories, accompanied by claims of collective worth contesting the stigmatization, its discursive sources are quite different.[25]

Religious identity is also a distinct domain of cultural identity, overlapping with ethnicity in some instances where religion demarcates a group also possessing ethnic characteristics and self-consciousness (Jews or Armenians, for example). Since community is defined by theology, elaborated in sacred texts, affiliation comports very distinctive obligations. The world religions possess sophisticated institutional structures for their perpetuation and reproduction, as well as anointed specialists for their leadership. The divine nature of their calling opens them to struggle over doctrine and frequent sectarian splintering. As the frequency of communal riots pitting Hindus against Muslims in India attests, religion can also serve as a mobilizing idiom for violent confrontation. In the early modern age, religion was the prime source of communal conflict, tamed only in the Western state by secularization and religious toleration.

Concluding reflections

In this chapter, I have endeavoured to explain the conflict potential of ethnicity. In closing, one must return to the variability in degree to which ethnic groups in presence within a nation-state arena have constantly conflictual relations. In the great majority of cases, conflict which exceeds the bounds of the civil is unusual. Further, there is evidence that, with a greater acknowledgement throughout the world that cultural pluralism is 'normal', and not a threat to the polity requiring erasure or repression through exclusionary 'nation-building' projects, one may discern a global process of political learning in the accommodation of cultural diversity.[26] A large repertoire of policy options for this purpose is available: decentralization, asymmetric federalism, electoral systems, affirmative action, legal pluralism, among others. Ted Gurr in a quantitative survey of ethnic conflicts concludes that they have significantly diminished in number in the 1990s, a counterintuitive finding he attributes in part to political learning.[27]

A modicum of political learning occurs at the level of the international community and a doctrine of humanitarian intervention to halt ethnic violence takes form. The education process is marked with failures, as in the early stages of a Bosnia intervention, and more disastrously in Rwanda, where the United States and France in particular pursued policies which exacerbated the calamity.[28] But an acceptance of a global responsibility to contain ethnic violence, however difficult its implementation, is an important development.

But these encouraging developments do not eliminate the possible perils of ethnicity which escapes the bounds of civility. Insensitive policies and ethnic extremists can form a lethal cocktail. A sustained and robust commitment to conflict containment and resolution will remain indispensable to a peaceful world.

Notes

1. P. R. Shaw & Y. Wong, *Genetic Seeds of Warfare: Evolution, Nationalism, and Patriotism* (Boston: Unwin Hyman, 1989).
2. A. D. Smith, *The Ethnic Origin of Nations* (Oxford: Basil Blackwell, 1986).
3. N. Glazer & D. P. Moynihan (eds), *Ethnicity: Theory and Experience* (Cambridge: Harvard University Press, 1975), p. 1.
4. F. Barth (ed.), *Ethnic Groups and Boundaries* (Boston: Little, Brown and Company, 1969).
5. L. Greenfeld, *Nationalism: Five Roads to Modernity* (Cambridge: Harvard University Press, 1992), and E. J. Hobsbawm, *Nations and Nationalism since 1780* (Cambridge: Cambridge University Press, 1990).
6. W. Connor, *Ethnonationalism: the Quest for Understanding* (Princeton, NJ: Princeton University Press, 1994).
7. Greenfield, op. cit.; B. Yack, 'The Myth of the Civic Nation', in R. Beiner (ed.), *Theorizing Nationalism* (Albany: State University of New York Press, 1999), pp. 103–18.
8. B. Anderson, *Imagined Communities: Reflections on the Origin and Spread of Nationalism* (Cambridge: Cambridge University Press, 1983).
9. C. Young, *The African Colonial State in Comparative Perspective* (New Haven: Yale University Press, 1994).
10. W. Kymlicka, *Multicultural Citizenship: a Liberal Theory of Minority Rights* (Oxford: Oxford University Press, 1995).
11. M. Waters, *Ethnic Options: Choosing Identities in America* (Cambridge: Harvard University Press, 1990).
12. S. Cornell & D. Hartmann, *Ethnicity and Race: Making Identities in a Changing World* (Thousand Oaks: Pine Forge Press, 1998), and C. Young (ed.), *The Rising Tide of Cultural Pluralism* (Madison: University of Wisconsin Press, 1993).
13. H. R. Isaacs, *Idols of the Tribe: Group Identity and Political Change* (New York: Harper & Row, 1975).
14. D. Chirot & M. E. P. Seligman (eds), *Ethnopolitical Warfare: Causes, Consequences, and Possible Solutions* (Washington: American Psychological Association, 2001).
15. L. A. Hirshfeld, *Race in the Making: Cognition, Culture, and the Child's Construction of Human Kinds* (Cambridge: MIT Press, 1996).
16. C. Young, *The Politics of Cultural Pluralism* (Madison: University of Wisconsin Press, 1976), pp. 467–8.
17. D. L. Horowitz, *Ethnic Groups in Conflict* (Berkeley: University of California Press, 1985).
18. S. Olzack & J. Nagel (eds), *Competitive Ethnic Relations* (Orlando: Academic Press, 1986).
19. A. Rabushka & K. A. Shepsle, *Politics in Plural Society: a Theory of Political Instability* (Columbus: Charles E. Merrill Publishing Company, 1972).
20. R. Hardin, *One for All: the Logic of Group Conflict* (Princeton: Princeton University Press, 1995), p. 5.
21. On Rwanda see G. Prunier, *The Rwanda Crisis: History of a Genocide* (New York: Columbia University Press, 1995), and on Burundi see R. Lemarchand, *Burundi: Ethnocide as Discourse and Practice* (Washington: Woodrow Wilson Center Press, 1994).
22. D. L. Horowitz, *The Deadly Ethnic Riot* (Berkeley: University of California Press, 2001).
23. P. R. Brass, *Theft of an Idol: Text and Context in the Representation of Collective Violence* (Princeton: Princeton University Press, 1997).
24. Cornell & Hartmann, op. cit., pp. 31–5.
25. A. W. Marx, *Making Race and Nation: a Comparison of South Africa, the United States and Brazil* (Cambridge: Cambridge University Press, 1998), and M. Omi & H. Winant, *Racial Formation in the United States from the 1960s to the 1990s* (New York: Routledge, 1994).

26. C. Young (ed.), *Ethnic Diversity and Public Policy: a Comparative Inquiry* (Basingstoke: Macmillan – now Palgrave Macmillan, 1998), and C. Young (ed.), *The Accommodation of Cultural Diversity: Case Studies* (Basingstoke: Macmillan – now Palgrave Macmillan, 1999).
27. T. R. Gurr, 'Ethnic Warfare on the Wane', *Foreign Affairs*, 79, 3 (May/June 2000), 52–64.
28. S. Power, 'Bystanders to Genocide', *Atlantic Monthly*, 288, 2 (September 2001), 84–108 and Prunier, op. cit.

2
The Timing of Peace Initiatives: Hurting Stalemates and Ripe Moments

I. William Zartman

While most studies on peaceful settlement of disputes see the substance of the proposals for a solution as the key to a successful resolution of conflict, a growing focus of attention shows that a second and equally necessary key lies in the timing of efforts for resolution.[1] Parties resolve their conflict only when they are ready to do so – when alternative, usually unilateral, means of achieving a satisfactory result are blocked and the parties feel that they are in an uncomfortable and costly predicament. At that ripe moment, they grab onto proposals that usually have been in the air for a long time and that only now appear attractive.

The idea of a ripe moment lies at the fingertips of diplomats. 'Ripeness of time is one of the absolute essences of diplomacy', wrote John Campbell.[2] 'You have to do the right thing at the right time', without indicating specific causes. Henry Kissinger did better, recognizing that 'stalemate is the most propitious condition for settlement'.[3] Conversely, practitioners are often heard to say that certain mediation initiatives are not advisable because the conflict just is not yet ripe. In mid-1992, in the midst of ongoing conflict, the Iranian Deputy Foreign Minister noted, 'The situation in Azerbaijan is not ripe for such moves for mediation.'[4]

The concept of a ripe moment centres on the parties' perception of a mutually hurting stalemate (MHS), optimally associated with an impending, past or recently avoided catastrophe.[5] The concept is based on the notion that when the parties find themselves locked in a conflict from which they cannot escalate to victory and this deadlock is painful to both of them (although not necessarily in equal degree or for the same reasons), they seek an alternative policy or way out. The catastrophe provides a deadline or a lesson indicating that pain can be sharply increased if something is not done about it now; catastrophe is a useful extension of MHS but is not necessary either to its definition or to its existence. Using different images, the stalemate has been termed the plateau, a flat and unending terrain without relief, and the catastrophe the precipice, the point where things suddenly and predictably get worse. If the notion of mutual blockage is too static to be realistic, the concept may be stated dynamically as a moment when the upper hand slips and the lower hand rises, both parties moving towards equality, with both movements carrying pain for the parties.[6]

The MHS is grounded in cost–benefit analysis, fully consistent with public choice notions of rationality[7] and public choice studies of war termination and negotiation,[8] which assume that a party will pick the alternative which it prefers, and that a decision to change is induced by increasing pain associated with the present (conflictual) course.[9] In game theoretic terms, it marks the transformation of the situation in the parties' perception from a prisoners' dilemma (PDG) into a chicken dilemma game (CDG),[10] or, in other terms, the realization that the status quo or no negotiation (DD, the south-east corner) is a negative-sum situation, and that to avoid the zero-sum outcomes now considered impossible (CD and DC, the north-east and south-west corners) the positive-sum outcome (CC, the north-west corner) must be explored.

Ripeness is necessarily a perceptual event, and as with any subjective perception, there are likely to be objective referents to be perceived. These can be highlighted by a mediator or an opposing party when they are not immediately recognized by the party itself, and resisted so long as the conflicting party refuses or is otherwise able to block out their perception. But it is the perception of the objective condition, not the condition itself, that makes for an MHS. If the parties do not recognize 'clear evidence' (in someone else's view) that they are in an impasse, an MHS has not (yet) occurred, and if they do perceive themselves to be in such a situation, no matter how flimsy the 'evidence', the MHS is present.

The other element necessary for a ripe moment is less complex and also perceptional: a way out. Parties do not have to be able to identify a specific solution, only a sense that a negotiated solution is possible and that the other party shares that sense and the willingness to search too. Without a sense of a way out, the push associated with the MHS would leave the parties with nowhere to go. Spokespersons often indicate whether they do or do not feel that a deal can be made with the other side and that requirement – i.e. the sense that concessions will be reciprocated, not just banked – exists, particularly when there is a change in that judgement.[11]

Ripeness is only a condition, necessary but not sufficient for the initiation of negotiations. It is not self-fulfilling or self-implementing. It must be seized, either directly by the parties or, if not, through the persuasion of a mediator. Thus, it is not identical to its results, which are not part of its definition, and is therefore not tautological. Not all ripe moments are so seized and turned into negotiations, hence the importance of specifying the meaning and evidence of ripeness so as to indicate when conflicting or third parties can fruitfully initiate negotiations.[12] Although ripeness theory is not predictive in the sense that it can tell when a given situation will become ripe, it is predictive in the sense of identifying the elements necessary (even if not sufficient) for the productive inauguration of negotiations. This type of analytical prediction is the best that can be obtained in social science, where stronger predictions could only be ventured by eliminating free choice (including the human possibility of blindness and mistakes). As such it is of great prescriptive value to policy-makers seeking to know when and how to begin a peace process.

Finding a ripe moment requires research and intelligence studies to identify the objective and subjective elements. Subjective expressions of pain, impasse and inability to bear the cost of further escalation, related to objective evidence of stalemate, data on numbers and nature of casualties and material costs, and/or other such indicators of MHS, along with expressions of a sense of a way out, can be researched on a regular basis in a conflict to establish whether ripeness exists. Researchers would look for evidence, for example, whether the fluid military balance in conflict – such as mountainous Karabagh, or the Burundian or Sri Lankan civil war, for example – has given rise at any time to a perception of MHS by the parties, and to a sense by authoritative spokespersons for each side that the other is ready to seek a solution to the conflict, or, to the contrary, whether it has reinforced the conclusion that any mediation is bound to fail because one or both parties believes in the possibility or necessity of escalating out of the current impasse to achieve a decisive military victory. Research and intelligence would seek to learn why Bosnia in the war-torn summer of 1994 was not ripe for a negotiated settlement and mediation would fail, and why it was in November 1995 and mediation could use that condition to achieve agreement.[13] Similarly, research would indicate that there was no chance of mediating a settlement in the Ethiopia–Eritrean conflict in the early 1980s and the early 1990s, or in the southern Sudan conflict in the 1990s, the skills of President Carter notwithstanding, because the components of ripeness were not present.[14]

While ripeness has not always been seized upon to open negotiations, there have been occasions when it has come into play, as identified by both analysts and practitioners. A number of studies beyond the original examination[15] have used and tested the notion of ripeness in regard to negotiations in Zimbabwe, Namibia and Angola, Eritrea, South Africa, the Philippines, Cyprus, Iran–Iraq, Israel, Mozambique, among others.[16] Touval's work on the Middle East[17] was particularly important in launching the idea. In general, these studies have found the concept applicable and useful as an explanation for the successful initiation of negotiations or their failure, while in some cases proposing refinements to the concept.

The most important refinements carry the theory onto a second level of questions about the effects of each side's pluralized politics on both the perceptions and uses of ripeness. What kinds of internal political conditions are helpful both for perceiving ripeness and for turning that perception into the initiation of promising negotiations? The careful case study by Stephen J. Stedman of the Rhodesian negotiations for independence as Zimbabwe takes the concept beyond a single perception into the complexities of internal dynamics. Stedman[18] specifies that some but not all parties must perceive the hurting stalemate, that patrons rather than parties may be the agents of perception, that the military element in each party is the crucial element in perceiving the stalemate, and that the way out is as important an ingredient as the stalemate in that all parties may well see victory in the alternative outcome prepared by negotiation (although some parties will be proven wrong in that perception). He also highlights the potential of leadership change for the subjective perception of an MHS where it had not been seen previously in the same objective circumstances, and of the threat of domestic rivals – rather than threats from the enemy – to incumbent leadership as the source of impending catastrophe, points also applied by Lieberfield[19] in his more recent comparison of the Middle East and South Africa.

The original formulation of the theory added a third element to the definition of ripeness, the presence of a valid spokesman for each side. As a structural element it is of a different order than the other two defining perceptual elements. Nonetheless, it remains of second-level importance, as Stedman and Lieberfield have pointed out. The presence of strong leadership recognized as representative of each party and that can deliver that party's compliance to the agreement is a necessary (while alone insufficient) condition for productive negotiations to begin, or indeed to end successfully.

Diplomatic memoirs have explicitly referred to ripeness by its MHS component. Chester A. Crocker, US Assistant Secretary of State for Africa between 1981 and 1989, patiently mediated an agreement for the withdrawal of Cuban troops from Angola and of South African troops from Namibia, then to become independent. For years an MHS, and hence productive negotiations, had eluded the parties. 'The second half of 1987 was ... the moment when the situation "ripened".'[20] Military escalations on both sides and bloody confrontations in south-eastern Angola beginning in November 1987 and in south-western Angola in May 1988 ended in a draw.

> By late June 1988, the ... Techipa–Calueque clashes in southwestern Angola confirmed a precarious military stalemate. That stalemate was both the reflection and the cause of underlying political decisions. By early May, my colleagues and I convened representatives of Angola, Cuba, and South Africa in London for face-to-face, tripartite talks. The political decisions leading to the London meeting formed a distinct sequence, paralleling military events on the ground, like planets moving one by one into a certain alignment.[21]

In his conclusion, Crocker identifies specific signs of ripeness, while qualifying that 'correct timing is a matter of feel and instinct'.[22] The American mediation involved building diplomatic moves that paralleled the growing awareness of the parties, observed by the mediator, of the hurting stalemate in which they found themselves.[23]

Alvaro de Soto, Assistant Secretary-General for Political Affairs at the United Nations, also endorsed the necessity of ripeness in his mission to mediate a peace in El Salvador. After chronicling a series of failed initiatives, he points to the importance of the Farabundo Marti National Liberation Front's (FMLN) November 1989 offensive, the largest of the war, which penetrated the main cities including the capital but failed to dislodge the government.

> The silver lining was that it was, almost literally, a defining moment – the point at which it became possible to seriously envisage a negotiation. The offensive showed the FMLN that they could not spark a popular uprising.... The offensive also showed the rightist elements in government, and elites in general, that the armed forces could not defend them, let alone crush the insurgents.... However inchoate at first, the elements of a military deadlock began to appear. Neither side could defeat the other. As the dust settled, the notion that the conflict could not be solved by military means, and that its persistence was causing

pain that could no longer be endured, began to take shape. The offensive codified the existence of a mutually hurting stalemate. The conflict was ripe for a negotiated solution.[24]

In Yugoslavia, Secretary of State James Baker looked for a ripe moment during his quick trip to Belgrade in June 1991 and reported the same day to President George Bush that he did not find it: 'My gut feeling is that we won't produce a serious dialogue on the future of Yugoslavia until all the parties have a greater sense of urgency and danger.'[25] Richard Holbrooke calls this 'a crucial misreading', as he did the later moment created by the Croatian Krajina offensive in August 1995.[26] Holbrooke[27] had his own image of the MHS (or the upper hand slipping and the underdog rising): 'The best time to hit a serve is when the ball is suspended in the air, neither rising nor falling. We felt this equilibrium had arrived, or was about to, on the battlefield [in October 1995]', and he tried to instil a perception of the ripe moment in the mind of Bosnian President Izetbegovic. It took the Croatian offensive, coupled with NATO bombing, to create an MHS composed of a temporary Serb setback and a temporary Croat advance that could not be sustained. A State Department official stated, 'Events on the ground have made it propitious to try again to get the negotiations started. The Serbs are on the run a bit. That won't last forever. So we are taking the obvious major step....'[28]

In his parting report as Under-Secretary-General of the United Nations, Marrack Goulding[29] specifically cited the literature on ripeness in discussing the selection of conflicts to be handled by an overburdened UN.

Not all conflicts are 'ripe' for action by the United Nations (or any other third party)....It therefore behoves the Secretary-General to be selective and to recommend action only in situations where he judges that the investment of scarce resources is likely to produce a good return (in terms of preventing, managing and resolving conflict).

Some practitioners have given a more nuanced endorsement of the concept, although not all have read the conceptual fine print carefully. Itamar Rabinovich,[30] the careful historian and skilful ambassador in the failed negotiations between Israel and Syria, terms the concept 'a very useful analytical tool ... but ... less valuable as an operational tool', but he expects that 'ripeness will account for the success of negotiations' rather than simply provide a necessary but insufficient condition for their initiation.

Resistant reactions

There are intriguing problems raised by ripeness theory. One complication with the notion of a hurting stalemate arises when increased pain increases resistance rather than reducing it (it must be remembered that while ripeness is a necessary precondition for negotiation, not all ripeness leads to negotiation). Although this may be considered 'bad', irrational or even adolescent behaviour, it is a common reaction and one that may be natural and functional. Reinforcement is the normal response to opposition: 'don't give up without a fight', 'no gain without pain', 'hold the course, whatever the cost', 'when the going gets tough, the tough get going', and 'if at first you don't succeed, try, try again'. The imposition of pain to a present course in conflict is not likely to lead to a search for alternative measures without first being tested. The theory itself takes this into account by referring to the parties' perception that they cannot escalate an exit from their stalemate, implying efforts to break out before giving in (without being able to predict when the shift will take place).

Second, while escalation is commonly used in reference only to means of conducting the conflict, it also refers to other aspects of conflict behaviour, including ends and agents.[31] Pressure on a party in conflict often leads to the psychological reaction of worsening the image of the opponent, a natural tendency which is often decried as lessening chances of reconciliation but which has the functional advantage of justifying resistance. Particular types of adversaries such as 'true believers', 'warriors' or 'hardliners' are unlikely to be led to compromise by increased pain; instead, pain is likely to justify renewed struggle.[32] Justified struggles call for greater sacrifices, which absorb increased pain and strengthen determination. The cycle is functional and self-protecting. To this type of reaction, it is the release of pain or an admission of pain on the other side which justifies relaxation; when the opponent admits the error of its ways, the true believer can claim the vindication of its efforts which permits a management of the conflict.[33]

Implications

Inescapable as it may be, the most unfortunate implications of the notion of a hurting stalemate lie in its dependence on conflict. In itself, the concept explains the difficulty of achieving pre-emptive conflict resolution and preventive diplomacy, even though nothing in the definition of the MHS requires it to take place at the height of the conflict or at a high level of violence. The internal (and unmediated) negotiations in South Africa between 1990 and 1994 stand out as a striking case of negotiations opened (and pursued) on the basis of an MHS perceived by both sides on the basis of impending catastrophe, not of present casualties.[34] However, the greater the objective evidence, the greater the subjective perception of the stalemate and its pain is likely to be, and this evidence is more likely to come late, when all other courses of action and possibilities of escalation have been exhausted. In notable cases, a long period of conflict is required before the MHS sinks in.[35] Yet given the infinite number of potential conflicts which have not reached 'the heights', evidence would suggest that perception of an MHS occurs either (and optimally) at a low level of conflict, where it is relatively easy to begin problem-solving in most cases, or, in salient cases, at rather high levels of conflict. Thus, conflicts not treated 'early' appear to require a high level of intensity for an MHS perception to kick in and negotiations towards a solution to begin. To ripen for resolution at least those conflicts that have not been managed early, one must raise the level of conflict until a stalemate is reached, and then further until it begins to hurt, and then still more, to ensure the perception of pain, and then still more yet, to create the perception of an impending catastrophe as well. The ripe moment becomes the godchild of brinkmanship.

As the notion of ripeness implies, MHS can be a very fleeting opportunity, a moment to be seized lest it pass, or it can be of a long duration, waiting to be noticed and acted upon by mediators. The moment was brief in Bosnia but longer in Angola. In fact, failure to seize the moment often hastens its passing, as parties lose faith in the possibility of a negotiated way out or regain hope in the possibility of unilateral escalation. Worse yet, when a moment of joint perception of a hurting stalemate passes without producing any results, parties frequently fall back on their previous perceptions that the other side will never be ready and the only course left is to hope and fight for a total realization of one's goals, no matter how long it takes: 'Nothing is acceptable but a Palestinian/Israeli state with Jerusalem as its capital.' By the same token, the possibility of long duration often dulls the urgency of rapid seizure.

Another set of implications comes from the fact that the theory only addresses the opening of negotiations, as noted at the outset and often missed by the critics. Now that the initiation of negotiation is theoretically explained, people would like to see a theory that explains the successful conclusion of negotiations once opened. Can ripeness be extended in some way to cover the entire process, or does successful conclusion of negotiations require a different explanatory logic?

Practitioners and students of conflict management would also like to think that there could be a more positive prelude to negotiation, through the pull of an attractive outcome without the push of an MHS. Although examples are rare, as explained by prospect theory,[36] one case is the opening of the Madrid peace process on the Middle East in 1992[37] and another is the negotiation of the Jordan–Israel peace treaty of October 1994; still another may be boundary disputes which are overcome by the prospects of mutual development in the region.[38] But the mechanisms are still unclear, in part because the cases are so few. As in other ripe moments, these occasions provided an opportunity for improvement, but from a tiring rather than a painful deadlock.[39] In some views, the attraction lies in a possibility of winning more cheaply than by conflict (paradoxically, a shared perception), or else a possibility of sharing power that did not exist before.[40] In other views, enticement comes in the form of a new ingredient, the chance for improved relations with the mediating third party.[41] In other instances, the opportunity for a settlement grows more attractive because the issue of the conflict becomes dépassé, no longer justifying the bad relations with the other party or the mediator that it imposed. Such openings might be termed a mutually enticing opportunities (MEO), admittedly a title not as catchy as MHS and a concept not as well researched (or practised). Few examples have been found in reality.

But MEO is important in the broader negotiation process and has its place in extending ripeness theory. At most, ripeness theory can reach beyond the decision to negotiate into the negotiations themselves by indicating that the perception of ripeness has to continue during the negotiations if the parties are not to re-evaluate their positions and drop out, in the revived hopes of being able to find a unilateral solution through escalation. But negotiations completed under the shadow – or the push – of an MHS alone are likely to be unstable and unlikely to lead to a more enduring settlement. As Ohlson[42] and Pruitt[43] have pointed out, that is the function of the MEO. The negotiators must provide or be provided prospects for a more attractive future to pull them out of their conflict, once an MHS has pushed them into negotiations. The seeds of the pull factor begin with the way out that the parties vaguely perceive as part of the initial ripeness, but that general sense of possibility needs to be developed and fleshed out into the vehicle for an agreement, a formula for settlement and a prospect of reconciliation that the negotiating parties design during negotiations. When an MEO is not developed in the negotiations, they remain truncated and unstable, even if they reach a conflict management agreement to suspend violence, as in the 1984 and 1999 Lusaka agreements or the 1994 Karabakh ceasefire.[44]

The third set of implications have to do with the absence of ripeness. Unripeness should not constitute an excuse for second or third parties' inaction, even if one or both of the conflicting parties are mired in their hopes of escalation and victory. Crocker states very forcefully (in boldface in the original) that 'the absence of "ripeness" does not tell us to walk away and do nothing. Rather, it helps us to identify obstacles and suggests ways of handling them and managing the problem until resolution becomes possible'.[45] Crocker's own experience indicates, before and above all, the importance of being present and available to the contestants while waiting for the moment to ripen, so as to be able to seize it when it occurs. In the absence of a promising situation, either the 'second' party that is alone in feeling the hurt and perceiving the stalemate or the third party has a choice: either to ripen or to position.

Crocker lists a number of important insights for positioning:[46]

- give the parties some fresh ideas to shake them up;
- keep new ideas flexible to avoid getting bogged down in details;
- establish basic principles to form building blocks of a settlement;
- become an indispensable channel for negotiation; and
- establish an acceptable mechanism for negotiation and for registering an agreement.

Other strategies include preliminary explorations of items identified with pre-negotiations:[47]

- identify the parties necessary to a settlement;
- identify the issues to be resolved, and separate out issues not resolvable in the conflict;
- air alternatives to the current conflict course;
- establish contacts and bridges between the parties;
- clarify costs and risks involved in seeking settlement;
- establish requitement; and
- assure support for a settlement policy within each party's domestic constituency.

Since ripeness results from a combination of objective and subjective elements, both need attention. If some objective elements are present, persuasion is the obvious diplomatic challenge. Such was the message of Kissinger in the Sinai withdrawal negotiations[48] and Crocker in the Angolan negotiations,[49] among many others, emphasizing the absence of real alternatives (stalemate) and the high cost of the current conflict course (pain). If there is no objective indicator to which to refer, ripening may involve a much more active engagement of the mediator, moving that role from communication and formulation to manipulation.[50] As a manipulator, the mediator either increases the size of the stakes, attracting the parties to share in a pot that otherwise would have been too small, or limits the actions of the parties in conflict, providing objective elements for the stalemate. Such actions are delicate and dangerous, but on occasion necessary. US massive aid incentives to Israel and Egypt to negotiate a second Sinai withdrawal in 1975, NATO bombing of Serb positions in Bosnia in 1995 to create a hurting stalemate, or American arming of Israel during the October war in 1973 or of Morocco (after two years of moratorium) in 1981 to keep those parties in the conflict, respectively, among many others, are typical examples of the mediator acting as a manipulator to bring about a stalemate.

Practitioners need to employ all their skills and apply all the concepts of negotiation and mediation to take advantage of the necessary but insufficient condition in order to turn it into a successful peacemaking process when it exists, or to help produce it or stand ready to act on it when it does not as yet.

Notes

1. I. W. Zartman, 'Ripeness: the Hurting Stalemate and Beyond', in P. Stern & D. Druckman (eds), *International Conflict Resolution after the Cold War* (Washington, DC: National Academy Press, 2000).
2. J. Campbell, *Successful Negotiation: Trieste* (Princeton: Princeton University Press, 1976), p. 73.
3. H. Kissinger, *New York Times*, 12 October 1974.
4. AFP, 17 May 1992.
5. See I. W. Zartman & M. Berman, *The Practical Negotiator* (New Haven: Yale University Press, 1982); I. W. Zartman, 'The Strategy of Preventive Diplomacy in Third World Conflicts', in A. George (ed.), *Managing US–Soviet Rivalry* (Boulder, Colo.: Westview, 1983); S. Touval & I. W. Zartman (eds), *International Mediation in Theory and Practice* (Boulder, Colo.: Westview, 1985), pp. 11, 258–60, and I. W. Zartman, *Ripe for Resolution* (New York: Oxford University Press, 1985/1989).
6. The same logic has been identified in regard to domestic elite settlements, produced by costly and inconclusive conflict; 'Precisely because no single faction has been a clear winner and all factions have more nearly been losers, elites are disposed to compromise if at all possible.' M. Burton & J. Higley, 'Elite Settlements', *American Sociological Review*, LII, 2 (1994), 295–307 at 298.
7. See A. Sen, *Collective Choice and Social Welfare* (San Francisco: Holden-Day, 1970); K. Arrow, *Social Change and Individual Values* (Yale: Yale University Press, 1963), and M. Olson, *The Logical of Collective Action* (Schocken, 1965).
8. S. Brams, *Negotiation Games* (New York: Routledge, 1990) and *Theory of Moves* (Cambridge: Cambridge University Press, 1994); and Q. Wright, 'The Escalation of Conflicts', *Journal of Conflict Resolution*, IX, 4 (1965), 434–49.
9. Timing can refer to many things other than costs and benefits, including domestic political schedules, generational socialization and attitudinal maturation, among others.

For an excellent analysis based on the first, see W. Quandt, *Camp David* (Washington: Brookings, 1986). On the second, see R. Samuels et al., *Political Generations and Political Development* (Boston: Lexington, 1977). These are perfectly valid approaches, but ultimately they can be reduced to cost/benefits, calculated or affected by different referents. To note this is not to deny their separate value, but simply to justify the conceptual focus used here.

10. See J. Goldstein, 'The Game of Chicken in International Relations: an Underappreciated Model', MS, Washington School of International Service, American University (1998).

11. I. W. Zartman & J. Aurik, 'Power Strategies in De-escalation', in L. Kriesberg & J. Thornson (eds), *Timing the De-escalation of International Conflicts* (Syracuse: Syracuse University Press, 1991).

12. At the outset, confusion may arise from the fact that not all 'negotiations' appear to be the result of a ripe moment. Negotiation may be a tactical interlude, a breather for rest and rearmament, a sop to external pressure, without any intent of opening a sincere search for a joint outcome. Thus the need for quotation marks, or for some elusive modifier such as 'serious' or 'sincere' negotiations. It is difficult at the outset to determine whether negotiations are indeed serious or sincere, and indeed 'true' and 'false' motives may be indistinguishably mixed in the minds of the actors themselves at the beginning. Yet it is the outset which is the subject of the theory. The best that can be done is to note that many theories contain a reference to a 'false' event or an event in appearance only, to distinguish it from an event that has a defined purpose. Indeed, a sense of ripeness may be required to turn negotiations for side effects (F. Ikle, *How Nations Negotiate* (Harper & Row, 1964)) into negotiations to resolve conflict. In any case, unless the moment is ripe, as defined below, the search for an agreed outcome cannot begin.

13. S. Touval, 'Coercive Mediation on the Road to Geneva', *International Negotiation*, 3 (1996), 547–70; J. Goodby, 'When War Won out: Bosnian Peace Plans before Dayton', *International Negotiation*, 3 (1996), 501–23 and R. Holbrooke, *To End a War* (New York: Random House, 1998).

14. M. Ottaway, 'Eritrea and Ethiopia: Negotiations in a Transnational Conflict' and F. Deng, 'Negotiating a Hidden Agenda: Sudan's Conflict of Identities', both in I. W. Zartman (ed.), *Elusive Peace: Negotiating an End to Civil Wars* (Washington: Brookings, 1995).

15. Zartman & Berman, op. cit.; Zartman, 'Strategy'; Touval & Zartman, op. cit.; Zartman, *Ripe for Resolution*; I. W. Zartman, 'Ripening Conflict, Ripe Moment, Formula and Mediation', in D. BenDahmane & J. McDonald (eds), *Perspectives on Negotiation* (Washington, DC: Government Printing Office, 1986) and Zartman & Aurik, op. cit.

16. Touval & Zartman, op. cit.; R. Haas, *Conflicts Unending* (Yale: Yale University Press, 1990); S. Stedman, *Peacemaking in Civil War* (Lynne Rienner, 1991); Kriesberg & Thornson, op. cit.; T. Sisk, *Democratization in South Africa: the Elusive Social Contract* (Princeton: Princeton University Press, 1995); T. Norlen, *A Study of the Ripe Moment for Conflict Resolution and Its Applicability to Two Periods in the Israeli–Palestinian Conflict* (Uppsala: Uppsala University Conflict Resolution Program, 1995); F. Olser Hampson, *Nurturing Peace* (Washington, DC: USIP, 1996); Goodby, op. cit; M. Sala, 'Creating the "Ripe Moment" in the East Timor Conflict', *Journal of Peace Research*, XXXIV, 4 (1997), 449–66; K. Aggestram & C. Jönson, '(Un)ending Conflict', *Millennium*, XXXVI, 3 (1997), 771–94; M. Mooradian & D. Druckman, 'Hurting Stalemate or Mediation? The Conflict over Nagorno-Karabakh, 1990–95', *Journal of Peace Research*, XXXVI, 6 (1999), 709–27; N. Sambanis, 'Conflict Resolution Ripeness and Spoiler Problems in Cyprus', *Journal of Peace Research*, pending; and J. Stein & L. Pauly (eds), *Choosing to Cooperate: How States Avoid Loss* (Baltimore: The Johns Hopkins University Press, 1992).

17. S. Touval, *The Peace Brokers* (Princeton: Princeton University Press, 1982), pp. 228–32 and 328.

18. Stedman, op. cit., pp. 238 and 241–2.

19. D. Lieberfield, 'Conflict "Ripeness" Revisited: South African and Israeli/Palestinian Cases', *Negotiation Journal*, XV, 1 (1999), 63–82 and *Talking with the Enemy: Negotiation and Threat Perception in South Africa and Israel/Palestine* (New York: Praeger, 1999).

20. C. Crocker, *High Noon in Southern Africa* (Norton, 1992), p. 363.
21. Ibid., p. 373.
22. Ibid., p. 481.
23. Ibid., chapter 16.
24. A. DeSoto, 'Multiparty Mediation: El Salvador', in C. Crocker et al. (eds), *Herding Cats: the Management of Complex International Mediation* (Washington, DC: USIP, 1999), pp. 7–8.
25. J. Baker & T. deFrank, *The Politics of Diplomacy* (New York: Putnam, 1995).
26. Holbrooke, op. cit., pp. 27 and 73.
27. Ibid., p. 193.
28. *New York Times*, 19 August 1995, A7.
29. M. Goulding, *Enhancing the United Nations' Effectiveness in Peace and Security* (United Nations: Report to the Secretary-General, 30 June 1997), p. 20.
30. I. Rabinovich, *The Brink of Peace: the Israeli–Syrian Negotiations* (Princeton: Princeton University Press, 1998), p. 251.
31. J. Rubin, Z., Pruitt, G. Dean & S. H. Kim, *Social Conflict* (New York: McGraw-Hill, 1994).
32. E. Hoffer, *The True Believer* (New York: Harper Bros., 1951); H. Nicolson, *Diplomacy* (Oxford: Oxford University Press, 1960) and G. Snyder & P. Diesing, *Conflict among Nations* (Princeton: Princeton University Press, 1977).
33. R. L. Moses, *Freeing the Hostages* (Pittsburgh: University of Pittsburgh Press, 1996).
34. T. Ohlson & S. Stedman, *The New Is Not Yet Born* (Washington: Brookings, 1994); Sisk, op. cit., and Liberfield, op. cit.
35. Steiner & Pauly, op. cit.
36. D. Kahnerman & A. Tversky, 'Prospect Theory: an Analysis of Decisions under Risk', *Econometrica*, IIIL, 3 (1979), 263–91.
37. Baker & deFrank, op. cit.
38. K. J. Nordquist, 'Boundary Disputes: Drawing the Line', in I. W. Zartman (ed.), *Preventive Diplomacy: Avoiding Conflict Escalation* (Lanham: Rowman & Littlefield, 2000).
39. C. Mitchell, 'Cutting Losses', Working paper 9, Institute for Conflict Analysis and Resolution, George Mason University, appearing in a shorter version in *Paradigms: Kent Journal of International Relations*, IX, 2 (1995), 3.
40. Ibid., p. 7.
41. Touval & Zartman, op. cit., and H. Saunders, 'Guidelines B', unpublished manuscript (1991).
42. T. Ohlson, *Power Politics and Peace Politics* (Uppsala: University of Uppsala, Department of Peace and Conflict Research), Report 50.
43. D. Pruitt & P. Olczak, 'Approaching to Resolving Seemingly Intractable Conflict', in B. Bunker & J. Rubin (eds), *Conflict, Cooperation and Justice* (New York: Jossey-Bass, 1995).
44. Zartman, *Ripe for Resolution,* and Mooradian & Druckman, op. cit.
45. Crocker, op. cit., p. 471.
46. Ibid., pp. 471–2. See also Haas, op. cit. and Goulding, op. cit.
47. Stein & Pauly, op. cit.
48. M. Gatti, *The Secret Conversations of Henry Kissinger* (New York: Bantham, 1976).
49. Crocker, op. cit., pp. 381–2.
50. Touval & Zartman, op. cit. and D. Rothchild, *Managing Ethnic Conflict in Africa* (Washington: Brookings, 1997).

3

Cultivating Peace: a Practitioner's View of Deadly Conflict and Negotiation

John Paul Lederach

Introduction

'So do you think it may be possible to move towards dialogue, maybe initial, off record contacts to see what obstacles or possibilities exist for a negotiated process to end the conflict?' The question posed by our peace research team to the representatives of the Basque separatist movement was genuine though intuitively we knew the response. The heads shook slowly and the inevitable short answer emerged, 'No. It is going to be a hard two years', followed by a much more detailed justification and rationale.

The year of this conversation could have been 1991 prior to the Barcelona Olympic Games, or 1994 following the Olympics. Or it could have been January 2001, for the answer was much the same. The counterpart could just as well have been representatives of the Spanish government rather than the separatists. For that matter, the conversation could have taken place in Northern Ireland, Somalia or Colombia. In protracted conflict, the horizon of expectation is not the rise of peaceful change. The horizon is the regeneration of violence, steady and sure as the rising sun.

The conversation, much repeated in my experience as a conciliator, poses a dilemma that I often hear framed as a significant doubt and question from students in seminars and journalists in interviews. Is it possible to negotiate while the fighting is still raging, and when, for all practical purposes, neither side is expecting or even preparing for any significant change in the cycle of deadly conflict?

In this chapter I will formulate some initial responses to that question from the standpoint and perspective of a practitioner. Theoretically, the field abounds with suggestions. Most well known is the idea of 'ripeness' first articulated by Zartman in his important book *Ripe for Resolution*.[1] Over the past decade research and writing have focused on lessons gained from peace processes and the question of timing.[2] The arguments have suggested that negotiations, and in particular mediation and conciliation, need to read a situation with a capacity to determine whether the timing is right for nudging the conflict from violence to dialogue, and more specifically to agreements that end the open violence. Conditions, patterns and criteria have emerged to further develop this capacity, but in the end the metaphor created by 'ripeness' points towards a single important premise: change from cycles of deadly violence to negotiation is possible only when the conflict and its perpetrating actors have reached a certain maturation point, then conciliation and negotiation efforts can be introduced with greater effectiveness and success.

This chapter is not aimed at refuting the important research gained from the studies of peace processes in reference to criteria and patterns for successful intervention and negotiation in deadly conflict. I will provide a critique of the guiding metaphor – ripeness – and propose a reorientation of the practice of developing negotiated peace processes with particular reference to time periods prior to and following the opening of formal talks. These are reflections that emerge from my own direct experiences and I believe that while they provide an alternative view to the metaphor of ripeness they are complementary to the existing body of literature.

A critique of ripeness

I start with three observations as to why I have found ripeness a limited metaphor for practice and then suggest several alternative metaphors or guiding perspectives in reference to how practitioners might align their work when faced with the question of whether it is possible to work for peace and negotiations when fighting is still raging. Let me start with what I consider to be a few of the practical limitations of ripeness.

Ripeness is a rearview mirror

From the standpoint of practice ripeness theory and approaches present an awkward challenge and paradox. On the one hand, much of this theoretical emphasis has been pursued in order to create a 'predictive' capacity useful to conciliators and mediators as they engage with people involved in negotiation processes. Such a capacity offers the promise that if, as practitioners, we can recognize factors, conditions and characteristics of negotiation situations in settings of violent conflict we can effectively increase our capacity to achieve a settlement, or inversely, to know when it is not effective to proceed with the effort. In other words, ripeness proposes to provide a predictive capacity. This is a forward-looking skill orientation, one that assumes linearity of process capable of foretelling outcomes from conditions. To draw the metaphor, ripeness should serve as a large windscreen in a car providing a clear and expansive view of what is coming on the horizon such that the driver can adjust the manoeuvres to match the challenges of the approaching road.

However on the other side of the paradox, as I look back across my practical experience, unlike the metaphor suggests, peacebuilding generally, and negotiations in particular, have not entailed a 'ripeness' process where I have watched the process develop, like the seasonal maturation of an apple moving from blossom to red, juicy and ready-to-eat fruit. In fact, more often than not the opposite has been true. I have only recognized the keys to transformative change in retrospect and in differing ways in each context. For example, on several occasions in the Miskito/Sandinista negotiations, the times when all the conditions pointed to successfully opening the talks were precisely the moments when all our efforts as conciliations failed. They were, in fact, called off at least three times, and once within a day of starting. On the other hand, when they finally opened, what appeared to be a long-drawn-out entry in the airport where nearly everything fell apart again and seemed to point to a complete lack of ripeness, the talks that followed lasted about a week and were highly successful. 'Who would have known?' we commented time and again to ourselves.

To draw out the metaphor, 'ripeness' (as in recognizing that potential for change happened) was more like a rearview mirror than a windscreen. The roadway of protracted conflict, it seems, may be more akin to dynamic, nearly ameoba-like spaces than the linear and predictable development of fruit. And herein lies the limitation. Ripeness may be most useful in retrospect (as we look back we can account for things in our interpretation of the history), but is extremely weak in its predictive capacity from the standpoint of a practitioner and in fact may provide us with a lens that is not helpful for adapting constructively to the pathways of peacebuilding.

Time and again, in situations as varied as Northern Ireland, the Basque Country or the negotiations between the Philippine government and the communist insurgency, the moments when I thought there was the greatest potential for a significant move forward have been stagnant and even counterproductive. For a practitioner these time periods create an emotional roller coaster. The predictive view suggests significant change is near. Then just when hopes are high everything collapses, leading to a deep sense of despair and often urgent, at times inappropriate, responses to save the moment. Other times, exactly when all the predictive characteristics pointed to complete stagnation and even highly escalated cycles of violence, turned out to be the period when by way of some unexpected suggestion or event, a significant move forward was created.

These experiences have led me towards an attitude not driven by a predictive lens of visible factors but rather towards the development of a lens that does not focus excessively on what appear at any given moment to be the limitations of temporal conditions. In protracted conflict temporal conditions are ephemeral and non-linear, requiring paradoxical intentionality: a set of mediative attitudes that keep your feet on the ground (a realist view of the situation) and your head in the clouds (a hope-driven idealist view of the possible). Therefore, rather than orienting my action around predictive ripeness, I find the opposite is increasingly true in my work. I am carefully cautious when all appears ripe for settlement and innoculatingly naive when all appears hopelessly lost in the grip of calamity.

Ripeness is in the eye of the beholder

Among the many things I have learned in the school of hard knocks of protracted conflict is a simple idea with wide-ranging implications: the prevailing system is set up to create a permanently emerging crisis. This essentially has to do with time and response. I find that in situations with a long history of social division and violence the focus of attention is on the immediate situation and the crisis, event or impending disaster that just happened. This is accompanied by the common view that once this 'crisis' is dealt with we can move onto the deeper and longer-range concerns and needs. The tendency across the board is to be driven by the crisis. This I have found particularly true of people who are directly involved on one side or the other of the conflict, and as such there is a prevailing attitude that the situation is not ripe. In other words, ripeness is more often than not something perceived by outsiders with the luxury of dispassionate facts and factors. In the midst of week-to-week and month-to-month emergencies people rarely see their situations as 'ripe' for peace. Ripeness is in the eye of the beholder and few who live in the settings have the luxury of such vision.

This leads to practical and attitudinal dilemmas for the peacebuilder. The most critical shift required is to understand the process not as linear but *circular and linear*. Ripeness, however, depends exclusively on a linear metaphor of time and change. Circular and linear can be visualized as a horizontal spiral where there is circular movement creating at any given moment forward, upward, backward and downward movement *and* the whole of the circles is moving forward across time. These are actually the temporal experiences from within the situation that I have commonly experienced: things feel like they may be moving forward, then a crisis comes and it feels like everything has come to a standstill. At other times it can easily feel like it is moving backwards, or even collapsing. This is the immediate time circle, and it is continuous, a permanent feature of the system. The challenge is how to visualize the possibility of sustaining an overall forward movement over time visible in the lens of decades not months. This requires a capacity to envision a longer-term process and recognize opportunities for constructive change in the midst of crisis. In other words, it is a shift towards being crisis-responsive rather than crisis-driven. The key attitude and skill shift is that of adaptation of process that assumes and takes account of constant crisis rather than a linear view of maturation that assumes stepwise progression to resolution.

Ripeness sees mediator action as cherry picking

When I played basketball many years ago our coach had a phrase with which he provoked us whenever we missed an easy shot, 'I can't believe you missed that cherry picker.' Essentially it meant that a lot of work had gone into place and then just when everything was right and a giveaway opportunity was presented, the basket was missed.

There are times when I have the impression that the metaphor of ripeness leads towards an emphasis on mediator action as if it were 'cherry picking'. The impression emerges from two understandings about mediation that I believe have significant limitations and implications.

The first commonly held belief is that mediation lies primarily in the person, and often the personality of the mediator-as-the-actor rather than mediation-as-process with multiple roles, functions and activities carried out by a wide array of people.[3] Particularly critical to our discussion here is the idea that the mediator comes from outside the setting and outside the relationships in conflict, or what I have referred to as the 'outside–neutral' view of mediator role.[4] When the mediator provides an outside and neutral role in many cases they are 'in' and 'out' of the setting in terms of their actual physical presence. Ripeness is oriented towards providing terms of reference for this kind of action such that the mediator can gauge when it is most effective to push for agreement or renewed negotiation. What the ripeness metaphor does not provide is a sense of the long-term nature of the process, the building and sustaining of the relationships, nor the multiplicity of roles, activities and functions that may be necessary to make a sustained dialogue and change in the relationships possible.

The second commonly held belief is that the success of mediation is primarily judged by whether it produced an agreement rather than whether it helped create a space for constructive change in people, perceptions and relationships that are not always captured in the confines of a written negotiated document. Ripeness suggests the cherry is the agreement and that picking the cherry is like a mediation harvest. In my practical experience in conciliation work this tends to promote a measuring stick of success based on what is often the least important element for gauging the sustainability of the change process necessary to actually create the transformation from deadly conflict to respect, cooperation and increased peaceful interdependence. It is not a metaphor that provides a vision of cultivating the soil, planting the seeds or nourishing the seedling in the face of winds, burning sun or icy storms, all of which speak to process, relationship and sustainability rather than a momentary action.

Alternative metaphors to ripeness

What I just outlined suggests that from the standpoint of practice the ripeness metaphor has some limitations when applied to contexts of protracted deadly conflict. The metaphor suggests a focus on content and agreement making rather than being relationship and change-oriented. It places emphasis on the mediator's action and perception rather than on the mediation-as-process with multiple sets of action and people. It tends to have a shorter-term view of action in mind aimed at intense action in specific time frames (harvest) but not necessarily the slower and painstaking process of preparing and sustaining process. This suggests a need for additional and complementary metaphors emerging from and oriented towards the experience of practice. As I reflect on my own experience several come to mind.

Cultivation: the building of long-term authentic relationships

Over the past two decades my efforts at peacebuilding and conciliation have led me to the metaphor of cultivator more than harvester, towards nourishment of soil and plant more than picking the fruit. The images that accompany this complementary metaphor suggest an organic connection to context, the building of relationships, and a commitment to process over time. Each of the images provides an avenue towards answering the question posed at the beginning of the chapter: is it possible to pursue negotiations while deadly conflict is raging?

The cultivation metaphor suggests that a deep respect for, and connection to, the context is critical for sustaining a change process that is moving from deadly expressions of conflict to increased justice and peace in relationships. The context of protracted deadly conflict, like soil, is the people, commonly shared geographies but often sharply differing views of history, rights and responsibilities, and the formation of perception and understandings based on cultural meaning structures. Cultivation is recognizing that ultimately the change process must be taken up, embraced and sustained by people in these contexts. The cultivator, as a connected but outside element in the system, approaches this soil with a great deal of respect, the suspension of quick judgement in favour of the wisdom of adaptation, and an orientation towards supporting the change process through highs and lows, ebbs and flows of violence and thawing of tensions, whether or not the situation appears ripe. The cultivator gives attention to the well-being of the ecosystem, not just the quick production of a given fruit.

A relationship-centric orientation naturally emerges from the metaphor. This is built on a genuine concern for relationships, not an instrumentalist approach to people in order to achieve an external goal. This suggests a criterion of authenticity, which cannot be overstated from the perspective of cultivation. A relationship-centric orientation keeps the focus on people, realities of histories and perceptions as the source that generates and regenerates cycles of deadly conflict. The contentious content of specific agreements are often symbolic of this deeper level. In essence, you can resolve an issue but you till the soils of relationships if you are interested in sustained transformation and systemic health.

Both of the above images require a long-term commitment. I think this may be the single most important lesson learned over the years, a shift from thinking about negotiations as a 'ripe' moment in time towards understanding the preparation and support for a change process over a much longer period.[5] It requires you to shift from thinking in weeks and months to thinking in decades. If you have ever talked with farmers about their land you will hear them talking about years – decades and even a lifetime of relationship to the soil and the climate.

Accompaniment: the pace of presence

To understand accompaniment as a metaphor of peacebuilding and conciliation it is useful to break it down to its Latin origins. The word is built on two primary concepts *com* or with and *pani* or bread. A literal translation would be 'with bread'. In other words, this is a table metaphor. To accompany is to sit and share bread with another. In my mind there are a number of important images this metaphor places before us as practical guidelines.

First, sharing a table provides a sense of intimacy, of being inside a shared space of humanity with another. This takes us back to our earlier idea of relationship. But it goes further because the image suggests presence with another, a quality of what I once called 'alongsideness'.[6] This of course is very much a part of the image that the word 'accompany' creates: we walk alongside the journey of another. The image it suggests is a respect for the journey of others. It represents presence with others as they travel on their way.

The second intriguing aspect of this image is the idea of pace. When it is the journey of the other the pace is not forced or prescribed from outside, but must, if it is to be authentic, be directed from sources of leading that come from within.

In reference to peacebuilding this poses numerous difficult dilemmas, for more often than not the pace of moving from deadly cycles of conflict to more constructive, mutually beneficial and respectful cycles is extremely slow. And much of peacebuilding from outside is oriented towards getting that movement to happen more rapidly. However, if movement or compromise happens because one is obligated or forced, then the change is rarely authentic and sustainable, and plants the seeds of renewed destructive conflict that sprout at a later date. This becomes all the more complex when the accompaniment is with people across the lines of division, and when slowness towards change means a great deal of suffering for a lot of people.

Ripeness seems to answer this dilemma by suggesting that if we read the situation correctly we can determine when the greatest potential for change could happen and can then push for this change to take place. Accompaniment suggests an ongoing presence motivated by an interest in supporting a sustainable change process built on making opportunity available for genuine change motivated from within but not under obligation or external time frames. If we were to put this in more concrete detail it would suggest that conciliation work is not about moving in and out of a situation according to a measure of the potential for success. Rather, the activities of conciliation are about ongoing presence, a constancy of availability and a regularity of connection.

Naivety: the art of the possible

Naivety in the world of realpolitik is generally seen as foolishness, gullibility and weakness of understanding about the true character of politics, power relationships and even basic human nature. Those who are naive are those who with a Pollyannaish attitude make things worse and are usually taken advantage of and eaten up in the process. Applied to peacebuilding, this is a common critique of those who pursue peace, particularly at times when things appear to be falling apart and getting worse.

When I look back at my own experiences I should like to suggest the inverse may be true, that the key to significant change came not when I was capable of producing a hard, factual, objective view of a situation and the predictable outcomes. Rather it seemed to come from a kind of naivety that suspended the lens of presented reality, and with a commonsensical approach asked questions and pursued ideas that seemed out of line with reality as presented.

Paradoxically, naivety cuts both ways. It is equally naive for the little boy alongside the parade to point a finger and say out loud, 'the emperor has no clothes' (which is exactly what I felt when the Dayton Peace Accords were hatched), or the sustaining of hope and pursuing of a 'couple of ideas' as I heard from Irish colleagues when on numerous occasions the bombs in the ceasefire period seemed to bring everything to a halt.

For my own edification as a peacebuilder I have come to embrace the utility of naivety as the art of the possible. Naivety does not take what is presented on the surface and generally accepted as final truth as the primary measuring stick of how things work, are held together or fall apart. Naivety is unafraid of being perceived as stupid and has the courage the raise basic questions, both of optimism when all seems impossible and of common-sense realism when everybody expects peace to happen because a paper was signed. In both instances, the art is in seeking a way to reach towards a deeper source of what is possible and needed to keep a constructive change process alive and healthy.

Epilogue

So what do I say when the journalist asks, 'And do you really believe it is possible to talk about negotiation and peace when war is raging?' I say hope is not negotiated. It is kept alive by people who understand the depth of suffering and know the cost of keeping a horizon of change as a possibility for their children and grandchildren. Quick fixes to long-standing violent conflict are like growing a garden with no understanding of seeds, soils and sweat. This conflict traces back across decades, even generations. It will take that long to sort out.

Journalists generally do not quote me in their papers. Sound bites about ripeness, people coming to their senses, and the need for realism and pressure seem to find their way into print more often. But I believe in cultivation. Cultivation as a metaphor suggests that the core of the peacebuilding work – fostering and sustaining committed, authentic relationships across the lines of conflict over time – does not rise and fall with the temporal ups and downs of the conflict cycles. It answers the question – is it possible to pursue peace when things are bad – with a resounding 'Yes!' Just as it also suggests that when things are suddenly headed towards an agreement the work is hardly over. It has only begun.

Notes

1. I. W. Zartman, *Ripe for Resolution: Conflict and Intervention in Africa* (New York: Oxford University Press, 1989).
2. See, for example, L. Kriesberg & S. J. Thorson, *Timing and De-escalation of International Conflicts* (Syracuse: Syracuse University Press, 1991).
3. C. Mitchell, 'External Peace-making Initiatives and Intranational Conflict', in M. I. Midlarsky (ed.), *The Internationalization of Communal Strife* (New York: Routledge, 1992).
4. P. Wehr & J. P. Lederach, 'Mediating in Central America', *Journal of Peace Research*, 28, 1 (February 1991), 86–98.
5. J. P. Lederach, *Building Peace: Sustainable Reconciliation in Divided Societies* (Washington, DC: United States Institute of Peace, 1997).
6. J. P. Lederach, 'Qualities of Practice for Reconciliation', in R. Helmick (ed.), *Reconciliation* (New York: Templeton Press, 2001).

4
New Contexts for Political Solutions: Redefining Minority Nationalisms in Northern Ireland, the Basque Country and Corsica

John Loughlin

Introduction

Ethnic conflicts, and the peace processes that attempt to end them, always occur within specific geopolitical or regional contexts and can be fully understood only by being situated within these contexts. Although it might be possible to compare conflicts and peace processes and to draw lessons from them across these different contexts, it remains that our analysis should start within them. Furthermore, the regional contexts themselves have been dramatically changing and whether these changes are leading to convergence or divergence remains to be seen. This chapter illustrates these general remarks through an examination of three case studies in the Western European context, and its central argument is that the significant political changes both at the regional level of the European Union and at the level of the EU member states have profoundly affected the nature of these struggles and have opened up new opportunities for a peaceful resolution of the conflicts, although the peace processes themselves have been very long and distinctly jagged in their outcomes.

The nation-state and minority nationalism

Nationalism is a complex phenomenon capable of several definitions. At least two are relevant to this chapter: the nationalism of those countries which have become 'fully fledged' nation-states (for example, the United Kingdom, France and Spain) and the nationalism of territorially based groups within these states which have aspired to nation-state status (Northern Irish Catholics, Corsicans and Spanish Basques). Both types of nationalism appeal to the normative principle of the 'nation-state', that is, that nations ought to have states and that states ought to be coterminous with nations.[1]

In practice, there has been a wide variation both in terms of the application of the principle and in the institutional expression given to liberal democratic nation-states (from simple unitary states to more complex regionalized and federal states).[2] Furthermore, even in a country such as France, allegedly the 'nation-state' par excellence, there has never been a perfect match between 'state' and 'nation' with cultural and linguistic minorities contesting their appartenance to the French 'nation'.[3] It is, a fortiori, difficult to apply the 'nation-state' model to either the UK or Spain, which are more properly categorized as 'union' states.[4] In the UK, it is highly problematic whether there exists an overarching (British) 'nation' coterminous with the UK 'state', given that England, Scotland and Wales and, before 1921, Ireland, were constitutionally accepted as the constituent nations of the kingdom. The 'state',[5] too, is far from homogeneously unified but consists rather of a heterogeneous collection of administrative arrangements which differed across the different territories of the UK. Spain, too, has never been a completely united or unitary state, although from the nineteenth century onwards, and certainly during the Franco dictatorship, Spanish elites aspired to the French Jacobin model. This aspiration, however, was frustrated by the existence of Catalonia, the Basque Country and Galicia.[6] When Spain made the transition to democracy in 1976–78, political decentralization and, in particular, the recognition of the national rights of the three historic nations of Catalonia, the Basque Country and Galicia[7] were key elements of the democratization process. Nevertheless, despite the innovative character of the Spanish 'autonomic state', the 1978 Constitution still remained somewhat confused and ambiguous about the relationship between the Spanish 'nation' and the 'nationalities' and 'regions'.[8]

Besides these ambiguities in defining and giving constitutional and legal expression to the nation-state idea, as illustrated by these three country case studies, the concept and political programme deriving from it have also been strongly contested by various ideologies and political movements such as federalists, regionalists and advocates of a united Europe. In France, the UK and Spain, minority nationalists challenged their respective nation-states in a variety of ways. Ideologically, they refused to recognize the legitimacy of the state's presence in their territories, arguing that this had come about by conquest. Each group generated an alternative 'founding myth' of their 'nation': in Northern Ireland, it was the physical force tradition which had expressed itself in various nineteenth century rebellions but especially the 1916 Easter Rising and the first Dáil of 1919; in the Basque Country, it was the existence of a 'unique' people whose ethnic origins were shrouded in mystery; in Corsica it was the short republic of Pascal Paoli (1749–69) which had been inspired by Rousseau's writings. The nationalists rejected both the symbols and the institutions of the nation-state of which they were part. However, their most serious challenge was to the state's monopoly of the use of force through the setting up of secret armies. In each case, the circumstances surrounding the violence and the forms it took differed. In Northern Ireland, the Provisional Irish Republican Army (IRA) could draw on a long tradition of political violence going back to the nineteenth century. In the Basque Country, the adoption of violent tactics happened only in the 1960s with the formation of Euskadi ta Askatasuna (ETA or 'Basque Homeland and Freedom').[9] In Corsica, it was only in 1962 that the first bombings took place in protest at French governmental policies on the island.[10] Various clandestine groups appeared in the 1960s and 1970s which, in 1976, coalesced into the Front de Libération Nationale de la Corse (FLNC).

Whatever the origins of violence, the results were similar in each case: a cycle of violence, state repression and further violence. Although the violent separatists were a minority in each region, their actions were sufficient to influence and even dominate the political agenda and to prevent solutions to their regions' problems arrived at by the national governments and other regional groups. Furthermore, agents close to the state often retaliated with violence, thus further undermining the legitimacy of the state in the eyes of more moderate regionalists or nationalists.[11] The impunity with which these anti-nationalist forces operated damaged trust in either the judiciary or the police in all three cases, thus unintentionally playing into the hands of the separatists. Finally, these 'wars' all had the effect of producing large numbers of prisoners, regarded as 'criminals' by the state and its supporters and as 'prisoners of war' or 'political prisoners' by the separatists and their supporters. Prisoners' issues became a fundamental element of the separatists' campaigns and the prisoners themselves in all three cases were granted a legitimacy by their movements as a result of the sacrifice which they had made for the 'cause'.[12]

By the 1980s, the violent conflicts in all three regions seemed insoluble as the protagonists were opposed not only in their sets of demands but also in their very conception of the nature of the problems. At root were two conflicting sets of claims about nationhood, sovereignty, legitimacy and control of the means of coercion. It is remarkable, then, given the complexities of the different conflicts, that breakthrough became possible in all three cases in the 1990s, even if these are still experiencing great difficulties and, in the case of the Basque Country, seem to have been reversed, at least for the moment. The remainder of this chapter will attempt to explain the context which made these breakthroughs possible.

A new geopolitical context

A series of developments from the early 1980s changed the context in which these conflicts were being fought out. We have dealt with these elsewhere[13] but it is worthwhile to draw attention briefly to the following. Since 1945, advanced capitalist states have, to use Thomas Kuhn's phrase, gone through at least two and perhaps three 'paradigm shifts'.[14] The first paradigm we have called the 'Welfare State' model which was adopted by most Western states from the early 1950s until the late 1970s/early 1980s (see Table 4.1). This was replaced by the 'neo-liberal' paradigm, associated with the ideas of the 'New Right' and politicians such as Ronald Reagan and Margaret Thatcher, and which spread across Western states in the 1980s and 1990s. Today, we seem to be witnessing what may be called the 'communitarian/ social' state paradigm which is in effect a synthesis of traditional social democratic values and some neo-liberal policy approaches. It has also been called 'The Third Way'.[15]

Each of these paradigms conceives the relationship between the state, the economy, society and culture/values in a distinct manner. They also conceptualize the role of regions and regional policy in a particular way. The shift refers to a

Table 4.1 Changing paradigms of the state–society relationships, 1945–2000

	Economy	State Features	Society	Culture/values
The 'expansive' Welfare State	Fordist production methods heavy industries: coal and steel geographical factors of production important Keynesian approaches of macro-economic management nationalization full employment goal rise in incomes and living standards top-down regional policy founding of EEC	equality of opportunity government intervention progressive income tax citizens' right to services and expanding definition of 'needs' centralization and bureaucratization of public administration managerialism in public sector fiscal overload (1970s) crisis of ungovernability	freedom of the individual urbanization sexual 'revolution' expansive definition of human 'rights' growing importance of mass media mass travel and tourism secularization student revolutions and 'youth' culture social engagement	new values based on freedom and choice new lifestyles (clothing, living patterns) cosmopolitan culture regional cultures devalued – reduced to 'folklore' for tourists regionalist reactions to revalidate their cultures regional culture seen (by elites) as obstacle to regional development
The 'contracting' neo-liberal state	post-Fordist deregulation and privatization new technologies and systems of communication new (non-geographical) factors of production predominance of service industries	the 'hollow', 'elusive', 'anorexic' state no government intervention reduction of taxation privatization; deregulation; cutting back of services decentralization regionalization	'no such thing as society' (Thatcher) individualism glorification of greed decline of notions of 'common good' and community fragmentation of communities	the neo-liberal project = propagation of values rich less willing to pay for welfare services through taxation reactions to this – e.g. election of Blair, Jospin 'remoralization' in Britain culture as variable in economic development

Table 4.1 cont.

	Economy	State Features	Society	Culture/values
	globalization and 'glocalization' *bottom-up models of regional development* importance of knowledge: the 'learning' and innovative region accelerated European integration (1985–)	'New Public Management' 'marketization' of public services citizens as consumers	creation of an underclass in cities increasing gap between poor and rich (individual and geographical)	*new appreciation of and opportunities for regional cultures* *Europe of the Cultures 2002 (Flanders)*
The 'communitarian/social' state	acceptance of capitalism and the market low taxation end of class struggle innovative entrepreneurship social dimension and institutional economics role for trade unions and local authorities *economic regionalism*	claims to pursue equality of opportunity and social justice but through competition concept of the *enabling* state no return to the old Welfare State; slimming down of bureaucracy new public–private partnership decentralization and devolution revalidation of local authorities and rebuilding local democracy and sense of citizenship; pro-European	perhaps limits to individualization and fragmentation remoralization of society concept of community – communitarianism new approach to law and order issues – zero tolerance	acceptance of individualistic trends toleration of different lifestyles new concepts of human rights *revalidation of regional and local cultures* personalism

fundamental reordering of these relationships and a reconceptualization of regions and regional policy. The evolution of our three case studies might also be understood in the context of the evolution of the three paradigms as a way of clarifying some of their most salient features and of understanding how solutions now seem to be within their grasp.

In the Welfare State paradigm, economies were in full expansion and states also expanded to provide and manage sets of needs and demands emanating from society. However, Welfare States were also bureaucratic, top-down and centralizing. Regional policy was conceived as the territorial expression of social policy, and both regional and social policies were aimed at integrating the weaker individuals and territories into the national society. In many respects the Welfare State model represents the epitome of the nation-state idea but also perhaps its limits.[16] By concentrating on *national* goals, it tended to exclude other perspectives such as those that might be found at the regional or local levels. The regional development programmes were often formulated and carried out by national elites with only token representation and even exclusion of regional and local elites. During this period, regional languages and cultures were regarded as obstacles to economic and social development. At most, they were relegated to quaint folkloric customs that might have a role in amusing tourists.

France, the UK and Spain (even at the time of Franco) all adopted versions of this model despite their very different political systems. In both France and the UK, there was an overall increase in the standard of living and social benefits available to many citizens. In Spain, during the last years of Francoism, there was a modernizing, technocratic elite, close to the Catholic organization Opus Dei, who tried to put into effect similar approaches, although the country as a whole remained quite poor by West European standards. Whatever the circumstances, in all three countries the arrival of Welfare States affected the three regions under consideration in a number of ways. In all three cases, there appeared new political movements which mobilized important sections of the population: in Northern Ireland, the Civil Rights Movement demanded equal treatment for Catholics on the basis of their membership of the UK; in Corsica (as in other French regions such as Brittany and the French Basque Country), regionalists demanded equal treatment with the French mainland on the basis of their French citizenship; in the Basque Country, moderate nationalists demanded recognition of their language and culture. In all three cases, however, these movements were really coalitions of disparate groups. The demands of the different groups within the coalitions were still couched in 'stato-national' terms, ranging from the full implementation of their rights as citizens of that state, to complete separatism but in the form of setting miniature 'nation-states'. The national governments first responded to these demands with repression and then (at least in the UK and France) with concessions which were usually too little too late. A cycle of violence, repression and further violence was initiated. By the 1980s, all three regions were experiencing high levels of violence. This led to the disintegration of the coalitions into moderate and radical factions, with the latter gradually increasing the intransigent nature of their demands. These radical demands and the equally intransigent responses of the national governments were so irreconcilable that solutions seemed impossible to reach. National governments claimed absolute sovereignty over the territories in which the conflicts were happening and the nationalist movements made the same claim. Both resorted to coercion or violence to back up their claims. In all three regions, significant sections of the population withdrew their consent to be governed.[17]

Did the European Community (EC) play a role during this period in either the exacerbation or calming of these conflicts? The answer is that 'Europe' was a dimension which tended to be in the background even if it was not altogether absent. During the Welfare State period of state development, the EC was reduced to the role of attempting to complete the Common Market and ensuring harmonization of trade activities across states. The dominant mode of European politics and policy-making was then definitely intergovernmental, that is, firmly based on the predominance of the national governments.[18] At the same time, some moderate regionalists were also European federalists while European federalists, such as the European Federalist Movement, were also sympathetic to regionalism. The more hardline minority nationalists, however, such as ETA, the FLNC and Sinn Fein (even before the split into Officials and Provisionals) were opposed to European integration. This opposition had two main sources. Some espoused a Marxist analysis which saw the European Community as a capitalist 'rich men's club'. Others opposed it because they saw it as a threat to the nationalist idea and therefore to what might emerge as their own mini-nation-states. In other words, their opposition mirrored that of nationalists such as de Gaulle and, later, Mrs Thatcher and Tory Euro-sceptics.

The Welfare State model of the state entered into crisis at the end of the 1970s and found itself unable to provide the range of benefits to citizens on which it had been premised. This crisis was probably part of a wider crisis of the capitalist system, which had been based on 'Fordist' methods of production and the smoke-stack industries of coal and steel. While capitalism successfully renewed itself through the development of new technologies and globalization, the political and administrative systems of Western European states were still based on the old Welfare State model and were much slower to change. Furthermore, these states found themselves increasingly facing stiff economic competition from the United States and Japan, which had succeeded in adapting themselves to the new economic realities. Western states responded to these challenges in two ways. First, they adopted, in different ways, what we have called the 'neo-liberal' paradigm to restructure their states.[19] Second, and related to this, they decided that they could achieve more by collaboration rather than as single, small or medium-sized countries. As a result, and with the encouragement of other elites such as the European Round Table of Industrialists, they 'relaunched' the process of European integration in the early 1980s. When he became President of the European Commission in 1985, Jacques Delors took up this challenge and decided that European integration would be pushed forward through the Single European Act and the implementation of the Single Market in 1992. Thus, 'Europe' became an increasingly important variable in a growing range of policy sectors, including regional policy. It was during this period of state and economic restructuring that the notion of a 'Europe of the Regions', an old federalist idea, was resurrected by the German *Länder* in order to advance both the cause of a federalist Europe and to enhance the position of subnational authorities generally.[20]

Although not intended by neo-liberals such as Mrs Thatcher when she signed the Single European Act in 1986, these political and institutional developments had enormous consequences both for the institutions and policies of the European Community and for the position of nation-states and their regions. First, the notion of national 'sovereignty' was further transformed. This had already changed from being the absolute exercise of power by national governments over fixed territories to being 'pooled' over an increasing range of areas. Decisions were increasingly taken in 'Brussels' and simply incorporated into national law by member state parliaments. Second, the institutions of the Community, especially the European Commission and the European Court of Justice, were immensely strengthened even if the Council of Ministers, which allegedly represents the principle of 'national interest', probably continued to be the most important EU institution.[21] Third, regions and local authorities were given a new lease of life both through the Structural and Cohesion Funds, operated through the new principles of partnership and subsidiarity, but also through the setting up of the Committee of the Regions by the Treaty of Maastricht.[22] What occurred here is neither the disappearance of the nation-state (the old dream of regionalists and European federalists) nor the creation of a European federation along the lines of a Europe of the Regions.[23] Rather, what has emerged is a new system of European governance (rather than government), in which the European institutions, national governments and subnational authorities have distinct and new roles. This system of governance has both state-like and federal features without itself being either a state or a federation.

With the election of Clinton and his programme of 'reinventing government' in the United States and a succession of centre-left leaders such as Blair, Jospin and Schröder in Europe, the dominance of the 'neo-liberal' paradigm seems to be giving way a new formulation of the role of the state and its relationship with civil society. We have called this the 'communitarian social state' since, unlike neo-liberalism, it allows the state a positive role in economic and social processes but one that is based, unlike the Welfare State, on 'partnership', 'subsidiarity' and mobilization 'from below' and accepting some of the key features of neo-liberalism such as the market and competition. In other words, the communitarian social state attempts to combine neo-liberalism with some of the traditional values of 'social democracy', without returning to the Welfare State model. These approaches might also be found in the debate about the future European model and the whole question of governance which is exercising the minds of the European Commission President Prodi and his collaborators.

The transformation of the state, European integration and minority nationalist conflict

These developments have provided a new context in which the violent conflicts in Northern Ireland, the Basque Country and Corsica have been played out, although, once again, each case is very different from the others. First of all, they permit new ways of defining the nature of the problems themselves. Whereas, previously, the conflicts revolved irreconcilably around claims of national sovereignty, the redefinition of sovereignty itself allows the protagonists to reformulate their claims in a different kind of way. The pooling of national sovereignty at the European level means that sovereignty itself has been relativized. What, then, is the sense in engaging in violent conflict to assert one's 'sovereign' rights? In the case of Northern Ireland, this was at least one strand of the complex process that began with the 1985 Anglo-Irish Agreement and fed into the Good Friday Agreement.[24] In Corsica, too, the wider transformation of the European system of governance allowed politicians and activists from different parts of the political spectrum, as well as French national politicians, to redefine the nature of the Corsican problem.[25] In the Basque Country, a peace process was launched in the 1990s, mainly by the moderate Partido Nacionalista Vasco (PNV) Basque government which was partly inspired by the Northern Ireland peace process and partly by the wider developments at the level of Europe.[26]

The second positive development is that the emerging European system of governance provides a new forum within which new identities, or new combinations of complex identities, may be formed which do not threaten the national or regional identities of the various protagonists of the conflict. In this way, what were previously zero-sum relationships between say Irish, Northern Irish, Ulster or British identities which had become intensified and solidified as a result of the conflict can now be expressed in a very different manner because there is an even wider overarching identity which is 'European'. This is the case even if, as most attitude surveys suggest, the protagonists do not (yet) feel a strong European identity.[27] Nevertheless, 'Europe' provides a new frame of reference and, as we have seen, a new set of opportunities for political action for regions and local authorities. Political elites in our regions, as well as elsewhere in Europe, have seized these new realities as tools in a vast process of regional mobilization to assert and promote the interests of their regions in the new Europe. Regional identity and culture, in the new paradigm of the communitarian social state, are no longer considered an obstacle to regional economic development but may be, on the contrary, an asset, with Catalonia serving as a kind of model in this regard. These opportunities and the mobilizations stimulated by them have, to some extent, taken the sting out of identity conflicts and permit minority groups to develop a new self-confidence and pride in themselves. The existence of bodies such as the Committee of the Regions and the European Parliament and interregional associations such as the Assembly of European Regions, gives them new fora to express their identities, thus reducing the temptation to use the weapon of political violence. Of course, not all minority nationalists are convinced by these developments but these are increasingly reduced to a hard core isolated, to a large extent, from the wider population which had hitherto given them support.

Finally, the new European context and the changing nature of nation-states present a challenge to those minority nationalist movements who had opposed European integration and had tried to set up their own mini-nation-states. It is increasingly recognized by these groups that the goal of complete independence is unrealistic. This has now been reformulated as 'independence within Europe'. 'Europe' and the slogan 'Europe of the Regions' have been used by minority nationalists as a way of repositioning themselves towards, and putting pressure on, their own national governments. This is seen strikingly in the case of the Catalan and Scottish nationalists but it may also be found in our three case studies. Furthermore, often national governments and regions collaborate in seeking greater funding opportunities from the EU, leading to a new type of relationship between them. Thus, the ideological basis of minority nationalism is changing and this makes the conflicts much less of a zero-sum game.

Most of the leading protagonists of peace in our three regions have been national and regional politicians deeply imbued with this European perspective. On the regional level may be found: John Hume and the Social Democratic and Labour Party (SDLP) in Northern Ireland; the PNV in the Basque Country (largely inspired by John Hume); and Claude Olivesi and Paul Giacobbi in Corsica. On the national level: the pro-European Tony Blair; and Pierre Joxe and Lionel Jospin; while in Spain, Aznar has not yet made the link between his Europeanism and the Basque peace process. It is true that Sinn Fein remains somewhat Euro-sceptic but, for the moment, they seem to have decided on a new pragmatism which tones down their previous intransigent republicanism and accepts the opportunities of the new European context.

Conclusions

These remarks should not be taken to imply that the transition from armed struggle to non-violent political action in our three regions has gone smoothly. Indeed, in Northern Ireland, it is over 17 years since the Anglo-Irish Agreement was signed and over eight years since the first IRA ceasefire in 1994, and peace is not yet definitively installed. In Corsica, the process has been much more rapid but scarcely less rocky. In the Basque Country, after a shaky beginning, the ETA ceasefire broke down and violence had even intensified.[28] Nevertheless, in all three cases a huge amount of progress has been achieved. Northern Ireland has new institutions, in part modelled on the institutions of the European Community, in part on the Nordic Council, which are now more or less functioning. These institutions may be regarded as kind of laboratory for testing some of the propositions concerning the emergence of a new kind of state dealt with in this chapter. The IRA and Loyalist ceasefires are still in operation while dissident groups such as the 'Real' IRA and the Loyalist Volunteer Force have little support in the wider population. In Corsica, the French government has come to an agreement with the majority of the Corsican political class with regard to radical institutional reforms of the island's status and the ceasefire by the main groups is still holding. The Bill giving effect to these reforms was successfully voted in by the French Parliament in June 2001. In the Basque Country, there is a new awareness of the possibilities of peace and the moderate Basques are still pursuing this vigorously. The success of the PNV in the regional elections of June 2001 are an indication that the majority of the Basque population is willing to follow the moderate nationalist party's peace line and rejects the return to violence of ETA.

Nevertheless, difficulties remain. In all three cases, it would not be an exaggeration to say that these are caused by factions or individuals who have not managed to adapt to the contemporary political realities outlined in this chapter. In Northern Ireland, unionists have undergone a traumatic challenge to their traditional identity as 'British', and an important minority has tried to resist the changes. In Corsica, while the majority of the political class, both nationalist and non-nationalist, have adapted, an important faction have resisted. The former French Minister of the Interior, Jean-Pierre Chevènement, vigorously opposed any concessions to Corsican autonomy and eventually resigned in protest at the deal that was struck in the end between the Prime Minister, Lionel Jospin, and the Corsican Assembly. In the Basque Country, the hardliners are the radical nationalists ETA/Herri Batasuna (HB) but also the Spanish Prime Minister Aznar. However, in all three countries, there is a wide-ranging debate, at least among academics and politicians, if not the general public, on the meaning of nationhood, regionalism and identity in the context of a changing nation-state and increasing European integration. This debate opens the possibility of a new form of civic republicanism and the discussion of the place of minority groups in European society in which political violence is abandoned as a method of making claims, to be replaced, hopefully, by rational and peaceful discussion.

Notes

1. P. Alter, *Nationalism*, 2nd edn (London: Edward Arnold, 1994).
2. J. Loughlin, *Subnational Democracy in the European Union: Challenges and Opportunities* (Oxford: Oxford University Press, 2001).
3. J. Loughlin, *Regionalism and Ethnic Nationalism in France: a Case Study of Corsica* (Florence: European University Institute, 1989).
4. D. Urwin, 'Territorial Structures and Political Developments in the United Kingdom', in S. Rokkan & D. Urwin (eds), *The Politics of Territorial Identity* (London: Sage Publications, 1982) and L. Moreno, *Federalizing the Spanish State* (London: Frank Cass, 2000).
5. It is a moot point as to whether the UK even possesses a 'state', at least in the sense in which this word is understood in the countries of continental Europe, which possess *l'État, lo Stato, el Estado*, etc. In the UK and, in the Anglo-Saxon tradition in general, we refer more to 'government' or, perhaps, to the 'Crown' (UK) or the 'Constitution' rather than the state.
6. D. Conversi, *The Basques, the Catalans and Spain: Alternative Routes to Nationalist Mobilisation* (London: Hurst, 1997) and Moreno, op. cit.
7. Galicia did not have the same degree of nationalist mobilization as the other two regions and, in fact, was quite pro-Franco. Nevertheless, it received the same favourable treatment of recognition after the transition to democracy.
8. The Constitution defines Spain (including the Catalans, Basques and Galicians) as a unitary and indivisible 'nation' within which exist 'nationalities' and 'regions', without specifying which is which.
9. F. Letamendia, *Historia del nacionalismo vasco y de ETA*, 3 vols (San Sebastian: R&B Ediciones, 1994).
10. Loughlin, *Regionalism*.
11. In Northern Ireland, various branches of the British security forces carried out clandestine activities against republicans and often assisted loyalist groups in their attacks on the Catholic community. In the Basque Country, the GAL (Anti-terrorist Liberation Groups – *Grupos Antiterroristas de Liberación*), a secret police group operating with the

connivance of parts of the Spanish government, carried out assassinations of nationalists, sometimes on French soil. In Corsica, there were suspicions that nationalists were
attacked and sometimes killed by *barbouzes*, secret militias opposed to nationalism.

12. In Northern Ireland, the death of Bobby Sands on hunger strike consolidated this aspect
    of the struggle.
13. Loughlin, *Subnational Democracy*.
14. J. Loughlin, 'Regional Autonomy and State Paradigm Shift in Western Europe', *Regional
    and Federal Studies*, 10, 2 (2000), 10–34.
15. A. Giddens, *The Third Way: a Renewal of Social Democracy* (Malden, Mass.: Polity Press, 1998).
16. It represents the epitome of the nation-state as a democratic system because it attempted
    to develop the notion of 'social' citizenship as opposed to purely formal 'political' citi-
    zenship. It represents its limits because the Welfare State, in the end, failed to deliver on
    this promise and, instead, became an excessively centralized and bureaucratic system
    from which the majority of citizens were excluded.
17. This is especially true of Northern Ireland and the Basque Country. In Corsica, only a
    small minority withdrew their consent.
18. It would take us too far outside the scope of this chapter to deal with this issue. Suffice
    it to say that in the 1960s it was General de Gaulle, as President of France (1962–69),
    who left his mark by asserting the notion of a *Europe des Patries* rather than a suprana-
    tional or federal Europe.
19. We speak here of the neo-liberal paradigm but it is important to remember that this is
    not a completely coherent model, was not fully implemented even in the UK, and took
    several different expressions depending on which country it was applied to. Nevertheless,
    there are a number of broad ideas which its adherents promoted: less and even no state
    intervention in the economy and society; the centrality of entrepreneurship; the pre-
    dominance of markets as a mechanism for the allocation of value; competition, etc.
20. J. Loughlin, 'The Europe of the Regions and the Federalization of Europe', *Publius: the
    Journal of Federalism* (Fall 1996).
21. It could be argued that despite its role of representing 'national interests', the Council
    has become, in effect, a supranational institution, since, in an increasing number of pol-
    icy areas, its decisions override the decisions of individual national governments.
    Furthermore, national governments increasingly frame their so-called 'national inter-
    ests' in 'European' terms, that is, they arrive at meetings of the Council of Ministers with
    proposals couched in terms that are likely to be acceptable to their colleagues.
22. J. Loughlin & D. L. Seiler, 'Le comité des Régions et la supranationalité en Europe', *Etudes
    Internationales* (Décembre 1999).
23. Loughlin, 'The Europe of the Regions'.
24. Ironically, the process was launched by two rather traditional nationalists: Charles
    Haughey and Margaret Thatcher. In the case of the latter, however, it is doubtful whether
    she fully grasped the consequences of the agreements she was entering into, just as she
    failed to grasp the full consequences of signing the Single European Act. John Hume
    probably played an important role in the background of these developments as did
    senior British and Irish Civil Servants working in the European Community.
25. J. Loughlin, C. Olivesi & F. Daftary (eds), *Autonomies Insulaires: vers une politique de dif-
    ference pour la Corse?* (Ajaccio: Editions Albiana, 1999).
26. J. Loughlin & F. Letamendia, 'Peace in the Basque Country and Corsica', in M. Cox,
    A. Guelke & F. Stephens et al. (eds), *A Farewell to Arms? From 'Long War' to Long Peace in
    Northern Ireland* (Manchester: Manchester University Press, 2000).
27. It is interesting that those with the strongest European identity are those sections of the
    population that are most highly educated and found in the higher social groups, in
    other words, among social elites. But it is precisely these elites who must be the bearers
    either of a nationalist project or the main protagonists in a peace process.
28. Loughlin & Letamendia, op. cit.

Part II
Negotiations

Many attempted peace initiatives fail to reach the negotiation stage. Indeed, the conditions laid down for entry to negotiations are often the main stumbling block. In a perfect world, negotiations provide a forum for antagonists to reach a comprehensive set of compromises in a stable environment. The reality is often complicated by suspicion, continuing violence or tension, and politicking within camps. Moreover, the high-stakes nature of negotiations, involving the possibility of gains or losses over power and resources, means that the location, timetable, participant list, chair and status of any negotiations are likely to cause as much conflict as the issues on the agenda.

While desirable, trust between negotiating partners is not essential. Instead it is important that they trust the ability of the negotiations, whether embodied by the chair or guaranteed by third parties, to deliver and implement a peace accord. To this end, ground rules for negotiation, procedures for 'troubleshooting' or addressing impasses, and techniques to ease communication become important. In some circumstances, face-to-face negotiations prove impossible, requiring the involvement of mediators. The media are a potential complicating factor. On the one hand negotiations may prosper away from the glare of publicity. On the other, secret negotiations can generate suspicion and cause confusion, something that may have severe implications if a subsequent peace accord is dependent on public support.

Ultimately it is the quality of the negotiations that matters, and whether they tackle the core issues of the conflict, include the main participants of the conflict, and have sufficient local and international backing to implement any agreement.

5
Negotiations and Peace Processes

Adrian Guelke

The connection between negotiations and peace processes rests on two apparently straightforward and seemingly persuasive propositions. They are that tangible evidence of a commitment to peace on the part of the major combatants is needed to create the right climate for negotiations to end violent political conflict and that the pursuit of a negotiated settlement is needed to sustain any peace process. They imply a more or less symbiotic relationship between negotiations and peace processes. It is a small step from these propositions to argue that the way to peace itself lies through negotiations culminating in a political settlement. However, not merely are political settlements frequently challenged by violence, but the two propositions themselves are more problematic than they appear at first sight. Thus, in practice, the circumstances in which parties are willing to enter into negotiations vary widely. What is acceptable in one political context may prove insufficient in another. As far as the assumed relationship between political settlements and peace is concerned, even the converse relationship does not necessarily hold. The consequence of failure of the parties to reach a negotiated settlement may not be the renewed outbreak of violent conflict, as the case of Cyprus's long, largely bloodless conflict since partition in 1974 underlines.

The failure of negotiations to end protracted violent political conflicts is typically attributed to a variety of factors, including most commonly the pursuit of irreconcilable aims by the major antagonists, obdurate political leadership, and the stage of the conflict. The obverse of these propositions is that successful negotiation depends on a readiness of the parties to compromise; political leadership capable of developing a relationship with the other side and the right timing. In particular, numerous writers have focused on the process of refining the positions of the parties so as to achieve an outcome that meets the aspirations of all of the parties.[1] In the language of conflict resolution this is referred to as a 'win–win' solution or slightly more realistically as a positive sum solution, i.e. a formula that gives more to the parties than a simple splitting of the difference between their positions. Other studies have focused on the importance of developing trust between those engaged in the negotiations, on breaking down what is sometimes labelled the psychological dimension of the conflict.[2] Finally, the issue of timing has received considerable attention, most notably in the writings of William

Zartman and his very widely quoted notion of ripeness allied to that of a mutually hurting stalemate.[3]

What these approaches have in common is their rationalistic view of the process of negotiations and the positive value they place on the objective of a negotiated settlement. From this perspective, negotiations are seen as a learning process and their success depends on a maturing of the views of the protagonists during the conflict that opens the way firstly to mediation, then to direct engagement with their enemies and finally to a settlement. A remark typifying such a perspective was made by the Deputy Leader of the Social Democratic and Labour Party, Seamus Mallon, in relation to the Good Friday Agreement in Northern Ireland. He described the settlement as 'Sunningdale for slow learners'. This was a reference to the Sunningdale Agreement of December 1973, which was opposed at the time by both the republican movement and a majority of unionists. Another implication of this perspective is that there is a sharp distinction to be drawn between negotiation and coercion. (However, on this point there are important differences among writers whose approach to negotiations can be categorized as fundamentally rationalistic. Thus, Zartman accords a much greater role both to power politics in establishing the context for negotiation and to the use of incentives in the case of mediation than do the followers of John Burton to either.) Even if it is accepted that a consequence of the breakdown of negotiations may be further violence, the readiness of the parties to settle their differences by negotiations is regarded as an indicator of their peaceful intentions. Further, the process of negotiations itself is frequently accompanied by a suspension of hostilities in the form of ceasefires and the like.

However, it is possible to present the process of negotiations, not as separate from coercion, but as integral to it. This realpolitik, as opposed to conflict resolution, model of negotiations is encapsulated in the realist precept of 'negotiations from strength' and in a catchphrase of South African policy during the 1980s, 'thump and talk'. The most eloquent advocacy of negotiations not as an alternative to power politics but their continuation by other means is to be found in Henry Kissinger's memoirs.[4] In *The White House Years* Kissinger strongly criticized American foreign policy during the 1950s when it was the policy of the government to eschew negotiations with the Soviet Union. He argued that the failure of the United States to engage the Soviet Union in negotiations resulted in missed opportunities to capitalize on the relative weakness of the Soviet Union. In particular, the existing division of Europe remained frozen in place when a more dynamic policy might have forced the Soviet Union into making concessions to the West. Kissinger blamed the notions that trust was necessary to negotiations and that friendship was a necessary component of negotiations for the attitude taken by both American government and public to the question. He used the case of the Korean War to underline his argument.

> Our perception of power and diplomacy as distinct and separate phases of foreign policy prevented us from negotiating to settle the Korean War after the landing at Inchon when we were in the strongest military position; it tempted

us to escalate our aims. A year later it also caused us to stop military operations except of a purely defensive nature the moment negotiations got under way, thus removing the enemy's major incentive for a rapid diplomatic settlement. We acted as if the process of negotiation operated on its own inherent logic independent of the military balance – indeed, that military pressures might jeopardize the negotiations by antagonizing our adversary or demonstrating bad faith. Not surprisingly, a stalemate of nearly two years' duration followed, during which our casualties equalled those we had endured when hostilities were unconstrained. Treating force and diplomacy as discrete phenomena caused our power to lack purpose and our negotiations to lack force.[5]

The gulf between this position and that of the Burtonian, Mark Hoffman, could hardly be greater. Hoffman defines conflict resolution as follows: 'the attainment of a non-hierarchical, non-coercive integrative solution that is derived from the parties themselves through a process of analytic problem-solving'.[6]

Another position exists. It is possible to argue that in some situations negotiations are undesirable in principle. In particular, it is frequently asserted that governments should not negotiate with terrorists, especially in the context of demands backed up by threats to the lives of hostages. In the course of the Second World War, the Allies ruled out any possibility of negotiations with the Axis powers by committing themselves to the objective of unconditional surrender. The nature of the regimes the Allies faced meant that this approach encountered little criticism. While these might be seen as exceptional cases, it is possible to extend this approach to apply to almost any conflict and it is important to take this perspective into account since its influence among communities or societies resisting change is often very considerable. Parties in internal conflicts frequently argue the case for 'victory before peace', a slogan used by the followers of Ian Paisley in 1976 when they protested against the Peace People, a movement formed to demand an end to political violence in Northern Ireland. A common theme of opponents of peace processes is that they entail the appeasement of evil groups whose demands ought to be resisted. Opposition to peace processes usually includes the demand that there should be no negotiations with any groups which have not completely and fully repudiated violence, or, if such negotiations have already begun, that they should be ended forthwith. One reason why such demands are made so fervently is the belief that the initiation of negotiations with such groups, regardless of the outcome of any talks, confers a measure of legitimacy upon them that is not warranted

It might fairly be suggested that the two models of negotiations described above apply in different contexts, in particular, that the realpolitik model of negotiations is most appropriate to the realm of international relations, the conflict resolution model to that of domestic politics. In support of this proposition, it is evidently the case that the settlement of international disputes through negotiations or the achievement of other objectives through negotiations, such as arms control, does not require the parties to abandon an overall relationship of antagonism. That was apparent during the period of superpower détente in the 1970s and 1980s. By contrast, in a domestic context, without an abatement of the power struggle between the parties, the prospects for the survival of a negotiated political settlement are likely to be poor. However, the distinction between the two contexts can be over-drawn. Thus, Anwar Sadat's initiative in going to Jerusalem in 1977 was credited with achieving a vital psychological breakthrough in the Arab–Israeli conflict. The continuing influence of this example on international relations of the Middle East is reflected in debate on whether a symbolic gesture on behalf of either of the parties might contribute to a breakthrough in relations between Israel and Syria.[7] The agreement reached between representatives of the United States, South Vietnam, North Vietnam and the Viet Cong on a ceasefire and elections, though directed at the domestic political context of the future government of South Vietnam, fits the realpolitik model of negotiations much better than the conflict resolution model. The same is true of the Dayton Agreement of December 1995 on Bosnia. The former barely provided the decent interval the Americans were seeking to effect their withdrawal; the latter remains critically dependent on external imposition.

In the case of failed settlements, there is often plenty of room for argument over whether power politics or a failure to address the root causes of the conflict sufficiently comprehensively or inclusively is to blame. In practice, most settlements achieved through a process of negotiation both entail the application of agreed normative political principles and reflect the balance of power among the parties. But while the existing balance of forces in any conflict places limits on what can be achieved through negotiations and while, conversely, a change in the balance of forces may make a settlement possible in a previously intractable conflict, settlements that do not rest on some normative foundation that is separate from the power political considerations are unlikely to prove durable. Of course, a commitment to some normative element, such as power-sharing, may be made in bad faith by one or more of the parties, so the mere existence of normative elements as part of a negotiated settlement does not guarantee their success, as the examples of Rwanda and Sierra Leone in the 1990s underline. However, such failures do not provide grounds for discounting the significance of the normative dimension to peace processes.

Common reasons why people resort to violence are the perception that they will continue to be denied justice under the existing political system, or, alternatively, that rebellion threatens a valued way of life. Certainly, calculation of the consequences of the use of violence plays a part, but it is secondary to the normative considerations. This is also evident in the phases that typically accompany the negotiated settlement of a violent political conflict within a polity. In difficult cases at least seven phases of the process can be identified. They are:

1. the pre-talks phase;
2. an era of secret talks;
3. the opening of multilateral talks;
4. negotiating to a settlement;
5. gaining endorsement;
6. implementing its provisions; and
7. the institutionalization of the new dispensation.

Each phase will be analysed briefly below.

Pre-talks

The unwillingness of both parties to the conflict to enter into negotiations in the early stages of a conflict may be explained by the belief of both parties in their ability to achieve their aims through other means, typically physical coercion. It is on the basis of this assumption that Zartman argues that ripeness, entailing the perception by the parties of the existence of a mutually hurting stalemate, is a necessary condition for the initiation of meaningful negotiations. However, the symmetrical avoidance of negotiations by both sides tends to be exaggerated in the literature. External backers of insurgents may insist on their side's being willing to enter into negotiations. Thus, the front-line states supporting the ANC and other liberation movements in southern Africa insisted that the 1969 Lusaka Manifesto should contain an offer to Pretoria of a willingness to settle the issues causing conflict in the region by negotiations. A motive for insurgents to seek negotiations at the outset of the conflict is that it gives them a measure of legitimacy, by underscoring both the political nature of their demands and by the implication that the conflict cannot be ended without their participation in a settlement. From a very different perspective, a government may calculate that it is better to engage insurgents in negotiations at an early stage in order to be able to deal with their demands from a position of relative strength. (In the conflict between Israel and neighbouring Arab states – admittedly a conflict in which the parties were governments – the stance of the Israeli government for many years was that there should be bilateral negotiations between the parties, based on the belief that such a context was favourable to Israel.)

Of course, for agreement to be reached on the initiation of negotiations, the desire of the parties to negotiate has to coincide and their very different motives for entering into talks tend to militate against such a coincidence. Further, negotiations that take place in such circumstances rarely, if ever, produce positive results. Zartman acknowledges the possibility that negotiations may take place for what he calls tactical reasons, but he argues that a crucial ingredient for serious talks will generally be absent, the intent of the parties to arrive at a joint outcome. However, even tactical negotiations are relatively uncommon in the early stages of a conflict and may not even occur as the conflict matures. This is because a characteristic of the initial phases of conflict is mobilization by the parties of their supporters behind mutually exclusive objectives and the demonization of the other side. The persistence and seeming permanence of such factors tend to be features of the most intractable conflicts. It was well described by Meron Benvenisti in 1990 in the case of the conflict between Israelis and Palestinians:

> There is a perpetual conflict, not necessarily violent, between the Jewish majority group that seeks to maintain its superiority, and the Arab minority group (Israeli Arabs and Palestinians in the territories) that seeks to free itself from majority tyranny. The majority community perceives the struggle as one of 'law and order'. The minority community, which does not regard the regime as legitimate, seeks to destroy it. Both communities deny each other's standing as a

legitimate collective entity. Hence, the Arabs define Zionism (the expression of the collective aspirations of the Jewish people) as racism – ergo illegitimate. The Israelis, in their turn, define Palestinian nationalism as Palestine Liberation Organisation (PLO) terrorism – ergo illegitimate. The delegitimisation is vital for both sides, for it enables them to believe in the exclusivity of their claim and in the absolute justice of their position.[8]

While the destructiveness of the conflict may seem an unavoidable cost to the antagonists themselves, external parties may be less sanguine than the combatants about the consequences of the conflict's persistence. Mediation may be pursued at this or any other phase of the conflict by such parties. For the reasons alluded to, it is unlikely to prove fruitful. A common way for governments at the centre of conflicts to deflect pressure from external parties for a resolution is the promotion of an alternative partner to that of its principal antagonist. In many conflicts the search for a 'moderate' alternative turns out to be a chimera. However, it is by no means always the case that the insurgents represent the majority of those on behalf of whom they have taken up arms. Thus, throughout Northern Ireland's troubles it was clear that the republican movement represented a minority of the Catholic population of the province.

Secret talks

Both the desire not to accord legitimacy to the other side and the fear of the reaction of supporters provide two reasons why the first stage in a peace process tends to take the form of secret talks between the main combatants or those who conceive themselves as such. A further reason for secrecy is their exploratory nature. By this point, the parties usually have not committed themselves irrevocably to a negotiated settlement as a way out of conflict. That is reflected in the absence of a truce or ceasefires. Communication through a third party or contact at a level of officials in the case of the government side are common in this phase. To begin with, both the fact that talks between the parties have taken place and their content tend to be hidden from public view. However, what distinguishes this phase from the previous one is that by this point there is usually a strong desire by both parties simultaneously for an exit from the conflict.

In the later stage of this phase, the general public is likely to become aware that secret talks between the parties have been taking place, though without learning a great deal about the content of the talks. How the public reacts to this knowledge has an important bearing on whether the parties proceed further along the path of negotiations. In situations where the public's overriding concern is that there should be an end to violence, there may be a very positive response to the revelation of secret talks since it can be taken for granted that a central objective of talks between the parties will be to establish the terms for an end to the violence. Where ending violence is not quite so high a priority for the whole of the society, fears about the political compromises discussed in secret between the parties may produce a strongly negative reaction, at least from a section of public opinion.

Multilateral talks

Formal, multilateral negotiations are a necessary phase in practically any peace process. Formality is necessary to provide a public assurance of the commitment of the parties to the successful outcome of the process. How inclusive the process is of significant strands of political opinion has a strong bearing on perceptions of its legitimacy, both internally and externally. Even when the process is largely being driven forward by two parties within a multilateral framework, they will often take great pains to ensure the participation of minor parties in the settlement, as in the case of South Africa, where the National Party government and the African National Congress amended the transitional constitution in the run-up to the 1994 elections so as to facilitate the participation of the Inkatha Freedom Party and the extreme right Freedom Front. Another consideration is that few conflicts are so simple that the two sides which engaged in secret talks to end the violence are also in a position to construct a comprehensive political settlement that will command widespread acceptance. Other parties need to be drawn into the process if the objective is to achieve a lasting settlement and, in fact, some of them may have to be involved even to achieve the minimal objective of sustaining a temporary truce.

Symbolic issues loom large in formal, multilateral negotiations. Arguments over representation, the venue, procedures and the agenda may delay the tackling of substantive questions. The initiation of negotiations on the future of South Vietnam in the early 1970s became deadlocked on how the parties should be represented at the talks which famously took the form of an argument over the shape of the table at which the negotiations were to take place. The unwillingness of certain parties to engage in face-to-face talks may require the mechanism of proximity talks, in which a third party shuttles between two delegations, as occurred at Dayton. Further, it is often the case that much of the real business of the negotiations is conducted outside of the structures of the multilateral negotiations. In particular, the crucial compromises between the main political parties frequently take place in secret talks, the existence of which only becomes apparent when they seek endorsement of these agreements in meetings of the multilateral negotiations. The need to establish as wide support for any agreements as possible rules out the option of bypassing a multilateral process altogether. However, while formal, multilateral negotiations are usually a necessary condition for the creation of lasting political settlements, they are not a sufficient condition.

Settlement

The existence of inclusive negotiations by no means guarantees movement towards a political settlement. Indeed, particularly if there is little likelihood, in the absence of a settlement, of a return to violent conflict on a scale unacceptable to both sides, the process itself may come to be seen as almost a substitute for a settlement, an attitude encapsulated in the Turkish Cypriot aphorism, 'no solution is a solution'. Even if the two sides do in fact passionately share the desire for an end to the conflict through a negotiated settlement, this may prove beyond their capabilities. Just as parties miscalculate what they might achieve through coercion, they can also miscalculate what they can achieve through negotiations. What each side requires as a minimum to be able to present a settlement as legitimate to its supporters may not be reconcilable. Thus, it is difficult to imagine how Greek Cypriot insistence on freedom of movement and the right of refugees to return to their homes can coexist with Turkish Cypriot demands for territorial separation to underwrite the community's security. The United Nations has put forward the ambiguous formula of a bizonal, bicommunal federation in an attempt to overcome this difficulty.

External parties may play a role in bridging the gulf between the principal antagonists, particularly where they have their own interests in wishing to see the conflict ended, such as the capacity for the conflict to affect the stability of an entire region. Thus, during the Lancaster House negotiations on the future of Zimbabwe–Rhodesia, promises of large-scale financial assistance for the purchase of land were made by the British and American governments to the Patriotic Front to persuade the alliance of the main African nationalist parties to accept provisions in the constitution safeguarding white farmers against the expropriation of their land. While they played an important role in the negotiations, the promises were never fulfilled on the scale envisaged during the talks. This case also illustrates well the problem of enforcing such promises once the conflict is over and the interests that impelled the external parties to make their promises are no longer threatened.

An important strategic choice in negotiations towards a settlement is whether the parties should seek to arrive at a comprehensive and detailed blueprint for the future government of the entity in question or simply the outline of a settlement. These represent opposite ends of a spectrum. Commonly, settlements fall between these two extremes. A related issue is whether the parties should set a time limit to negotiations. An advantage of the detailed approach is that the settlement is less likely to unravel as a result of disagreements over the interpretation of its provisions. A disadvantage is that the time needed to reach such a settlement may threaten the peace process itself by causing one or other of the parties to suspect that the purpose of the talks is not to reach a settlement, but to use the truce that accompanies the talks to bring about a shift in the balance of power between the two sides.

Endorsement

Elections usually constitute an important element in the negotiated settlement of peace processes. They provide an obvious way of legitimizing a new dispensation. Even agreements that are the product of power politics such as the 1970s agreement on the future of South Vietnam may pay lip-service to the principle, though the actual holding of elections may prove another matter. Elections to a new legislature and of a new President may perform the dual function of providing retrospective endorsement of the settlement and its partial implementation. This is what happened in South Africa in 1994. However, in some settlements, there is special provision for the separate endorsement of the settlement by referendum, as in the case of Northern Ireland's Good Friday Agreement of 1998. The Good Friday Agreement provided for the simultaneous holding of referendums on the settlement in Northern Ireland and the Republic of Ireland.

This approach had a number of advantages in the particular context of the Irish question. The promise by the British government that any settlement coming out of the multi-party negotiations would be put to the Northern Irish electorate provided a means of allaying Protestant fears as to the purpose of the talks. The simultaneous holding of referendums in Northern Ireland and the Republic of Ireland provided a means of addressing the issue of Irish self-determination. The position taken by nationalists since Northern Ireland had come into existence in 1920 was that the province was not a legitimate political entity. This was because partition had been imposed against the wishes of a majority of the population of the island of Ireland as a whole. The 1998 settlement committed Irish nationalists to accept the existence of two jurisdictions on the island, at least for the time being, while the referendums undercut the position of fundamentalists who asserted that partition continued to be illegitimate. There was also a practical dimension to the holding of the referendum in the Republic: it provided the authority for the changes to the Irish constitution which the government had negotiated as a part of the settlement. Another instance of the use of referendums to underwrite a settlement were the series of referendums that accompanied the negotiation of Commonwealth status for Puerto Rico in the 1950s. However, neither these nor subsequent referendums have entirely succeeded in quelling international criticism of Puerto Rico's status as semi-colonial.

Implementation

The less detailed the terms of the negotiated settlement, the greater the difficulties are likely to be at the stage of implementation. A continuing process of negotiations leading to series of new agreements will be needed to put flesh on the bare bones of the original settlement. It is at this stage that disputes over the interpretation of the settlement are likely to arise. Overcoming these obstacles may present a much larger challenge for the parties and external mediators than arriving at the broad outlines of a settlement had been. Indeed, the reason for confining the original agreement to an outline is most likely to have been the perceived gulf between the parties on the substantive issues. The obvious example in this context is the Declaration of Principles agreed between the government of Israel and the Palestine Liberation Organization (PLO) in September 1993. In this case, the parties acknowledged that what they agreed fell far short of a final settlement and that was reflected in their agreeing to a timetable for the negotiation of a final settlement, though this proved unsustainable almost from the outset.

The process of implementation itself may have a profound effect on how a particular political settlement turns out because of its impact on the balance of power among the parties. Elections usually constitute an early element in the implementation of a settlement. How the parties fare in such elections will almost inevitably have a very large bearing on their influence on the rest of the process. South Africa provides a case in point. As Christopher Saunders has noted, interpretations of the country's transition tend to vary with when they were written, with later authors viewing the process in the light of the ANC's overwhelming electoral predominance and the influence that had on the shape of the final constitution agreed in 1996. By contrast, authors who wrote about the settlement before its implementation tended to portray it as a compromise between the forces of African and Afrikaner nationalism.[9]

Shifts in the balance of forces during the implementation stage may consolidate the settlement by making it apparent that one side has won. Indeed, from this vantage point, a negotiated settlement may come to be seen less as entailing the creation of a 'win–win' solution in which the political aspirations of both sides are accommodated as a process enabling a formerly political dominant group to surrender its position gracefully. In this context, the settlement may simply be transitionary to more fundamental change. That possibility may have a significant influence on both sides during the course of the negotiations, the hope of one and the fear of the other. More generally, the normative rationale of the settlement may be undermined by the actual balance of forces in the situation which results in the settlement being implemented in a way that falls far short of what one side or the other and perhaps the outside world see as legitimate. Thus, Palestinian critics of Arafat such as Edward Said have argued that the PLO is simply in too weak a position to secure a legitimate outcome to the Middle East peace process.[10]

Institutionalization

The final stage in any settlement is the point at which it becomes apparent that the new order has taken root and the change that has come with it is seen to be irreversible. A necessary condition for institutionalization is that the settlement is perceived as legitimate internationally, a perception that will itself in part depend on internal reaction to the settlement. Should internal opponents of a settlement be able to sustain an insurgency against the government, a question mark is likely to exist over the legitimacy of the new dispensation even if it meets other tests of legitimacy. Conversely, the appearance of stability and peace may persuade international opinion of the legitimacy of a new political dispensation even if it does not accord fully with international norms of governance. Nevertheless, the issue of legitimacy remains of greater importance than whether the government is seen to accord with the balance of power within the society in question. The durability of even the most powerful government will be in doubt if it does not appear to command widespread acceptance among the people it rules.

That is why in reaching agreement on a new dispensation, parties find that addressing fundamental principles of what constitutes legitimate governance in a divided society is as, if not more, important than constructing arrangements that reflect existing power realities. Of course, international norms as to what constitutes good governance are not unchanging and a settlement that reflects the norms which existed at the time it was reached may be undermined by their sub-sequent evolution and reinterpretation. By contrast, changes in norms may facil-itate a settlement by altering the frame of reference. Thus, a looser interpretation of sovereignty within the context of European integration helped to make pos-sible the compromises on cross-border bodies and the British–Irish Council in the Good Friday Agreement.

Of course, what might appear to some to be a ground-breaking settlement involving the creation of novel political structures to accommodate the different parties may appear to others to be a desperate attempt to reconcile mutually incom-patible positions and far from being politically principled to rest on the unstable foundations of the existing balance of power among the parties. Similarly, it is dif-ficult to know where to place the blame when such a settlement breaks down. Almost inevitably, the judgement that a new political dispensation has become institutionalized tends to be a retrospective one. As far as negotiations are con-cerned, institutionalization forms the point at which politics starts to be conducted in terms of the acceptance of agreed rules, superseding negotiations on what rules should be.

Conclusion

The seven phases of negotiations described above are not intended to provide a rigid model of how all negotiations to end violent conflicts either are or should be conducted. Further, the order of the different phases is not meant to imply a strict separation in time among these phases. In practice, different phases over-lap and what are presented above as discrete processes may be collapsed into one another, so that, for example, endorsement is often a part of the implementation process. While primacy has been given to the role of current norms in the nego-tiation of the settlement of violent political conflicts, the realm of power politics cannot simply be set aside. At every stage in the process, the parties are likely to consider the implications of any development for the balance of forces in the soci-ety. The fear of negotiations as a one-way street is by no means confined to inter-national politics. In domestic politics, it tends to take the form of the suspicion that the other side is pursuing a hidden agenda and that its engagement in negotiations is tactical. Indeed, even the acceptance of a settlement may be per-ceived as tactical, i.e. designed to extract benefits that will shift the balance of forces in the party's favour, while seeking to evade any obligations that place it at a disadvantage.

Precisely because of these possibilities, issues of trust and good faith have an importance in negotiations to end violent political conflicts that they do not have in limited international negotiations between adversaries where the complications are often largely technical in character. Thus, while there is not an automatic incompatibility between negotiations and the continued use of violence, in prac-tice, suspension of hostilities is typically a precondition for the initiation of nego-tiations or, at the very least, the first item on the agenda if negotiations start in the absence of ceasefires. Just as a shifting balance of power may affect the durability of any negotiated settlement, so too may changes in norms. Thus, much greater importance is attached these days to the recognition of minority rights than was the case in the aftermath of the Second World War. Further, for good or ill regional ethno-nationalisms are credited with much greater legitimacy than before the end of the Cold War, with a consequent softening of the international community's hostility towards secession. In fact, the current fluidity in the interpretation of key international norms such as self-determination makes it peculiarly hard to predict the outcome of current peace processes and whether the settlements that emerge from negotiations among the parties will prove durable.

Notes

1. See, for example, J. Burton, *Deviance, Terrorism and War: the Process of Solving Unsolved Social and Political Problems* (New York: St. Martin's Press – now Palgrave Macmillan, 1979) and R. Fisher & W. Ury, *Getting to Yes* (New York: Bantam, 1991).
2. J. P. Lederach, *Building Peace* (Washington, DC: United States Institute of Peace, 1997).
3. I. W. Zartman, 'Ripeness: the Hurting Stalemate and Beyond', paper presented to the International Political Science World Congress, Quebec City (August 2000).
4. H. Kissinger, *The White House Years* (London: Weidenfeld & Nicolson, 1979).
5. Ibid., pp. 63–4.
6. M. Hoffman, 'Third Party Mediation and Conflict Resolution in the Post-Cold War World', in J. Baylis & N. J. Rengger (eds), *Dilemmas of World Politics* (Oxford: Clarendon Press, 1992), p. 265.
7. S. Al-Azm, 'The View from Damascus . . . Continued', *New York Review of Books*, XLVII, 13 (10 August 2000).
8. M. Benvenisti, 'The Peace Process and Intercommunal Strife', in H. Giliomee & J. Gagiano (eds), *The Elusive Search for Peace: South Africa, Israel and Northern Ireland* (Cape Town: Oxford University Press, 1990), p. 123.
9. C. Saunders, 'Of Treks, Transitions and Transitology', *South African Historical Journal*, 40 (May 1999).
10. E. W. Said, *Peace and Its Discontents* (London: Vintage, 1995).

6

Rules and Procedures for Negotiated Peacemaking

Pierre du Toit

Introduction

Rules and procedures provide structure to the process of negotiating for peace. Some rules, such as time frames and deadlines, are primarily intended to provide a formal structure for the *process* of negotiations, while others, such as preset constitutional guidelines, aim to shape the *outcome* of the negotiating process. Often this seemingly neat distinction becomes blurred, as when tight deadlines affect the thoroughness with which negotiators deal with the details of a constitutional settlement. The aim of this chapter is to consider the impact of the structuring of peace processes through such rules and procedures, with special emphasis on the role of time frames and deadlines. The following questions will be taken up:

- Who makes the rules and procedures? Participants, or external third parties?
- Do these rules and procedures apply to the process or to the outcome of peacemaking, and what effect, if any, do they have on each other?
- Who acts as the enforcement agency, ensuring that the rules and procedures are upheld?

The two primary cases which are selected for comparative insights are South Africa and Namibia. Comparability is enhanced by virtue of both countries being considered as very successful cases of democratic transition, and hence of peacemaking. Both are African states and both experienced a long period of colonial rule, one German, the other British. Colonial rule ended in white minority government in both of them, where authority was asserted by coercion and resisted by revolt, thus producing violent transitions. Peacemaking and democratic transition, although analytically distinct, went together. These two cases were also both among the very earliest post-Cold War transitions.

Significant differences allow us to make measurable comparisons. The character of white minority rule differed sharply between the two cases. In South Africa the ruling minority was an indigenous one, entrenching its position through the policies of apartheid, based on racial division and exclusion. This same power elite ruled over Namibia, a position achieved in the First World War, when they invaded the then German colony and were awarded a trusteeship by the League of Nations. Although this mandate was not recognized by the UN, the successor to the League, the apartheid rulers of South Africa extended this style of domination over the territory, in the face of worldwide opposition and condemnation. This was instrumental in shaping the single outstanding contrast in the peace processes in the two cases. The Namibian conflict became hugely internationalized, resulting in the eventual peace process being shaped by rules and procedures which were drawn up and laid down entirely by outsiders, acting as *third parties*. South Africa, being a sovereign state, allowed the peacemakers to choose whether to engage third parties in setting rules and procedures. They decided to do this themselves. The contrast between the two cases is almost extreme, but the outcomes for them almost identical in that they both led to successful peace settlements.

Time frames and deadlines

Negotiators usually have three ways of responding to offers: accept, refuse or continue to talk in order to improve subsequent offers. This last option is affected by deadlines. A deadline is a mechanism for imposing time costs on negotiators. It is a jointly recognized ultimatum, tied to a particular calendar date which, upon expiry, sets the incurring of costs into operation. Time frames are subsets within this ultimatum, consisting of the requirement that specific targets be met within a particular chronological sequence. Deadlines convert proposals into final offers, potential sanctions into actual costs, and turn the alternative to negotiated settlements into reality. As they face a deadline, the options narrow down to two: agree to the proposal, or refuse, take it or leave it.[1]

Deadlines have two dimensions, reasonableness and seriousness.[2] The *reasonableness* requirement holds that enough time must be made available to find a quality settlement, that is, one that deals effectively with the basic issues of conflict. When this is not met, and negotiators are forced into rushing a decision, agreements of poor quality may result. Problems of *ownership* may arise when large concessions made under pressure leave one party alienated from the outcome and unable to justify it to their own audiences. They then have every incentive to later disown the agreement, or to actively undermine it. Problems of *detail* may also crop up. If some matters cannot be dealt with adequately because of time pressure, and remain unclarified, unresolved and/or are carried over to new negotiating arenas in this form, problems may re-emerge.

Seriousness refers to the extent to which the deadline puts pressure on the negotiators to conclude a settlement. Pressure can only result from credible sanctions behind the deadline. Data from experimental settings confirm that impending deadlines induce negotiators to increase the rate of concessions made, thus facilitating movement towards agreement.[3] The implied negative sanction here is that if a party were not to concede, and no settlement is forthcoming, then it may end up being labelled as a *spoiler*. However, when parties anticipate that deadlock or breakdown due to their inability to meet a deadline is imminent and inevitable, then a deadline may produce a hardening effect.[4] Parties adopt a tough position for if and when negotiations fail, so that they can appear to look strong in the eyes of their home audiences. This allows them to claim that they did not capitulate under undue pressure, and that they did not sacrifice vital interests 'just to get a settlement'.

Rule-making by outsiders: Namibia

The German colony of South West Africa was established in 1884, after the Berlin Conference in which Africa was carved up into colonial domains by the European powers. The then Union of South Africa invaded the territory in 1915, as part of its contribution to the First World War, and as reward for its efforts the League of Nations granted a 'C' class mandate over the territory to the Union. This stipulated that the area be governed as an integral part of the country, extending its own laws over the mandated people and territory.[5]

This became a highly internationalized issue once South Africa, under its defunct mandate, proceeded to implement its racial policies in the occupied territory. In 1950 the International Court of Justice (ICJ) ruled that South Africa could not retain control over the territory under the new UN mandate system. In 1966 the UN General Assembly voted to assume control over the administration of the territory, and in 1971 the ICJ ruled South Africa's continued occupation of Namibia as illegal. South Africa resisted these international pressures, as well as those emerging from within Namibia in the shape of nationalist movements, led by the South West African People's Organization (SWAPO).

The escalation to violent confrontation was again influenced by international forces. In 1966 SWAPO decided to take up arms against South Africa's occupation of the territory. In 1975 Angola's independence dramatically changed the military context. The Popular Movement for the Liberation of Angola (MPLA), with Soviet backing, seized power and a civil war against its rivals, led by the National Union for the Total Independence of Angola (UNITA) ensued. SWAPO and South Africa's African National Congress (ANC), both also with Soviet backing, then relocated their military bases to southern Angola, strategically well placed close to the northern Namibian border. War escalated when the South African forces invaded Angola with two objectives: to destroy SWAPO military bases and to aid UNITA in its fight against the MPLA government. Cuba eventually entered in direct military support of the MPLA, while the USA acted in providing logistical support to UNITA.

Peacemakers entered into this complex conflict arena in two ways. Firstly, the UN Security Council passed Resolution 385 in 1976 and Resolution 435 in 1978, setting out rules, procedures and a time frame for the independence of Namibia. Secondly, the informal Western Contact Group (WCG), comprised of the USA, Britain, France, Canada and West Germany, was set up with the objective of facilitating the implementation of these resolutions. As the name suggests, their primary task was to engage with the recalcitrant South Africans to get them to accede to the UN peace plan.[6] This they did, most visibly by exercising their veto in the Security Council when South Africa refused to accept Resolution 385. At the same time the South Africans were facilitating the establishment of internal political parties with interests more to their own liking, such as being outside the orbit of Soviet influence, not promoting socialist economic plans, and not considering an independent Namibia as a military base for the ANC. The WCG did produce a plan for Namibian independence by early 1978, which was approved by the Security Council, and came to be the core of the eventual UN plan.

The key ingredients of the UN plan, as far as rules and procedures go, were the following:

- A time frame allowing the setting up of a UN force responsible for the sequential implementation of a ceasefire, followed by the demobilization of military forces, then the holding of an election, the drafting of a constitution, and culminating in independence.
- The demobilization did not make provision for a de facto condition of dual power, i.e. 'liberated areas' under effective SWAPO control within Namibia. SWAPO forces were to assemble in Angola and Zambia.
- The elections would be run by the incumbent South African administration through the office of the Administrator-General, whose activities would be 'supervised and monitored' by the UN. For this purpose a designated UN military force, UNTAG, would be assembled.
- SWAPO would lose its UN privileges, starting with its recognition as the 'sole and authentic representative' of the Namibian populace, and hence, UN funding.
- Elections would be held for a Constituent Assembly, not for an independent government. This Assembly would have to draft a constitution which, once enacted, would provide the framework within which a government would be established, based on the results of the election.
- The principles on which this constitution would have to be based are prescribed to the political parties. The final constitution would need the approval of two-thirds of the Assembly's members.
- The deadline for the implementation of Resolution 435 was set at 23 October 1978.

With this set of overarching rules the crucial question of who would be the enforcement agency in control of the peace process was settled. In the words of one set of analysts: '. . . the plan brokered by the WCG downplayed the role of the UN in the transition to that of linesman, with South Africa, itself a protagonist, as stage manager'.[7] These rules also reflected the interests of the WCG themselves, with South Africa being their least disliked option as a decolonizing agent.[8]

The implementation of this peace plan was thwarted for about 11 years, coming into effect only on 1 February 1989. Why such a comprehensive collapse of a UN Security Council deadline? Primarily because of a lack of consensus within the ranks of the international actors comprising the collective third party intervenor (that is, the WCG) about how to proceed. Both South Africa and SWAPO agreed with great reluctance, and under pressure from their backers, to accept Resolution 435, and then only in principle. Part of the international community's problem was agreeing how to deal with South Africa's apparent stalling tactics. These tactics evolved from the rules and procedures set out in the UN plan. For the South Africans to shape the peace process to their liking, they had to ensure that in the eventual election SWAPO did not get two-thirds of the vote. This required credible electoral opposition from domestic parties with interests close to the South African position. This in turn required time to build, as there were no such parties in the early 1980s. They bought this time by, among other things, escalating the military conflict in southern Angola. This strategy bore fruit once the USA entered the conflict arena and succeeded in linking the Namibian peace process to the withdrawal of Cuban forces from Angola.[9] France objected to this linkage, and eventually withdrew from the WCG in December 1983.

The linkage strategy was effective but costly. Military conflict escalated to full conventional warfare, culminating with the battles at Lomba and Cuito Cuanavale in 1987, by which time a mutually hurting stalemate had set in.[10] Two other factors conducive to peacemaking also came into effect at that stage. Gorbachev's initiatives in the Soviet Union had by that time contributed to a considerable thawing of the Cold War, and the South Africans had, in their view, established a credible set of electoral opponents to take on SWAPO in an election.

The result was another set of peace agreements, all concluded in 1988, setting further rules and procedures for the peace process, with yet more specific time frames and deadlines. These included:

- The Geneva Protocol of 5 August 1988, signed by South Africa, Cuba and Angola, stipulating, among other things, that, in preparation for a ceasefire, SWAPO forces would be withdrawn to north of the 16th parallel within southern Angola, the complete withdrawal of South African forces from Namibia, and of Cuban forces from Angola, all according to specified dates, as well as a new date for the implementation of Resolution 435.
- The Brazzaville Accord of 13 December 1988, drawn up between the same three parties, revised these target dates, and set the deadline for the implementation of Resolution 435 at 1 April 1989.
- The Bilateral Agreement between Cuba and Angola of 22 December 1988, setting a time frame for the withdrawal of Cuban troops, starting on 1 April 1989 and to be concluded on 1 July 1991.
- The Tripartite Agreement of 22 December 1988 between South Africa, Cuba and Angola, reaffirming all the above, and calling on the UN Security Council to implement Resolution 435 on 1 April 1989.

The official implementation of the UN plan started on 1 February 1989. Three aspects of the transition/peace process, all bearing on the rules of the transition, are worth noting here. The first is the military invasion by SWAPO on 1 April 1989, the day of the commencement of the ceasefire. The second is the element of what Cliffe et al. have called 'structural intimidation' by the South African government in its management of the process. The third notable feature was the huge momentum which carried the process through to its successful conclusion.

April 1 was a crucial deadline, the date set for the commencement of the ceasefire, ending all hostilities, and setting in motion the phased withdrawal of foreign military forces from the conflict arena. United Nations Transition Group (UNTAG) forces were required to monitor this process. However, by the due date less than 1000 of the 4560 military personnel had arrived, and only 12 of the 500 police monitors were deployed.[11] UNTAG were thus vastly unprepared for the invasion by about 1600 SWAPO soldiers on 1 April. The UN responded to the crisis by authorizing the remobilization of some of the internal military units created by the South Africans in the territory. These units effectively dealt with the invaders in the ensuing battles, which stretched over nine days, resulting in a further death toll of close to 300 soldiers (about 250 from SWAPO and 35–40 from the domestic units). The peace process was salvaged when SWAPO retreated in accordance with the Mount Etjo Agreement of 9 April, but the actual implementation of the process was only resumed in mid-May.[12]

The rules and procedures for the transition gave South Africa, through its administrative bureau of the Administrator-General (AG), the opportunity to wield the power of incumbency. As the effective host of the peace process, subject only to monitoring by UNTAG, the AG had to draw up the detailed rules and procedures governing the election and had access to the officials who were implementing these, most notably the local police force, which was the remaining coercive unit after the effective containment of SWAPO units and repatriation of South African forces. This provided opportunities for 'structural intimidation' in various forms, ranging from clandestine financing of anti-SWAPO political parties by the South African government, control over the media, dirty tricks to harass SWAPO and to boost the Democratic Turnhalle Alliance (DTA), which was the primary electoral opponent of SWAPO, pressure on farm workers and employees by their employers to vote against SWAPO, and so on. A climate of violence also persisted, with intermittent shootings, beatings and kidnappings taking place.[13]

Despite all of these, the most striking overall feature of the peace process, once set in motion, was its almost inexorable momentum. Having been created, structured, sponsored and endorsed by the most influential actors in both the regional and international community, the process was virtually unstoppable. Despite the 1 April ceasefire breakdown and despite the electoral climate of intimidation, the elections went smoothly, the result was declared free and fair, and the parties duly assembled to draft a constitution within the laid down perimeters. Such was the momentum that it took them only 80 days to complete this process, leaving the details mostly to a trio of constitutional experts![14] On 21 March 1990 Namibia became independent.

Rule-making by insiders: South Africa

In the South African transition rules and procedures relevant to the *process* also had a remarkable impact on events. Firstly, South Africans reached early agreement that they would establish these rules themselves, without the intervention of outsiders.[15] Secondly, the substance of these rules was a source of intense disagreement; they became the single largest issue of contention in the constitutional negotiations and provided the source of the breakdown in the talks in mid-1992. Thirdly, only after this matter was resolved, did the peace process gain momentum towards a successful settlement.

The public peace process got under way in early 1990 when State President F. W. de Klerk rescinded the bannings on the African nationalist movements such as the African National Congress (ANC) and its allies, and unconditionally released

Nelson Mandela from serving a term of life imprisonment for high treason. This was preceded by about five years of secret negotiations between Mandela and various state agencies. All of 1990 and most of 1991 were spent in negotiating various non-aggression pacts aimed at curtailing public violence (in the absence of a ceasefire to end an undeclared war), and in sorting out preconditions to formal constitutional talks, such as the release of political prisoners.

Formal negotiations on a democratic constitution were instituted in December 1991 with the multi-party Congress for a Democratic South Africa (CODESA). One of the vital issues at stake was the rules and procedures for the democratic transition. From the outset the ANC and the National Party (NP) government were, for tactical reasons, at loggerheads about the nature of the transition. The ANC, keen to utilize its expected electoral strength from among the black electorate, wanted an elected constitutional body to draft a new constitution within a very short time frame. The NP government, anticipating their own minority position after any electoral contest, wanted a multi-party conference, such as CODESA, to negotiate a constitution under which elections would take place. This body would then rule, within an almost unspecified time frame, while a final constitution is enacted. They calculated that their interests could in this way be written into a constitutional form *before* the electoral power of the ANC could be brought to bear on the process. In this way each one wanted to set rules and procedures allowing for itself to control the process to its own advantage.

At CODESA five working committees were established. Working Groups 2 and 3 were assigned to deal with rules and procedures for the transition. Here the tactical differences between the major protagonists came to a head. The parties agreed that an interim parliament had to be set up to govern during the transition. They also agreed that this elected interim body had to be set up in terms of constitutional principles negotiated by CODESA and that it would serve as a constitutional assembly which had to negotiate a 'final' constitution. They could not agree, however, on the proportion of votes required to ratify such a final constitution. The NP wanted a white minority veto, either in a direct form or indirectly, by way of very high decision-making percentages. In Working Group 2, for example, they insisted that the powers and functions of regions be protected by a 75 per cent majority vote requirement. At this the ANC balked, along with a dispute about majorities built into a deadlock-breaking mechanism.[16] At the end of May 1992 the ANC declared CODESA a failure, and on June 16 started with its mass action campaign, aimed at putting pressure on the NP government to relent. The next day the Boipatong massacre took place, thus renewing the cycle of public violence.

This contest over rules and procedures was not just about a de facto white minority veto, expressed in tangible constitutional procedures. It was also about the intangible matters of the power relationship between the major contenders and about the nature of the negotiating process. The question of who set the rules and following from that, who controls the peace process, was fundamentally about power. As one analyst noted, at CODESA both the ANC and the NP thought that they were going to talk their opponents into their own agenda for change, set on their own terms.[17] Neither was prepared to accept the other as a negotiating partner of equal strength and standing, and both thought of the negotiating process as one of talking the opponent into defeat.

The campaign of mass mobilization beyond the negotiating table produced a series of violent confrontations, culminating in the Bisho massacre of 7 September 1992. Huge international pressure was brought to bear on the ANC and NP government to return to the table. This bore fruit and on 26 September the Record of Understanding, a bilateral agreement between the two parties, was signed. This was essentially an agreement on rules for guiding the transition.[18] It was agreed that:

- There would be a constitution-making body which had to be democratically elected;
- This body would function as a single body for this purpose;
- It would be bound by constitutional principles set by a multi-party conference preceding the election of the constitution-making body;
- It would work within a fixed time frame;
- This body would have adequate deadlock-breaking mechanisms for dealing with differences on substantive constitutional matters;
- It would arrive at its decisions democratically with certain yet to be agreed on majorities;
- It would be elected within an agreed predetermined time period.

During the transitional period this constitution-making body would act:

- as an interim parliament;
- with an executive which would be a government of national unity;
- with a constitution providing for both national and regional levels of government.

With this the two heavyweights came to terms on rules for the transition. From there on the process rapidly gained momentum. In November 1992 the ANC announced that it was prepared to engage in executive power-sharing during the transition, and in the same month State President De Klerk produced a timetable for the transition, starting with a reconvened multi-party conference in March 1993 and culminating in elections for the Government of National Unity in March or April 1994.[19] With a few changes, this time frame came to be implemented, with the historic elections taking place over three days, starting on 26 April 1994.

Settling on rules and procedures for the transition in this way also had its costs. The most important was that this bilateral agreement between the NP and the ANC alienated the third heavyweight in the arena, the Inkatha Freedom Party (IFP). Shortly after the release of the Record of Understanding the IFP announced their withdrawal from the negotiating process.[20] They stayed outside and proceeded to play a very high-risk game of brinkmanship, along with their right-wing allies up until the very end, declaring their willingness to take part in the election only six days before balloting started.

Nonetheless, the NP and ANC, having learnt the hard way that deadlocks over matters of detail can lead to a breakdown in the entire peace process, proceeded with great caution. The reconvened multi-party negotiating process (MPNP) functioned with the aid of some innovative informal deadlock-breaking rules and procedures to facilitate the process *within* the agreed-upon negotiating arena. These included the rule of 'sufficient consensus', which held that proposals which carried the joint support of the NP and ANC were carried despite objections by any number of smaller parties. Their objections would be registered, debated and considered, but could not thwart the adoption of the proposals.[21] Another procedure was the so-called 'channel', an informal subcommittee of the planning committee of the MPNP, comprised of three, and later two, members who met every day to anticipate deadlocks, and to devise pre-emptive strategies for overcoming them. Finally, the device of *bosberade*, informal bilateral summits, held at luxury resorts in the African bush veld, running parallel to the formal negotiating process, helped to smooth formal proceedings.[22]

The deadline posed by the 26 April 1994 date for the election also impacted on the transition process. Having decided early on at CODESA to utilize outsiders only as observers at the eventual elections, the South Africans had to find their own internal umpire to act as enforcement agent for the transition. This took the form of newly created institutions, the most important being the Transitional Executive Council (TEC) and the Independent Electoral Commission (IEC). The first was to serve as a multi-party executive authority during the run-up to the election, while the latter had to serve as the actual administrative body for the conduct of the election. The IEC was only established during December 1993, and was given a bare four months to create an entirely new institution comprised of close to 300,000 employees. They had to execute a triple function: administer the election, monitor it and provide for adjudication of conflicts. In the end they succumbed under time pressure and the result was an election that was much flawed in meeting its procedural requirements. In the end the peace process was salvaged by the major stakeholders, who negotiated informally to accept the declared result as legitimate, thus ensuring a successful conclusion to South Africa's messy miracle.[23]

Comparative insights

Ownership

The Namibian rules and procedures for peacemaking had a crucial flaw. They were drawn up by third parties alone. Not a single domestic stakeholder (i.e. a political party which would be represented in Parliament after independence) was a signatory to any of these agreements. This was specially relevant in the case of SWAPO, which was required to remove its armed units to above the 16th parallel within Angola, prior to the 1 April 1989 ceasefire. This status of being a non-signatory arguably created a lack of a sense of ownership in the organization, and has been said to account for their military invasion on the day of the ceasefire, in direct violation of the standing agreements.[24] Likewise, the withdrawal of the IFP from the constitutional negotiations in South Africa in late 1992 can also be taken back to the fact that they were not party to the agreement contained in the Record of Understanding.

Seriousness

In the Namibian case, disagreement within the ranks of the collective third party, the Western Contact Group, affected their ability to implement rules, and especially to apply the sanctions required to come into effect with the failure to meet the deadline of implementing Resolution 435. In the South African case all the parties held to the deadline set by the election date of 26 April 1994, again with the exception of the IFP and its right-wing allies in the Freedom Alliance. The latter pursued a strategy of what can be called in retrospect, *brinkmanship*, joining the elections at the very last moment. However, had they pushed harder and boycotted the election, the end result would have been judged as *spoiling*. The fact that they stood down at the very last moment is an indication of the seriousness with which the deadline was taken by other parties – they refused to postpone the election date at the demands of the Freedom Alliance.

Reasonableness

The election deadline in South Africa did create problems of reasonableness. Within the preset time frame the IEC just did not have adequate time to set up a competent administrative machinery with which to run the election. When they duly failed, it was only the pragmatism of the major electoral contestants themselves, who negotiated to accept the election result, that saved the day.

Control

Both the Namibian and South African cases show that the rules governing the peace process provide the key to control of the process and hold huge potential power implications. The party that can shape the rules can control the process and is provided with an opportunity to bring to bear whatever sources of power it has at its disposal to maximum effect. This was in essence what the contest between the ANC and NP was about, and was also at the heart of the South African government's strategy in Namibia.

Momentum

Once the major powers in a conflict arena have reached basic agreement on the rules and procedures to govern a peace process, and once such a process has been set in motion, it can rapidly generate substantial momentum. Both cases confirm this proposition. In neither case did potentially major crises divert the peace process. The 1 April 1989 invasion by SWAPO was arguably the most direct threat to the transition, but was effectively contained by the parties driving the peace process. In South Africa the assassination of Chris Hani, general secretary of the South African Communist Party, on 10 April 1993 became the single most important crisis which the MPNP had to overcome. With the adept leadership of Mandela in particular, it did so without faltering.

Conclusion

Rules and procedures shape the arena within which negotiators cooperate and compete with each other on their way to searching for amicable settlements. The negotiations over such rules and procedures are as decisive to the outcome as the negotiations *within* the stage set by these rules and procedures. Rule-setting by outsiders can be equally successful as those set by the protagonists themselves, as this comparative overview shows, but both ways of establishing the negotiating arena need to demonstrate an awareness of problems of ownership, reasonableness and seriousness that may arise. Both cases also show that once the playing field has been accepted as being level by the major players, then such agreement on rules can generate momentum towards successful peacemaking.

Notes

1. I. W. Zartman & M. R. Berman, *The Practical Negotiator* (New Haven: Yale University Press, 1982), pp. 191–2.
2. Ibid., pp. 193–7.
3. A. E. Roth, J. K. Murnighan & F. Schoumaker, 'The Deadline Effect in Bargaining: Some Experimental Evidence', *The American Economic Review*, 78 (September 1988), 806–23; S. Ghee-Son Lim & J. K. Murnighan, 'Phases, Deadlines and the Bargaining Process', *Organizational Behaviour and Human Decision Processes*, 58 (1994), 153–71.
4. Zartman & Berman, op. cit., pp. 195, 196.
5. J. Barber & J. Barratt, *South Africa's Foreign Policy – the Search for Status and Security 1945–1988* (Johannesburg: Southern, 1990), p. 22.
6. The plan came to be centred on the contents of three documents, the so-called Western Settlement Plan, drawn up by the WCG and approved by the Security Council as Document S/12636, of April 1978; Resolution 435 of 1978, and the Supplement to this resolution, Security Council Document S/15287, titled 'Constitutional Principles', of 1982. See L. Cliffe et al., *The Transition to Independence in Namibia* (Boulder, Colo.: Lynne Rienner, 1994), pp. 239–46. Resolution 385, calling for South Africa's withdrawal from Namibia, is an essential precursor to this plan.
7. Ibid., p. 69.
8. V. Jabri, *Mediating Conflict – Decision-making and Western Intervention in Namibia* (Manchester: Manchester University Press, 1990); Cliffe et al., op. cit., pp. 68, 69.
9. C. A. Crocker, *High Noon in Southern Africa – Making Peace in a Rough Neighborhood* (Johannesburg: Jonathan Ball, 1992).
10. According to Crocker this stalemate was the decisive catalyst in moving the regional powers to search for a peaceful settlement. See Crocker, op. cit., p. 486. For a review of the different assessments of the significance of the Cuito Cuanavale confrontation see W. Breytenbach, 'Cuito Cuanavale Revisited: Same Outcomes, Different Consequences', *Africa Insight*, 27, 1 (1997), 54–62.
11. Cliffe et al., op. cit., p. 84.
12. For a number of different viewpoints on this controversial incident and its implications for both the Namibian and South African peace processes consult A. Seegers, *The Military in the Making of Modern South Africa* (London: I. B. Tauris, 1996), pp. 261–5; Cliffe et al., op. cit., pp. 84–94; and J. Geldenhuys, *A General's Story – from an Era of War and Peace* (Johannesburg: Jonathan Ball, 1995), pp. 265–74.
13. Cliffe et al., op. cit., pp. 81–3, 94–113.
14. L. Doubell, 'SWAPO in Office', in Colin Leys & J. S. Saul (eds), *Namibia's Liberation Struggle – the Two-Edged Sword* (London: James Currey, 1995), pp. 171–95, at 176; Cliffe et al., op. cit., pp. 199–214.
15. This is not to say that outside forces did not impact on the South African process. Influence from outsiders was pervasive but indirect. At no stage did effective decision-making pass into the hands of foreign actors. See D. Geldenhuys, *Foreign Political Engagement – Remaking States in the Post-Cold War World* (London: Macmillan – now Palgrave Macmillan, 1998), pp. 73–99.

16. C. Cooper et al., *Race Relations Survey 1992/93* (Johannesburg: South African Institute of Race Relations, 1993), pp. 503, 504.
17. S. Friedman (ed.), *The Long Journey – South Africa's Quest for a Negotiated Settlement* (Johannesburg: Ravan Press, 1993), p. 174.
18. B. W. Kruger, 'Prenegotiation in South Africa (1985–1993) – a Phaseological Analysis of the Transitional Negotiations', unpublished MA thesis (University of Stellenbosch, 1998), pp. 178, 179; T. D. Sisk, *Democratization in South Africa – the Elusive Social Contract* (Princeton, NJ: Princeton University Press, 1995), pp. 219, 220; Cooper et al., op. cit., pp. 35, 36.
19. Cooper et al., op. cit., pp. 38, 39.
20. Ibid., p. 36.
21. D. Atkinson, 'Brokering a Miracle? The Multiparty Negotiating Forum', in S. Friedman & D. Atkinson (eds), *South African Review: 7 The Small Miracle – South Africa's Negotiated Settlement* (Johannesburg: Ravan Press, 1994), pp. 13–43, at 22.
22. P. du Toit, 'South Africa: in Search of Post-Settlement Peace', in J. Darby and R. Mac Ginty (eds), *The Management of Peace Processes* (London: Macmillan – now Palgrave Macmillan, 2000), pp. 16–60, at 29, 30.
23. S. Friedman & L. Stack, 'The Magic Moment – the 1994 Election', in Friedman and Atkinson, op. cit., pp. 301–30.
24. Cliffe et al., op. cit., pp. 53, 54, 64, 75, 86.

7
Mediation and the Ending of Conflicts

Christopher Mitchell

Progress towards the settlement of protracted and violent social conflicts usually takes one of two basic forms. In one, the adversaries manage to arrive at some solution through direct, inter-party discussion of the issues in contention. They then bargain towards an accommodation of their competing goals that, at the very least, satisfies enough of their underlying interests to make the resultant settlement acceptable to leaders and rank and file followers, and thus durable over time. This process of *negotiation* is usually an extremely complex one, subject to many vicissitudes and liable, because of its fragility, to break down frequently and disastrously, as in the Basque Country and in Sri Lanka. Perhaps for this last reason, a directly negotiated bilateral settlement is something of a rarity.

Far more usually, the adversaries in any protracted conflict find themselves in need of the assistance of others to begin, conduct and conclude successfully what has fashionably become known as a 'peace process'. Hence, what is often seen as a bilateral negotiating process becomes trilateral, with the introduction of some third party as a 'go-between', 'facilitator' or 'mediator'. Again, the actual mediation of historic protracted conflicts usually turns out, on examination, to be a much more complex process than a simple interaction between two clearly defined and well-articulated adversaries plus one mediating party. This seems especially to be the case in violent and protracted conflicts that take place between communities or ethnicities within the formal boundaries of so-called 'nation-states' – the Bosnias, Sri Lankas and Colombias of today's world. It is possibly for this reason that sure and systematic knowledge about the nature and dynamics of 'mediation processes' in protracted social conflicts is relatively scarce, compared with, for example, our understanding of the work of mediators in other fields, such as industrial or intra-family conflicts. What follows is a brief discussion of some of the issues in the current debate about appropriate and effective mediation practices in protracted social conflicts[1] – otherwise somewhat loosely described as 'civil strife', 'intra-state conflicts' or 'ethnopolitical conflict'.

Mediation: the dominant model

Much current thinking about mediation processes in protracted social conflicts remains strongly influenced by the kind of mediation that has, throughout history, been practised in violent conflicts *between* formally independent 'sovereign' societies. In these, leaders from other societies 'outside' the conflict offer intermediary services to help bring the adversaries together with the aim of concluding an acceptable agreement to end the violence and to compromise on the issues. In the world of classical Greece, leading city states such as Sparta, Athens and Corinth frequently acted as powerful intermediaries in conflict between their lesser neighbours, thus providing a classical model for mediators with considerable leverage on the adversaries – 'outsider' intermediaries whose offer of services could not easily be rebuffed, whose advice could not easily be ignored and whose blueprints for a settlement could not simply be rejected or amended. The model of the 'Great Power' mediator was thus first constructed in the world of the Greek city states.

Similar types of mediator and mediatory processes can be seen operating in the world of separate and formally equal states that came into being in Europe and elsewhere following the end of the Thirty Years War, although the reality of the powerful and influential mediator tended to be politely masked on many occasions. The best known of these was Bismarck's use of the concept of the 'honest broker' to describe Germany's role at the Congress of Berlin in 1878 and his claim of disinterested activity for the good of Europe – against which one can set the more cynical but probably more accurate comment of Nikita Khrushchev that 'There are no neutral men!'

The world of nineteenth- and twentieth-century diplomacy saw the development of other mediatory models than that of the Great Power 'intermediary with leverage', however. Intermediary action by a group of governments – what might be termed the multi-government model – can be traced to the post-Napoleonic conception of 'the Concert of Europe' and be most recently exemplified by the successful activities of the Contadora Group in Central America and the less successful efforts of the Western Contact Group in attempting to assist the search for a solution in the conflict over Namibia.[2] Similarly, the same period has seen the frequent use of major international figures as intermediaries, utilizing reputation and prestige to accomplish ceasefires and settlements in violent and volatile situations – Theodore Roosevelt helping to end the Russo-Japanese War in 1905, the Emperor of Ethiopia presiding over the process resulting in the 1972 agreement ending the First Sudanese Civil War, Presidents Nyerere and Mandela brokering an agreement between antagonistic factions in Burundi at the very end of the twentieth century. The 'eminent persons' model is another variant of the theme of outside mediation developed to deal with wars and even – on occasions – with civil wars.

However, while it is clearly the case that both thinking about and practice of mediation in protracted social conflicts have been much influenced by the various models of appropriate mediator activity derived from international practice, questions have been raised in recent years about the utility of any of these models or approaches. This is especially so when the conflict in question takes place within the formal boundaries of one of the 'members of the international community' [i.e. a territorial state]; when it involves the formal government of the state as one of the parties to the conflict opposed by ethnic or other types of insurgent; and when the issues in conflict revolve around the preservation of the unity of the state as opposed to its division or disintegration. In such circumstances it becomes even more difficult to discover an appropriate government as 'honest broker', given the tendency of the governments of existing states – and those international organizations such as the United Nations, the Organization of African Unity (OAU) or the Organization of American States (OAS), that consist of the representatives of the governments of existing states – to be somewhat biased in favour of the principles of continuing territorial integrity and of non-interference in the internal affairs of any other country. Both these principles raise major barriers to intermediary action even in situations where the effects of protracted social conflicts spill over borders and disrupt neighbours through raids, refugees, reinforcements, routes for arms and general mayhem.

Much of the current intellectual and practical debate about the role of mediation in protracted social conflicts thus revolves around the question of who – or more accurately what type of entity – might be most appropriate to perform mediatory tasks in conflicts that are violent, protracted and dangerous to a region, but which take place within the confines of an existing state or country, no matter how collapsed the former or disintegrated the latter. Three aspects of this debate currently predominate, and the next sections of this chapter will briefly discuss each of these in turn. They are the debates about (1) the timing of mediation, (2) 'external neutrals' vs 'insider partials' as effective intermediaries, and (3) appropriate forms of intermediary activity and their relation to various stages of a 'peace process'.

When can mediation help?

Since William Zartman wrote his pioneering work on the timing of interventions into protracted social conflicts,[3] the issues of timing or a conflict's 'ripeness' for resolution have been much discussed and written about. One focus for debate has naturally taken the form of asking when there exist appropriate conditions for successful intermediary actions, and much of the writing of Ron Fisher and Loraleigh Keashley has concentrated on developing a contingency approach to peacemaking interventions.[4] They argue that the type of initiative (whether from benevolently inclined outsiders or indirectly involved insiders) most likely to have a positive impact on a conflict depends on the stage that particular conflict has reached. For example, Fisher and Keashley suggest that once conflicts have crossed the threshold from hostility and threats to direct violence, only low-key efforts to dampen the violence and – perhaps – restore non-provocative communications between the adversaries are likely to be effective, although in another work on the issue of timing, Jeff Rubin takes a more hopeful view of what might be attempted.[5]

In spite of this body of work, the dominant concepts about 'ripeness' and when third parties might best intervene remain firmly those initially proposed and later elaborated by Zartman[6] himself and his colleague Stephen Stedman.[7] Mediators and other types of third-party intermediaries should best await the development of a 'hurting stalemate' for both adversaries, perhaps accompanied by an approaching mutual catastrophe. Such circumstances offer the best context for mediatory activity, as they will have set leaders on at least the intellectual course of considering alternatives and searching for a way out. In such circumstances mediators are less likely to encounter a discouraging – if conceptually ambiguous – 'lack of will' on the part of the adversaries and are more likely to be able to move the conflict nearer a solution.

There seem to have been many protracted social conflicts that bear out Zartman's contentions that only mutual pain and a sense of 'no end in sight' will make parties in violent conflict open to the possibilities of mediation and a brokered solution. However, there are clearly other cases that do not fit this model and where mediators have been able to move adversaries towards an alternative process to continuing mutual coercion and harm. In another contribution I have suggested alternative ideas about 'ripe moments', arguing that circumstances that enable leaders to abandon entrapping commitments or to envisage creative alternatives may also provide openings for well-crafted intermediary initiatives.[8]

More generally, it might be that while a situation of stalemate and cost may bring about a change of mind on the part of the leaders of embattled adversaries, other external forms of change can also produce rethinking and reconsideration so that those leaders thus become more receptive to offers of mediation, conciliation, good offices or facilitation. At the moment there seems to be very little systematic examination of the relationship between contextual changes affecting a conflict system and reconsiderations on the part of decision-makers therein. However, both anecdotal evidence and some theoretical formulations suggest that such a link does exist and should be explored. Change does beget change, as the old saying has it, and it seems only commonsensical to argue that major alterations in circumstances can become the occasion for leaders locked in a conflict to ask whether alternative courses of action – perhaps involving help from third parties – might exist.

For example, it seems clearly to have been the case that the ending of the Cold War and the collapse of the Soviet Union had a not unimportant effect on British strategic thinking about the conflict in Northern Ireland, while the growing importance of the EU and the progressive integration of Western Europe did much to affect nationalist thinking about the whole set of relationships involving northwestern Europe's offshore islands. We need to know more about the dynamics of this kind of linked change.

Elsewhere, I have argued that three levels or types of change can have a profound effect upon the thinking of both leaders and constituents of parties in conflict.[9] Changes at the systemic, structural and tactical levels in a conflict system can all bring about a situation in which leaders jerk themselves out of an *incremental continuation* mode of decision-making and into a *comprehensive reconsideration* mode. The latter is not unlikely to involve a search for alternatives and a potential opportunity for mediators to become involved in a search for such alternatives. At the moment, unfortunately, we know too little about the types of contextual change which lead towards the search for new ideas about solutions and those which lead to decisions about 'more of the same' and an intensification of struggle. However, the idea that change can provide mediators with an opening does seem to offer an interesting alternative to the idea that openings only open when parties recognize hurt.

Appropriate mediators

A second major intellectual puzzle currently being faced is the whole issue about whether it is more appropriate that mediatory tasks are carried out by outsiders, rather on the 'classical' model of international mediation discussed above, or whether success is more likely when insiders – individuals and organizations that are themselves part of the society or community within which the conflict is being fought out – act as intermediaries between warring factions. The 'outsider-neutral' versus 'insider-partial' debate is too frequently carried out as though the existence of these two types of intermediary presented an 'either–or' choice, at least in those situations where choice is possible. More fruitfully, enquiry might well start with the assumption that there are circumstances in which one rather than the other is more likely to be successful, while the reverse is true in other circumstances.

Of course, a preliminary question ought to be whether the distinction is as clear-cut as the ongoing debate implies. Where is the dividing line between those who are genuinely 'insiders' and those who, for some unambiguous reason, can be regarded as 'outside' the conflict, in the sense that they are not even a 'peripheral' as opposed to a 'core' party to that conflict? For example, it is clearly the case that the United States government is not exactly 'neutral' in the protracted Israeli/ Palestinian conflict, but is it even 'outside' that conflict, given the substantial influence on domestic US politics wielded by the Jewish community in the USA and by the number of Florida-registered voters that appear to reside normally in Tel Aviv and its environs?

A similar definitional dilemma arises from the intermediary activities of many successful third parties. For example, Kare Loder reports on the successful mediatory role played by Norwegian Church Aid (NCA) in helping to end the civil war in Mali in 1996.[10] He notes that NCA had been working in northern Mali on drought relief since 1984, had '... saved the various communities in the area from disintegration and the nomads in particular from extinction...'[11] and had made a point of using Malians rather than Norwegian expatriates in senior positions. Thus, the 'NCA team' that began to act as facilitators of a traditional peacemaking dialogue in the autumn of 1995 consisted of four individuals, three of whom were respected Malians and only one a Norwegian. Was this a case of an outsider-neutral or an insider-partial initiative? Or might it have been a hybrid case of an insider neutral? Similar questions might even be asked about the Norwegian team from FAFO that had been working in the Gaza Strip for over ten years before some of its members launched the informal talks that made up the Oslo Process and led, in 1993, to the tragically undermined Oslo Accords.[12]

Be that as it may, the issue of what kind of mediators are most appropriate for what circumstances remains a baffling and contentious one. Outsiders have problems obtaining access to intra-state conflicts, although the doctrine of non-inter-ference in the internal affairs of an independent state is beginning to fray at the edges, especially when it is hard to argue that a state still exists, as in the cases of Somalia, Rwanda or parts of former Yugoslavia. Still, the steadfast refusal of the Madrid government to allow outsiders to act as intermediaries in the Spanish–Basque conflict indicates that in many situations only insiders (or, at the most, relatively powerless and unofficial 'Track Two' intermediaries) can even obtain access to the parties involved in a protracted intra-state conflict. The continuing insulation of the Sri Lankan conflict from external mediation – mainly at the behest of the Colombo government rather than the Liberation Tigers of Tamil Eelam (LTTE) – also indicates the tenacity of this 'domestic jurisdiction' obstacle.[13]

Wehr and Lederach[14] have argued persuasively that in many protracted con-flicts, only intermediaries that understand the cultural nuances of the society and who enjoy the *confianza* (something more than simply 'trust') of the antagonists can hope to carry out intermediary roles successfully. Certainly experiences of the success of local intermediaries in developing peace at least at the local level in parts of north-eastern Kenya,[15] in northern Ghana, and in the Atlantic provinces of Nicaragua[16] back up the claim that insider-partials have advantages denied out-siders. On the other hand, there are enough cases of outsiders – usually outsiders who do not conform to the classical model of an 'outsider with leverage' – play-ing a successful part in processes achieving peace at the national level to raise again the question of what circumstances do favour one type of mediator over the other. Obvious examples of effective outsider mediation range from the work of the San Egidio Community in helping to bring about the Mozambique Peace Accords[17] to the Vatican's role in helping to arrange an agreement between Argentina and Chile over their disputed boundary in the Beagle Channel.[18] However, the exam-ples are many, the overall picture a confusing one, and any precise matching of type of intermediary to set of circumstances so that success is likely seems a long way off, even at the theoretical level.

Mediator roles and functions

The final puzzle for students and practitioners of mediation is a variant of the tradi-tional query: what do mediators actually do? In this connection it has been clear for some considerable time that the answer to this apparently simple query is that it depends on *when* a mediator chooses to take an initiative – that is, that there are clearly appropriate roles and functions – tasks to be undertaken, in plain language – depending upon what stage a peace process has achieved.

Even 30 years ago the then sparse literature on mediation recognized that medi-ators would be called upon to do different things for the conflicting parties, depending on the recent history of their conflict. If negotiations had taken place but had broken down then the task of an effective intermediary was to restore communications between the adversaries and explore the conditions each was imposing for the resumption of talks. If the antagonists had yet to explore even the possibility of conversations, then the task of the mediator was to sound out both sides to see if there might be any readiness to engage in talks – if the elusive 'will' existed on both sides, and if it did what conditions for meeting might be imposed.

At this time, and subsequently, the vast preponderance of attention was paid to the tasks of mediators once representatives of the parties in conflict were 'at the table' and much time and effort were spent in delineating what skills a mediator required in the role of chairperson or moderator of the actual face-to-face talks. Issues over the appropriate place for third-party 'power' or 'leverage' developed out of these analyses and still occupy a central place in today's diverse and controversial literature about what makes a successful mediator, and whether adroitness and creativity can make up for the absence of resources to be promised or withheld as ways of inducing agreement between rivals. The debates over 'pure' versus 'power' mediation have been well summarized by Ron Fisher,[19] while Marieke Kleiboer has proposed a sophisticated explanation of why different analysts take up very different positions on this and other debates on the nature of appropriate and successful mediation practices.[20]

The publication of Hal Saunders's[21] seminal article on pre-negotiation and of James Wall's[22] analyses of mediation systems derived from his studies of industrial and organization mediation further complicated ideas about mediators' tasks and roles from the early 1980s. Both analyses suggested that mediators could and do carry out a far wider range of tasks than merely acting as a go-between for parties unwilling – perhaps temporarily – to meet face to face or moderating face-to-face exchanges when these became a possibility. Wall's analysis suggested strongly that one of the tasks facing many mediators involved dealing not merely with the relationships between negotiators or between negotiators and their own decision-makers 'back home', but also between negotiators, their leaders and their constituents, so that this became a further complicating task for mediators aiming for success in ending a conflict. Saunders, in turn, raised questions of what mediators needed to do in the pre-negotiation stages of any peace process; and how various types of intermediary might best prepare parties to be ready to conduct a fruitful negotiation by bringing the most appropriate attitudes, expectations and skills to any formal, official 'table'.

Finally, some of the recent literature on conflict transformation and the aftermath of achieving an agreement has added a list of still further roles for third parties. Mediators' tasks now do not end with the signing of the agreement or a set of accords. Part of the result of all this has been the suggestion that it might be helpful to think of a mediator less as a single person or organization and more as a set of roles to be fulfilled or tasks to be performed. Furthermore, these necessary tasks may actually be carried out by a variety of individuals or organizations, acting – one hopes – in concert with one another, a hope that Susan Allen-Nan has characterized as involving *complementarity* of intermediary initiatives.[23] Different writers characterize this list of tasks somewhat differently, but there is general agreement that there are essential tasks to be undertaken and that these need not necessarily all be carried out by the one mediator.

My own suggested list (below) clearly contains some tasks that would not have been regarded as proper for classical mediators even 20 years ago, but I would argue that all have an important impact on the likely success of mediation in moving a conflict towards a resolution. Moreover, this list has become somewhat less startling with the recognition – again brought about by recent work on peacebuilding at the grass roots and opinion leader levels – of the importance of multilevel intermediary tasks that need to be carried out so as to improve the chances of a lasting and generally accepted resolution of a conflict.

Core mediator tasks in conflict resolution[24]

Pre-negotiation

Explorer.   Determines adversaries' readiness for contacts; sketches range of possible solutions.

Reassurer.   Reassures adversaries that other not wholly bent on 'victory'.

Decoupler.   Assists external patrons to withdraw from core conflict. Enlists patrons in other positive tasks.

Unifier.   Repairs intra-party cleavages and encourages consensus on interests, core values, concessions.

Enskiller.   Develops skills and competencies needed to enable adversaries to reach a durable solution.

Convener.   Initiates process of talks, provides venue and legitimizes contacts and meetings.

During talks or negotiations

Facilitator.   Fulfils functions within meetings to enable a fruitful exchange of versions, aims and visions.

Envisioner.   Provides new data, ideas, theories and options for adversaries to adapt. Creates fresh thinking.

Enhancer.   Provides additional resources to assist in search for positive-sum solution.

Guarantor.   Provides insurance against talks breaking down and offers to guarantee any durable solution.

Legitimizer.   Adds prestige and legitimacy to any agreed solution.

Post-agreement

Verifier.   Reassures adversaries that terms of agreement are being fulfilled.

Implementer.   Imposes sanctions for non-performance of agreement.

Reconciler.   Assists in long-term actions to build new relationships among and within adversaries.

Conclusion

The list of mediator tasks – what mediators do and when – will undoubtedly soon be modified and extended as we analyse more examples of successful and unsuccessful initiatives, and then draw some general lessons from the wealth of case material currently becoming available. This book is clearly part of this necessary consolidation of knowledge about mediators and mediation and equally clearly will contribute to our obtaining a better understanding of the nature of mediation work and its role in resolving protracted and dangerous social conflicts. I can only hope that this present chapter makes a contribution to the task of understanding what we know and, more importantly, what we still need to know about these issues.

Notes

1. E. E. Azar, *The Management of Protracted Social Conflict* (Aldershot: Dartmouth Publishing Co., 1990).
2. V. Jabri, *Mediating Conflict: Decision Making and Western Intervention in Namibia* (Manchester: Manchester University Press, 1990).
3. I. W. Zartman, *Ripe for Resolution: Conflict and Intervention in Africa* (New York: Oxford University Press, 1985).
4. R. J. Fisher & L. Keashley, 'The Potential Complimentary of Mediation and Consultation within a Contingency Model of Third Party Consultation', *Journal of Peace Research*, 28, 1 (1991), 21–42.
5. J. Z. Rubin, 'The Timing of Ripeness and the Ripeness of Timing', in L. Kriesberg & S. J. Thornson (eds), *Timing the De-escalation of International Conflicts* (New York: Syracuse University Press, 1991).
6. Zartman, op. cit.
7. S. J. Stedman, *Peacemaking in Civil Wars* (Boulder: Lynne Reinner, 1991).
8. C. Mitchell, 'The Right Moments: Notes on Four Models of "ripeness"', *Paradigms*, 9, 2 (Winter 1995), 38–52.
9. C. Mitchell, *Gestures of Reconciliation* (London: Macmillan – now Palgrave Macmillan, 2000).
10. K. Loder, 'The Peace Process in Mali', *Security Dialogue*, 28, 4 (1997), 409–24.
11. Ibid., p. 416.
12. J. Corbin, *The Norway Channel* (New York: Atlantic Monthly Press, 1994).
13. P. Saravanamuttu, 'Sri Lanka: the Intractability of Ethnic Conflict', in J. Darby & R. Mac Ginty (eds), *The Management of Peace Processes* (London: Macmillan – now Palgrave Macmillan, 2000), pp. 195–227.
14. P. Wehr & J. P. Lederach, 'Mediating Conflict in Central America', *Journal of Peace Research*, 28, 1 (1991).
15. D. Ibrahim & J. Jenner, 'Breaking the Cycle of Violence in Wajir', Ch. 10 in R. & J. Z. Herr (eds), *Transforming Violence* (Scottdale, Pa: Herald Press, 1998).
16. Wehr & Lederach, op. cit.
17. C. Hume, *Mozambique's War: the Role of Mediation and Good Offices* (Washington, DC: USIP Press, 1994).
18. T. Princen, 'Mediation by a Transnational Organization: the Case of the Vatican', Ch. 7 in J. Bercovitch & J. Z. Rubin (eds), *Mediation in International Relations* (New York: St. Martin's Press – now Palgrave Macmillan, 1992).
19. R. Fisher, *Inter-Active Conflict Resolution* (New York: Syracuse University Press, 1997).
20. M. Kleiboer, *International Mediation: the Multiple Realities of Third Party Intervention* (Boulder: Lynne Rienner, 1997) and M. Kleiboer & P. t'Hart, 'Time to Talk? Multiple Perspectives on Timing of International Mediation', *Cooperation and Conflict*, 30 (1995), 307–48.
21. H. H. Saunders, 'We Need a Larger Theory of Negotiation: the Importance of the Pre-negotiation Phase', *Negotiation Journal*, 1, 1 (July 1985), 249–62.

22. J. A. Wall, 'Mediation: an Analysis, Review and Proposed Research', *Journal of Conflict Studies*, 25, 1 (March 1981), 157–80 and J. A. Wall & A. Lynn, 'Mediation: a Current Review', *Journal of Conflict Resolution*, 37, 1 (March 1993), 160–94.
23. S. Allen-Nan, 'Complimentarity and Coordination of Conflict Resolution Efforts in the Conflicts in Abkhazia, South Ossetia and TransDniestria', PhD dissertation, George Mason University (1999).
24. Adapted from C. Mitchell, 'The Process and Stages of Mediation: Two Sudanese Cases', Ch. 6 in D. R. Smock (ed.), *Making War and Waging Peace* (Washington, DC: USIP Press, 1993).

8
The Role of the News Media in Peace Negotiations: Variations over Time and Circumstance

Gadi Wolfsfeld

One of the most common premises of all peace negotiations is that it is imperative to keep the news media out. The greater the level of media involvement, it is claimed, the more likely the talks will fail. This assumption is, for the most part, correct. It is much more difficult to conduct negotiations within the glare of a spotlight than behind closed doors. It is important, however, for researchers and policy-makers to move beyond this truism and look deeper into the issue.

The role the news media play in negotiations, it turns out, is only one piece in a more complicated puzzle.[1] One cannot separate the influences the press will have on peace talks from what is happening outside the negotiating room. When the news media are playing a generally constructive role in the process, and the talks are being held in a mostly supportive environment, press coverage is less likely to have a negative influence on the negotiations. If, on the other hand, the news media are playing a relatively negative role in the overall process, they are also more likely to have a negative influence on talks. Policy-makers who focus exclusively on the technical issue of how to keep the talks secret are in danger of missing the bigger picture.

The relationship between the press and government can be described as a 'competitive symbiosis'.[2] On the one hand each side depends on the other to achieve certain goals. The government depends on the news media to pass on information to a variety of audiences and the press depends on the government to provide it with information and events that can be turned into interesting news stories. Nevertheless, each would like to obtain the most services for the smallest price. The government would like to have total control over the information the press receives and to have it transmitted without criticism or analysis. The media want to have access to all information from as many sources as possible and to process those data as it sees fit. The relationship between governments and the media is an ongoing struggle over who tells the story.

The outcome of this struggle will determine the role the news media play in any political process, including a peace process. It is helpful to think of that role in terms of a continuum of independence. On one side of that continuum would be those situations in which the news media become *government tools* that simply pass on whatever they are told. The opposite extreme would be devoted to those cases in which the news media were *unwelcome intruders* in the process. Here the media become major obstacles as government leaders find themselves constantly reacting to stories either uncovered by the press or planted by other actors. In the middle of the continuum one finds those cases in which the press play the role of *informative intermediary* whereby it provides relatively helpful information about the process. In these situations – which many would consider an ideal role for the news media – the media provide independent reports and analyses about what is going on. The news media combine information from a variety of sources that allows them to construct more balanced and sophisticated stories about what is happening.

The key goal for researchers is to better identify those factors that have the greatest influence on the role the media will play both inside and outside the negotiating room.[3] The ideas that will be presented are based on research that I have conducted concerning the role of the news media in political conflicts and peace processes. The political contest model[4] attempts to explain how and why the role of the news media in political conflicts varies. The more recent studies have focused specifically on the role of the news media in peace processes.[5]

The empirical research centred on three peace processes. The first case was the Oslo peace process between Israel and the Palestinians that began in earnest in the summer of 1993. The second was the peace process between Israel and Jordan that led to the signing of a peace treaty between those two countries in November of 1994.[6] The final case comes from the process in Northern Ireland that led to the Good Friday Agreement that was signed in April of 1998. The methodology in each of these cases included in-depth interviews with political leaders, advisors and journalists as well as content analyses of media coverage. The varied circumstances surrounding each of these processes provide important insights about how the role of the media can change.

The political environment and media independence

Political control leads to media control. While this relationship is the most obvious in regard to non-democratic countries, it can also be applied to those enjoying democratic rule. The most important factor determining a government's level of control over the news media is the extent to which it is able to take control over the political environment. The political environment can be defined as the aggregate of private and public beliefs, discourse and behaviours concerning political matters within a particular setting and time. It is a 'macro' concept referring to the political situation that confronts political actors attempting to promote their own agenda. What is the distribution of opinions on a particular issue? Who are the major groups and institutions working for and against the government on this topic? What are the most important events that can be linked to the issue? Government leaders and the opposition are in a constant battle to take control over the political environment. The struggle over the news media should be seen as simply one element within this more general competition for political control.[7]

One reason why it is so important to look first at the state of the political environment is because this is exactly what journalists do. The press is much more likely to *react* to political developments than to *initiate* them. A useful way to understand the role of the news media in any political process is to start by looking at the political context, attempt to understand how political actors and journalists interact within the situation, and then examine how the resulting news stories influence the process itself. This idea can be labelled as the 'politics–media cycle'. Changes in the political environment lead to changes in the role of the news media that then lead to further changes in the political environment. This approach differs from others by placing more weight on the political dimension.

There are two major indicators of governments' level of control over the political environment surrounding a peace process: (1) their ability to mobilize consensus among elites in support of the process; (2) their ability to take control over events and the flow of information associated with the process. The first factor shapes the general political context in which journalists are operating, while the second determines the nature of the inputs journalists will use to construct news stories. The greater the leaders' success in each of these areas, the more likely the news media will do their bidding. If they fail in these tasks, the news media have the potential of becoming serious obstacles. As always, it is best to think of success and failure in terms of a continuum rather than as a dichotomy.

By far the most important challenge is to mobilize as many elites as possible in support of the peace process. This sets the stage for everything that follows. Journalists depend on their elite sources to give them a sense about which policies are controversial and which are not.[8] They not only reflect those beliefs, they advance them. They often become advocates for the cause and help define the borders of legitimacy by treating dissenters as deviants.

The role of the United States news media in two different wars helps demonstrate this principle. Hallin's work on the Vietnam War shows how in the early years of that conflict,[9] the American news media were extremely supportive of government efforts to 'stop communism'. Anti-war protesters were framed as either crazy or dangerous. Only when respectable elites began to raise questions about the war did the role of the media begin to change, which (I would argue) increased the rate of political change. There was a reverse trend in the Gulf War, albeit in a much shorter time frame.[10] The debate in the Senate over the decision to use force was extremely intensive and the news media reflected that level of dissent and division. Once the hostilities began, however, most elites decided to come together in support of the war effort and the resulting coverage would best be described as celebratory. These are both good examples of the politics–media cycle.

There is good reason to believe that the level of consensus has a similar influence on the role of the news media in a peace process. When there are deep divisions over the process the news media will justifiably focus on these divisions and thus play a more critical and independent role. In those cases in which the opposition to a peace process is relatively small, on the other hand, the news media will feel obligated to run with the tide and become part of the consensus. As noted, this may involve marginalizing those who disagree.

The high level of consensus should also have an influence on the role the news media play in negotiations. First, journalists may be less aggressive looking for stories that raise serious questions about the process. Once a storyline has been established, journalists search for information that fits and either ignore or underplay information that runs in a different direction.[11] Second, even when journalists do publish negative stories about the negotiations, they are likely to be less damaging. Without a serious challenger able to exploit such information for political advantage, such stories are unlikely to resonate with the general public. Finally, leaders enjoying a high level of political support are in a much better position to take some flak and move on. While negative coverage can completely undermine a weak government, its effects on a powerful government will be considerably less significant.

A second goal for leaders is to take control over events and the flow of information. When governments are in a position to *initiate* events it provides them with important advantages in their relations with the news media. It allows them to carefully orchestrate what happens in the field and to prepare the accompanying spin.

When, on the other hand, governments either lose control over events, or are forced to react to the actions of others, they find it more difficult to control media coverage. Journalists become less dependent on official sources when they find stories elsewhere.

The control over events and the flow of information can be especially important with regard to the negotiations. Governments must keep the negotiations moving smoothly so both parties feel that they have an interest in working together. They also must keep a tight lid on information coming out of the talks. The greater the friction between the two sides the more each will turn to the news media in an attempt to mobilize outside support for their position. The news media are seen as weapons that can be used against the other side.

There is an important lesson here. The path of influence between the level of media involvement and the success of the negotiations runs in *both directions*. Not only does increased media involvement decrease the likelihood of success, but the lower the level of success, the more the media are likely to become involved. When this does take place, the resulting coverage has the potential of making matters even worse. This is another example of the politics–media cycle that was mentioned earlier: difficulties in the negotiations lead to damaging press leaks that make it even more difficult to move forward in the negotiations.

When people think about the role of the news media in negotiations they usually focus exclusively on the flow of information. The fact that this topic comes up relatively late in this discussion places this issue within the proper perspective. The struggle for control over information takes place on many fronts, not only in negotiations. News about the peace process is also based on what journalists gather from opposition leaders, from alternative local and foreign sources, from movement leaders, and from public opinion polls. Whoever provides the best news stories is in the best position to compete for the public agenda.

Here too one must also take into account the level of elite consensus. The greater the level of elite support for a peace process the less likely there will be massive protests that cast a negative light on the situation and place the government on the defensive. Even more importantly, when things do go wrong the media will emphasize the need to get the process back on track. A crisis will probably be framed very differently, however, when a peace process is considered controversial. There will be an intensive debate over the meaning of the crisis and more critical and pessimistic storylines will emerge.[12]

Every government that is involved in peace talks, however, must inevitably cope with the trade-off between the need for secrecy and the need for transparency. If all negotiations are kept completely secret it violates the public's right to know. It also limits the ability of governments to prepare people for the types of concessions that will have to be made in order to move the process forward. If, on the other hand, there is no secrecy, the talks have very little chance of succeeding.

Why is secrecy such an essential element in such negotiations? The most important reason has to do with leaders' needs for public posturing. The public wants to achieve peace by paying the smallest price possible. Political leaders interested in moving forward must continually try to convince the public that they are 'winning'. When speaking to their constituencies, leaders stress the need to remain firm and often place their messages within a colourful wrap of patriotic myths and symbols. Above all, they will avoid any appearance of weakness that would play into the opposition's hands. Premature leaks of concessions will severely undermine this strategy.

When both sides begin playing to their constituencies it sours the atmosphere surrounding the talks. Valuable time can be wasted in dealing with public declarations that are offensive to the other side. Negotiators will also find themselves severely limited in their ability to compromise when leaders have promised to remain firm. The type of communication required within the negotiating room is in many ways the exact opposite of what is needed when speaking to the public. Genuine negotiations demand flexibility and at least a minimal amount of empathy. Messages tailored for the public usually entail steadfastness and ethnic loyalty.

The struggle for control over events and the flow of information concerning a peace process is in many ways a microcosm of the overall conflict between officials and journalists. The most important commodity governments have to offer the press is newsworthy information. When leaders are able to maintain a monopoly on that information, it provides them with tremendous power over the media. When, on the other hand, journalists are in a position to cultivate alternative sources of information it increases their ability to play an independent role. The government loses its power to dictate storylines. This is, for the most part, a healthy development for it provides citizens with a more balanced picture of what is happening. Nevertheless, when governments lose all control over the flow of information media coverage can become a serious obstacle to moving forward.

From the Middle East to Northern Ireland

The three cases alluded to earlier will be used to illustrate the theoretical arguments. One of the most important differences among the three cases was the governments' level of control over the political environment. The Oslo peace process represents a case in which the Israeli government had the least control. That same government, on the other hand, had a tremendous amount of control over the environment surrounding the peace process with Jordan. The level of control in the Northern Ireland peace process appears to fall between the other two, but not in the middle. For reasons detailed below, I will argue that the situation facing leaders in that part of the world falls closer to the Jordanian case than to that of Oslo. The goal of the analysis is to demonstrate the close relationship between control over the political environment and the role the news media play in a peace process.

Israel and the Palestinians

The Rabin government did have quite a bit of control over the environment during the initial negotiations in Oslo. The talks in Oslo, it will be remembered, were kept completely secret until the breakthrough was announced in August of 1993. One of the intriguing elements in that process was that there were also 'talks' going on in Washington at the same time. The news media were all covering these meaningless talks in the United States, which allowed the actual negotiations to be carried out in complete privacy. There can be little doubt that the fact that the negotiators were kept completely isolated contributed to the success of the talks.[13]

There was also quite a bit of enthusiasm among the public and the press when the initial agreements were announced. The government had a complete monopoly on all of the information about the talks and was able to exploit the complete surprise to their advantage. This short period came to be known as the 'peace festival'; the Israeli news media were filled with euphoric stories about massive economic growth and predictions that a final settlement was just around the corner. The government was also able to initiate a number of grand peace ceremonies that provided wonderful vehicles for promoting peace to the news media and the public. The opposition was caught completely off guard during these first few weeks, and appeared to be running against the political stream.

It was not to last, however. The negotiations that followed were carried out within a very different political environment from the one in which they began. The government was never able to mobilize a broad level of elite consensus in support of the process, had very little control over the flow of events and information about the process. All of these factors led to the news media playing an extremely problematic role in the process. Based on the interviews and content analyses that were carried out, it is fair to conclude that the role of the news media fell closest to the 'unwelcome intruders' end of the continuum.[14]

The lack of elite consensus was not surprising. The dispute over how to deal with the occupied territories represents the key division between right and left in Israel. For many years the Israeli public and the Knesset were split completely down the middle over whether or not the country should be willing to make territorial concessions in the West Bank and Gaza. The decision to recognize the PLO as the legitimate representative of the Palestinian people was also an extremely controversial one. Arafat was still seen by many in Israel as the leader of a terrorist organization and Rabin himself had expressed similar views before the elections. Given the historical context, any leader would have found it extremely difficult to mobilize a wide level of consensus in support of Oslo.

The atmosphere became even more negative because of terrorist bomb attacks on Israeli civilians. The government's inability to take control over these events was its greatest failure. The Israeli news media, which had been so enthusiastic at the start, turned hostile. The coverage of the attacks was nothing short of hysterical, and the various news media appeared to be competing with one another over who could produce the most shocking coverage.[15] These terrorist attacks provided tremendous advantages to Oslo's opponents, especially given the way they were covered. The Rabin government was continually on the defensive trying to justify the process.

The level of control over the flow of information coming from the negotiations themselves tended to vary. There were two different sets of negotiations in the first years of Oslo and it is interesting to compare them.[16] The first set ended with the signing of the Cairo Agreement in May of 1994. The media were very involved in these negotiations with both the Israelis and the Palestinians providing journalists with leaks and continual briefings. Both sides agreed that this was a mistake; they decided to keep the press out during the talks that led to the Oslo B Agreement that was signed in September of 1995. In this case none of the details of the negotiations were revealed and all agreed that this was a more effective mode of operation.

Once again, however, these problems should be understood within the larger context. The government's problems with the flow of information from the negotiations were relatively small compared to what was going on elsewhere. Most of the negative information about the peace process came from members of the opposition, the extremely active and vocal movements working against Oslo, and the terrorist attacks being carried out by Hamas and the Islamic Jihad. The fact that the press became too involved in certain aspects of the negotiations may have made things worse, but it was relatively unimportant in the total scheme of things.

The peace process with Jordan

The political environment surrounding the negotiations with Jordan was completely different and so was the role of the news media.[17] The most important feature was the extremely high level of consensus surrounding the agreement. In direct contrast to the other accords, the peace agreement with Jordan received an overwhelming majority in the Knesset: 91–3. There were also no major protests against the agreement and no violence during either the negotiations or the final signing. It is hard to imagine a more problem-free peace process between two enemies.

The generally positive relationship between Israel and Jordan was also reflected in the way the negotiations were conducted. The press was informed about where and when the talks would take place, but almost nothing about their substance. Some issues, such as the amount of water that was to be given to Jordan, could have proven quite controversial if they had been leaked to the press. Both sides had a genuine interest in keeping these issues out of the news until they were completed. These talks provide a wonderful illustration of how the causal relationship between media involvement and the negotiation success runs in both directions. The negotiations went extremely well, which meant that neither Israel nor Jordan had any motivation to leak stories to the news media and this contributed to the success of the talks.

This case also provides a good example of how political success leads to media success. The Israeli press not only reflected the high level of consensus, it also reinforced it. News stories about the agreement and the numerous ceremonies that followed were tales of celebration. A content analysis of newspaper articles that appeared in the final weeks of that process found that a remarkable 74 per cent of the items were positive and only 5 per cent were negative.[18] Governments rarely enjoy this level of support, especially in peacetime.[19]

The role of the news media in this process falls as close as one can get to the 'government tools' end of the continuum. A particularly revealing incident concerns the major signing ceremony held in the Arava desert on 17 October 1994.[20] The master of ceremonies for the event was Haim Yavin, the most respected anchorman in Israeli television. The fact that a journalist would take an active part in such a ceremony says it all. Any journalist who participated in the ceremonies connected with Oslo would have been tainted with political bias. But when 'everyone' agrees, the news media have no need to even feign objectivity.

Northern Ireland

The final case is the Northern Ireland peace process. The authorities had a fair amount of control over the political environment surrounding the process, especially after the signing of the Good Friday Agreement in April 1998. Multi-party talks, chaired by former US Senate majority leader George Mitchell, were held over two years.[21] His efforts eventually proved successful and the agreement received more support across the political spectrum than any previous attempt. Not only was the agreement supported by the major parties from each camp (the Ulster Unionist Party and the Social Democratic and Labour Party), it was also endorsed by the political parties associated with paramilitary groups (Sinn Fein, the Progressive Unionist Party and the Ulster Democratic Party). The only major groups to oppose the accord were the Democratic Unionist Party (DUP) and the United Kingdom Unionist Party (UKUP). The level of political consensus was reinforced by the decision to carry out a national referendum on the Good Friday Agreement in both Northern Ireland and the Republic of Ireland. The accord received 71 per cent support in the North and 94 per cent in the South.

The relatively high level of consensus also provided the authorities with a good deal of control over both events and the flow of information. The fact that the paramilitary groups were part of that consensus ensured that the level of violence would be kept relatively low. There were also very few public protests against the agreement. This sense of common purpose was also felt in the negotiating room and from all accounts Mitchell was able to keep a fairly tight lid on the discussions.[22] Early on he set up a very strict set of ground rules for all of the participants to ensure the maximum level of secrecy for the talks.

The news media in Northern Ireland became an enthusiastic supporter of the Good Friday Agreement. This was especially notable in the newspapers that are identified with the different communities. One of the most significant examples of this change was when the unionist paper the *Belfast Newsletter* and the nationalist *Irish News* published a series of common editorials in favour of the peace process. As the political camps began to move closer on the peace process, so did the newspapers. The culmination of this cooperation was the fact that both newspapers asked the readers to vote yes in the referendum.[23]

Previous agreements, such as the Anglo-Irish Agreement of 1985, were much more controversial, especially among Protestants. The *Belfast Newsletter* constantly criticized that agreement, while the *Irish News* was much more positive. As the major political parties moved together so did the media, and there is good reason to believe that this made it easier for the government to mobilize public support.

It was argued earlier that the level of consensus sets the stage for everything that follows. One of the most telling demonstrations of this point concerns the manner in which the Northern Ireland press dealt with the terrorist bombing at Omagh that took place in August 1998. The goal of that attack was to derail the peace process. However, examining the news coverage of that incident and listening to the interviews that were carried out, it seems that the bomb had exactly the opposite effect. The major lesson for the news media was the need to *speed up the process* so that such tragedies would never happen again. This was very different from what happened in Israel, where terrorist attacks led the press to raise serious questions about the wisdom of the peace process.

Thus, the fact that the news media played a relatively supportive role for the peace process in Northern Ireland can be related to the fact that those journalists were working in a very conducive atmosphere. This does not mean that they played an ideal role. Interviews with those who were opposed to the Good Friday Accords are replete with charges of pro-government bias. When the news media move closer to the 'government tools' end of the continuum they are more likely to either ignore or discredit opponents. One would need more evidence before deciding that this is what happened in Northern Ireland. However there is good reason to suspect that the pro-peace enthusiasm of the media may have made it more difficult for the 30 per cent who opposed the accord to express their opinion.[24]

The evidence suggests that the role of the news media in the Northern Ireland peace process falls closest to the Jordanian case. The major difference is that in Northern Ireland, there was a certain amount of debate over the process. It may not have been a fair debate, but citizens were exposed to other opinions. While making such evaluations is far from an exact science, the amount of discord expressed in the news media provides a reasonable indicator of where to place the media in each of the three peace processes.

Conclusion

The major point of this essay was to encourage peace scholars and practitioners to adopt a broader perspective when looking at the role of the news media in negotiations. The optimal approach is to start by looking at the surrounding political environment concerning the peace process, then attempt to understand how this influences the production of news and only at the end examine the more specific influences on the process. Governments who are able to mobilize a good deal of political consensus in support of their efforts and to exert a fair amount of control over events and information have little to fear from the news media.

There is both good and bad news here for those interested in the promotion of peace. The good news is that the media can, in some circumstances, play an extremely constructive role in a peace process. In the Jordanian peace process and the one in Northern Ireland, the news media were important agents in creating a conducive atmosphere for reconciliation. The bad news is that there is no simple means of mobilizing the news media to one's cause. The hard work of politics comes first. Only when leaders have been successful on the political front can they expect to get help from the news media.

One could argue that from a normative point of view this is as it should be. The storylines adopted by the press *should* reflect the distribution of opinions and beliefs in the general society. An agreement that enjoys a good deal of political support should receive much more positive coverage than one that is marred by controversy. There is something to that point.

It is not that simple, however. The role the news media play in such conflicts begins long before leaders can even consider initiating a peace process. The news media are more interested in conflict than in peace. They are much more likely to deal with threats than opportunities especially in coverage of the enemy. The news media are more likely to reinforce national stereotypes than to change them. Therefore, news media make it more difficult for leaders to begin a peace process. Perhaps this is at least one of the reasons why there are so many international conflicts and so few peace processes.

Thus, the fact that the news media played a positive role in two out of the three cases is misleading. First, one must think about all of the instances in which the news media make it more difficult to even initiate a serious peace process. Such cases are automatically excluded from such studies. Second, one must bear in mind the role of the media in the many years preceding these breakthroughs. There is good reason to believe, for example, that the news media played a much more inflammatory role in previous attempts to bring peace to Northern Ireland.

The news media, then, are best thought of as fair-weather friends. When the sun is shining and everything is going well they are all too happy to participate in the celebration. In times of trouble, when they could do the most good, they only make things more difficult. The news media can make a positive contribution to a peace process. However, they only do so when most of the difficult work has already been done.

Notes

1. There is relatively little written on the topic of media and peace, especially compared to what has been written on the role of the media in conflict and war. There are a number of studies that deal with such topics as the role of the media in foreign policy and

diplomacy: Y. Cohen, *Media Diplomacy: the Foreign Office in the Mass Communications Age* (London: Frank Cass, 1986); R. Cohen, *Theatre of Power: the Art of Diplomatic Signaling* (London: Longman, 1987); J. Fromm et al., 'The Media Impact on Foreign Policy', in H. Smith (ed.), *The Media and the Gulf War* (Washington, DC: Seven Locks Press, 1992); E. Gilboa, 'Mass Communication and Diplomacy: a Theoretical Framework', *Communications Theory*, 10 (2000), 275–309 and 'Media Diplomacy: Conceptual Divergence and Applications', *Harvard International Journal of Press/Politics*, 3 (1998) 56–75; N. Gowing, *Media Coverage: Help or Hindrance in Conflict Prevention?* (New York: Carnegie Commission on Preventing Deadly Conflicts, 1996); G. Henderson (ed.), *Public Diplomacy and Political Change: Four Case Studies, Okinawa, Peru, Czechoslovakia, Guinea* (New York: Praeger, 1973); P. O'Heffernan, *Mass Media and American Foreign Policy* (Norwich, NJ: Ablex, 1991) and 'Mass Media and US Foreign Policy: a Mutual Exploitation Model of Media Influence in US Foreign Policy', in R. J. Spitzer (ed.), *Media and Public Policy* (Westport, Conn.: Praeger, 1993); S. Serfaty (ed.), *The Mass Media and Foreign Policy* (New York: St. Martin's Press – now Palgrave Macmillan, 1991) and W. P. Strobel, *Late Breaking Foreign Policy: The News Media's Influence on Peace Operations* (Washington, DC: United States Institute of Peace Press, 1997). Several studies relate to the problems peace movements face in attempting to mobilize the news media: Glasgow University Media Group, *War and Peace News* (Philadelphia: Open University Press, 1985); T. Gitlin, *The Whole World Is Watching* (Berkeley: University of California Press, 1980); R. Hackett, *News and Dissent: the Press and Politics of Peace in Canada* (Norwood, NJ: Ablex, 1991); C. Ryan, *Prime Time Activism: Media Strategies for Grassroots organizing* (Boston, Mass.: South End Press, 1991) and M. Small, 'Influencing the Decision-making: the Vietnam Experience', *Journal of Peace Research*, 24 (1987), 185–98. A few articles deal with the role of the news media in disarmament and international cooperation: P. A. Bruck, 'Strategies for Peace, Strategies for News Research', *Journal of Communications*, 39 (1989), 108–29; P. A. Bruck & C. Roach, 'Dealing with Reality: the News Media and the Promotion of Peace', in C. Roach (ed.), *Communication and Culture in War and Peace* (Newbury Park: Sage, 1993); W. Dorman et al., *American Press Coverage of US–Soviet Relations, the Soviet Union, Nuclear Weapons, Arms controls, and National Security: a Bibliography* (New York: Center for War, Peace and the News Media, 1988) and W. A. Gamson & D. Stuart, 'Media Discourses a Symbolic Contest: the Bomb in Political Cartoons', *Sociological Forum*, 7 (1992), 55–86. Several studies focus on images of the enemy: R. W. Ayres, 'Mediating International Conflicts: Is Image Change Necessary?', *Journal of Peace Research*, 34 (1997), 431–47; W. Eckhart, 'Making and Breaking Enemy Images', *Bulletin of Peace Proposals*, 22 (1991), 87–95 and R. Ottosen, 'Enemy Images and the Journalistic Process', *Journal of Peace Research*, 32 (1995), 97–112. There is also some work on the topic of 'peace journalism', which talks about the need to change journalists' norms and routines for covering peace and conflict: G. F. Adam & R. Thamotheram, *The Media's Role in Conflict: Report Reviewing International Experience in the Use of Mass-media for Promoting Conflict Prevention, Peace and Reconciliation* (Geneva: Switzerland: Media Action International, 1996); Bruck & Roach, op. cit.; J. Galtung, 'High Road, Low Road: Charting the Course of Peace Journalism', *Track Two*, 7 (1998), 7–10; S. Himmelfarb, 'Impact is the Mantra: the "Common Ground" Approach to the Media', *Track Two*, 7 (1998), 38–40; J. Lynch, 'Findings of the conflict and Peace Journalism Forum', unpublished manuscript (Talow, England: 1998); R. Manlow, *The Mass Media and Social Violence: Is There a Role for the Media in Preventing and Moderating Ethnic, National, and Religious Conflict?* (New York: Center for War, Peace, and the News Media, New York University, 1996), 'The Media's Role in Preventing and Moderating Conflict', *Crossroads Global Report* (March/April 1997), 24–7, and 'Role Plays: Potential Media Roles in Conflict Prevention and Management', *Track Two*, 7 (1998), 11–16; C. Roach, 'Information and Culture in War and Peace: Overview', in C. Roach (ed.), *Communication and Culture in War and Peace* (Newbury Park: Sage, 1993); and D. Shinar, 'Media Diplomacy and "Peace Talk": the Middle East and Northern Ireland', *Gazette*, 62 (2000), 83–97.

2. G. Wolfsfeld, *Media and Political Conflict: News from the Middle East* (Cambridge: Cambridge University Press, 1997).
3. In this chapter I relate specifically to the *political* factors that influence the role of the media. Elsewhere 'The News Media and Peace: from the Middle East to Northern Ireland', *Peace Works No. 37* (Washington, DC: United States Institute of Peace, 2001). I also deal with the *professional* factors that influence how journalists relate to a peace process. Different media organizations, for example, have different goals and audiences and the role of the press in a peace process tends to reflect such variations.
4. Wolfsfeld, *Media and Political Conflict*.
5. Wolfsfeld, 'The News Media and Peace'.
6. I do not deal with the role of either the Palestinian or Jordanian press in this chapter. This is because the rules governing the role a controlled press will play in a peace process different from those that apply to a free press. I do deal with the role of the Jordanian press elsewhere: *News about the Other in Jordan and Israel: Does Peace Make a Difference?* (forthcoming).
7. Wolfsfeld, *Media and Political Conflict*.
8. W. L. Bennett, 'Towards a Theory of Press–State Relations in the United States', *Journal of Communications*, 10 (1990), 103–25.
9. D. Hallin, *The Uncensored War* (New York: Oxford University Press, 1986).
10. Wolfsfeld, *Media and Political Conflict*.
11. See, for example, H. Brosius & P. Epp, 'Prototyping through Key Events: News Selection in the Case of Violence against Aliens and Asylum Seekers in Germany', *European Journal of Communications*, 10 (1995), 391–412; H. M. Kepplinger & J. Habermeir, 'The Impact of Key Events on the Presentation of Reality', *European Journal of Communications*, 10 (1995), 371–90; J. Lederman, *Battle Lines: the American Media and the Intifada* (New York: Henry Holt, 1992) and G. Wolfsfeld, 'Political Waves and Democratic Discourses: Terrorism Waves during the Oslo Peace Process', in W. L. Bennett & R. Entman (eds), *Mediated Politics: Communications in the Future of Democracy* (New York: Cambridge University Press, 2000).
12. Wolfsfeld, 'The News Media and Peace'.
13. D. Makovsky, *Making Peace with the PLO: the Rabin Government's Road to the Oslo Process* (Boulder, Colo.: Westview Press, 1995) and U. Savir, *The Process* (New York: Random House, 1998).
14. It is worth noting that this conclusion runs completely against conventional wisdom in Israel. The assumption is that because many Israeli journalists are thought to identify with the political left they make a concerted effort to provide positive coverage. However, when professional considerations compete with ideological considerations, the former will normally win out, see Wolfsfeld, 'The News Media and Peace'.
15. Wolfsfeld, 'Political Waves and Democratic Discourses'.
16. Wolfsfeld, 'Promoting Peace through the News Media: Some Initial Lessons from the Oslo Peace Process', *Harvard International Journal of Press/Politics*, 2 (1997), 52–70.
17. Wolfsfeld, 'Fair Weather Friends: the Varying Role of the Media in the Arab–Israeli Peace Process', *Political Communication*, 14 (1997), 29–48.
18. Ibid.
19. This analysis refers to the role of the news media in the relatively short negotiating process between Jordan and Israel. When one looks at this question from a more long-term perspective, one finds that the role of the Israeli news media was much less positive. Once peace was established the Israeli press tended to mostly ignore Jordan, and when that country was covered it was often within a rather negative context. The role of the Jordanian press was even more problematic: Wolfsfeld, *News about the Other*.
20. An interesting side note concerns the timing of the event. It was held in the middle of the afternoon – despite the predictably oppressive heat – so that the ceremony (and President Clinton) could be shown live on 'Good Morning America'.
21. G. Mitchell, *Making Peace* (New York: Knopf, 1999).

22. Some might argue that it was relatively easy to keep the talks secret because for a good part of the time there was little progress, and thus little to leak.

23. There are other important differences between the cases that have to do with the nature of the media environments. One of the more important has to do with the fact that there are more 'shared' news media in Northern Ireland: many Protestants and Catholics turn to the same media as a source of information about the conflicts. This forces such news organs to make a concerted effort to bridge the gaps between the two populations. In most conflicts, however (including the one in the Middle East) each set of antagonists depend on their own news media and this serves to reinforce existing cultural assumptions about the other side.

24. A content analysis of editorials appearing in a number of newspapers provides support for this proposition (Wolfsfeld, in press). A study of editorials that were written in the wake of 22 key events found 126 editorials in favour of the process, 23 expressing a more ambivalent attitude, and only two that were opposed.

Part III
Violence

Long-running conflicts are often characterized by the structural nature of violence. Whether from state or non-state sources, many forms of violence are subtle and embedded in political and social dynamics. Peace initiatives can be interpreted as a threat and spark an increase in violence. An ending of major violence from the main militant groups is almost always a prerequisite for their inclusion in peace negotiations. The state will be expected to tone down its security measures too. But parties and militants in peace processes are rarely the homogeneous blocs they might seem to outsiders. Peace initiatives place participants under enormous strain and can prompt dissent and breakaways.

Armed spoilers, dedicated to derailing any peace initiative, have become a feature in many peace processes. Popularly derided as 'wreckers', they are often sophisticated in the targeting of their violence. The purpose is to shock public opinion, through deliberately gratuitous acts of violence, into applying pressure on participants to withdraw from talks. Beyond that, the spoiler's agenda may reflect vested interests in the continuation of the conflict or a manoeuvring for power within a bloc. Neutralizing spoiler violence is often dependent on the spoiler's military capability and popular support, and the ability of the negotiators to build a process capable of withstanding the spoiler's assault.

The legacy of violence stretches from human costs and opportunity costs such as lives lost or devoted to an armed struggle, to criminality fuelled by former combatants or farmland wasted through landmines or pollution. The solutions to these problems tend to be expensive, politically sensitive and long term, but failure to address them can jeopardize the survival of a peace accord.

9
Peace Processes and the Challenges of Violence

Stephen John Stedman

Violence poses fundamental challenges to peace settlements. Peace processes are often rife with strategic and tactical deception and even those who sign peace agreements may cultivate violence in order to undermine their new 'partners' in peace. Multiple actors in civil wars rarely simultaneously choose peace; those who seek to end a violent conflict will often face opposition from parties who are excluded or who exclude themselves from peacemaking. Such spoilers – leaders and factions who view a particular peace as opposed to their interests and who are willing to use violence to undermine it – pose a grave threat to those who risk making peace.[1] Beyond strategic and tactical uses of violence, there is the obvious need to convince those with the guns to lay them down and reconstruct their lives in a peaceful manner. War may end, but if former combatants lack jobs and skills and if weapons are easily available, then violent crime may increase and rob citizens of their security and their hopes for a robust peace dividend. Finally, there are the effects of past violence: addressing the needs of victims and examining issues of accountability and culpability for atrocity and murder.

Not all peace processes, however, are equally vulnerable to violence. Just as there are cases where analysts assert that violence destroyed incipient coalitions for peace, there are others where scholars assert that violence pushed hesitant elites to full settlement.[2] This then is the puzzle identified by Tim Sisk and John Darby, among others: when and why does violence sometimes act as a catalyst for making peace and when and why does violence destroy potentially promising peace processes? Possible answers include environmental variables such as number of parties, issues at stake and economic interdependence; the strategies of elites in the face of violence; and attitudes and support for peace among followers.

In this chapter I approach this question with an emphasis on the short-term implementation of peace agreements. I do so for two reasons. First, I approach the question of violence and peace processes from a belief that peace is most vulnerable in the short term. When countries emerging from civil war revert to large-scale bloodshed, it is usually within the first five years of reaching a peace agreement. Second, I think that we know more about protecting peace in the short term than we know about healing societies in the long term. It is not that longer-term processes associated with peacebuilding, such as establishing a culture of accountability, reconciling former enemies, consolidating democracy and fostering human rights, are unimportant. But precisely because they are long-term processes, our ability at any given time to have a large effect on the success or failure of such processes as reconciliation is limited. Moreover, we certainly do not want our evaluation of short-term implementation held hostage to the achievement of processes that likely take decades.

I argue that peace processes differ in their vulnerability to violence; the presence of spoilers, spoils and hostile neighbours pose the gravest threats to fledgling peace processes. These threats tend to be more manageable by local parties when there is a high degree of economic interdependence, a local tradition of formal democratic politics and a lively civil society. When such factors are absent, the role of international actors in combating spoilers becomes paramount. Based on research on successful peace implementation, I argue that there are clear priorities to sustaining peace processes. The first is to overcome or minimize the threat of spoilers; the second is to demobilize soldiers and reintegrate them into civilian life; and the third is to sow the seeds for future long-term peacebuilding by assisting the reform of police and judiciaries, supporting wider disarmament in society and building local capacity for human rights and reconciliation. These priorities address the problems of violence that I mention in my opening paragraph: the strategic and tactical use of violence to undermine peace, the potential rise in criminal violence that can rob peace of its value and finally, undoing the psychological and physical traumas of violence.

I begin by reviewing several strands of literature on implementing peace agreements. I first discuss what we know about environmental factors that make the realization of peace more or less difficult in war-torn societies. I then turn to the key tasks of implementing peace agreements and briefly review insights from three different literatures: spoilers in peace processes, demobilization of combatants and peacebuilding. Finally, I present a new avenue of research on peace implementation that focuses on how different constituencies view the meaning of implementing peace agreements.

The conflict environment and the effect of violence on peace settlements

Early research on peacemaking in civil wars viewed conflicts in a differentiated manner and hypothesized that efficacy of mediation was related systematically to the presence or absence of important variables endogenous to the conflict. The pioneering work in this regard was I. William Zartman's work on ripeness, which posited that, all things being equal, civil wars were more amenable to mediation when the parties had reached a hurting stalemate – where no party sensed it could win, but where all parties sensed that they would be dramatically worse off if conflict continued.[3] My own early work on peacemaking in civil wars took a different tack, but, like Zartman, hypothesized that civil wars differed in terms of likelihood of settlement. My first book focused on group dynamics within warring parties, as well as the presence or absence of leaders who either suffered from decision-making pathologies or simply saw the conflict in all-or-nothing terms and were unable to make necessary concessions to settle.[4]

Beginning in the mid-1990s a second wave of scholarship in civil war termination rejected the insights of the ripeness approach and approached civil war in an undifferentiated manner: El Salvador was Angola was Northern Ireland was Rwanda. The challenges of making peace were generic – overcoming the security dilemma and related commitment problems, building trust and confidence among adversaries, and problem-solving to address the security needs of the warring parties. The most potent weapons for overcoming those challenges were provided by outsiders in the form of attention, resources and guarantees.[5] The problem for this research is that given an undifferentiated treatment of the problem, prescribed solutions tend to be open-ended. That is, more resources, more attention and stronger guarantees are always suggested, with a resulting danger of tautology: if international actors are willing to do all it takes to make peace, then peace will be made.

Recent work has made great progress in identifying attributes of civil wars that make them more or less amenable to peacemaking. The implication for those concerned with violence and peace processes is that some peace settlements are more vulnerable to extremist violence than others. A study of international implementation of peace agreements in civil wars finds that successful ending of civil wars is much more difficult when there are more than two warring parties; when at least one of the parties is fighting for secession; when coercion has played a large role in producing the peace agreement; when there are more than 50,000 soldiers; when the state has collapsed; when there are easily identifiable spoilers; when there are neighbouring states that oppose the peace settlement; and when there are valuable, easily marketed commodities such as diamonds or timber.[6] The study found that the last three variables – spoilers, spoils and hostile neighbours – often found in tandem, posed the greatest dangers to peace settlements. Spoilers are more likely to oppose peace when they are assured of support from neighbouring states and if they can grab valuable spoils that can enable them to continue their fight.

A new exciting line of research asks the question in a different way: what variables might provide some peace settlements with greater immunization against extremist violence? Elizabeth Wood, for example, argues that economic interdependence between or among warring parties provides a powerful incentive for them to cooperate in the face of spoilers.[7] Wood contrasts South Africa, where the well-developed industrial economy created incentives for the parties to work together for a mutually beneficial outcome, with Angola, where the lack of economic development and the economy's reliance on oil and diamond exports forged a winner-take-all, zero-sum approach to the conflict. The lack of economic interdependence and an endgame that will likely produce separation help to explain why the parties in the Israeli–Palestinian conflict are unable to sustain cooperation against spoilers and collapse into mutual recrimination in the face of extremist violence.[8]

Another contextual variable that may help parties overcome spoiler threats is the provision of international resources. Usually, scholars do not treat international attention and commitment as a contextual variable, and by defining it as international will make the error of treating it as completely voluntarist. Yet research shows that cases will vary predictably in the amount of international resources and attention they receive.[9] To the extent that the case engages the national interests of a major or regional power, the more likely the case will receive adequate attention and resources. The United States and Europe have provided more than $16 billion to peace implementation in Bosnia since 1995, which by 2001 translates into more than $4200 a person in that war-torn country. In contrast, international actors provided about $35 million to implementing the Arusha Accords in Rwanda during 1993–94, or about $4 a Rwandan.

It may be possible that when international actors do too much, and play too great a role in implementing peace, as in Bosnia, it creates perverse incentives for local parties not to take cooperative steps in making peace themselves: an excess of international involvement can deter local ownership of a peace settlement.[10] The international role in implementation should be fine-tuned to the difficulty of the implementation environment. As Doyle and Sambanis argue, where difficulty is high, and local capacities are weak, international actors must increase the resources allotted to making and building peace.[11]

Priorities in peace implementation

Peace agreements often involve multiple pledges, which then translate into implementation sub-goals: demobilization, disarmament, elections, human rights, refugee repatriation, economic reconstruction, reforming police and establishing accountability. Given a world of limited resources and time, what tasks in peace implementation should receive priority? To protect an incipient peace against the threat of violence, priorities must be given to overcoming spoilers, demobilizing soldiers, providing civilian security and building up local capacity for peace.

Priority 1: overcoming the threat of spoilers

In previous works I have called attention to the role of spoilers as destroyers of peace agreements and have put forth a typology of spoilers based on their position in the peace process, number of spoilers, type based on intent, and whether the locus of spoiling behaviour lies with the leader or followers of the party. Of crucial importance is the motivation and intent of the spoiler. Does it have limited demands that can be met through inducements? Is it a total spoiler, who sees power as indivisible, and will use any inducement to its strategic advantage? Or is the spoiler greedy, that is, possessing goals that expand based on the prospect of appeasement?[12]

Several articles have taken issue with, or attempted to refine, the spoilers concept. In particular, four aspects of the original formulation have come under criticism. First, it is said that since it is impossible to identify *ex ante* what type of spoiler one faces, then the concept has little predictive or prescriptive value.[13] Second, it is argued that the definition of total spoiler type as immutable is problematic, given the propensity of what are described as total spoilers at one time to change.[14] Third, it is argued that too much attention to spoiler motivation detracts from the much more important considerations of capability and opportunity to spoil.[15] Fourth, some have questioned my emphasis on the role of international actors in overcoming spoiler problems; that attention needs to be paid to strategies that local peacemakers can pursue to moderate spoiler threats.[16]

Marie-Joëlle Zahar calls into question the usefulness of the typology by arguing that *ex ante* it is impossible to know what kind of spoiler one is confronting.[17] This seems to me an academic criticism distant from the realities of peacemaking, deception and violence. Indeed, if I understand the criticism correctly, it is that the spoiler concept does not eliminate the possibility of strategic deception in peace negotiations. After all, if there was a magic indicator of type, then no party could act to deceive; they would all wear Ts, Ls or Gs on their chest.[18]

It is impossible to know any type that is based on intention: we are not mind-readers. Given that fact, the search for scientific indicators of type misses the point: if we are uncertain about intention, we need to look for intelligence (not indicators) about intention; and then we must update our prior assessments on new intelligence. Intelligence will always be fallible; if it were not the case, intelligence failures would be a thing of the past and the world would be a safer place.

Let me walk through this step by step. We need to enter into peace implementation with an appreciation of uncertainty and incomplete information. This seems to me superior than blithely assuming that all parties that sign peace agreements do so in good faith, or are equally trustworthy. In some cases we will want to be particularly vigilant to greater likelihood of spoiler behaviour, for instance when a rebel group such as the Revolutionary United Front in Sierra Leone hacks off the arms and legs of non-combatants, including children and infants, as a standard tactic, or for instance, when a rebel group such as the Khmer Rouge is responsible for millions of deaths by implementing an economic development policy based on forced evacuation of cities and the killing of people who wear eyeglasses. We will also want to be aware that rebel leaders who spend decades in the bush, surrounded by sycophants who assure them that the world revolves around them, may not be able to conceive of power as divisible.

But since the goal at the beginning of implementation is to keep an open mind to the possibility of insincere signatories to an agreement, even where we have good reason to doubt that sincerity, mediators need to try to move forward by including the party. We then judge compliance, and assess motives for non-compliance, best accomplished through intelligence – informants, surveillance, reading of documents, etc. For instance, if an informant comes to a peace implementer and describes in detail arms caches, militias and lists of ethnic opponents who are to be killed at a rate of 50,000 a week, we should probably update our prior assessment about spoiler likelihood and type. This, of course, happened in Rwanda in January 1994, and the failure of the UN to update its belief in the commitment of the Rwandan government to peace contributed to the ensuing genocide.

But can some total spoilers change? Zahar and Darby argue that there are examples of factions who are labelled total spoilers at one time, who then years later are willing to negotiate a settlement. Accordingly, they call into question whether there is such a thing as a total spoiler that holds immutable preferences for total power. There are several issues here that deserve discussion. The mere fact that some analysts describe a faction as a total spoiler at a given time seems irrelevant for two reasons best referenced through the examples that Zahar provides: the PLO in the 1970s and 1980s and the IRA or UDA in Northern Ireland. First, my article went to great lengths to insist that spoilers can only be defined in relationship to a given peace agreement. In the absence of an agreement, the concept of spoiler should not apply. Second, the main fact of abhorrent behaviour and totalistic rhetoric in the past does not in and of itself create a total spoiler. Again, as I pointed out, most parties in civil wars engage in atrocities and many use total rhetoric; the early dismissal of a faction as totalistic is usually done for political reasons to delegitimize it rather than to provide any objective sense of whether there is a compromise to which it might agree. Third, in each of these examples, just as there were critics who portrayed the PLO, IRA and UDA as irreconcilable, totalistic factions, there were those who were sympathetic with them and characterized them as reasonable, justice-seeking, parties capable of weighing costs and benefits of war and concessions.

In my article I did point out a route whereby a party that is a total spoiler can change. When the locus of the spoiler problem lies with a single leader who, for whatever reason, sees a war in an all-or-nothing fashion, there is the potential for the party to change type when the leader changes.

A third criticism holds that intent may not be as important in determining threat as capability and the opportunity structure available to would-be spoilers. This I think is an important refinement of the concept; it calls attention to aspects of the conflict environment that make spoilers a greater threat in some cases than others. Where spoilers have access to easily tradable valuable commodities, and where they can rely on the support of neighbouring countries who oppose peace, then spoilers are more likely and a greater threat to peace.

Finally, a fourth criticism holds that my article placed too great an emphasis on the role of international actors in overcoming spoiler threats. Cetinyan and Stein, citing evidence from the Middle East and Northern Ireland, note that if peacemakers anticipate challenges from spoilers, then they can create strategies to isolate them and prevent them from destroying agreements. Zahar argues that since there are a few agreements that have been implemented without international custodians, they are neither necessary or sufficient to marginalize spoilers.

The fact that there are two to three peace processes where domestic peacemakers were able to marginalize spoilers does not mean that in the great majority of cases international custodians are irrelevant. Again, taking a differentiated view of civil wars is needed. The examples that are cited of self-implementing agreements are usually South Africa, Northern Ireland and the Middle East. We will disregard the problematic evaluation of the latter two as processes in motion, difficult to measure as successful. These examples suggest that spoilers have different origins and pose different threats to peace depending on the level of development; in a war-torn country where there is a history of democracy and some democratic accountability to constituents, where there is a baseline minimum of industrialization, and where there exists a thriving civil society, the threat of spoilers is very different from where none of these variables obtain. Where power and resources seem indivisible, where leaders lack democratic constraints and where there are few groups who are independent of the men with guns, spoilers pose a greater threat.

Priority 2: demobilization of soldiers

Beyond overcoming the threat from spoilers, the demobilization of soldiers and their reintegration into civilian life is the *single most* important sub-goal of peace implementation.[19] The ending of a civil war hinges on the willingness of competing armies to relinquish self-help solutions to their insecurity, to demobilize their soldiers, and in most circumstances, to create a new, integrated army. These are processes, however, that are fraught with risks for antagonists. International implementers can reduce such risks by acting as guarantors – by deterring any party from taking advantage of their adversary's vulnerability and by protecting any party that is taken advantage of during demobilization. Such guarantees, however, are seldom forthcoming from implementers. With the exceptions of NATO in Bosnia, Syria in Lebanon and ECOWAS (on occasion) in Liberia and Sierra Leone, implementers have not committed to such guarantees. Most implementers of peace agreements limit their role to monitoring, verifying and facilitating demobilization.

Such monitoring has been flawed by the lack of an intelligence capacity to assess the motives behind violations of demobilization agreements and by the unwillingness of implementers to set and maintain strict standards of compliance. An assessment of motives is important because cheating is pervasive in the demobilization of soldiers. There are different motives for cheating – motives that have important implications for the prospects of successful war termination. Starting with the most benign among them, warring parties may hold troops back from demobilization as a form of insurance against adversary attack. Less benignly, parties may keep troops in reserve in order to gain a potential advantage in elections, even deploying them for the purpose of electoral intimidation. Finally, the most malignant motive for cheating is a deliberate effort to sucker an opponent or take military advantage of a rival who, already having complied with demobilization accords, is strategically vulnerable.

Since motives are important for outcomes, a premium should be placed on the robust monitoring and verification of demobilization. The greatest danger stems from implementers who are lax in acknowledging, reporting or responding to violations of demobilization agreements. In Angola, implementers did not call the parties to account for such violations for fear that condemnation would hinder the implementers' ability to act as impartial brokers. Worse, the implementers would later falsely verify UNITA's demobilization in order to claim the mission as a success. In Rwanda, the UN Department of Peacekeeping Operations (DPKO) prohibited its peacekeepers from aggressively investigating reports of hidden arms caches for fear that such investigation might provoke violence by extremists.

Priority 3: sow the seeds of long-term peacebuilding

Implementers of peace agreements can make important contributions in the short term and with relatively low costs that can prove to have large pay-offs for longer-term peacebuilding: the reform of civilian police and judiciaries, reduction of light weapons and the strengthening of local civil society organizations. The former two contributions address the problem of increased violent crime that is often found in the aftermath of negotiated settlements; the latter contribution goes to the heart of building local capacity to address the lingering psychological, institutional and physical effects of war-related violence.

Reform of police and judiciaries

For good reasons, international implementers of peace agreements focus on assuring the security of ex-combatants. But research has found that assuring the security of the general population is a neglected aspect of peace implementation.[20] This is problematic, however, given that many civil war settlements are based on liberal norms and institutions which depend on citizens' forgoing group-based protections and accepting individual assurances of security by the newly reformed state. In the absence of a police force which can effectively provide those assurances, new post-war arrangements seem unjust and in violation of group rights. In an insecure environment, political entrepreneurs can engage in protection racketeering that undermines the credibility and authority of the new state.

As Charles Call and William Stanley observe, 'virtually all post-1989 cases of negotiated civil war termination experienced perceptions of heightened public insecurity, often as a result of documented increases in violent crime'.[21] As they point out, civil war settlements offer unique opportunities for redesigning and reforming civilian security institutions. The inclusion of civilian security reform into peace agreements provides implementers with clear guidelines for assistance programmes. Their work suggests important lessons for such programmes: the need to design and implement judicial, penal and police reforms in tandem; and the importance of creating specialized police units, especially criminal investigative units and oversight offices (e.g. Internal Affairs, Inspectors-General and Civilian Commissions).

Societal disarmament

Countries that emerge from civil wars are usually awash in light weapons. The availability of such weapons contributes to crime, lawlessness and civilian insecurity. When such crime becomes oppressive, citizens question the value and legitimacy of peace. While disarmament of soldiers and police and judicial reform are necessary to reduce the overall supply of weapons in a country, they are not enough. As Virginia Gamba explains in her chapter, governments, citizens and international organizations must make special efforts to specifically reduce the numbers and availability of weapons.[22]

Local capacity building: civil society organizations

At a relatively low cost, implementers can support local civil society organizations that can play key roles in sustaining peace after the implementers leave.[23]

Civil society organizations can help to sustain peace agreements by working at the grassroots level to legitimize peace and make it more than an elite concern. Local organizations can address key issues such as reconciliation, justice and human rights – issues that go to the heart of what many consider to be the root causes of civil wars. Moreover, local organizations tend to have a longer time horizon and are more adept at sustaining long-term processes that are integral to peacebuilding.

New research direction: the meanings of peace implementation

I would like to conclude this chapter with some thoughts about the different connotations of peace implementation; in particular, the very different lenses that people in war-torn societies bring to bear on the question of putting peace into practice. When enemies in civil wars sign peace agreements, leaders, supporters and people caught in the middle often view implementation as three distinct things: compliance, process or peacebuilding.

Peace is extremely fragile during implementation of agreements. After the immediate euphoria of agreement and high expectations for what the agreement will bring, comes the basic political reality that putting peace into practice requires cooperation among former enemies, that leaders must still bring followers with them, that disaffected groups may attack those who would make peace; that those who have the guns must be persuaded to lay them down. Inevitably, peace takes time; inevitably, frustrations rise, expectations are not met; and paradoxically, a sense of loss may arise in key constituencies: loss of status, control, identity and meaning. If such perceptions are not addressed, the likelihood of violence triumphing again persists.

For some people implementation is compliance, nothing more, nothing less: whether or not the parties to an agreement put into practice what they promised in the agreement. Emphasis is placed on the legalistic fulfilment of obligation. Disputes may arise in interpretation of what was promised, but nonetheless implementation is judged on the benchmark of how much that is written and mutually agreed to is carried through.

For others implementation is not about compliance per se, but rather about commitment to a process of continuous negotiation of differences. Those who emphasize process insist that peace agreements are often vague, incomplete and expedient and that they are often built on purposive ambiguity. Such ambiguity, derisively described by some as 'fudging', is included in agreements in order for leaders to protect their positions within constituencies, to buy time to bring supporters along, or simply to kick difficult issues ahead in the hopes that tackling smaller issues and building confidence will someday allow them to revisit their largest sources of disputes. Proponents of implementation as process insist that differences of opinion will always arise about the content of agreement; indeed, some go further to insist that agreements themselves are context-bound and when contexts change, leaders should be willing to revisit their original promises. Adaptation and flexibility are hallmarks of this vision of implementation; enemies are judged by their willingness to discuss their positions, learn their adversaries' needs, and commit themselves to ongoing, non-violent negotiation.

Finally, there are those who see implementation as peacebuilding; that is, the forging of meaningful long-term relationships between former enemies. Those who judge implementation through the lens of peacebuilding are seldom satisfied with compliance with a peace agreement; indeed, the demands and expectations of peace tend to be far greater than clauses in a written agreement. Indeed, in so far as peace agreements silence issues of truth, reconciliation, justice and account- ability, many hope that during implementation moral and ethical values of peace may trump narrow fixation on compliance. The standards for judging successful implementation are broad and long term: will efforts at making peace create the conditions that will allow new identities and relationships to prosper?

My purpose here is not to argue for one perspective over another. It is simply to acknowledge that in conflict-ridden societies, people will disagree about what implementation entails, and to suggest that when such disagreement exists we ignore progress on all three dimensions at our peril. Narrow compliance without process or relationship building runs the risk of medium- to longer-term instabil- ity and fails to address underlying senses of loss and fear among citizens. Process without compliance runs the risk of severe alienation of constituents from the peace agreement as they see elite political deals without tangible actions behind them. In the worst of conditions, people fear that process trumps substance, and any hopes for a peace dividend are perpetually postponed and unattainable. Relationship building without process or compliance subjects those who would make peace in society to attack from their own groups who label them traitors.

Notes

1. S. J. Stedman, 'Spoiler Problems in Peace Processes', *International Security*, 22, 2 (Fall 1997), 5–53.
2. See the pioneering works of T. Sisk, 'The Violence–Negotiation Nexus in Divided Societies', research in progress and J. Darby, *The Effects of Violence on Peace Processes* (Washington, DC: United States Institute of Peace Press, 2001).
3. I. W. Zartman, *Ripe for Resolution* (New York: Oxford University Press, 1985). For Zartman's history of the concept and his reflections on its strengths and weaknesses, see I. W. Zartman, 'Ripeness: the Hurting Stalemate and Beyond', in Paul C. Stern & Daniel Druckman (eds), *International Conflict Resolution after the Cold War* (Washington, DC; National Resource Council, 2000), pp. 225–50.
4. S. J. Stedman, *Peacemaking in Civil Wars: International Mediation in Zimbabwe, 1974–1980* (Boulder: Lynne Rienner, 1991). For a comparison of South Africa and the Middle East that argues for the importance of group dynamics in conflict resolution, see D. Lieberfeld, 'Conflict "Ripeness" Revisited: the South African and Israeli/Palestinian Cases', *Negotiation Journal*, 15, 1 (1999), 63–82.
5. See, for example, F. O. Hampson, *Nurturing Peace* (Washington, DC: USIP, 1996) and B. Walter, 'The Critical Barrier to Civil War Settlement', *International Organization* (Summer 1997), 335–65.
6. S. J. Stedman, 'Implementing Peace Agreements in Civil Wars: Lessons and Recommen- dations for Policymakers', IPA Policy Paper on Peace Implementation (New York: International Peace Academy, May 2001).
7. E. J. Wood, 'Civil War Settlement: Modeling the Bases of Compromise', paper presented at the 1999 Annual Meeting of the American Political Science Association (2–5 September 1999).

8. J. Lewis, 'Peace Processes and the Challenge of Credible Commitments: South Africa and Israel/Palestine', Stanford University, Senior Honors Thesis (May, 2000).

9. Stedman, 'Implementing Peace Agreements'.

10. S. Woodward, 'Avoiding Another Cyprus or Israel', *Brookings Review* (Winter 1998), 45–8.

11. M. Doyle & N. Sambanis, 'International Peacebuilding: a Theoretical and Quantitative Analysis', *American Political Science Review*, 94, 4 (December 2000), 779–802.

12. Stedman, 'Spoiler Problems in Peace Processes'.

13. See Marie Joëlle Zahar's chapter in this volume.

14. Ibid., and Darby, op. cit.

15. G. Downs & S. J. Stedman, 'Evaluation Issues in Peace Implementation', paper presented at the annual meetings of the American Political Science Association, Washington, DC, 30 August 2000.

16. R. Cetinyan & A. Stein, 'Assassins of Peace?: Spoilers and the Peace Process in the Middle East', paper presented at the Annual Meeting of the American Political Science Association, 3 Sept. 1999, Atlanta, Georgia.

17. Zahar, op. cit.

18. That is, total, limited or greedy spoilers.

19. J. Spear, 'Demobilization and Disarmament: Key Implementation Issues', in Stedman, Rothchild & Cousens, *Ending Civil Wars*: Vol. II (Boulder, Colo.: Lynne Rienner, 2002).

20. C. Call & W. Stanley, 'A Sacrifice for Peace? Security for the General Public during Implementation of Peace Agreements', in *Ending Civil Wars*: Vol. II.

21. Ibid.

22. See Virginia Gamba's chapter in this volume.

23. J. Prendergast & E. Plumb, 'Civil Society Organizations and Peace Agreement Implementation', in *Ending Civil Wars*: Vol. II.

10
Reframing the Spoiler Debate in Peace Processes

Marie-Joëlle Zahar[1]

Why do some peace agreements end civil conflict while others break down? Empirical evidence underscores the importance of sustainability: the Rwandan genocide succeeded the 1992 Arusha peace agreement; likewise, some of the worst violence in Angola, Sri Lanka and Cambodia (among others) followed the breakdown of peace accords.

To date, the most powerful answer to the failure of many a peace settlement points to the emergence of actors who decide to spoil the peace process. Spoilers are leaders who believe that peace 'threatens their power, worldview, and interests, and use violence to undermine attempts to achieve it'.[2] This chapter reviews current research on violence in peace processes, and proposes to reframe the debate by focusing on the interaction between three important concepts: spoiler intent, opportunity and capability.

Diagnosing spoilers

When peace agreements collapse, analysts and practitioners point a finger to spoilers. The typical spoiler acts in one of two ways: either systematically refusing to negotiate or, alternatively, entering into agreements and then reneging on promises.[3] There are spoilers galore in civil war settings, as the behaviour of UNITA in Angola and of the RUF in Sierra Leone, among others, amply demonstrates. Building sustainable peace requires bringing the parties threatening to peace into the negotiation process (thus managing outside spoilers) and preventing them from developing incentives to renege during the implementation stage (or managing inside spoilers).

Stedman's pioneering study on the topic argues that international custodians of peace are the decisive factor in the success or failure of a spoiler's attempt to derail peace. Where international custodians have created and implemented efficient strategies for protecting peace and managing spoilers, damage has been limited and peace has triumphed. Where international custodians have failed to develop and implement such strategies, spoilers have succeeded.[4]

Critics suggest that a central weakness of current research on spoilers is its inability to determine spoiler types *ex ante*. While the criticism may be read as a purely academic concern with the predictive power of theories, it is also prompted by practical concerns for the sustainability of peace. Indeed, this author agrees with Stephen Stedman's assertion that information and *a correct diagnosis of the type of spoiler* are crucial for the choice of an appropriate strategy of spoiler management. In reality, however, most parties to a civil war both desire peace (as war is costly) and want to get away with as much as they can in the event of an agreement (they have incentives to defect for unilateral gains).[5] How can we then tell who is a spoiler and who is a peacemaker? When a spoiler emerges, how can we tell what strategy to adopt? These issues are consequential for the success of peace agreements and they deserve further elaboration.

In his earlier work on the topic, Stedman introduced three types of spoilers who vary on two dimensions: their goals (limited or total) and their commitment to the achievement of these goals (high, and low) (see Table 10.1). Total spoilers pursue *total power* and *exclusive recognition of authority* and hold immutable preferences. Limited spoilers have *limited goals* – for example, recognition and redress of a grievance, a share of power or the exercise of power constrained by a constitution and opposition, and basic security of followers. *Limited goals do not imply limited commitment to achieving those goals, however.* Finally, greedy spoilers lie between the limited spoiler and the total spoiler. *The greedy spoiler holds goals that expand or contract based on calculations of cost and risk.*[6]

Critics argue that the typology is problematic as a diagnostic tool, especially if intended to provide assistance to custodians in determining the adequate strategy of spoiler management. Indeed, two supposedly different types of spoilers share the same characteristics (cell 1); moreover, the same spoiler types often span two cells of the typology (cells 1 and 3 and 1 and 2). It has been suggested that this inconsistency derives from the fact that some spoiler types are defined according to their preferences over actions while others are defined according to their preferences over outcomes.[7] This critique is only useful to separate the total spoiler type from the rest. Of the three types in the typology, this is the only one that exhibits fixed preferences over both outcomes and actions. To this reader, however, the typology suggests something different. I read this classification attempt as evidence that spoiler tactics and objectives can change in the course of a peace process. This prompts the question 'what affects spoiler tactics and objectives?' Stedman's typology is useful as a descriptive tool, but it does not help elucidate this question.

The typology also raises the issue of total spoilers. Is it inconceivable that total spoilers could be induced under certain conditions to become peacemakers? High commitment to the achievement of total goals does not, by definition, exclude a

Table 10.1 Stedman's typology of spoilers

	Limited goals	*Total goals*
Low commitment	1 Greedy or limited spoilers	2 Greedy spoilers
High commitment	3 Limited spoilers	4 Total spoilers

notion of costs and risks. All it suggests is that total spoilers are willing to incur higher risks and bear heavier costs than most in pursuit of their objectives. Stedman insists that the concept of spoiler can only be defined in relation to a given peace agreement. Actors can therefore act as total spoilers in relation to one agreement but not the other. I would like to raise two issues in this respect. First, given Stedman's definition of total spoilers and his emphasis that such spoilers tend to be individuals, I wonder if such actors would accept any agreement other than one that perfectly meets their objectives. Would such unbalanced deals deserve the label 'peace agreements' or would they be tantamount to surrender? Second, empirical evidence suggests that even in the short term a faction's attitude towards a given agreement can fluctuate wildly. A study of the PLO's attitude regarding peace with Israel might prove interesting in this regard. A cursory look at the organization's behaviour between 1993 and 2001 reveals the kinds of fluctuations that I have in mind. The same PLO, which was the Palestinian cornerstone of peace negotiations with Israel, is now accused (albeit by some not all) of acting as a total spoiler. Should we accept the premise that the PLO has become a total spoiler, how do we account for this change in attitude towards the Oslo process? Some would suggest that Yasir Arafat was never interested in peace. Others would argue that the Israeli–Palestinian peace process was particularly unstable in view of the lack of interdependence of the parties and of an endgame which would produce separation. Both explanations can be countered convincingly, leaving the initial question unanswered.[8] Finally, spoiling does not necessarily involve actual widespread violence. In Northern Ireland, for example, the attitudes of the Irish Republican Army towards demobilization can be read as an attempt to spoil the Good Friday Agreement. In short, empirical evidence demonstrates that actors do go back on (or revert to) extreme positions under (admittedly often exceptional) circumstances. It is thus important to ask, 'What circumstances can bring about such drastic changes in an actor's commitment to peace?'

Managing spoilers: the role of third parties

Current research on spoilers places excessive weight on the role of third parties in spoiler management. Most analyses of failed peace settlements determine that third parties are critical to the success of peace settlements and the management of spoilers.[9]

Where Stedman focused on spoilers' beliefs that peace is contrary to their interests, a variation on the theme has framed spoiling in the context of the security dilemma. According to proponents of this approach, civil wars reproduce the anarchy of the international system where self-help is the only logical course of action.[10] The greatest problem that civil war opponents encounter is 'how to write an enforcement contract under conditions of extreme risk'. Negotiations would succeed in designing peaceful transitions if the participants could be protected during the implementation period.[11] Demobilization is an especially thorny issue. Even adversaries who truly wish to resolve their wars remain wary of disarmament as weapons are their only means of protection against the unilateral defection of others. Hence, the emergence of spoilers is less an act of malevolence vis-à-vis the peace process and more a function of the rules of the game in an anarchic context. In this framework, outside intervention can serve the purpose of enforcing the terms of the contract.[12]

The security dilemma is a potentially important obstacle to civil conflict resolution. However, there are problems with the approach as well as with proposed solutions. The problems with the approach are aptly summarized in Stedman's contribution to this volume. Security dilemmas and commitment problems offer an undifferentiated analysis of civil wars. They also offer undifferentiated solutions. Third parties are not sufficient and may not even be necessary to prevent the emergence of spoilers. The involvement of external actors may go a long way to reassure former enemies; nevertheless, the strategic situation of actors continues to matter for decision-making even with the presence of custodians. Angola is a case in point. Following the 1994 Lusaka Protocol, sustained UN presence on the ground was not sufficient to allay the fears of Jonas Savimbi and to ensure his continued commitment to the peace process. There have also been cases – albeit few – of self-enforcing peace agreements that succeeded, cases in which one cannot invoke the presence of an external enforcer as the solution to the commitment problems faced by the factions. South Africa is probably the clearest illustration of such success. This suggests that some peace agreements may be more vulnerable to spoiling than others. It also suggests that it is not international presence per se that may be determining but what third parties do on the ground. On this point I agree with Stedman, 'scholars do not treat international attention and commitment as a contextual variable, and by defining it as international will make the error of treating it as completely voluntarist'. Yet, third parties can do too much or too little and their actions will affect the opportunity structure available to would-be spoilers. In other words, implementers need to be attuned to the context in which they are operating.[13]

This brings up a neglected aspect of third-party involvement in the implementation process. It can directly contribute to the creation of spoilers. Most analytical frameworks of outside implementation take 'neutral' UN missions as their frame of reference. However, a number of peace settlements have been implemented by regional powers such as Syria in Lebanon, India in Sri Lanka or Nigeria in Liberia. These actors are not only often partial to one faction; they are also less philosophically opposed to the use of force in implementation. This sort of custodianship may heighten the insecurity of some actors who do not see the third party as a custodian but as a hostile neighbour. In Lebanon, for example, the presence of some 35,000 Syrian troops was central to General Awn's rejection of the Ta'if Accord. It also played a central role in the Lebanese Forces' hesitation to comply with the demobilization and disarmament clauses of the Ta'if Accord and can be largely blamed for troubles in summer 2001.[14] In brief, the mere presence of third parties is not sufficient for overcoming the commitment problem faced by factions to the peace process. External implementation may, in some cases, directly contribute to the consequent security dilemma. This variation in the role of custodians should be investigated further.

Winners, losers and spoilers

Peace implementation is at heart a political process. While most settlements attempt to create incentives for all factions to support peace, they are bound to create winners and losers. Foremost among those losers are parties that were not invited to the negotiating table, those factions that Stedman labelled 'outside spoilers'. Little analysis has focused on the differences between inside and outside spoilers. Yet they differ, not only in their motives to spoil, but also in their evaluation of the costs and benefits (and therefore the opportunity structure) associated with spoiling.

Inside spoilers, outside spoilers and incentives to spoil

Why do spoilers emerge? Are they attempting to overturn a peace process or to register dissatisfaction? We can sketch a preliminary answer by probing the differences between inside and outside spoilers.

Warring factions that were not brought in the fold of peace negotiations may see peace as a threat for a number of reasons. Ideologically, their survival may be premised on the continuation of strife. Extremist Islamist groups illustrate this contention. For such movements as the Palestinian Hamas, peace with Israel would undermine the very bases of their existence. If we accept that political actors are ultimately interested in remaining politically relevant,[15] such groups see compromise as political suicide. Financially, warring factions that benefit from the war have no interest in a peace that may unravel the war economy,[16] especially if they have not negotiated side agreements that allow them to partake in the financial benefits of peacetime. In Sierra Leone, for example, the RUF opposed agreements that would have decreased the group's control over diamond mining and ultimately secured the nomination of its leader to the post of Minister of Natural Resources. Finally, groups that are sidelined for strategic considerations (either because they are considered relatively insignificant or because their presence at the table may prevent the inclusion of other factions) fear negotiations the result of which may disregard their demands. Conflict provides even the most marginal organizations with the potential to gain power and influence.[17] For such groups, peace holds the prospect of losing whatever marginal influence and power they yielded during the course of the conflict.

In contrast, parties to the talks have a venue to express their demands and they are usually ensured some sort of political representation in the post-agreement phase. Peace settlements are in essence elite pacts.[18] Actors who are involved in these pacts negotiate terms that allow them to maximize their gains in light of the conditions under which they are negotiating. In other words, peace negotiations occur at a time when both sides, for whatever reason, agree to accept the military outcome be it symmetrical or asymmetrical as the basis for determining the political pay-offs accruing to each.[19] It is indeed possible for the parties to reach stable peace settlements in which the leaders of warring factions develop vested interests.[20] If these actors fear the post-agreement phase, it is for a different set of reasons.

One reason that is frequently advanced is the problem of credible commitment that develops in the course of peace implementation.[21] When parties are genuinely interested in peace but cannot trust each other to keep promises, they face a commitment problem.[22] Custodians are supposed to help the parties overcome this issue, but as I noted earlier there are problems, both analytical and empirical, associated with current conceptualizations of the role of custodians.

Capability and opportunity

Not all would-be spoilers resort to violence in their opposition to the negotiation or implementation of a given peace process. If spoiling is not only a function of capability, what are the factors that influence such a decision? I argue that the opportunity to spoil can be thought of in terms of costs and benefits. Not only do inside and outside spoilers have different reasons to spoil a peace process, they also have different assessments of the costs and benefits associated with such a decision. The benefits from spoiling have already been discussed at length elsewhere. The existence of valuable, easily marketed commodities is one such benefit. Less systematically addressed are the costs associated with such a decision, costs that often loom large especially where the spoils are negligible. Once again, the Palestinian and Northern Irish cases come to mind. What do would-be spoilers stand to gain from derailing such peace processes? Are their potential gains larger than the losses associated with such a decision? I argue that there are 'standard' categories of costs and benefits that an analyst or a policy-maker ought to consider in any assessment of would-be spoilers. I especially draw attention to the role of third parties and intra-factional politics.

1. Assessing the costs of spoiling

Leaders who consider spoiling as an option have a number of costs to consider. These costs can be regrouped in two categories. The first category is those costs associated with the resumption of fighting; the second category is those costs associated with the loss of peace dividends.

Fighting is a costly decision, especially when actors have committed to disarm and demobilize. In a post-conflict situation, the cost of fighting includes international audience costs and straightforward military costs. An actor who reneges on his commitment to peace runs the risk that international interlocutors will question his reliability as a partner in future talks. His credibility and legitimacy are at stake. Thus, in Sierra Leone, RUF leader Foday Sankoh damaged his credibility by repeatedly spoiling agreements. If such an actor decides to spoil peace and fails in its attempt, it runs serious risks of being sidelined in future peace talks. In other words, the group's political survival may be at stake.

The military strength of the custodians and their willingness to use force determine the military costs associated with a decision to spoil. It is more difficult to challenge a custodian who shows resolve to militarily enforce peace if need be. As important as this factor may be, few implementers are willing to commit to do so. The deterrent effect of the willingness to use force has been invoked in understanding the Bosnian Serb compliance with the Dayton Peace Agreement (the resolve of IFOR and SFOR having been opposed to the 'irresolute' attitude of the UN forces in Bosnia).

Time is another important factor. Indeed, the earlier the decision to spoil, the less likely implementers of the agreement will have had the opportunity to carry out a full demobilization. The longer an actor waits before taking a decision, the higher the military costs associated with the resumption of fighting.

The second category is costs associated with the loss of peace dividends. As stated earlier, peace agreements are in essence elite pacts and those pacts include a range of benefits for their signatories. Power-sharing agreements guarantee that the actors will have political influence in the post-conflict polity. They also guarantee access to funds and other financial assets through control of, or privileged access to, the resources of the state. This aspect was paramount in the Bosnian Serb decision to go with the Dayton Peace Agreement (DPA). Indeed, Republika Srpska was the means through which the Bosnian Serb leadership amassed power and riches. The DPA guaranteed the survival of the entity and the continued inflow to the Bosnian Serb leaders of material advantages resulting from their control over the institutions of Republika Srpska.[23] Likewise, there are political and financial gains for the PLO from staying within the peace process with Israel. Indeed, not only did the position of insider give the PLO recognition as a political actor, it also provided the organization's leadership with control over international aid to the occupied territories.[24]

2. The role of intra-factional politics

It has often been argued that conditions of civil war dispense leaders from seeking democratic approval from their would-be constituencies. Thus, most of our analyses of leaders' choices have focused on inter-faction negotiations to the expense of intra-factional politics. However, intra-factional politics remain important,[25] especially in a peace implementation setting when democratic norms of accountability are likely to be fostered by custodians. Domestic audience costs depend on the specifics of a given situation. However, we can stipulate that a leader whose incumbency depends on popular support (or on preventing an internal coup that would remove him from power) might thus be especially sensitive to the internal audience costs associated with his decisions, especially on the eve of an electoral deadline. If the leaders' constituency perceives peace to be a net benefit, they will not take lightly to a decision to spoil the peace process. If, on the other hand, they believe they are being wronged, the leader might be putting his political survival at stake if he fails to respond to their grievances. The tightrope that Palestinian Authority President Yasir Arafat had to walk during the tenure of former Israeli Prime Minister Benjamin Netanyahu and his dilemma since the election of Prime Minister Sharon vividly illustrate this situation.

3. Cost, benefits and decisions

A better assessment of intent, opportunity and capability is required to forge ahead with current research on spoilers. As noted in Stedman's contribution to this volume, not all peace agreements are equally vulnerable to spoiling. Not all actors are keen to spoil a peace process either, even when they possess the capability to this effect. Insiders and outsiders may have different reasons for spoiling but they both have to assess the opportunity structure with which they are faced.

When the implementation of peace agreements proceeds as planned, insiders are given voice – or the means to express their concerns and the access necessary to redress grievances. In such cases, the longer peace lasts, the more likely that insiders will develop loyalty to the institutions of the negotiated peace pact. The dividends of peace deepen and the cost of spoiling increases accordingly. If the negotiation process achieves a stable outcome, the leaders' exit options become 'costly and disadvantageous'. Decision-makers find that 'just as they were once trapped in a cycle of conflict, now the structure of incentives works to trap them in the politics of moderation'.[26] In brief, insiders who consider the option of spoiling have to assess their options not only by considering the cost of fighting but also by factoring in the loss of peace dividends.

In counter-distinction, actors who are left out of the negotiated settlements have no stakes in peace and may have extensive stakes associated with the continuation of the conflict. From their perspective, the cost of peace is extremely high and its benefits low. Should they demobilize, these actors are ensured that they will lose the military power that (1) underpins whatever benefits they were gaining from the conflict, and (2) would provide them with the only bargaining edge to secure benefits from peace. For them, the cost of peace is the potential loss of all benefits from war added to the prospect of demobilization. Spoiling, on the other hand, does not really cost them much. Actors who are not invited into the negotiations process do not have to worry about international audience costs (incurred when reneging on one's commitment to peace). The imminence of peace negotiations constitutes a finite horizon against which these actors assess their choices and strategies. If several other factions enter into peace negotiations, an excluded party will ultimately either have the choice to take the agreement or leave it. In all likelihood, these actors do not have to concern themselves with domestic audience costs either. Since the actor's exclusion is usually an outside decision, his or her domestic constituency will not fault the actor for not participating in the peace talks. A decision to spoil peace might even be interpreted as standing up to outsiders who fail to acknowledge the actor as a legitimate part of the conflict, and therefore of the peace process.[27] For excluded parties, or outsiders, the only cost to consider is that of a military escalation.

This line of reasoning echoes the fundamental lessons of research on mediation and intervention. The narrower the basis of a peace agreement, the more difficult it will be to sustain. Likewise, the clearer the benefits to various factions from the peace deal and the stronger the commitment of third parties to providing the factions with security guarantees, the greater the chances that their evaluation of the opportunity structure will deter these factions from resorting to spoiling.

Charting future research

These observations chart new directions for research on spoilers. I surmise that any attempt at a typology should start with two fundamental questions. Why do actors want to spoil the process? How do they assess the costs and benefits of spoiling? Initial findings point to the importance of the distinction between inside and outside spoilers. Further research on the incentives and cost–benefit evaluations of these two categories of spoilers should pave the way for a better understanding and (hopefully) more successful management of spoilers.

Though not directly addressed in the chapter, the issue of spoiler management is very much part and parcel of the research. Third-party commitment to a given peace process can shape the opportunity structure of would-be spoilers. When third parties offer credible guarantees to the factions, they increase the costs of spoiling and thus decrease its likelihood. But third parties do not only shape the opportunity structure of would-be spoilers, they also affect the incentives of factions. Peace implementation involves an intricate exercise in sequencing. Implementation is not limited to compliance with the terms of a given document; it is also about fostering commitment to a negotiating process and ultimately laying the foundations for peacebuilding. However, lack of compliance in the short term will undoubtedly affect the actors' medium to long-term commitment to the process as well as the chances for peace to take root. Likewise, third-party decisions to privilege one aspect of peace implementation at the expense of others is a consequential element that deserves further analysis in relation to the emergence of spoilers.

Notes

1. The author would like to thank Lynn Eden, Page Fortna, Barry O'Neill and Steve Stedman for many useful discussions. The financial assistance of the Social Science and Humanities Research Council of Canada is gratefully acknowledged.
2. S. J. Stedman, 'Spoiler Problems in Peace Processes', *International Security*, 22, 2 (Fall 1997), 5.
3. This 'tactical acceptance' thesis is mostly promoted by D. Horowitz, *Ethnic Groups in Conflict* (Berkeley: University of California Press, 1985).
4. Custodians have pursued three major strategies to manage spoilers: (1) inducement – entails giving the spoiler what he wants (default mode); (2) socialization – requires the establishment of a set of norms for acceptable behaviour by which to judge the demands and the behaviour of parties; involves material and intellectual components to elicit normatively acceptable behaviour, and (3) coercion – that relies on the use or threat of punishment to deter or alter unacceptable behaviour or reduce the capability of spoilers to disrupt the peace process.
5. I owe this observation to Page Fortna.
6. A greedy spoiler may have limited goals that expand when faced with low costs and risks; alternatively, it may have total goals that contract when faced with high costs and risks.
7. See N. Sambanis, 'Conflict Resolution Ripeness and Spoiler Problems in Cyprus: from the Intercommunal Talks (1968–1974) to the Present', paper presented to the American Political Science Association (25 September 1998).
8. For a rebuttal of the thesis that Arafat has never been interested in peace see D. Sontag, 'Quest for Mideast Peace: How and Why It Failed', *New York Times*, 26 July 2001; see also H. Agha & R. Malley, 'Camp David: the Tragedy of Errors', *The New York Review of Books*, 9 August 2001. While separation is indeed the endgame on paper, the territorial reality of the zones A, B and C created under Oslo belies such separation. The Palestinian economy is also highly dependent on Israel in terms of both labour and trade. Although the Palestinians are much less important to the Israeli economy, Israel still exports $2 billion/year to the West Bank and Gaza. See R. Brynen, *A Very Political Economy. Peacebuilding and Foreign Aid in the West Bank and Gaza* (Boulder: Lynne Rienner, 2000), p. 40; see also 'Downsizing amid the Uprising', *The Economist*, 10 August 2001.

9. See especially B. F. Walter, 'The Critical Barrier to Civil War Settlement', *International Organization* 51, 3 (Summer 1997).

10. For a discussion of the security dilemma in civil wars see Barry Posen, 'The Security Dilemma and Ethnic Conflict', in Michael Brown (ed.), *Ethnic Conflict and International Security* (Princeton, NJ: Princeton University Press, 1993).

11. B. F. Walter, *Designing Transitions from Violent Civil War*, IGCC Policy Paper 31 (San Diego: UC Institute on Global Conflict and Cooperation, 1998), available at http://www-igcc.ucsd.edu/igcc2/PolicyPapers/pp31.html; Internet. A modified version of the argument was subsequently published in *International Security*, 24, 1 (1999).

12. Walter, 'The Critical Barrier to Civil War Settlement'. See also Fen Osler Hampson, *Nurturing Peace* (Washington: USIP, 1996). This argument is very similar to the standard IR argument about the role of institutions or regimes in fostering cooperation under anarchy.

13. On the differentiated role of implementers see particularly the conclusions of the Stedman et al. study. S. J. Stedman, 'Implementing Peace Agreements in Civil Wars: Lessons and Recommendations for Policymakers', IPA Policy Paper on Peace Implementation (New York: International Peace Academy, May 2001).

14. M. Zahar, 'The Problem of Commitment to Peace: Lessons from Bosnia and Lebanon', paper presented to the Annual Meeting of the American Political Science Association, Atlanta, 2–5 September 1999.

15. This assumption is common in game-theoretic analyses of decision-making. It is also eminently reasonable, as no leader should be expected to sign on his demise. See R. Putnam, 'Diplomacy and Domestic Politics: the Logic of Two-Level Games', *International Organization*, 42, 3 (Summer 1998).

16. The financial rewards gleaned by the Khmer Rouge in the ruby-mining business, by UNITA in the diamond trade and by the Shan United Army in the opium trade illustrate the importance of the war economy. For a discussion of this phenomenon see M. Berdal & D. Keen, 'Violence and Economic Agendas in Civil Wars: Some Policy Implications', *Millennium*, 26, 3 (1988); S. W. R. de A. Samarasinghe and R. Coughlan (eds), *Economic Dimensions of Ethnic Conflict* (London: Pinter Publishers, 1991), p. 184.

17. This holds especially true for organizations that would have otherwise been sidelined from politics.

18. T. D. Sisk, *Power Sharing and International Mediation in Ethnic Conflicts* (Washington, DC: United States Institute of Peace, 1996), especially Ch. 5; C. Hartzell & D. Rothchild, 'Political Pacts as Negotiated Agreements: Comparing Ethnic and Non-Ethnic Cases', *International Negotiation*, 2 (1997), 147–71; E. J. Wood, 'Civil War Settlement: Modeling the Bases of Compromise', paper presented to the Annual Meeting of the American Political Science Association, Atlanta, 2–5 September 1999.

19. P. Kecskemeti, 'Political Rationality in Ending War', in W. T. R. Fox (ed.), *How Wars End* (Philadelphia: The Annals of the American Academy of Political and Social Science, 1970), pp. 105–15.

20. See M. Zahar, 'Fanatics, Mercenaries, Brigands ... and Politicians: Militia Decision-Making and Civil Conflict Resolution', PhD dissertation, McGill University, Canada, 2000. See also Wood, 'Civil War Settlement', and Sisk, *Power Sharing and International Mediation in Ethnic Conflicts*.

21. Walter, 'Designing Transitions from Civil War'; M. Zahar, 'The Problem of Commitment to Peace: Actors, Incentives and Choice in Peace Implementation', paper presented to the Annual Meeting of the American Political Science Association, Washington, DC, 31 August–3 September 2000.

22. J. Fearon, 'Commitment Problems and the Spread of Ethnic Conflict', in D. Lake & D. Rothchild (eds), *The International Spread of Ethnic Conflict: Fear, Diffusion, and Escalation* (Princeton, NJ: Princeton University Press, 1998), pp. 107–26.

23. See Zahar, 'The Problem of Commitment to Peace'.

24. See Brynen, *A Very Political Economy*.

25. In my dissertation research, I established the importance of intra-factional politics for leaders' decisions to accept or reject peace settlements. See also S. Stedman, *Peacemaking in Civil Wars: International Mediation in Zimbabwe, 1974–1980* (Boulder: Lynne Rienner, 1991).

26. Sisk, *Power Sharing and International Mediation in Ethnic Conflicts*.

27. For a discussion of similar dynamics in international crises see J. Fearon, 'Domestic Political Audiences and the Escalation of International Disputes', *American Political Science Review*, 88, 3 (September 1994), 579–81.

11

Managing Violence: Disarmament and Demobilization

Virginia Gamba

Introduction

Multinational peace processes have not often been accompanied by either comprehensive disarmament or the adequate control of weapons by the appropriate authorities; nor have they benefited from comprehensive and far-reaching demobilization and integration programmes for ex-combatants.

As a result, literally millions of weapons are in constant circulation either because one of the belligerent parties has lost control over them (as happened in Angola); because peacekeepers themselves have been robbed of them (as happened in Sierra Leone[1]); or because they are no longer required politically and acquired commercial value (as happened in Mozambique).

Whatever the reason, arms not taken and destroyed during peace processes most often than not end up restarting intra-state conflicts (like in the case of Angola, Liberia and Sierra Leone), are used for fuelling other conflicts (as is the case in D.R. Congo and Sudan) or have found their way into the illegal arms market in neighbouring states thereby contributing to the problem of arms proliferation at regional level and mounting armed crime at national level.

Even in the case of the transition in South Africa towards a fully democratic system there have been problems in the post-transitional phase in regards to the proliferation and misuse of arms. It is important to note that perhaps South Africa is one of the few countries that have engaged in a full and peaceful demobilization and integration effort that proved successful and did not require external assistance. Nevertheless, this example cannot be used as a lesson for future demobilization processes since South Africa never lost either the infrastructures to support full demobilization and integration processes nor the authority to manage the transition in peace: two elements that seldom are present in conflict situations elsewhere. And yet, despite the fact that South Africa managed its demobilization and military integration without outside assistance, it did not place a great onus on the disarmament and destruction of the tools of war. For this reason, the years following the transition consistently showed an increase in the theft of arms from both state and private sources as well as an influx of illicit arms from South Africa's more unstable neighbours. The concomitant increase in violent armed crime – particularly cash in transit heists and car-jacking – led the government to review its firearms and ammunition legislation in the year 2000 as well as the commencement of a government programme to identify and destroy surplus small arms in state possession. Had these measures applied to the transition, it would have contained the spiral of armed crime which followed elections.

Aside from the special case of South Africa, a further link can be made between lack of disarmament and the absence of a well-planned and well-funded demobilization and reintegration programme for ex-combatants. If demobilization is not complete and arms are available, it is very possible that this combination will lead to renewed conflict and/or to increased banditry among unemployed and dissatisfied armed ex-combatants (as was the case of the UN Observer Group in Central America – ONUCA – and the UN Operation in Mozambique, ONUMOZ). The increase in armed banditry is inextricably linked to alternative employment opportunities (or the lack of employment opportunities) for ex-combatants, and to the availability of weapons, which in turn is a consequence of ineffective arms control and disarmament at a time when these were both possible and crucial to the well-being of an entire region.

Multinational peace efforts and disarmament

Contemporary political violence occurs primarily at sub-state or intra-state level, as is illustrated by the fact that the majority of contemporary multinational peace support operations have been mandated by the UN – or by others at the UN's request – to support peace efforts in intra-state wars.

Because the UN mirrors the international conflict resolution processes of the past, multinational peace support operations mandated in intra-state or failed state situations often apply the same principles to peacekeeping as they would have done in an international conflict. Thus every belligerent party to a conflict is treated on equal footing and elevated to the same degree of status, irrespective of its representation or past.[2] This seriously undermines the potential for gaining authority – one of the most crucial elements to allow for successful disarmament in peace support operations. To understand why this is so, it is imperative also to comprehend the changing nature of contemporary peace support operations and their needs.

From 1956 (the Suez crisis) to the watershed year of 1990 (UN Transition Assistance Group (South West Africa/Namibia) UNTAG, ONUCA and UN Observer Mission in El Salvador, ONUSAL), each individual peacekeeping mission has been different. Therefore, it is possible to say that peace support operations, since their inception, have always been a chameleon of possibilities only restrained by the political context of troop contributors and by regional imperatives.[3] Thus, all of the missions that have – up to now – passed as peacekeeping operations have, in reality, been a mix of peacekeeping, peacemaking, peacebuilding and peace-enforcing tasks. The real challenge has always been how to know when to apply each task in each operational and tactical level at the right moment.

It could also be said that the evolution and changes in peacekeeping operations have not stopped with the pre- and post-1989 divide. In the analysis of operations from 1989 to 2000 for example, another difference is beginning to emerge aside from size, task and non-military mandate: that of a continued effort by the Security Council at gaining greater specificity on disarmament issues in the mandates for each operation.

In a series of studies conducted by the UN between 1994 and 1996,[4] a number of UN (and non-UN) peacekeeping operations since 1989 were analysed to determine the way in which these missions had undertaken disarmament and demobilization activities. The results of this study shed light on one main dilemma in the management of arms during peace processes:

> in contemporary intra-state peace missions, warring parties and paramilitary forces refuse to be disarmed, cantoned and controlled by peace forces even if consensus for doing so has been agreed to by the belligerent factions at the strategic level. [This dilemma partially explains why] ... although most peace operations studied had strategic consent and had mandates to undertake disarmament and demobilisation missions, they normally failed to implement them as originally envisioned.[5]

The study showed that the problems in the way disarmament and demobilization tasks were tackled during UN peacekeeping operations spanned successive layers of decisions and levels within the operation. Peace agreements often had mention of disarmament needs but when these same agreements were mentioned as part of UN mandates establishing an operation, the same were perceived as diluted for operational purposes (as in the UN Angola Verification Mission II, UNAVEM II). By the same token even if mandates specified the disarmament needs of an operation, problems in interpretation of these needs emerged in successive levels of command (from the strategic to the operational and, finally, tactical levels, the rules of engagement had a propensity for change (as in the UN Protection Force (Croatia, Bosnia/Hercegovina) UNPROFOR).

More often than not, as mandates diluted disarmament and demobilization tasks, or as rules of engagement suffered changes down the line of command, a peacekeeper on the ground had more of an awareness of *what he was not supposed to do* than *what he had to do* to ensure the success of his/her mission. This alone can explain why some UN missions mandated under Chapter VII operations of the Charter, were dealt with as if they had been normal Chapter VI operations (as in UNOSOM). Conversely, the lack of clarity in the peacekeepers' mandates and rules of engagement, and the lack of coordination between military and civilian components and between different contingents sometimes led to Chapter VII activities during Chapter VI operations (as in the UN Transitional Authority in Cambodia (UNTAC) and in UNPROFOR).

The studies also showed that disarmament and demobilization efforts during a peacekeeping operation had a greater or lesser success of taking root in direct relation to the way the neighbouring states shared and supported the peace process that was under way (as in ONUCA, ONUSAL, UNTAG). All successful UN operations during the 1990s have shared one common issue: they had the support of the region. In terms of disarmament and demobilization, this support is crucial.

Authority and the provision of a secure environment for the people and for the peacekeepers; the use of consent-promoting techniques; obtaining effective regional support; and ensuring the willingness of the peacekeepers to do their job as mandated all the way down to the tactical level, seem to be the right environment for disarmament tasks during peace processes to flourish. Of all of these, none is as important as the acquisition of authority: the will to disarm and demobilize.

Authority to disarm and demobilize

A multinational peacekeeping force must gain authority as soon as it is deployed in the field. This is achieved through the provision of very clear guidelines as to the force's role vis-à-vis the population as well as vis-à-vis the warring parties themselves. These guidelines must be constructed from the peace agreements 'down' – that is, they must be expressed and agreed upon in the documents that are formulated with the warring parties initially and also expressed in the mandate of the ensuing international operation as well as the operational instructions of the operation – particularly when the agreements are brokered by the UN and/or are then taken up in the Security Council resolution that mandates the operation. In operations where there is clarity as to authority, the possibility of sustaining adequate arms management controls (as seen in Cambodia) is greater than when either the mandate or the peacekeepers are unclear as to the nature and power of their presence in the field (as in Somalia, Angola, Liberia and Sierra Leone, among others).[6]

When the UN fails to establish authority over and above that of the parties to a dispute, it reduces its chances of promoting peace; it makes any disarmament and demobilization component of the mission hostage to the whims of the belligerents; and it seriously reduces the security of the population and the peacekeepers themselves, as happened in Somalia, former Yugoslavia, Liberia, Angola and Sierra Leone.

The establishment of authority is particularly important in contemporary peace support operations where the boundaries between peacekeeping and peace enforcement are blurred. Similarly, there have been numerous occasions where an agreed-upon ceasefire has broken when peacekeepers were already deployed. Even with authority granted to a multinational mission, the monitoring of tenuous ceasefires, and of those components in an operation that directly relate to the deflation of tension – such as disarmament and demobilization tasks – proves to be an operational nightmare. Without such authority, they become a political one. Peacekeepers are left in the dangerous position of having to monitor a fictitious situation and being unable to do anything to revert to the *status quo ante*.

In some major operations undertaken under both Chapter VI and Chapter VII mandates, there have been instances of the successful application of an enforcement capability to ensure compliance with agreed conditions (as seen in some cases of Sector West monitoring by the UNPROFOR[7] mission, and some of the tactical decisions undertaken by the UNTAC[8] commanders, among others). This might lead to the conclusion that the enforcement of weapons control at the tactical level, *when there is strategic and operational consent*, is possible. But for this to happen consistently in situations pertaining to the slippery slope between Chapter VI mandates and Chapter VII-type actions in the field, the element of establishing a UN authority over and above the parties, and the willingness of the mission to engage in permanent consent-promoting techniques between belligerent parties, become mandatory. This is also particularly true of Chapter VIII operations as was the case in ECOMOG (Economic Community of West African States Monitoring Group, also known as the ECOWAS monitoring group).

Since 1988 only four 'second generation' peacekeeping missions succeeded in establishing this type of authority: UNTAG (Namibia), UNTAC (Cambodia), ONUCA (Central America) and ONUSAL (El Salvador).[9] All of these were mandated and implemented between 1988 and 1992. From then onwards very few of successive peacekeeping operations have established the same norm. Thus, a lack of authority seems to have become a standard for most multinational peace support operations since 1993.

Not surprisingly, a lack of established authority early on in the process has also conditioned the approach of deployed personnel in the first crucial months of an operation. This lack of authority[10] has led to the development of a timorous approach by peacekeepers in the field which has ultimately damaged the credibility, evolution and future of the whole operation. This was clearly seen in UNOSOM I, UNPROFOR, UNAVEM II, UNAVEM III, ONUMOZ, UNOMIL (UN Observer Mission in Liberia), UNAMSIL (UN Observer Mission in Sierra Leone) and ECOMOG.[11] All of the above contained some disarmament or demobilization components which ultimately became the first casualty of their respective missions.

It is obvious, by contrast, that those peace support operations which are conducted by a unilateral force have a greater natural authority to them. Unfortunately there is more interest in unilateral intervention examples than in unilateral peacekeeping operations and one often fails to consider how the latter might yield good lessons for contemporary multinational operations. A case in point is the record of the British mandated and led Commonwealth Monitoring Force (CMF) which oversaw and assisted the political transition in Rhodesia/Zimbabwe. Here, the 'cohesion of the British-led mission with its clear lines of authority and relative lack of inter-state bickering could be seen to contrast favourably with a number of [UN operations] efforts... [thus] with a few exceptions, the British conception of the mission was not challenged by national contingents'.[12] Although highly focused and extremely professionally conducted, the CMF had many salient points which partially account for its relative success – monitors relied on diplomacy and the development of personal relationships to influence the parties towards acceptance of final settlement and elections; it therefore was one of the first operations of this type to adopt consensuality as its major modus operandi. And, although the operation itself was of short duration, the British commitment to the post-electoral reconstruction period lasted for 20 years through the presence of the British Military Assistance Training Team (BMATT) structure.

Nevertheless, the CMF put its attention into the development of three major tasks: demilitarization, integration and reconciliation, not placing enough weight on the fundamental needs of disarmament. If the CMF can be judged a success in creating the conditions that permitted elections to take place, it was less success-ful in specific modalities of the operation such as maintaining containment. A more telling criticism of the mission was that its mandate was concluded through forcing a disproportionate number of concessions from one party over another. The CMF then, although seen as an impartial force thanks to its professionalism, was still obliged to implement an inequitable mandate. Had not the strongest war-ring party won the election, it is doubtful that it would have agreed to demobilize and demilitarize to the extent that the other parties to this dispute did. Thus, although unilateralism enhances the potential for the creation and retention of authority with the people and the parties to a dispute, it does not altogether pro-vide for all the solutions. Invariably, it also demands long-term commitment of the unilateral force in the post-conflict reconstruction period: a commitment which not many are prepared to sustain.

The lack of a clearly established authority has repeatedly undermined the power of international contingents of peacekeepers in engaging in consent-promoting techniques between the belligerent parties, a sine qua non of successful disarma-ment and demobilization needs. To have both the authority and the ability to build consent as the mission progresses[13] is the single most important factor in disarma-ment operations because 'to implement their mandated tasks, peacekeeping and multi-function missions unlike peace enforcement operations rely on having the consent of the belligerent parties, at least at the strategic and operational levels'.[14]

From the above, it can be gauged that disarmament and demobilization com-ponents in a 'second generation' peacekeeping mission are difficult to implement because they are the first to fall by the wayside should the mission fail to com-mand authority and build consent. By the same token, without serious disarma-ment and demobilization, the peace support operation itself will most probably fail, as has repeatedly happened in the case of Angola, for instance.

Angola and Sierra Leone: no disarmament, no peace

Angola is a good example of repeated failures of missions because of ineffective disarmament and demobilization, both due fundamentally to the inability to gain authority. At the end of the UNAVEM II mission, the UN Secretary-General reported to the Security Council on 25 November 1992 that a root cause for the deterioration in the security situation in Angola had been the incomplete fulfil-ment of key provisions of the Peace Accords. Ineffectual demobilization and dis-armament were another serious contributing factor.[15] Of the 34,425 weapons collected from UNITA troops and police in the disarmament effort, 97 per cent were personal or light crew weapons and between 30 and 40 per cent were old and/or unserviceable.[16] These problems would continue during the UNAVEM III mission. Compared to the previous UN mission, UNAVEM III was much larger, costing some US$1.5 billion over four years and had as many as 7000 troops, 350 military observers, 65 minesweeping experts, 260 civilian police and 100 staff members in Angola.[17] Despite this commitment by the international community the peace process unravelled from the start. It was delayed in deployment and the UN systematically turned a blind eye to acknowledged breaches of the accord by both parties.[18] Furthermore, as the first combatants entered the assembly camps for disarmament and demobilization, as early as January 1995, it became clear that there was going to be little demobilization and almost no disarmament.[19]

At the opening of the Movimento Popular pela Liberacao d'Angola's (MPLA) Fourth Congress in Luanda on 5 December 1998 President dos Santos called for the termination of UNAVEM III's successor MONUA (UN Observer Mission in Angola) and an end to the Lusaka peace process. MONUA withdrew for safety from all UNITA-held areas on 6 December. With the resumption of war, the instruments of the peace process crumpled and faded away. Following the shooting down of two UN-chartered aircraft, the UN Secretary-General decided that MONUA could achieve little and recommended that its mandate be terminated on 26 February 1999, to be followed by a phased withdrawal. UNAVEM III went the same way as its predecessor:

> The failures of UNAVEM II and UNAVEM III occurred for many different reasons but one of them was the lack of willingness of the parties to take disarmament and demobilisation seriously, and the lack of commitment in the UN itself to pursue these objectives. By early 1999 with the resumption of war in Angola, it would be possible to judge part of the United Nations failure as directly related to the parties' intention to use the 'lull' in hostilities prevalent during UNAVEM II and III to re-equip and re-train in order to escalate the level of the fighting in the procurement of decisive victory. What is interesting is that the warring parties seem to have exploited the international attention awarded to them by UNAVEM II and III to obtain clear political and military objectives. The Angolan government, conscious of the fact that it had retained power over the years due to external support, attempted to freeze this status through the UN Operations; while UNITA used the defects in the UN mission, particularly related to disarmament and demobilisation, to buy time to re-equip and re-train in the hope of escalating conflict and acquiring a decisive victory when the time was judged ripe.[20]

In the summary of his recent work on Sierra Leone, Berman states a similar situation in Sierra Leone:

> On 7 July 1999, the government of Sierra Leone and the Revolutionary United Front (RUF) signed the Lomé Peace Agreement in an effort to end over eight years of civil war between the government and the RUF. This conflict resulted in tens of thousands of deaths and the displacement of more than 2 million people – well over one-third of the total population many of whom are now refugees in neighbouring states. A central component of this agreement called for the RUF to disarm. But this did not happen. Instead, a year later, the RUF leader, Foday Sankoh, was in the custody of the Sierra Leonean government and the future of the peace accord was in grave doubt.

One thing was clear, however: far from disarming, all parties – the RUF, as well as the government and its allies – have been re-arming at an alarming rate. They are doing so in contravention of a 1997 UN arms embargo (amended in June 1998 to exclude the Sierra Leonean government) and despite a 1998 regional moratorium on the production, procurement and sale of small arms and light weapons. Over a year after the Lomé Peace Agreement, the political and security situation remains extremely fragile.[21]

One of the most interesting aspects of the Sierra Leone case is the fact that so many of the weapons used by the RUF were obtained by seizing arms from the peace-keeping force itself: the contingents of Guinea, Kenya, Nigeria, Jordan, Zambia and India have all suffered heavily in this regard.[22]

Clearly, if we take these two cases, it would be possible to prove that not only was authority not gained in these situations but that there was a direct link between its lack and the failure in disarmament and demobilization components crucial to peace in both Sierra Leone and Angola.

Disarmament in the post-conflict phase

But lack of effective disarmament at the right time has not only been responsible for the continuation of violent conflict; it can also postpone recovery in post-conflict situations as well as endanger regional dynamics among neighbours.

As states in post-conflict regions struggle to develop in harmony with each other, there is a growing realization that the negative impact of multinational peace support efforts that had inadequate disarmament components and ineffectual demobilization programmes, are taking a toll on the human and financial resources needed for post-conflict reconstruction. The increase in armed banditry and organized crime on the one hand, and the continued political violence in some sectors of society as well as an increase in corruption patterns, are undermining safety, security, governance and democracy at large.

In relatively calm regions such as Southern Africa, governments acting alone and in conjunction are now addressing these new threats to security. A principal pivot of regional and governmental strategies has to do with the management, control and reduction of illicit weapons flows.

During post-conflict reconstruction processes regional interactions and efforts acquire prominence over international ones. Therefore, it is at regional levels that the greatest number of control mechanisms may be applied to begin to put an end to the proliferation problem of existing stocks of arms. In other words, it is a question of 'what existing regional mechanisms and structures might do to control and reduce the damage already set in motion by the increased availability of light weapons across borders'.[23]

Increasingly, regional organizations are taking decisions to address the short- and long-term problems associated with small arms proliferation.[24] At subregional levels there has also been much movement among affected states. Thus, for example, South Africa has established bilateral agreements with Swaziland, Namibia and Mozambique to engage in information sharing and cooperative efforts to reduce cross-border smuggling of goods, including firearms. South Africa and Mozambique have cooperated in a series of operations in Mozambique to identify and destroy arms and ammunition caches left over from the war. Small arms recovered and destroyed so far are in their thousands.

The one area of demobilization that is currently being discussed in Southern Africa is that of rethinking the training and integration of demobilized soldiers. The examples of the past demobilization retraining and reintegration in Southern Africa have by and large been negative. It has been customary for international and governmental agencies assisting in the process of demobilization and reintegration to look at this issue as if it were a minor correction rather than a major overhaul of society. More often than not soldiers and paramilitary forces have been battling each other for decades: many men-at-arms that need to be demobilized have been soldiers since they were eight or nine years old, they know nothing else but combat and the only skill they have is the use of arms. For this reason, it is misleading to talk of demobilization and reintegration: there was no prior mobilization nor a prior role in society for these military men and women. The training of demobilized soldiers is therefore one that must be much more comprehensive than what has been applied so far to cover for the sometimes total lack of schooling, general education or skills in these people. By the same token, the integration of these people into society must be very well structured: conventional wisdom simplifies the issue of reintegration as one where healing and reconciliation are prioritized as if the demobilized soldier had been removed from a viable society creating a vacuum that can be filled with his/her return. More often than not, there is no place in society for these people except as bandits or criminals because they do not come back to a niche they left open when they took up arms. Issues of education, long-term training skills and programmes for the improvement of entire communities, so that there are places open to demobilized soldiers in that new community pattern, must become part of the new thinking on demobilization and reintegration.

An interesting issue is that presented by the demobilization and reintegration of women combatants. More often than not, the social stigma attached to girl/women combatants is such that they are barred from returning to the protection of their families and villages who tend to repudiate them as 'tainted' elements of society. Paradoxically, although cruelly abused and often psychologically disturbed, these young women who have had to learn to rely on themselves early on constitute a real 'threat' to post-conflict societies because they are the seed for a less dependent alternative to the social fabric. Not enough time or effort has been dedicated to the study of the contemporary demobilization and reintegration of women nor of the ultimate socio-economic changes that the insertion of this type of ex-combatant imposes on society at large.

Finally, the needs for disarmament and demobilization correction are so great in post-conflict reconstruction that they often take precious resources out of the development and socio-economic needs of emerging societies. This is one of the reasons why serious demobilization coupled to disarmament should be engaged in as early as possible in a peace process, allowing post-conflict reconstruction to start on the best possible footing.

By the same token, it is equally crucial to understand that regional initiatives in support of both a peace support operation and a national reconstruction process become fundamental to the establishment of adequate authority and for the implementation of disarmament during and after peace processes.

Disarmament processes during peace support operations are best served by coordination between the international mission and the region immediately bordering the stricken state. Regional powers and immediate neighbours should be aware of what is happening in their vicinity and deny the use of their territory, resources or facilities to any of the warring parties that have agreed to enter a peace process. This is particularly true in situations of honouring arms embargoes and sanctions imposed on belligerent parties.

If the multilateral peace mission is under the auspices of the UN, the region where the UN is operative should support this endeavour so as to close loopholes that will lengthen the resolution process and endanger disarmament and demobilization components. If the region becomes part of the problem and not part of the solution in conflict resolution, the chances that the conflict will eventually spill over to their own territories are very great. Thus, it is in the interest of regions to control the situation when they are in a position to do so.

By the same token, in post-conflict reconstruction processes such as that of Mozambique, it is in the interest of the neighbouring states to provide every assistance for continued disarmament and arms control operations as well as ensuring efficient demobilization and integration of ex-combatants. If this is not undertaken, those weapons and the men who use them, become a cross-border threat to the peace and stability of the region.

Although the operative brunt of these actions rests with regions, the international community can assist by ensuring that their part of the responsibility on disarmament and demobilization is better implemented during a multinational peace process and that arms and ex-combatants become a key focus of post-conflict reconstruction assistance agendas. The key here is to remember that the greater the number of weapons actually collected and destroyed, the less need for massive operations of recovery and destruction of weapons in the future. All of this can happen if the multinational peace operation gains the authority to disarm from the very beginning of its operation.

Conclusion

To sum up, judging the impact of imperfect disarmament and demobilization on the evolution of peace processes and their aftermath, it seems logical to suggest that there is an urgent need to improve the mechanisms within existing multinational peace support operations so that every mission can start with 'a clear understanding of what disarmament means for a particular operation, as distinct from demobilisation; a clear ... position on the destruction of weapons; ... [and] the financial resources to cover the costs of effective disarmament'.[25]

What is needed is to prioritize arms management processes during conflict prevention and resolution missions so that disarmament and demobilization become vital and comprehensive components of a mission from the outset and do not fall hostage to the timings and political manoeuvres of warring parties who are less than serious in their bid for lasting peace. Although clearly the principal responsibility in achieving these objectives lies with the Security Council when mandating peacekeeping operations, it also lies with troop-contributing countries in the way they implement the mandates they receive.

Finally, multinational peace support operations seldom occur in states that are islands; for this reason, a special effort must be undertaken by the states neighbouring the area where the peacekeeping operation is taking place. Without regional support for international missions, the latter will find its operations all the harder to sustain and to implement. By the same token, regional coordination and assistance must accompany post-conflict reconstruction processes. Nevertheless, the international community also has a major role to play in assisting countries to sustain disarmament, arms control and demobilization efforts well beyond the end of a multinational peace support operation.

It is in burden sharing and in sustaining the long-term objectives of disarmament and demobilization during conflict resolution *and* post-conflict reconstruction that both regional and international goals can meet to produce lasting peace.

Notes

1. E. G. Berman, 'Re-armament in Sierra Leone: One Year after the Lome Peace Agreement' Small Arms Survey, Occasional Paper 1, Geneva December 2000.
2. J. Potgieter, 'The Price of War and Peace: a Critical Assessment of the Disarmament Component of United Nations Operations in Southern Africa', in V. Gamba (ed.), *Society under Siege: Crime, Violence and Illegal Weapons* (Johannesburg: Institute for Security Studies, The Towards Collaborative Peace Series, Vol. I, 1997), p. 132.
3. For a good discussion on this issue see J. S. Sutterlin, 'Military Force in the Service of Peace', *Aurora Papers*, 18 (1993); and A. Kane, 'The United Nations and the Maintenance of Peace and Security: Challenges and Choices', in *Proceedings of the Forty-Third Pugwash Conference on Science and World Affairs – A World at the Crossroads: New Conflicts, New Solutions*, Hasseludden, Sweden, 9–15 June 1993 (London: World Scientific, 1994), pp. 175–84.
4. The studies were undertaken by the United Nations Institute for Disarmament Research (UNIDIR) in Geneva under the research area entitled 'Disarmament and Conflict Resolution Project' which I directed at the time. The publications produced by the project are as follows (all UNIDIR's Disarmament and Conflict Resolution Project Series, Geneva: UN): *Managing Arms in Peace Processes: the Issues* (1996); *Managing Arms in Peace Processes: Somalia* (1995); *Managing Arms in Peace Processes: Rhodesia/Zimbabwe* (1995); *Managing Arms in Peace Processes: Croatia and Bosnia-Herzegovina* (1996); *Managing Arms in Peace Processes: Cambodia* (1996); *Managing Arms in Peace Processes: Mozambique* (1996); *Managing Arms in Peace Processes: Liberia* (1996); *Managing Arms in Peace Processes: Psychological Issues and Intelligence* (1996); *Managing Arms in Peace Processes: Haiti* (1997); *Managing Arms in Peace Processes: Nicaragua and El Salvador* (1997); *Managing Arms in Peace Processes: Training* (1997), and *Small Arms Management and Peacekeeping in Southern Africa* (1996).
5. V. Gamba and J. Potgieter, 'Concluding Summary: Multinational Peace Operations and the Enforcement of Consensual Disarmament', in *Managing Arms in Peace Processes: The Issues* (UNIDIR's Disarmament and Conflict Resolution Project Series, Geneva: UN, 1996), p. 209.

6. See C. Adibe, *Managing Arms in Peace Processes: Somalia* (UNIDIR's Disarmament and Conflict Resolution Project Series, Geneva: United Nations, 1995) and A. Age et al., *Fighting for Hope in Somalia* (Oslo: NUPI, 1995).
7. See A. Raevsky & B. Ekwall-Uebelhardt, *Managing Arms in Peace Processes: Croatia and Bosnia-Herzegovina* (UNIDIR's Disarmament and Conflict Resolution Project Series, Geneva: UN, 1996).
8. See J. Wang, *Managing Arms in Peace Processes: Cambodia* (UNIDIR's Disarmament and Conflict Resolution Project Series, Geneva: UN, 1996).
9. V. Gamba & J. Potgieter, 'Multi-Functional Peace Support Operations: Evolution and Operations', *ISS Monograph Series 8* (January 1997), South Africa, p. 22.
10. See D. Cox, 'Peacekeeping and Disarmament: Peace Agreements, Security Council Mandates, and the Disarmament Experience', in *Managing Arms in Peace Processes: the Issues* (UNIDIR's Disarmament and Conflict Resolution Project Series, Geneva: UN, 1996).
11. See Adibe, op. cit.; Raevsky & Ekwall-Uebelhardt, op. cit.; E. Berman, *Managing Arms in Peace Processes: Mozambique* (UNIDIR's Disarmament and Conflict Resolution Project Series, Geneva: UN, 1996); C. Adibe, *Managing Arms in Peace Processes: Liberia* (UNIDIR's Disarmament and Conflict Resolution Project Series, Geneva: UN, 1996).
12. J. Ginifer, *Managing Arms in Peace Processes: Rhodesia/Zimbabwe* (UNIDIR, 1995), p. 54.
13. It is important to note that the failure to establish authority and to provide a secure environment for the peacekeepers as well as the population not only compromises the success of the mission itself, but has, at times, also led to the institution of parallel enforcement missions in the middle of the process, such as that presented by UNITAF. By contrast, non-UN operations such as those of the CMF in Rhodesia and Operation Uphold Democracy in Haiti, were successful, in that they did manage to establish both authority and a secure environment before handing the effort to multinational forces and the UN itself to consolidate the peace that had been gained.
14. Gamba & Potgieter, op. cit., p. 213.
15. Document UN S/24858, 25 November 1992.
16. UNAVEM III Force HQ, Q Cell, File c:\QWP\R97.WB2\12 March 1997; Potgieter, op. cit., p. 153.
17. One of the reasons for the change to the UN Observer Mission in Angola (MONUA) in June 1977 was the estimated US$1 million per day costs.
18. Human Rights Watch, *Angola Unravels* (New York, 1999), p. 2.
19. H. de Beer & V. Gamba, 'The Arms Dilemma: Resources for Arms or Arms for Resources', in J. Cilliers & C. Dietrich (eds), *Angola's War Economy: the Role of Oil and Diamonds* (Johannesburg: ISS, 2000).
20. Ibid., p. 85.
21. Berman, 'Re-armament in Sierra Leone', op. cit., p. iv.
22. Ibid., pp. 19–20.
23. Potgieter, op. cit., p. 162.
24. See V. Gamba (ed.), *Society under Siege: Licit Responses to Illicit Arms* (Johannesburg: Institute for Security Studies, TCP series, Vol. II, 1998).
25. Ibid., pp. 163–5.

Part IV
Peace Accords

At one level a peace accord is a technical document, often negotiated by lawyers and signed by elites. It is also a political document with the capacity to have a real impact on people's lives. Its success or failure depends on the seriousness of negotiators to sell any accord to their constituents and to deliver on any concessions or reforms.

The extent of any agreement is important, particularly in terms of the degree to which it deals with the constitutional, territorial and security issues that lie at the core of a conflict or is merely concerned with the manifestations of the conflict. There has been a tendency in recent years to stretch the remit of peace accords to issues of cultural and economic inclusion that define the developmental aspect of conflicts.

One doughty problem is the inflexibility of state sovereignty. The fixity of state boundaries in the face of demands for separation steers states towards the granting of limited autonomy and provision for minorities within established boundaries. This leads to the question of 'how much autonomy is enough' and whether or not it satisfies or encourages demands for devolution and independence from the centre. A number of workable power-sharing formats have been designed over the past few decades, although many have the side effect of perpetuating rather than challenging ethnic politics. The electoral validation of a peace accord conforms to wider international trends towards democratization. Yet electoral mechanisms may complicate a delicate situation, especially if organized prematurely. Although the counting of heads is important, more important is the broadening and deepening of democracy and participation.

12
Power-sharing after Civil Wars: Matching Problems to Solutions

Timothy D. Sisk

If and when the antagonists waging today's wars grow weary of violence and seek peace, they often end up at the negotiating table trying to craft political settlements that define the terms sharing power. Recent evidence suggests that contemporary wars – most of which are internal, and most of those are fought in the name of ethnicity or religion – are much more likely to end at the peace table than on the battlefield. Peter Wallensteen and Margareta Sollenberg – scholars who track such trends – report that of the 108 conflicts since 1989, 75 had ended by 1998. 'Of these,' they write, '21 were ended by peace agreements, whereas 24 ended in victory for one of the sides and 30 had other outcomes (ceasefire agreements or activity below the level for inclusion). Many new peace agreements were signed in the middle and late parts of the period, particularly 1995–96.' In sum, today some 50 per cent of wars end at the peace table, a dramatic increase over the broad historical average of only about 15 per cent.[1]

Ostensibly, power-sharing solutions are designed to marry principles of democracy with the need for conflict management in deeply divided societies. Power-sharing involves a wide array of political arrangements – usually embodied in constitutional terms – in which the principal elements of society are guaranteed a place, and influence, in governance. From South Africa to Sri Lanka, from Bosnia to Burundi, from Cambodia to Congo, it is difficult to envisage a post-war political settlement that does not, or would need to, include guarantees to all the major antagonists that they will be assured some permanent political representation, decision-making power and often autonomous territory in the post-war peace. Indeed, the gist of international mediation in such conflicts is to encourage parties to adopt power-sharing in exchange for waging war. Why would parties to such wars concede at the bargaining table – or in post-war elections – what they had not lost on the battlefield?

The problem is that, as described below, power-sharing systems are sometimes prone to failure. If power-sharing is necessary, but unlikely to endure, how can sustainable peace be built in post-war situations? This chapter assesses recent experience with power-sharing as a means of living together after deadly ethnic conflict. It describes how new political institutions are a critical element of negotiated settlements, it offers a typology of power-sharing models, and it includes examples of various approaches in practice. The chapter critically evaluates the common pro-position that power-sharing is a long-term solution to ethnically based wars that do not result in separation. While power-sharing may be desirable, and necessary, as an *immediate* exit to deadly ethnic wars, power-sharing is not a viable *long-term* solution to managing uncertainty in ethnically divided societies.

The problem with power-sharing

Sadly, there is a serious problem with power-sharing as the outcome to deadly eth-nic conflicts. In sum, the long-term political guarantees inherent in many power-sharing systems sometimes contain the seeds of their own destruction. They are not very durable solutions.[2] A key feature of power-sharing – the mutual veto, whereby decisions are only taken with the widest possible consent and only with a near consensus – often leads to the use of 'political blackmail'. Unable to get con-sensus, governance stagnates and policy-making drifts; the result is a 'cold peace', in which the parties do not continue to employ violence but neither have they embarked on a serious process of reconciliation. When power-sharing agreements lead to such political *immobilism* (the inability to make or implement policy due to protracted disagreement), frustration emerges and tensions rise; one or more parties defect from the accord. Eventually war can erupt anew. The outbreak of civil wars in Angola, Cyprus, Lebanon, Sierra Leone and Sudan have all been the result of broken power-sharing agreements that led to renewed violence.

At best, power-sharing solutions make for good transitional devices, but in the long run the best outcome is a much more fluid form of democracy that allows for the creation of flexible coalitions that bridge the ethnic divide. *A central ques-tion that has yet to be fully explored is the terms under which power-sharing, consensus-oriented forms of democracy can evolve into more flexible institutions that can foster reconciliation and a broader national identity.* If sustainable peace comes through 'conflict transformation', as argued by John Paul Lederach,[3] power-sharing is often a too rigid system of governances to allow for the social and political changes nec-essary for addressing the underlying causes of conflict that give rise to war.[4]

How can the rigid structures of political power-sharing wither over time to the point where the guarantees for group security they contain are no longer neces-sary? This is not a purely academic question. In Bosnia, for example, the ability of NATO's international peacekeepers to end their occupation is premised on the ability of the power-sharing institutions forged in the 1995 Dayton Agreement – now dominated by nationalists – to melt into more moderate and ethnically mixed political institutions.[5]

If power-sharing is at best a transitional device, this conclusion begs the question of what types of political institutions can be expected to allow democratic decision-making to prosper in post-war environments in which politics remains deeply divided. How can we match problems inherent in certain types of civil war situa-tions? The remainder of this chapter highlights a broad range of political institu-tions which, if tailored to the specific conditions they are meant to serve, can move beyond formalized power-sharing to foster inclusive multiethnic coalitions that amount to an informal system of sharing power while ensuring equity and distributive justice among contending groups. How can power-sharing wither away, leading to a more normal system of liberal democracy?

Negotiating peace: partition or power-sharing

Parties in internal conflicts face essentially two choices for the settlement of underlying disputes: 'separation', that is partition, and power-sharing, or creating the structures for living together.[6] In very rare and special circumstances, contemporary civil wars end in partition that rearranges international frontiers. Outcomes to civil wars that feature total separation have been seen recently only in Eritrea and East Timor, and both of these instances involved historical claims to self-determination that go back to what was essentially botched efforts of decolonization.[7] Other instances of total political separation are also *sui generis*: the former Soviet Union and the former Yugoslavia were dissolving federations, and the Israeli–Palestinian dispute is also a matter of unresolved, colonial-era self-determination claims.

Partition refers to the creation of an entirely new state that enjoys full sovereignty and international recognition. As noted above, secession remains a strong taboo in the international system. Some question the prevailing policies of the international community that systematically works to keep troubled states together. Chaim Kaufman writes that:

> Stable resolutions of ethnic civil wars are possible, but only when the opposing groups are demographically separated into defensible enclaves. Separation reduces both incentives and opportunity for further combat, and largely eliminates both reasons and chances for ethnic cleansing of civilians. While ethnic fighting can be stopped by other means, such as peace enforcers by international forces or by a conquering empire, such peaces last only as long as the enforcers remain. This means to save lives threatened by genocide, the international community must abandon attempts to save war-torn multiethnic states.[8]

Others disagree with the Kaufman thesis, citing the need to defend the principle of tolerant, multiethnic diversity and the importance of not rewarding disputants with territorial ambitions who may have committed war crimes; these are the principal reasons why the international community insisted upon the maintenance of Bosnia's territorial integrity at the Dayton talks.[9]

In all other wars today, partition – despite being sometimes advocated by secessionist forces – is simply unlikely and improbable. The bias against partition by all the major world powers, and particularly the five Permanent Members of the UN Security Council – remains incredibly strong. The stark consequence of this basic reality of the international system is clear: in most civil wars, the terms of settlement will involve living together and some kind of agreement to share political power. Even after civil war, antagonists are destined to live together.

The purpose of a substantive settlement is to reconstitute 'normal' politics in a society after war and to create new, mutually beneficial rules of the political game. Ultimately, parties in a negotiation process to resolve deep-seated conflict arrive at institutional solutions: rules and procedures through which to arbitrate their differences peacefully in Parliament rather than violently on the street. These institutional solutions may be augmented with agreements to undertake more long-term socio-economic change, as has been the case in South Africa and El Salvador. Negotiated settlements as power-sharing agreements have certain common features.

First, they are the product of negotiation. Settlements in internal conflicts reflect the convergence point of the parties at the negotiating table among their preferences for new rules, structures or institutions, to constitute the post-war peace. Waterman argues that 'civil wars are conflicts over political order', and settlements in them entail the 're-creation of the conditions for a viable, common political order'.[10] Importantly, settlements do not end conflict; they are simply agreements to continue bargaining under consensually defined rules of interaction. The aim of power-sharing in peace agreements is clearly conflict management, not conflict resolution.

Not surprisingly, settlements in internal conflicts often take the form of new constitutions or significant packages of amendments to existing constitutions. As constitutional laws, however, the settlement may 'freeze' in time the balance of power among the parties, which may have shifted dramatically during the subsequent phases of a peace process. Even though parties may have entered negotiation because of a perception of relative parity in power, subsequent events may have strengthened or weakened one side or another. This change in fortunes may well be reflected in the terms of a settlement. The settlement reflects the new constellation of forces and codifies and institutionalizes the relative bargaining power of the disputants.

Second, power-sharing settlements reflect the interests and expectations of the parties. In formal substantive negotiations, parties formulate their positions based on their expectations of how the structure of the new institutions will serve their interests; they exercise 'analytical imagination' about the costs and benefits of alternative institutions, such as the electoral system.[11] Therefore, settlements do not end conflicts; they are *promises* to end conflicts by creating new rules of the game to which all parties at the table can agree.

Third, power-sharing settlements in internal conflicts can be either 'interim' or 'final'. In interim settlements, parties are able to arrive at some basis for reconstituting normal politics but cannot agree on, or prefer to defer, highly sensitive or unresolved issues. The best example of an interim agreement, which has not seen a happy period of implementation, is the October 1993 Oslo Accord in the Israeli–Palestinian dispute. Interim settlements are usually partial agreements, whereas final settlements purport to be comprehensive in scope. In contrast, the 1995 Dayton Agreement for Bosnia is wide-ranging, but it is so final in its terms that it has been widely criticized as too inflexible and insufficiently dynamic.

Fourth, they establish systems of incentives. All settlements seek to formalize patterns of interaction and in this respect they seek to establish new incentive structures in their own right, resolving some of the uncertainty about the new rules of the game that characterize earlier phases of the peace process. In many cases, they are package proposals that resolve multiple issues simultaneously by linking them. Similarly, many of the more celebrated settlements in recent years have featured 'democratization as conflict resolution', explicitly marrying the goals of conflict amelioration with the introduction of competitive, multi-party politics. These features of power-sharing are illustrated well by the three 'stands' in the Northern Ireland peace process that led to the 1998 Good Friday Agreement. With linked issues and complex decision-making rules, this accord has created a power-sharing system, which seeks to provide incentives for bargaining in several arenas on a wide range of issues.

Settlements are attractive for all parties when they contain the likelihood of greater benefits for parties than they would achieve by abrogating negotiations and returning to the battlefield. Successful settlements are a formula of positive-sum gain for all parties. Many suggest that it is the genius of the April 1998 Good Friday Agreement in Northern Ireland that all parties could defend the agreement as containing the elements of what they had fought for all along. Moderate republicans could claim that the agreement represents the first step towards accession to Ireland; moderate loyalists could claim that the agreement preserves British sovereignty.[12] These elements of power-sharing help us understand the key components of such agreements. In sum, negotiated settlements that create power-sharing institutions:

- Create political institutions that are broadly inclusive of all major mobilized groups in society, and decisions are made through negotiating, issue trading and the search for consensus or near-consensus decision-making.
- The key elements of power-sharing institutions are: (1) inclusion of all major mobilized actors; (2) influence in decision-making, not just representation in governing institutions; (3) moderation, and the search for common ground; and (4) ongoing bargaining or negotiation within the new rules of the game that the peace agreement has established.

Options for settling ethnic conflicts

A long-standing misconception of power-sharing institutions is that they are all of a specific type, which for many years has been called 'consociationalism'.[13] The elements of this approach to power-sharing are well known: grand coalitions, proportional representation, cultural autonomy or federalism, and the mutual veto. Yet this prototype of power-sharing is but one of what is in fact a very broad range of political options for settling ethnic conflicts, the gist of which can be exceptionally different in terms of aims, structures and effects on promoting inter-group moderation and compromise.[14] What are the principal options for sharing power?[15]

Autonomy

For many conflicts today, such as Azerbaijan (Karabagh), Sudan or Sri Lanka, autonomy is often seen as a reasonable way to balance the claims of states for territorial integrity and the claims of rebel forces for secession. Autonomy, as eminent scholar Yash Ghai suggests, is not a term on which there is a consensus definition.[16] Nonetheless, his best effort at one is useful: 'Autonomy is a device to allow an ethnic group or other groups claiming a distinct identity to exercise direct control over important affairs of concern to them while allowing the larger entity to exercise those powers which are the common interests of both sections.' Among the forms of autonomy include symmetrical federalism in which all units enjoy similar powers, and asymmetrical federalism that might provide enhanced powers to a particular region.[17]

Probably the most appealing candidate for autonomy as a solution is the Kosovo imbroglio. United Nations and Organization for Security and Cooperation in Europe proposals for the solution of the Kosovo problem are an example of potential autonomy solutions in ethnic conflicts in which territory and ethnicity largely overlap. United Nations Security Council Resolution 1244, of 10 June 1999, clearly defines the mandate of the UN Interim Administration Mission in Kosovo (UNMIK) as promoting autonomy and self-government within the limits of territorial integrity for Yugoslavia. The resolution authorizes UNMIK to:

> establish an international civil presence in Kosovo in order to provide an interim administration for Kosovo under which the people of Kosovo can enjoy substantial autonomy within the Federal Republic of Yugoslavia, and which will provide transitional administration while establishing and overseeing the development of provisional democratic self-governing institutions to ensure conditions for a peaceful and normal life for all inhabitants of Kosovo.

Yet as the continuing tensions and as yet unresolved status of Kosovo demonstrate, the idea of autonomy as a solution is more common than its actual acceptance by the parties in conflict. Autonomy is a difficult option for power-sharing precisely because it fails to satisfy the preferences of either states which fear a 'slippery slope' towards disintegration of their territory, and secessionist groups which demand nothing less than full sovereignty and statehood. While autonomy must remain on the table as an option, it has in practice seen little success as a means of resolving the issues on the table in settlement negotiations.

Power-sharing: group building-block approach

Another possible option is a looser form of autonomy, not always explicitly territorial, termed 'consociationalism'. The option is in essence a *group building-block approach* that relies on accommodation by ethnic group leaders at the political centre and guarantees of group autonomy and minority rights; in essence, this approach is 'consociational' in that it encourages collaborative decision-making by parties in conflict. The key institutions are: federalism and the devolution of power to ethnic groups in territory that they control; minority vetoes on issues of particular importance to them; grand coalition cabinets in a parliamentary framework, and proportionality in all spheres of public life (e.g. budgeting and civil service appointments).[18]

Like Bosnia, Lebanon has a political system in which representation and autonomy for the country's main religious groups are guaranteed in the constitution.

Table 12.1   Consociational power-sharing

Principles	Practices	Problems
Broad-based coalitions among ethnic political parties	Grand coalition governments	Elites may initiate conflict to bolster their power at the centre
Minority or mutual veto on matters of importance to the group	Group rights defined in constitutional terms for named ethnic, racial, religious or cultural groups	Can reify ethnicity, reinforcing the divisions in society rather than promoting cross-cultural understanding
Proportionality	Proportional representation (PR) electoral system and the proposed allocation of jobs, spending, representation and participation by ethnic group leaders	PR may reflect well the divisions in society but does not provide incentives for building bridges across community lines
Group autonomy	Federalism, territorial or 'corporate'	May contain disincentives for contending groups to live peacefully together

Systems of communal representation have been attempted in many settings over the years, as described by scholar Arend Lijphart, an advocate of this approach, in his seminal book *Democracy in Plural Societies* (1977). Some criticize an approach that structures the political system around ethnic identities, arguing that mechanisms such as communal representation 'reify' and help harden ethnic differences, and the use of the mutual veto will lead to gridlock in decision-making. Table 12.1 summarizes the consociational model.

Power-sharing: integrative approach

In contrast, the integrative approach eschews ethnic groups as the building blocks of a common society and purposefully seeks to integrate society along the lines of division. In South Africa's 1993 interim constitution, for example, ethnic group representation was explicitly rejected in favour of institutions and policies that deliberately promote social integration across group lines. Election laws (in combination with the delimitation of provincial boundaries) have had the effect of encouraging political parties to put up candidate slates – if they want to maximize the votes they get – that reflect South Africa's highly diverse society. And the federal provinces were created so as not to overlap with ethnic group boundaries (South Africa's groups are more widely dispersed in any event). In Ben Reilly's chapter on 'Democratic Validation' in this volume, he outlines further how the key to such integrative approaches (or 'centripetalism', because it tries to engineer a centre-oriented spin to political dynamics) is the electoral system; its strongest possible effect is to engender the development of multiethnic political parties.

The integrative approach seeks to build multiethnic political coalitions (again, usually political parties), to create incentives for political leaders to be moderate

Table 12.2   Integrative power-sharing

Principles	Practices	Problems
Incentives for elite and mass moderation on divisive ethnic or racial themes	A president who stands for all groups and who emphasizes moderation and reconciliation (like a Mandela)	Leaders who can rise above the fray of inter-group enmity are hard to find; they cannot be simply invented
Intra-group contestation and inter-group moderation in electoral contests	The use of vote-pooling electoral systems, such as the single transferable vote or the alternative vote	People may be unwilling to vote for candidates who are not from their community
Minority influence, not just representation	Federalism is a way to give all minority groups access to power in various regions; the regions serve as a training ground for national-level moderates	Political leaders and key publics may not be willing to respond to the incentives for moderation, preferring that minority representation will remain token or symbolic

on divisive ethnic themes, and to enhance minority influence in majority decision-making.[19] The elements of an integrative approach include electoral systems that encourage pre-election pacts across ethnic lines, non-ethnic federalism that diffuses points of power, and public policies that promote political allegiances that transcend groups. Some suggest that integrative power-sharing is superior in theory, in that it seeks to foster ethnic accommodation by promoting cross-cutting interests. Others, however, argue that the use of incentives to promote conciliation will run aground when faced with deep-seated enmities that underlie ethnic disputes and that are hardened during the course of a brutal civil war. Table 12.2 summarizes this option and its related practices and problems.

The group building block and integrative approaches can be fruitfully viewed as opposite poles in a spectrum of power-sharing institutions and practices. Which approach is best? To make such a determination, it is useful to consider power-sharing practices in terms of three dimensions that apply to both approaches: territorial division of power, decision rules and public policies that define relations between the government and the ethnic groups.

Power-sharing practices: an overview

Consociational

1. Granting territorial autonomy to ethnic groups and creating confederal arrangements;
2. Adopting constitutional provisions that ensure a minimum level of group representation (quotas) at all levels of government;
3. Adopting group proportional representation in administrative appointments, including consensus-oriented decision rules in the executive;
4. Adopting a highly proportional electoral system in a parliamentary framework; and

5. Acknowledging group rights or corporate (non-territorial) federalism (e.g. own-language schools) in law and practice.

Integrative approach

1. Creating a mixed, or non-ethnic, federal structure, with boundaries drawn on other criteria such as natural features or economic development zones;
2. Establishing an inclusive, centralized unitary state without further subdividing territory;
3. Adopting winner-take-all but ethnically diverse executive, legislative and administrative decision-making bodies (e.g. a purposefully diverse language board to set policies on language use);
4. Adopting a semi-majoritarian or semi-proportional electoral system that encourages the formation of pre-election coalitions (vote pooling) across ethnic divides; and
5. Devising 'ethnicity-blind' public policies and laws to ensure non-discrimination on the basis of identity or religious affiliation.

Although this typology presents two conceptually distinct approaches, it is clear power-sharing options can be pieced together in a number of ways. Like any menu, levers of democratic influence can be combined to suit individual tastes. In deciding which power-sharing institutions and practices might work, there is no substitute for intimate knowledge of any given country. In multiethnic Fiji, for example, a four-year expert review of the country's political system produced a set of recommendations for a recently adopted constitution that combines measures to guarantee a minimum level of traditional Fijian (as opposed to Indo-Fijian) representation in Parliament (a group building-block option) with measures to promote the formation of political alliances across group lines (an integrative option). The Fiji experience points to how a well-conceived process, featuring a balanced panel of experts with firm political support, can arrive at creative solutions specifically tailored to a unique set of problems.[20] The Fiji case is instructive precisely because the efforts of spoilers (see the chapter on 'Violence' by Stephen Stedman in this volume) to disrupt integration along ethnic lines was only temporarily successful; as Fiji recovers from the attempted *coup d'état* of 2000, it has returned to an integrationist formula for resolving its ethnic tensions.

Conclusion: matching problems to solutions

The practical differences among various types of power-sharing systems, and their implications for managing conflict in divided societies, could easily be lost on even the most interested observer. Most complicated are the issues of electoral system choice and the implications of various alternatives for potentially lessening ethnic tensions and buttressing moderate forces against the cries of betrayal of ethnic solidarity inevitably mounted by ethnic hardliners.[21] But the differences are important, even pivotal, in determining whether some societies will progress beyond negotiated settlements to sustainable peace.

The underlying differences between the consociational and the integrative approaches to living together are essential for post-settlement peace. The differences revolve around these questions:

- What are the fundamental building blocks of the political system, homogeneous, powerful ethnic parties or fluid, issue-based political parties and movements that cross-cut ethnic divisions?
- In governance, how are coalitions formed? Are coalitions forged between or among ethnic parties after elections, or does multiethnic coalescence occur before elections in the creation of multiethnic political parties?
- Most important, is it possible to forge sustainable political institutions that induce moderation and empower tolerant political leaders, effectively penalizing ethnonationalist politicians by marginalizing them in the pursuit of political power?

In sum, consociational power-sharing solutions see ethnic groups as the building blocks of society; in integrative systems, ethnicity is recognized, but it is not the basis of post-war politics.

There is no way to say prima facie which type of power-sharing system – consociational or integrative – is inherently best. Moreover, it should be acknowledged that in the most desperate cases, partition should not be abandoned as a viable option to end the violence of an ethnic civil war (as in Sudan). The challenge to all observers of a particular conflict must be to match problems to solutions. What might be possible in South Africa as a settlement to that country's transition from apartheid to democracy (which did away with ethnic representation, state-sanctioned racial differentiation and ethnic title to territory), is not possible to transplant in a complex arena like Bosnia in which it has been virtually impossible to induce the parties to accept a more integrative approach.

In matching options to solutions, much depends on the level of enmity between the contending groups, the trajectory of the war (e.g. the extent of ethnic separation that occurred) and whether or not in their negotiations they can accept any degree of uncertainty or vulnerability to political loss. Critical to analysis of the problems is a coherent assessment of the role that ethnicity plays in the turn to violence and the salience of identity as a cause of conflict.[22] At some point, it becomes impossible to live together in broad, tolerant, multiethnic coalitions; in such cases, perhaps consociational democracy is the best alternative to violence. When consociationalism cannot work, autonomy might be a solution. When even autonomy is not possible, the time may be ripe to consider partition.

Ideally, power-sharing will work best when it can, over time, wither away. Whether in South Africa, Northern Ireland, Bosnia or Lebanon, in the immediate term formal power-sharing has been a necessary confidence-building device to ensure that all groups with the capacity to spoil a peace settlement should be included in the institutions and given influence in decision-making. Over time, however, post-war societies need to move beyond the mutual hostage taking that a guaranteed place at the decision-making table implies, the *immobilism* it inevitably creates, and the construction of post-war societies around the fixed and unyielding social boundaries of ethnicity. Integrative power-sharing solutions have an inherent advantage, if they can be achieved. Simply put, when successful, they engineer a moderation-seeking, centripetal spin to the political system, one that allows for ethnicity but promotes fluid coalitions that transcend the cleavages of conflict in war-torn societies.

One method for achieving a subtle but steady move towards a more integrative power-sharing goal is to keep the process of constitution-making going well into the post-war order. Peace agreements cannot freeze in time the conditions that pertain at the end of the war. Peace settlements need to resolve the war with certainty, but they also need to be imbued with a certain set of provisions for flexibility, continued bargaining and opportunity for amendment. They need an incentive structure that encourages ongoing bargaining, moderation and ethnic conflict management.[23] A practical way to begin is to purposefully manipulate the electoral system to provide new incentives to moderate and coalesce across group lines, as suggested above. Electoral systems should be designed to give politicians real incentives to motivate, moving beyond a perhaps natural instinct to play the communal card to attain power.[24] Yet a third is to engender cooperation by designing multiethnic territorial divisions of power within a country, eschewing practices of 'ethnic federalism'.

None of these methods will ensure success. Institutional choice and design, no matter how careful, cannot resolve some of the inherent commitment problems that occur in post-war societies; rules on paper cannot address the deep-seated fear that opponents will win in elections or in Parliament what they had not won on the battlefield or in the streets. But with a willingness to escape from violence, the right set of power-sharing institutions – one that carefully matches problems to solutions – can provide incentives to tip the balance from war to peace, from rigid ethnic bargaining to a more fluid democracy in which moderation trumps extremism.

Notes

1. P. Wallensteen & M. Sollenberg, 'Armed Conflict 1989–1998', *Journal of Peace Research*, 36, 5 (1999), 593–606. On the historical averages, see S. J. Stedman, *Peacemaking in Civil War: International Mediation in Zimbabwe, 1974–1980* (Boulder: Lynne Rienner, 1991) and B. Walter, 'The Critical Barrier to Civil War Settlement', *International Organization*, 51, 3 (Summer 1997), 335–64.
2. Military victories are arguably more unstable than negotiated settlements because they leave grievances among the vanquished unresolved, only to re-erupt at the first opportunity when strength has been regathered. For the argument that military victories are more durable than peace agreements, see R. Harrison Wagner, 'The Causes of Peace', in Roy Licklider (ed.), *Stopping the Killing: How Civil Wars End* (New York: New York University Press, 1993).
3. J. P. Lederach, *Building Peace: Sustainable Reconciliation in Divided Societies* (Washington, DC: United States Institute of Peace Press, 1997).
4. For an excellent summary of underlying causes of ethnic conflicts, see M. Brown (ed.), *Ethnic Security and International Security* (Princeton: Princeton University Press, 1993).
5. For example of the practical policy challenges, see 'Turning Strife to Advantage: a Blueprint to Integrate the Croats in Bosnia and Herzegovina', an International Crisis Group Report (15 March 2001), available at www. intl-crisis-group.org.

6. T. D. Sisk, *Power Sharing and International Mediation in Ethnic Conflicts* (Washington, DC: Carnegie Commission on Preventing Deadly Conflict and the United States Institute of Peace Press, 1996).

7. See S. Chesterman, T. Farer & T. Sisk, 'Competing Claims: Self-Determination and Security at the United Nations', an International Peace Academy Policy Brief, May 2001.

8. C. Kaufman, 'Possible and Impossible Solutions to Ethnic Civil Wars', *International Security*, 20, 4 (Spring 1996), 136–75 at 137.

9. For example, S. Burg, 'The International Community and the Yugoslav Crisis', in M. Esman & S. Telhami (eds), *International Organizations and Ethnic Conflict* (Ithaca, New York: Cornell University Press, 1995).

10. H. Waterman, *The Political Geography of Peace and Conflict* (New York: John Wiley, 1991), p. 292.

11. For further on this approach to analysing the origins of power-sharing agreements, see T. Sisk, *Democratization in South Africa: the Elusive Social Contract* (Princeton, NJ: Princeton University Press, 1995). For a more recent assessment that includes an emphasis on the importance of strategic interaction, see P. du Toit, *South Africa's Brittle Peace* (London: Palgrave – now Palgrave Macmillan, 2001).

12. See J. Darby & R. Mac Ginty, 'Northern Ireland: Long, Cold Peace', in J. Darby & R. Mac Ginty (eds), *The Management of Peace Processes* (London: Macmillan – now Palgrave Macmillan, 2000), especially pp. 78–9.

13. A. Lijphart, *Democracy in Plural Societies* (New Haven, Conn.: Yale University Press, 1977).

14. Sisk, *Power Sharing*.

15. For a more thorough overview of power-sharing options, see Sisk, *Power Sharing*, and P. Harris & B. Reilly (eds), *Democracy and Deep-Rooted Conflict: Options for Negotiators* (Stockholm: IDEA, 1998).

16. See also R. Lapidoth, *Autonomy: Flexible Solutions to Ethnic Conflicts* (Washington, DC: USIP Press, 1997) and H. Hannum, *Autonomy, Sovereignty, and Self-Determination: the Accommodation of Conflicting Rights* (Philadelphia: University of Pennsylvania Press, 1990).

17. J. Coakley (ed.), *The Territorial Management of Ethnic Conflict* (London: Frank Cass, 1993).

18. For a recent assessment of consociational power-sharing in Europe, see U. Schneckener, 'Making Power Sharing Work: Lessons from Successes and Failures in Ethnic Conflict Regulation', *Institut für Interkulturelle und Internationale Studien*, University of Bremen (Working Paper No. 19/2000).

19. D. Horowitz, *Ethnic Groups in Conflict* (Los Angeles and Berkeley: University of California Press, 1985).

20. See the report of the Constitutional Review Commission, *The Fiji Islands: toward a United Future* (Suva, 1996).

21. For details on the importance of electoral system choice for conflict management, see B. Reilly & A. Reynolds, 'Electoral Systems and Conflict in Divided Societies' (Washington, DC: National Academy Press, 1999) (Papers on International Conflict Resolution).

22. M. J. Esman, *Ethnic Politics* (Ithaca, NY: Cornell University Press, 1994).

23. D. Rothchild, *Managing Ethnic Conflict in Africa* (Washington: Brookings, 1997).

24. Human Rights Watch, *Playing the Communal Card: Communal Violence and Human Rights* (New York City: Human Rights Watch, 1995).

13
Peace Accords and Ethnic Conflicts: a Comparative Analysis of Content and Approaches

Fernand de Varennes

Introduction

Most peace accords fail. More precisely if less dramatically, of the hundreds of agreements, ceasefires and declarations which have been concluded between hostile parties since the Second World War, relatively few of them have led to durable settlements.[1] There are some notable successes: South Tyrol in Italy did succeed in completely avoiding an escalation of violence in the 1960s through an autonomy package, and Guatemala has succeeded in ending more recently a horrific period of widespread atrocities. Other conflicts such as those involving Palestinians and Israel, and the Muslim minority in the Philippines, have endured for decades, despite the myriad of agreements. Nevertheless, there does appear to be a definite, observable and positive trend worldwide, as pointed out in the 2001 report from the Center for International Development and Conflict Management.[2] The number of conflicts and their intensity have lessened in the last decade, usually as a result of agreements offering greater autonomy or some other form of power-sharing to minorities.

This chapter proposes to examine this trend by considering the content of various peace agreements and offer suggestions as to available options in constitutional designs during peace processes. The approach will be on 'substance' rather than process, an approach which is perhaps contrary to prevailing views but which may offer more specific recommendations as to why some accords are successful, and why many others are not.

It is also contended that the suggestions that 'ethnic differences often provoke violence' and that 'ethnonationalism' causes conflicts are unhelpful, since in the first case it is factually incorrect, and in the latter fails to identify the conditions under which the use of violence becomes a viable path to achieve political goals in preference to non-violent means.

Trends in peace agreements since 1946

Peace agreements concluded since the end of the Second World War have not changed fundamentally: as indicated earlier, the near-constant demand has been for autonomy. Early documents such as, for example, the 2 January 1946 Turkestan

Peace Agreement (China), the 28 June 1947 Naga-Akbar Hydari Accord (India) and the 1947 Panalong Agreement (Myanmar) all focus on autonomy guarantees, as they also do almost universally today. There are, however, a notable number of trends which appear to have been developing in the last decades.

Whether dealing with the 1991 Peace Accords (Angola), the Dayton General Framework Agreement for Peace in Bosnia and Hercegovina, the 1995 Israeli–Palestinian Interim Agreement on the West Bank and the Gaza Strip and many others, they show the following common features:

- increased reference to and inclusion of human rights standards, especially non-discrimination and respect for the rights of minorities and indigenous peoples;
- in the case of 'comprehensive' peace agreements, more recent texts are increasingly detailed as compared to earlier ones, sometimes even incorporating a precise timetable for compliance with commitments entered into under the agreement;
- increased similarity in format and wording, especially the adoption of international concepts such as self-determination, etc....

Whereas earlier documents tended to be more general and focused almost entirely on guarantees for autonomy, contemporary agreements seem to be converging in terms of substance and language. This phenomenon may in part be explained by the presence of international mediators and organizations which are often involved in the long negotiations preceding the conclusion of these agreements. The presence of UN, EU and OSCE officials, as well as from other organizations, means that officials who often have training in international law or conflict resolution, tend to provide a background under which the various provisions of agreements are ironed out.

Furthermore, there is undeniably the additional impact of the language of human rights. While human rights as an international concern after the Second World War was still in its infancy, in the space of 50 years it appears to have permeated societies in all parts of the world and become a reference point for groups such as minorities who feel that the state has been treating them unjustly. Unavoidably, human rights and self-determination have provided the tools to better express the nature of the claims of minorities, and what needed to be done to correct the failures and inadequacies of government policies as well as the structures of the state.

Finally, it seems certain that increased means to access these agreements, provided in part by the growing intervention of international actors, but also the greater ease in obtaining and building upon past accomplishments with the circulation of people and information, has meant that parties whether in Mindanao in the Philippines or in Arusha, Tanzania, can easily 'borrow' from useful models worldwide.

The above gives some indication of a few observable trends from a perusal of peace agreements from 1946, but it does nothing to explain why conflicts occur and why they can be so difficult to control.

Why minorities kill

Most conflicts are no longer international. It is clear that the vast majority of armed conflicts, which have plagued the world in the last two decades, are within states rather than between states. While a number of these internal conflicts involve revolutionary groups attempting to overthrow the central government (Tajikistan; Congo-Kinshasa; Angola), most are ethnonationalist in the sense that there is a minority group fighting for independence or autonomy. In a number of cases, minorities (Mohajirs of Pakistan; Dayaks of Indonesia; Albanians in Macedonia) assert they are struggling for their rights in a country where they are the victims of active discrimination by the government in areas such as employment, land use and property rights or language use.

It must be pointed out that conflicts do not go hand in hand with the presence of minorities, or to use the same language as earlier, ethnic differences do not, per se, cause conflicts. Any systematic examination of the linkage between the presence of minorities and conflicts in Asia, Europe, Africa or the Americas makes it clear that there is no such linkage. What stands out in every continent is that despite the thousands of various 'minority combinations' worldwide, there are currently relatively so few conflicts. Many ethnic conflicts have in fact ended, or at least been 'suspended' through peace agreements with independence/autonomy being achieved (Azerbaijan/Nagorno-Karabakh, Bangladesh/the Chittagong hill tribes, Bosnia, Georgia/Abkhasia, Moldova/Transdniestr, Papua New Guinea/Bougainville, Yugoslavia/Kosovo, etc.). There are only just over 40 active conflicts of varying intensity involving minorities worldwide, a miniscule number compared to the thousands upon thousands of minority groups.[3]

As the next sections will indicate, a dissection of various peace accords from around the world shows a fairly consistent pattern in terms of fundamental demands which are indicative of the underlying causes of tension and the structures and approaches that are most likely to be successful. This is critical to reaching a durable settlement, since no long-term solution will be found unless one addresses the underlying source(s) of a conflict.

From examining more than 200 peace accords concluded since the end of the Second World War, one finds once again a great deal of consistency. The accords that go beyond negotiating processes and immediate cessation of hostilities almost always tend to include one or more of the following, in order of prominence:

- independence/autonomy/power-sharing
- human rights guarantees
- 'fair' distribution of resources/employment

One could conclude of course that it is self-evident that any struggle for political power would include some kind of power-sharing formula. However, that ignores a more subtle signal that the almost universal prominence of autonomy and power-sharing demands by minorities indicates: the belief among some segments of the minority population that the state itself does not represent their interests properly, and therefore the minority must control its 'own affairs' via a devolved or autonomous political structure within the state – or outside of it in the case of independence movements.[4] In other words, it is a loss of trust in the ability of the state to accommodate their interests which often drives minorities into the path of violence.

Failure of inclusive governance

In most states, governments are seldom completely neutral in ethnic terms.[5] In the distribution of power within their structures, states almost inevitably reflect the dominant groups within society.[6] France is not an ethnically neutral state, since the French language and culture are very much part of its 'national personality', and in fact reflect the cultural attributes of the majority, but not the totality, of the French population. France is still the scene of armed groups (Corsicans and very sporadically Breton hardliners) using violence to uphold demands dealing with minority rights.

Even in countries like the United States with 'civic' forms of nationalism, the argument that all minorities, especially racial and linguistic ones, have been or still are treated neutrally is historically impossible to sustain. On the contrary, the United States had a number of extremely violent ethnic conflicts involving its traditional minorities on its territory during the nineteenth century. These armed insurrections only came to an end when the various indigenous peoples were either exterminated or accepted a modicum of autonomy when they were no longer in a position to offer any resistance to the overwhelming power and numbers of the 'European Americans', much in the same way as Aboriginal peoples in Australia were first conquered, then subdued and eventually almost annihilated as distinct communities.

The context most if not all states have in common where a conflict has erupted is that numerically large and concentrated minorities are systematically underrepresented or outvoted and discriminated against. This might not have very serious consequences if the fiction of a neutral or ethnically, religiously or linguistically blind modern state were true, and all citizens were to be treated equally without any disadvantages because of these personal characteristics. This is, however, clearly not the case: states usually tend to reflect and protect to a greater extent the interests of the majority, including in some cases demonstrating definite cultural, linguistic or religious preferences. Persons who belong to minorities therefore find themselves in a double dilemma: they have interests in a number of areas that may be different from those of the majority, while in the electoral process and the political sphere, persons who belong to minorities tend to be outvoted and under-represented. This means on the one hand that they are unable to exercise a great deal of political leverage in the political system, while on the other hand they have different interests which they need to assert against the politically dominant majority. Minorities tend therefore to suffer disproportionately from a 'deficit' in terms of numbers and influence in many if not most political systems, democratic or not.

A number of peace agreements actually refer to some of the reasons why an ethnic minority has engaged on the path of violence.[7] Among the most often repeated deep-laid sources of tension which have fuelled violence are the following:

- Exclusion from employment opportunities because of language requirements or subtle 'ethnic' preferences, both in the civil service or in private activities (discrimination);
- Actual exclusion of members of a substantial minority from most state employment positions, especially in the higher echelons (discrimination);

N3!

- Denial of landownership, or refusal to recognize traditional landownership;
- Refusal to allow minorities to hold elected office because of language or other discriminatory criteria;
- Economic development projects in minority regions which benefit the majority instead of the minority (discrimination);
- Expropriation of traditional lands without proper compensation, and/or a transmigration programme which results in the arrival of vast numbers of migrants (discrimination);
- Refusal to use minority language in public schools and administration where warranted by substantial number of speakers of a minority language;
- Denial of citizenship and corresponding rights on a discriminatory basis;
- Prohibition of use of minority languages, symbols or of minority religious practices in private activities.

What minorities want

From the above, it is not difficult to see that it is not 'nationalism' as such which is the root source of most violent ethnic conflicts, but rather in most cases the discriminatory distribution of power and resources and other violations of the rights of minorities which have in the end led to violent conflict. The 'subtext' one can detect from many peace agreements is that in almost all conflicts ethnic groups do not actually demand more democracy, or more economic development; more subtly, their demand is for more effective political participation, and a fairer share and distribution of education, employment opportunities and resources. It seems that in almost all situations of conflict, ethnic minorities operate on the belief that only with independence or autonomy will they be guaranteed more effective political representation and control and a fair share of the benefits and resources of the state.

The almost universal prominence of power-sharing arrangements in peace accords suggests that minorities usually revert to violence in frustration at not being able to change their government's policies because they are outnumbered and outvoted. They usually react to defend their interests in a legal and political environment that they believe they cannot control nor even simply influence significantly.

Autonomy and power-sharing as part of the solution to an ethnic conflict suggest that these minorities no longer trust the 'national' government. They do not trust the government because the ethnic majority dominates it. And the ethnic majority's domination and ethnic preferences in countries raked by conflicts can usually be linked to a series of violations of the rights of minorities in areas of language, religion or culture, and especially discrimination in terms of employment and land rights.

Design for divided societies – what works

So what does a perusal of peace accords from around the world tell us about the types of structures or constitutional arrangements which work? The answer in part depends on what one judges as a success: is it merely the (more or less complete) cessation of widespread hostilities (Northern Ireland; Bosnia) which offers no

anvard/ comprehensive mediation of issues

guarantee of long-term settlement, or is it a more comprehensive arrangement which clearly seems to have brought permanent peace? In this chapter I will adopt the latter criterion in trying to define successful approaches and models. However, this is not to say that de-escalation of armed conflicts is not in itself an important objective. Indeed, it may often be a necessary prerequisite before a 'final solution' can seriously be embarked upon.

The structure of the state is usually the main demand that needs to be addressed. Countries where ethnic conflicts have been solved or have de-escalated greatly in the last 50 years are almost always those where autonomy or power-sharing has been implemented. In this category one could include, tentatively in some cases, Finland (Åland Islands), Nicaragua (Miskitos), France (New Caledonia), Italy (South Tyrol), India (Mizos), Niger (Tuaregs), Bangladesh (Chittagong hill tribes), Papua New Guinea (Bougainville), Solomon Islands (Guadanalcanese), United Kingdom (Northern Ireland). Some conflicts ended by outright independence, as with Bangladesh (1971), Slovenia (1991), Croatia (1991), Eritrea (1993) and East Timor (2000). In still others, de facto autonomy verging on independence has ended the conflict, as in Abkhasia, Nagorno-Karabakh and Transdniestr.

The clear, even undisputable, conclusion, contained in the 2001 *Global Survey of Armed Conflicts, Self-Determination Movements, and Democracy*, is that:

> ...the most common outcome of self-determination conflicts is a settlement between governments and group representatives that acknowledges collective rights and gives them institutional means for pursuing collective interests within states. Sometimes a group gains better access to decision-making in the central government, often it gains regional autonomy, and of course some settlements include both kinds of reforms. Thus the outcome of self-determination movements seldom is a redrawing of international boundaries, but rather devolution of central power and redrawing of boundaries within existing states.
>
> ...The greatest risk in autonomy agreements is not the eventual breakup of the state, rather it is that spoilers may block full implementation, thereby dragging out the conflict and wasting resources that might otherwise be used to strengthen autonomous institutions.[8]

Not all peace accords providing for autonomy succeed by any stretch of the imagination. Whether involving the Moros in the Philippines, the Catholics in Northern Ireland, Palestinians in the Occupied Territories or Southerners in Sudan, most peace accords do not result in a complete cessation of hostilities. There is one main and rather obvious reason for these failures: the peace accords are never fully implemented.

It is not possible in this brief chapter to examine case by case why there was a failure of implementation, or whether the fault for this lies with the failure in the negotiating process or a multitude of other factors.[9] Some scholars claim that ethnic leaders and rebels in protracted conflicts may have more to lose than to gain if peace is reached in terms of material benefits.[10]

However, and again perhaps contrary to prevailing orthodoxy, my examination of unsuccessful agreements tends to show a different picture: it is actually the central government which has 'more to lose' and often reneges on, or is unable to implement, concessions agreed to. The Addis Ababa Agreement of 1972 contained autonomy arrangements that led to a period of peace in southern Sudan. It was in 1983 after the government abrogated this agreement that the conflict reignited. The Punjab Accord of 1985 failed because the Indian government was unable to make the promised reforms due to obstruction from provincial authorities. Indeed, since most conflicts have ended with some form of devolution of power, and autonomy appears rather conclusively to be the most effective way of settling a dispute while maintaining the territorial integrity of the state, it is the central government that must adopt legislation and perhaps even modify constitutional provisions in order to make this possible.

Successful peace agreements are not those that have simply agreed to a cessation of hostilities: they tend to be those that address the root causes of the conflict and try to redress these, partly through autonomy arrangements and/or rights that protect the minority and responds to its demands. Thus governments that fail to deliver on the commitments made in peace accords as shown above almost inevitably invite a resumption of the conflict at some later point in time.

This is not an assertion that the state as opposed to ethnic rebel groups is more 'blamable' for the failure of peace accords. But because the ultimate concession must be made by government in 'giving up' some degree of political power and changing the structure of the state, government leaders sometimes face seemingly insurmountable institutional difficulties in terms of modifying their Constitution (which may be extremely difficult or almost impossible), ensuring enough support in their own central Parliament or provincial legislature to pass the necessary changes, or even ensuring their own political survival against accusations of weakness or 'giving in to terrorists'. In most if not all parts of the world, concessions to minority groups are seldom popular, and especially not once the cycle of violence has started in earnest.

The difficulties that face most governments in changing the state's political structure and even culture are indeed formidable, and perhaps tend to be ignored in much of the literature dealing with ethnic conflicts which more often than not view such conflicts as involving a 'minority problem'. In fact the root causes of most conflicts and the reason autonomy and power-sharing are seen as the ultimate solution, come from the central state's preferences and use of power which are seen as discriminatory and exclusionary.

Among other constitutional choices that successful peace accords suggest is that a system of proportional representation in terms of government ministries and public service positions and legislative veto in certain areas may be the best route in the case of non-territorial or more dispersed minorities (Northern Ireland).

Successful agreements involving indigenous peoples (Miskitos in Nicaragua, Kanaks in New Caledonia) usually provide, in addition to territorial autonomy, greater legal recognition and enforcement of their traditional or customary laws.

Finally, because absence of 'proportionate' access to the state's largesse figures prominently in most claims of discriminatory treatment by minorities, many agreements contain provisions which refer, in addition to the need for a devolution of power (autonomy), to increased representation in employment sectors controlled by government (civil service, army, police) as well as means to control the influx of 'outsiders' into the traditional territory of the ethnic minority.

The chimera of greater democracy and economic development

Before ending this chapter, there is another conclusion on constitutional design that can be drawn from studying various peace agreements. Contrary to prevailing views, the absence of 'good governance' and democratic traditions, or lack of economic development, do not in themselves breed ethnic conflicts. Almost no peace accord contains stand-alone provisions for increased economic development or democratic practices, or even prioritizes these, over some form of autonomy.

The above observation is probably controversial, and yet that is an obvious conclusion looking at the actual text of peace accords. Pure, unadulterated democracy of one person, one vote, hardly helps minorities ensure they are not simply outvoted by the ethnic majority controlling the state apparatus. Quite the contrary, autonomy of a territorial basis as is contained in most successful agreements, as well as some kind of legislative veto for non-territorial minorities, ensures that ethnic groups are protected from the excesses of democracy qua majoritarian rule. It is for this reason also that many peace accords refer to the need for stronger legislative and constitutional guarantees for the protection of the human rights of minorities, including such a fundamental right as non-discrimination (Albanians in Macedonia, indigenous peoples in Mexico, Guatemala, etc.).

Since the underlying roots of many, if not most, internal conflicts appear to be based on claims of discrimination and exclusion of minorities, it explains the quasi-universal prominence of structural measures in the form of an autonomous, usually territorial, political unit, as well as demands for constitutional provisions which offer to the minorities stronger guarantees for the protection of their rights. Thus, the 'distrust' that these ethnic minorities have towards central authorities is reflected in the demands for:

- constitutional guarantees that autonomy arrangements cannot be weakened easily by central government;
- constitutional guarantees in terms of a share of resources and taxation bases for the autonomous unit, whether it is a canton, province, region, etc.;
- constitutional guarantees that enshrine and strengthen the legal provisions dealing with human and minority rights and ensure access to independent judicial authorities;
- constitutional provisions, laws and other mechanisms to address the under-representation of ethnic minorities in civil service employment and political institutions.

As for economic development, most agreements will link it with measures involving autonomy or non-discrimination, in the sense that what is sought is control of economic development by ethnic groups via devolved competence to a regional or provincial authority or a fair proportion of the benefits of economic development, rather than economic initiatives from the central government with no guarantees as to who benefits from these.

Far from being caused by poverty, conflicts involving minorities resorting to armed opposition against central authorities may often find fuel in the perceived unfairness from economic development which is seen to benefit central government and members of the majority rather than the minority (Acehnese, Papuans and Dayaks in Indonesia; Chittagong hill tribes in Bangladesh; Tibetans and Uighurs in China; Ijaw in Nigeria, etc.). To put it more bluntly, it is hard to see why Tibetans should rejoice at the prospect of economic development projects, sometimes supported by the World Bank and other international institutions, which promise to bring into their region tens, perhaps hundreds, of thousands of Han Chinese who end up occupying most of the best employment positions, while Tibetans themselves tend largely to be bypassed.

Economic development without autonomy and without strong legal and constitutional guarantees of the rights of minorities has predictably been an ongoing contributing source of tension in many of the conflicts surveyed in this chapter. More often than not, economic development with no consideration of the impact on minorities has been part of the problem, rather than a solution.

Conclusion

Peace accords that have been successful in ending or at least suspending ethnic conflicts almost always involve devolution of political power and changes to the structure of the state through some kind of autonomy arrangement or power-sharing with an ethnic minority. It is only when the central government, normally controlled by a majority ethnic/cultural group, is willing to share with a minority its hold on the constitutional, legal and institutional levers of the state that some kind of successful modus vivendi is reached. Conversely, most unsuccessful models are those where the agreements are never fully implemented or fail to address the fundamental sources of tension which eventually give rise to most ethnic conflicts. More often than not, it is the government in power, and the governing group at its helm, which balks at being perceived as weak or making too many concessions to the demands of minorities.

Since the underlying roots of many, if not most, internal conflicts appear to be based on claims of discrimination and exclusion of minorities, it appears that the most successful attempts at solving these conflicts rely, in addition to structural guarantees in the form of an autonomous, usually territorial political unit, on demands for constitutional provisions which offer to the minorities stronger guarantees for the protection of their rights.

The often asserted claims that democracy and economic development are the answer to solving all of the world's conflicts appear to find little actual support in most peace agreements. Majoritarian democracy is not seen as a solution in any country where minorities are outnumbered and outvoted in conventional politics. This explains why almost all successful peace agreements offer autonomy where a territorial ethnic minority can control its own affairs.

Economic development by itself does not figure prominently in peace accords, probably because economic development without autonomy in many countries is seen as part of the problem rather than a solution. It has in many cases tended to benefit central government and members of the majority, and has thus exacerbated tension and contributed to a growing sense of alienation and anger rather than contributed to peace.

Notes

1. There has never been an attempt to count all peace agreements in ethnic or internal conflicts. In my own work I have collated over almost 300 documents, though this is by no means complete. These will appear in a series of books, the first one entitled 'Conflicts and Minorities in Asia', to be published by Kluwer Law International. The largest Internet source for some of these documents can be found at the site of INCORE (Initiative on Conflict Resolution) at http://www.incore.ulst.ac.uk/cds/agreements. A smaller number can be found at the US Institute of Peace's website at http://www.usip.org/library/pa.html.
2. T. R. Gurr, M. G. Marshall & D. Khosla, *Peace and Conflict 2001: a Global Survey of Armed Conflicts, Self-Determination Movements, and Democracy* (Integrated Network for Societal Conflict Research (INSCR) Program, Center for International Development and Conflict Management, University of Maryland, 2001).
3. The number would of course be much higher if one were to include those conflicts that are simply 'on hold', where a final status determination has not yet been made such as in the case of Abkhasia, Nagorno-Karabakh, Chiapas, Northern Ireland, etc. Current ethnic conflicts include: Rwanda (Hutus), Chad (Toubou), Comoros (Anjouan), Liberia (Krahn), Senegal (Casamançais), Sierra Leone (Mandingo), Uganda (Langi), Uganda (Acholi), Spain (Basques), France (Corsicans), Russia (Chechens), Macedonia (Albanians), Laos (Hmongs), Myanmar (Karens), Myanmar (Karenni), Myanmar (Shan), India (scheduled tribes), Indonesia (Papuans), Indonesia (Acehnese), India (Tripuras), Philippines (Moros), Sri Lanka (Tamils), Afghanistan (Tajiks), Myanmar (Chin/Zomis), India (Kashmiri Muslims), India (Bodos), India (Assamese), China (Uighurs), Thailand (southern Muslims), Afghanistan (Uzbeks), Israel/Occupied Territories (Palestinians), Turkey (Kurds), Ethiopia (Somalis), Ethiopia (Oromos), Sudan (Southerners), Sudan (Nubans), Angola (Cabindans), Nigeria (Ijaw), Solomon Islands (Guadanalcanese), Indonesia (Dayaks), Indonesia (Ambon Muslims/Christians), Yugoslavia (Albanians).
4. There are numerous publications dealing with these issues, including for example Y. Ghai (ed.), *Autonomy and Ethnicity: Negotiating Claims in Multi-ethnic States* (Cambridge: Cambridge University Press, 2000) and H. Hannum, *Autonomy, Sovereignty and Self-determination: the Accommodation of Conflicting Rights* (Philadelphia: University of Philadelphia Press, 1990).
5. On this issue see Y. Tamir, *Liberal Nationalism* (Princeton: Princeton University Press, 1995).
6. F. de Varennes, 'Minority Rights and the Prevention of Ethnic Conflicts', Working Paper, UN Working Group on the Rights of Minorities, E/CN.4/Sub.2/AC.5/2000/CRP.3 (Geneva, 2000).
7. See, for example, the agreements with the Kanaks of New Caledonia, the indigenous peoples of Chiapas.
8. Gurr et al., op. cit.
9. The often repeated view that some conflicts are simply intractable is unhelpful. Most of the accords examined in the research for this chapter in fact did not operate on such a basis and offered instead means to achieve some kind of modus vivendi. Rather than being intractable, it seems that in most cases both sides acknowledge that there are means of attaining a cessation of hostilities, though later on one side of the conflict refuses or for some other reason cannot actually implement concessions initially promised in a peace agreement.
10. J. M. Richardson Jr. & S. W. R. de Samarasinghe, 'Costs and Benefits of Violent Political Conflict: the Case of Sri Lanka', *World Development*, 21 (1995).

14
Human Rights and Minority Protection

Christine Bell

Human rights instruments seem to contemplate a relationship between justice and peace. The UN Charter itself opens with the objective of avoiding war and immediately references the concept of human rights. The Universal Declaration on HR makes a 'just peace' thesis more explicit. It claims that 'it is essential, if man is not to be compelled to have resources, as a last resort, to rebellion against tyranny and oppression, that human rights should be protected by the rule of law'.[1] More recently the Council of Europe's Framework Convention notes that 'the upheavals of European history have shown that the protection of national minorities is essential to stability, democratic security and peace in this continent'.[2]

While a connection between human rights and peace may seem obvious and is acknowledged in human rights instruments, in practice the precise nature of the connection is problematic and controversial. During conflicts, the linking of human rights protection to peacemaking is often challenged as partisan and/or idealistic. The view that international human rights law provides unnegotiable minimum standards is often presented as in tension with the need for a pragmatic peace involving compromise, including compromise on human rights. In 1996 an anonymous contribution to the *HR Quarterly* provided a stark example of this argument.[3] In it the writer castigated the human rights community for prolonging the war in former Yugoslavia by insisting that any settlement included requirements of justice. By judging every peace blueprint in terms of whether it rewarded aggression and ethnic cleansing, human rights 'pundits' and negotiators were accused of rejecting pragmatic deals which, with hindsight, were as good as or better than the eventual settlement. The anonymous writer argued that as a result 'thousands of people are dead who should have been alive – because moralists were in quest of the perfect peace'.[4]

The 1990s have been the decade of the peace agreement. A review indicates that peace agreements have been signed in over 60 situations, each typically having many agreements, making over 300 peace agreements of one description or another.[5] Most of these agreements took place in conflicts that, while having international dimensions, were not inter-state conflicts as traditionally defined but conflicts originating within existing state borders. These conflicts were twofold in nature: those involving a transition from an authoritarian regime to a democratic one, and conflicts involving self-determination challenges to the state by ethnic or indigenous groups, although some conflicts, such as in Guatemala, contained both these dynamics. Central to many of the resulting peace agreements is the language of human rights, suggesting that there is indeed some connection between human rights and peacebuilding. The agreements of Central America and South Africa, for example, provided for a transition to democracy. They were characterized by a constitutionalism designed to define, protect and enforce rights, and to replace the arbitrary use of power with its legal regulation through checks and balances. In conflicts involving a self-determination claim by ethnonational groups, as in Northern Ireland or Bosnia-Hercegovina, peace agreements also typically attempted to redefine the access of the groups to power and to state institutions. This was then coupled with the enforced protection of individual rights, aimed at creating a working polity out of a divided society, and at reassuring all citizens that they would not be penalized on the basis of their ethnicity.

A review of peace agreements indicates that the typical peace blueprint in both situations involves three elements. First, a central deal on democratic access to power. This can be a fairly straightforward transfer of power, as in South Africa, or also include provisions to ensure the effective participation of minorities, who in divided societies are often locked permanently out of power by majoritarian frameworks. Such measures can include consociational political arrangements or autonomous areas where minority groups enjoy a degree of self-government. Second, peace agreements typically include human rights institutions with measures such as bills of rights, constitutional courts, human rights commissions or other national institutions for protecting rights, and rights-based reform of policing and criminal justice. These aim to ensure the protection of rights and prevention of past human rights abuses in the future. Third, peace agreements often include some mechanisms to address past human rights violations, from prisoner release provisions, to provisions aimed at enabling refugees to return, through to truth and reconciliation commissions which aim to account for the worst abuses in the conflict.

This would suggest that negotiators in practice do find a connection between peace agreements or human rights, and that the normative claims of human rights law are not at odds with pragmatic approaches to resolving conflict. This chapter examines the types of human rights provisions that typically are found in peace agreements, and their relationship to negotiated political institutions. The chapter examines the combination of principle and pragmatism that puts human rights provisions in peace agreements.

Peace agreements: what are they?

It is useful to consider first of all, what constitutes a 'peace agreement', for the term is loosely used across a variety of different processes to describe quite different documents used at different stages of a peace process. I have suggested in an earlier work that peace agreements can usefully be thought of as in three categories, which correlate with three different stages of any process.[6]

Pre-negotiation agreements

The pre-negotiation stage of a peace process typically revolves around who is going to negotiate and with what status.[7] For face-to-face or proximity negotiations to take place each party must be assured that their attempts to engage in dialogue will not be used by the other side to gain military advantage. In order to get everyone to the negotiating table, agreement needs to be reached on matters such as: the return of negotiators from exile, or their release from prison; safeguards as to future physical integrity and freedom from imprisonment; and limits on how the war is to be waged while negotiations take place. Pre-negotiation peace agreements therefore typically include mechanisms such as: amnesties for negotiators; temporary ceasefire agreements; human rights protections; and monitoring of violations both of ceasefires and human rights. Pre-negotiation agreements also typically begin to set the agenda for talks as the parties begin to bargain, and sound out each other's positions on substantive issues. Often this takes the form of attempts to set preconditions on the negotiating agenda. Such agreements often do not include all the parties to the conflict, but are bilateral agreements between several parties; they are often not published but remain secret until a later date. Examples of pre-negotiation agreements from the South African process include: The Groote Schuur Minute, 4 May 1990, between the then South African Government (SAG) and the African National Congress (ANC), the Pretoria Minute, 6 August 1990, between the SAG and the ANC, The Royal Hotel Minute, 29 January 1991 between the ANC and the Inkatha Freedom Party (IFP), the DF Malan Accord, 12 February 1991 between the ANC and the SAG, and the National Peace Accord, 14 September 1991 between a broad range of political parties including the ANC, SAG and IFP, and civic society groups.

Where international mediation takes place while conflict is ongoing, the pre-negotiation agreements can be understood as including the various blueprints and attempts to structure ceasefires which precede any agreement eventually assented to by all the relevant parties. This trial and error settlement process takes place simultaneously with the war in which the parties continue to strive for military victory. Ongoing attempts to find possible frameworks for a settlement are engaged in by all parties in the shadow of their prospects for military victory. Examples of such agreements include the peace blueprints brokered by the international community, which were put on the table during the conflict in former Yugoslavia between 1992 and 1995.[8]

Framework/substantive agreements

The second type of peace agreement can be termed 'framework or substantive' agreements. These agreements tend to be more inclusive of the main groups involved in waging the war by military means, and usually are public. Their emergence is often marked by a 'handshake moment', signifying a 'historical compromise' between enemies. Those who stay outside the process are often those who choose to do so, so as to 'outbid' those within the process, such as the Democratic Unionist Party in Northern Ireland.

Framework/substantive agreements begin to set out a framework for resolving the substantive issues of the dispute. The agreement usually: reaffirms a commitment to non-violent means for resolving the conflict; acknowledges the status of the parties in the negotiations; begins to address some of the consequences of the conflict (such as prisoners, emergency legislation and ongoing human rights violations); provides for interim arrangements as to how power is to be held and exercised; and sets an agenda, and possibly a timetable, for reaching a more permanent resolution of substantive issues such as self-determination, democratization, armed forces/policing, rights protection and reconstruction. Examples of framework agreements include the Belfast Agreement in Northern Ireland,[9] the Dayton Peace Agreement in Bosnia-Hercegovina,[10] the Interim Constitution in South Africa,[11] and possibly the Declaration of Principles and some of the following Interim Agreements in the Middle East,[12] although these increasingly are moving towards breakdown and possible renegotiation, and in the future may even be regarded as pre-negotiation agreements akin to the failed constitutional frameworks attempted during the war in former Yugoslavia.

Implementation agreements

The final category of peace agreements is implementation agreements. These begin to take forward and develop aspects of the framework, fleshing out their detail. The Israel/Palestinian Interim Agreement (Oslo II) filled out and partially implemented the framework in Oslo I; the South African Final Constitution[13] filled out and implemented the Interim Constitution. By their nature implementation agreements involve new negotiations and in practice often see a measure of renegotiation as parties test whether they can claw back concessions made at an earlier stage. Implementation agreements typically include all of the parties to the framework agreement. Sometimes implementation agreements are not documented, and sometimes agreement takes other forms, such as agreed legislation.

Agreements do not, of course, fit neatly into the above classification; however, it does provide a basis for loosely identifying appropriate comparators across complex documentary trails of peace agreements, enabling comparison of the types of human rights provision they contain.

Human rights: what are they?

Just as the term 'peace agreements' is difficult to define, so the question of what are 'human rights' can be a fraught one. For the purposes of this chapter 'human rights' will be identified using the customary law, and international instruments relating to first-, second- and third-generation rights. However, it should be pointed out that some difficulty arises from the fact that international instruments clearly identify the right to self-determination as a 'human right'. This opens up a relationship between human rights as conventionally understood as individual rights, and human rights as including broader political arrangements aimed at group accommodation.

Human rights in peace agreements

When the texts of peace agreements are examined, a different role for human rights in each stage of agreement can be observed, leading to different types of human rights provision.

Pre-negotiation

As political scientists have pointed out, ethnic conflict is often characterized by 'multiple disagreements over what kind of conflict it is, and about whether it is "one" or "many"'.[14] That is, there is a 'meta-conflict' or 'conflict about what the conflict is about'. The different positions as to what the conflict is 'about' lead to different prescriptions for its resolution. If the conflict is about lack of democracy for example, that leads to one set of solutions; if it is about inter-group ethnic hatred, then that leads to others.[15] Any attempt to resolve the conflict on the basis of negotiations (rather than victory) must involve an attempt to 'meta-bargain', that is bargain over the nature of the conflict. Resulting agreements will often contain the seeds of such a meta-bargain, although it is usually not made explicit.

In pre-negotiation agreements human rights provisions usually enter as a result of principled demands based on the experience of past human rights abuses. The pressure for a human rights component within a peace agreement usually comes from one side's analysis of the causes of the conflict. Human rights therefore require to be addressed in any attempt to resolve the conflict. Given that many conflicts are asymmetrical, the demand for human rights protections is usually initiated by the weaker party, such as Irish nationalists, Palestinians or Bosniacs, which sees human rights as addressing a status quo against which they are battling.

However, because human rights issues often go to the substance of a conflict, addressing them substantively is usually not possible at a pre-negotiation stage. The human rights issues which come to be addressed tend to be confined to discrete issues which impinge on the negotiating context itself, such as measures to limit the waging of violent conflict (see Box 14.1). Any further agreement requires a package of issues to be addressed, and some agreement on what human rights are, and on what the conflict was about, and this is not possible at the pre-negotiation stage.

Substantive/framework

Unlike the pre-negotiation agreement, human rights rhetoric only takes hold in a framework agreement if it serves the interests of all sides for it to do so (see Box 14.2). Inclusion largely depends on some type of meta-bargain having been reached. While human rights arguments may initially emanate from the less

Box 14.1 Typical pre-negotiation agreement provisions relating to human rights

> Provisions to limit the conflict:
> - ceasefires
> - scaling back emergency legislation
> - compliance with humanitarian and human rights standards
> - monitoring of compliance
>
> Humanitarian relief to victims of conflict
>
> Ad hoc addressing of the past:
> - partial prisoner release
> - partial amnesties
> - independent commissions to investigate alleged abuses
> - return of bodies of disappeared

Box 14.2 Typical framework agreement provisions relating to human rights

---

Arrangements for access to power and territory

Provision of a human rights agenda:
- bill of rights
- human rights commission
- other commissions
- reform of policing
- reform of criminal justice
- reform of judiciary

Provision of an agenda for undoing the past:
- return of refugees
- return of land

Ad hoc measures addressed at the past:
- amnesties
- prisoner release
- measures for reconciliation
- measures addressed at helping 'victims'
- embryonic and partial truth processes

Provision for civic society to become involved in implementation

---

powerful, the generality, abstract impartiality and international basis of human rights standards mean that, as the process progresses, both sides may turn to the language of human rights to assert their claims. At the framework or substantive agreement stage an arrangement regarding access to government and territory aims to address the self-determination issues at the heart of the deal. At this point the language of human rights can provide a vital negotiating tool by helping to carve out win–win solutions from zero-sum demands. Individualized human rights protections can address fears of annihilation, domination and discrimination that motivate claims to territory and statehood, potentially diluting such claims. Institutions for protecting human rights can soften a power allocation at the centre of the deal by providing protections or safeguards against its abuses. Human rights frameworks at this stage therefore emerge not as 'add-ons' or 'sweeteners' to the political arrangements (although some parties to the agreement might view them as such), but as an integral part of how power is to be exercised and controlled. Interestingly, this link between political power and human rights is underwritten by current directions in international self-determination law, which is moving away from an emphasis on unresolvable questions of who are the peoples, and what is the territory. Instead focus is shifting to consideration of what peoples substantively get in terms of access to the power, equality and resources they need to exercise free choice over their future.[16]

The interrelationship of human rights institutions and political institutions can be illustrated by the cases of South Africa, Northern Ireland, Bosnia-Hercegovina and Israel/Palestine. In South Africa the deal most obviously provided for one person one vote and democratic constitutionalism. While consociational mechanisms with power-sharing provided a measure of group protection for the whites who were relinquishing power, these were all limited to five years, after which time straightforward majoritarian democracy was contemplated. In this democracy it was clear that the main mechanism to ensure protection for whites would be, not consociational tools of vetoes and balancing, but human rights protections. So, for example, a Bill of Rights took on increasing importance for the white minority as it became clear that the deal was moving towards majority rule without minority vetoes. For the African National Congress (ANC) human rights protections were also important as signalling a new regime which unlike its predecessor would be democratically legitimate and respectful of human rights. This is not to say that there was consensus on what should be in the Bill of Rights. While the generality of many core rights was accepted by both the ANC and the South African Government/National Party (SAG/NP) as necessary, the meta-conflict re-emerged with regards to whether certain rights, such as a right to property, should be protected and if so what the content of that right should be. However, the mutual self-interest in ensuring protection of human rights meant that agreement was reached in the Interim Constitution on a Bill of Rights with supremacy over other laws; a new Constitutional Court with new selection procedures to ensure independence of the judiciary; and a number of national human rights institutions – a public protector office, a Commission on Gender Equality and a Human Rights Commission. The Constitution also addressed criminal justice (through the Bill of Rights) and the restructuring and accountability of police and defence forces.

In Northern Ireland, the deal was classically consociational with an additional 'cross-border' element. This meant that future political institutions were to be shared between Irish nationalists and British unionists. As the deal moved towards this arrangement, human rights began to take a central place. What became known as 'the equality agenda' came to form an area of common ground between Sinn Fein and the various fringe loyalist parties, especially the Progressive Unionist Party (PUP) who particularly emphasized social inclusion. This was supported by pluralist parties such as the Women's Coalition, and by civic society operating in parallel outside the talks process. As McCrudden writes, for Sinn Fein and the PUP,

> a failure to address human rights and equality issues of importance to their communities would make it much more difficult to 'sell' any agreement. Once human rights was identified as an area that was important, particularly to Sinn Féin, it then became important for those who wanted to keep Sinn Féin 'on board' to include it for reasons of strategy as well as for reasons of principle in the final Agreement.[17]

Ulster Unionists were traditionally suspicious of human rights claims and did not tend to frame their own demands in such language. However, when negotiations intensified it became clear that human rights and equality issues could often be conceded more easily than areas that implicated sovereignty, such as cross-border bodies. They could even be traded against these bigger concessions. Furthermore, 'rights for nationalists' could be sold to constituents as a concession necessary to underwriting the international legitimacy of Northern Ireland within its present borders. As a result the Belfast Agreement has a strong rights emphasis, although it masks disagreement by avoiding substance and instead setting out principles and associated procedures for developing the rights framework – a task which is left to the post-agreement phase. The agreement provides for incorporation of the European Convention on Human Rights, provision for 'mainstreaming' of equality in public decision-making, and other policy measures to target social need, a Human Rights Commission which among other things is to 'consult and advise' on a Bill of Rights for Northern Ireland, an Equality Commission and commissions to examine criminal justice and policing, with agreed remits which include human rights issues. Interestingly, the agreement also provides for Republic of Ireland reciprocity in human rights, including the establishment of a Republic of Ireland Human Rights Commission and further attention to incorporation of the European Convention on Human Rights. It also provides for a joint committee of the two new Human Rights Commissions to examine the possibility of an all-Ireland Charter of Rights which would provide a rights framework for the island as a whole.

In contrast, in Israel/Palestine the focus of all parties on a 'separation' solution aimed at accommodating Palestinian claims for external self-determination with Israeli demands for security meant that, unlike the other examples, there was no reciprocal interest to see human rights protections instituted as part of the deal. The peace agreements in Israel/Palestine set up a form of autonomy for Palestinians. All difficult issues were postponed to final status negotiations – Jerusalem, settlements and military locations. Palestinian autonomy was limited geographically – only certain areas; it was limited personally – only Palestinians; and limited jurisdictionally – only certain spheres of operation. At time of writing the agreements appear to have collapsed despite the reluctance of either side to declare so.

What is interesting for this discussion is that the 'separation' nature of the deal undermined any mutuality in seeing human rights protections built into the deal. The focus on separation provided a distinct disincentive to incorporate human rights protections within the text of the deal. With Israelis excluded from the ambit of Palestinian authority there was no Israeli self-interest to protect human rights. Rather, the granting of a measure of autonomy to Palestinians brought with it Israeli security concerns as to whether autonomy would facilitate or decrease Palestinian attacks on Israelis. Conversely, for the Palestinian Liberation Organization (PLO), although building in human rights institutions could have provided the Palestinian authority with a buffer against unreasonable Israeli security demands, there were clear disincentives to do this. Having failed to secure international standards, such as the Fourth Geneva Convention providing humanitarian standards for civilian persons in times of war (and during occupation), as governing the interim period, there was no reason to further limit Palestinian autonomy by conditioning it on human rights as policed by Israel. Not only would this have been offensive to underlying claims of Palestinian statehood, it would also have reinforced Israeli arguments that Israel no longer had responsibility for human rights violations in the occupied territories. Provision for human rights in the Israeli Palestinian Agreements is therefore virtually non-existent. No overarching 'constitutional' framework for protecting or enforcing rights is provided. Criminal justice and policing are dealt with only so as to divide functions and powers between Israel and Palestinian authorities.

In Bosnia-Hercegovina (BiH) the deal itself must be understood as a compromise between opposing demands of separation (of ethnic groups) and sharing (pluralist approaches). The text of the Dayton Peace Agreement (DPA) affirms Bosnia and Hercegovina as a unitary international state with legal continuity – thus the international community appeared to get their key demand, triumphing over the secessionist demands of Croatians and Serbians.[18] However, the detail of the DPA reveals a compromise. The unitary state is to be comprised of two entities, one a Federation of cantons comprising mostly Croats and Bosniacs (themselves further separated through a cantonal structure); and the Republika Srpska – a Serb-dominated entity. The detail of the devolution of powers reveals the entities to be, in effect, ethnic mini-states with the unitary state structure left with very limited competencies. However, a number of human rights institutions are set up to operate at the state level and control the use and abuse of power at the entity level. Thus the DPA purports to incorporate a large number of international conventions into domestic law, including the European Convention on Human Rights. It provides for a Constitutional Court to stand superior to the governments of the entities and the unitary governmental structures, a Human Rights Commission comprising an adjudicative Human Rights Chamber and an Office of the Ombudsman, and a Commission for Displaced Persons and Refugees.

These human rights institutions are set up not just to police the entities, but to proactively attempt to reverse the ethnic cleansing which resulted in the entity division in the first place. Most notably this is to happen through provision for a right of return for refugees and displaced persons to pre-war locations, which is provided for in detail in Annex 7 of the DPA. Interestingly the human rights institutions all have provision for international membership, giving the international community an ongoing role in implementation.

However, in practice the territorial concessions underlined by the deal through the devolution of power to the entities mean that they can often frustrate the implementation and effectiveness of the human rights institutions and negate mechanisms for protection of rights. By September 1999 only 7 out of 37 decisions of the Human Rights Chamber had been fully implemented. Only 27 out of 57 final reports of the Ombudsperson had been complied with.[19] The UN High Commission on Refugees estimated that only 340,919 refugees and 270,001 displaced persons, out of an estimated 2 million plus displaced by the conflict, had returned, and of those most returns were to the Federation, with less than 0.7 per cent comprising non-Serbs returning to Republika Srpska. Out of 60,000 certificates in housing cases, less than 3 per cent had led to a changeover in land,[20] and the International Crisis Group calculated the number of 'minority returns', that is people returning to home areas where they would now constitute a minority, at less than 5 per cent of all refugees and persons displaced by the war.[21]

In summary, the case studies illustrate that if the deal is one where political institutions and a unified territory are to be shared between different groups, then both sides may have an interest in seeing rights language used, despite radically different notions of what human rights are, and of what their implementation will lead to in practice. In the text of a peace agreement such differences can often be masked and postponed by the general and universal language of rights. More cynically, the language of rights may be rhetorically useful to those who do not contemplate conceding the human rights demands of the other side. Those who have not framed their demands in human rights language during the conflict will often come to do so during the peace process, recognizing it as an internationally endorsed language. Rights language may signal the satisfaction of human rights claims at the heart of the conflict, even where substance has not been conceded. Human rights institutions may stamp an agreement with the badge of democracy, giving it international legitimacy. In other words, human rights mechanisms can be conceded as the universally recognized chic language in which to write peace agreements. Bosnia-Hercegovina and arguably Northern Ireland, provide two very different cases where human rights language was conceded by those who had not traditionally subscribed to such language, for some of these reasons.

Conversely, where the emphasis of the deal is on territorial separation of ethnically distinct groups then rights protections may be resisted or viewed by the parties as irrelevant, as Israel/Palestine and to some extent Bosnia-Hercegovina illustrate. The role of the international community in driving these deals and the lack of a 'mutually perceived hurting stalemate' between local parties also clearly contribute to the difficulties faced.

Implementation

At the implementation stage of a peace process, a measure of renegotiation often takes place, as parties explicitly renege on earlier commitments or more subtly try to reshape the agreement in their own image (see Box 14.3). Depending on how the agreement holds, the human rights institutions will continue to be implemented and begin their functions. Often this is the point at which civic society can become more involved in a more structural way in the peace process, through engagement with the new institutions established through the peace agreement. However, the nature of the 'deal' also helps to predict some of the difficulties that will arise at the implementation stage.

Box 14.3 Typical implementation–negotiation agreement provisions relating to human rights

---

Refinement/clarification/renegotiation of central deal

If agreement continues to move forward:
- demilitarization
- monitoring

Taking forward of human rights commitments:
- establishment of institutions
- institutions engage with society and continue to define human rights and implement human rights agenda

Increased involvement of civic society in human rights agenda (and process generally)

More measures to deal with past human rights abuses, including perhaps a unified holistic mechanism

---

As has already been noted, conflicts in divided societies are characterized by 'meta-conflict' (the conflict as to what the conflict is about), and the need for a meta-bargain (some level of agreement as to 'what the conflict was about'). Implementation of the human rights component of a peace agreement is largely dependent on some type of resolution of this conflict – a meta-bargain – having been reached. Without such a meta-bargain, as Horowitz notes, 'the antagonists will see the choice as being merely to dominate or to be dominated and so will engage in behavior that aims at hegemony'.[22] The human rights component of the agreement is just as likely to be a site for such conflict as within political institutions of government. Disagreements over what 'human rights' mean, who are the 'real' human rights abusers and what is necessary to securing or enforcing rights, are all likely to impede and delay coherent implementation, as the examples below illustrate.

In Bosnia-Hercegovina, it is clear from the text of the DPA that the human rights institutions which aim to cement the unitary state stand at odds with the powers of the entities and the scope of their autonomy. Given the lack of ethnonational consent to the unitary structure, it is not surprising that there is resistance to implementing the decisions of the human rights institutions, as the implementation figures bear out. In Northern Ireland, the Belfast Agreement documents a partial meta-bargain. There is agreement on political and other institutions that will give both nationalists and unionists access to power. There is also agreement on mutual recognition of citizenship rights and national identities, and on how the border could be changed in the future. However, there is no agreement on a common national identity or on the final borders or issue of sovereignty. The agreement's language is deliberately ambiguous as to sovereign aspirations and self-determination futures. The implementation of the human rights measures has rapidly exposed the lack of agreement in the Belfast Agreement. A recent example is found in the issue of policing. While the Belfast Agreement contained agreed general statements regarding principles for policing, these principles masked disagreement over whether the pre-agreement Royal Ulster Constabulary (RUC) did or could comply with those principles. While Irish nationalists signed up to the principles as a precursor to radical reform, or even replacement of the RUC, British unionists later claimed that they had signed up on the basis that the RUC already largely complied. When the Patten Commission established as a result finally made its recommendations, it was the recommendation to rename the RUC, thus providing a symbolic break both with the past and a British ethos, which proved the most difficult for unionists to accept. A similar tussle appears to be developing with regard for the need, or not, for a Bill of Rights, despite the fact that, unlike the controversy that surrounded policing, prior to the negotiations all the political parties were on record as agreeing that a Bill of Rights for Northern Ireland would be desirable.

What these struggles represent is not just ongoing negotiation around implementing the human rights dimension, but a more fundamental struggle over the meaning of the Belfast Agreement, and the type of transition it establishes. Does the agreement redefine the relationship of nationalists and unionists to the state? Does it herald a 'new beginning' or a reworked former order? Does it mark a creative attempt to transcend the conflict of the past and an innovative solution to a self-determination conundrum? Or does it represent devolution with a few 'tweaks', marking limited reform within a traditional British constitutional framework? The implementation, or not, of the human rights measures both indicate the type of transition, but also determine it.

In South Africa, where a meta-bargain can be identified involving, in essence, a clear transfer of power with human rights constraints, implementation of the human rights provisions of the Interim and Final Constitutions has confirmed the nature of the transition. It is a transition from minority rule and human rights abuses to majoritarian democracy constrained by a rights-based legal order. This is all evidenced by the functioning of the Constitutional Court, the primacy given to the Bill of Rights within the Constitution, and the signing of international human rights conventions. However, the failure of the new regime to deliver decisive movement towards socio-economic equality, and the accompanying high crime rate, indicate that while the conflict has been transformed, it has not been eliminated. The pressure for economic justice impacts on the work of human rights institutions and also on government policy, paradoxically at times resulting in calls for the limitations of human rights in the name of economic and social stability. Again, remaining ambiguities in the 'deal', such as whether political power was traded by the white minority for retention of economic power, will continue to be worked out but in significant part, although not exclusively, through the human rights institutions.

Conclusions

This brief account of the place and role of human rights institutions within a peace agreement cannot be separated from the proposed role and scope of the political institutions. Individual and group rights mesh together to form complex constitutional arrangements. These arrangements form, in essence, a contract between competing groups regarding access to power and, depending on the conflict, territorially based control. Individual human rights provisions (both forward- and backward-looking) are crucially shaped by the deal at the heart of the peace agreement. The central deal on access to territory and power controls whether human rights protections are addressed at all. Where the deal in essence moves towards a complete 'divorce' between peoples and partition of territory, as in the case of Israel/Palestine, and to some extent Bosnia-Hercegovina, then the political elites of both sides may not have an interest in seeing human rights protections written into the text of that divorce agreement. Conversely, where complete territorial separation is not contemplated, as in South Africa and Northern Ireland, then human rights institutions may be crucial to enabling agreement on access to government. Human rights protections can address past allegations of lack of legitimacy. They can also provide for future safeguards against abuse of power under the new governmental or territorial arrangements.

The protection and promotion of individual human rights are part of a bigger constitutional picture. Similarly, the political arrangements which form the other dimension of that picture are equally addressed to remedying past human rights abuses such as exclusion and domination. The overlap between law and politics does not evidence a lack of principle. Rather it indicates that peacemaking is often in fact, constitution-making, and that peace agreements at the framework stage are often distinctively 'transitional' constitutions.[23]

Notes

1. Preamble, Universal Declaration of Human Rights 1948.
2. Preamble, Framework Convention on the Rights of National Minorities, 1995 ETS No. 148.
3. Anonymous, 'Human Rights in Peace Negotiations', *Human Rights Quarterly*, 18 (1996), 249–58.
4. Ibid., p. 258.
5. For a list see C. Bell, *Peace Agreements and Human Rights* (Oxford: Oxford University Press, 2000), pp. 323–74.
6. Ibid., pp. 19–32. See also C. Mitchell, *The Structure of International Conflict* (London: Macmillan – now Palgrave Macmillan, 1981), p. 207, and T. du Toit, 'Bargaining about Bargaining: Inducing the Self-negating Prediction in Deeply Divided Societies: the Case of South Africa', *Journal of Conflict Resolution*, 33 (1989), 210–33.
7. Mitchell, op. cit., pp. 206–16.
8. Bell, op. cit., pp. 108, 110–11, 112–14.
9. Agreement Reached in Multi-party Negotiations 10 April 1998 (hereafter Belfast Agreement).
10. The General Framework Agreement for Peace in Bosnia and Hercegovina, 4 December 1995 (hereafter Dayton Peace Agreement).
11. Constitution of the Republic of South Africa, 1993 (200 of 1993) (hereafter Interim Constitution).
12. Declaration of Principles, 13 September 1993, see also Interim Agreement between Israel and the Palestinians, 28 September 1995 (hereafter Interim Agreement).
13. Constitution of the Republic of South Africa 108 of 1996 (hereafter Final Constitution).
14. J. McGarry & B. O'Leary, *Explaining Northern Ireland: Broken Images* (Oxford: Blackwell, 1995), p. 1.
15. Ibid., see J. McGarry & B. O'Leary, and *The Politics of Ethnic Conflict Regulation* (New York: Routledge, 1993); D. Horowitz, *Ethnic Groups in Conflict* (Berkeley: University of California Press, 1985) and *A Democratic South Africa? Constitutional Engineering in a Divided Society* (Berkeley: University of California Press, 1991), pp. 1–41.
16. See A. Cassese, *Self Determination of Peoples: a Legal Reappraisal* (Cambridge: Cambridge University Press, 1998); A. Eide, *New Approaches to Minority Protection*, Minority Rights Group International Report 93/4 (London: MRG International, 1995); and 1999 Lund Recommendations on the Effective Participation of National Minorities in Public Life, available at www.osce.org/henm/documents/lund.htm.
17. C. McCrudden, 'Mainstreaming Equality in the Governance of Northern Ireland', *Fordham International Law Journal*, 22 (1999), 1696–775 at 1724–7.
18. Article I, Dayton Peace Agreement.
19. Figures supplied by the Office of the High Representative for Human Rights Department, September 1999.
20. Figures supplied by the Office of the High Representative for Human Rights Department, September 1999.
21. International Crisis Group, *Is Dayton Failing? Bosnia Four Years after the Peace Agreement* (Sarajevo: International Crisis Group, 1999), p. 32.
22. Horowitz, *A Democratic South Africa*, p. 34.
23. See Bell, op. cit., pp. 293–321. On transitional constitutions, see R. Teitel, 'Transitional Jurisprudence: the Role of Law in Political Transformation', *Yale Law Journal*, 106 (1997), 2009–80 and *Transitional Justice* (New York: Oxford University Press, 2000).

15
Democratic Validation

Ben Reilly

In any transition from conflict to peace, the creation or restoration of some form of legitimate governing authority is paramount. While there are relatively few cases of peace deals themselves being put directly to a national vote for acceptance or rejection, at some time in the process of moving from conflict to peace, the support of the citizenry must be tested and obtained. In some form and at some point during every relatively successful process, and sometimes at more than one, the negotiators must seek public approval.

Post-conflict elections or referendums are a common, but not the only, vehicle for achieving this aim. But they are also fraught with problems which, if not appreciated, can easily undermine the foundations of any peace deal. Understanding the complex relationship between peace negotiations and the broader process of mass elections is thus a key step in crafting a lasting peace.

There is an inescapable linkage between the forging of peace deals and the process of democratic legitimation. For example, almost all peace treaties between formerly warring parties involve some changes to the apparatus of the state via revised arrangements for representative bodies, distribution of powers, territorial structure and the like.[1] States need governments, and governments need some form of validating mechanism to prove their democratic credentials – not least to the international community and its donors, for whom this has become an essential condition for post-conflict assistance.

The most important reason for some kind of democratic exercise, however, is to ensure that the new regime can derive some claim to legitimacy on behalf of the citizens it will represent and the polity it will govern. Indeed, the consent of the electorate, and the legitimacy of a new, post-conflict dispensation are a key – and underappreciated – variable in determining whether a peace deal will succeed or fail. How that consent can be obtained in the highly fraught atmosphere which characterizes most peace processes is the subject of this chapter.

'Legitimacy' is a difficult concept at the best of times, but in post-conflict situations it can be particularly thorny. Almost by definition, post-conflict societies are torn between competing conceptions of authority, and riven by deep societal cleavages and barely masked hostilities. Particularly in ethnically divided societies, competing visions of the state and the ideal make-up of its citizenry abound. These are often encapsulated in ethnically exclusive visions: Kosovo for the Kosovars, Fiji for the Fijians and so on.[2] Validating or legitimizing a peace deal under such conditions is thus both an unavoidable issue that must be confronted soon in any transition from war to peace, and an extremely fragile high-wire act that can easily derail a nascent peace.

Democratic legitimation in such circumstances usually requires some kind of election – be it a public plebiscite on a peace deal, the election of some kind of constituent assembly, or a fully fledged national election for a new government. And this is often where the problems of democracy in severely divided societies begin. Take, for example, the dilemma faced by UN peacekeeping operations, which are back in the spotlight in Europe (Bosnia and Kosovo), Africa (Sierra Leone and the Democratic Republic of Congo) and Asia (East Timor). In all of these cases, while the immediate focus of peacekeeping operations is, understandably, on the application of credible military force and the restoration of governing authority, the *political* dimension of peacekeeping missions quickly comes to the fore as soon as a basic peace is achieved. After all, the purpose of most such missions is to create a viable state apparatus that has the capacity to function without external assistance. A primary task of promoting international security is thus the establishment of domestic political order.

Not least because so many of today's conflicts take place within states, the overarching challenge of peacebuilding is to construct a sustainable democratic state that can function without direct international involvement. To achieve this, critical choices need to be made about how the internal politics of fragile states can be stabilized, how moderate and multiethnic political parties can be encouraged, and how the rhythm of democratic politics can be developed and made sustainable. This is a priority issue in both Kosovo and East Timor, for example, where UN missions have been confronted with the challenges of attempting to build functioning democracies in societies only recently ravaged by violent conflict, and suffering a history of incorporation and oppression by powerful neighbours.

Over the last decade, UN peacekeeping missions appear to have developed a kind of standard operating procedure in such contexts. Once a minimum level of peace has been obtained (which does not necessarily mean a full ceasefire agreement), and a basic level of infrastructure is in place, the next step is usually to hold some sort of elections – often within a year or two of the start of the mission – followed by a rapid handover to the newly elected authorities, and an even more rapid departure of UN troops and personnel. Thus in Kosovo today there has been strong pressure on the OSCE, the body tasked by the UN with organizing elections in the region, to hold elections for a new Parliament as quickly as possible, regardless of whether the social conditions that exist there are conducive to the cut and thrust of open electoral politics or not. A similar pressure to hold 'instant elections' has been felt in East Timor, where the UN Transitional Administrator, Sergio de Mello, has acknowledged that postponing elections beyond 2001 would be 'difficult', arguing that 'you can't hold back the horses' of political development indefinitely. (In both cases, elections were scheduled for the second half of 2001.)

Undoubtedly, real challenges are involved in such circumstances. In many cases the push towards holding rapid elections is fuelled as much as anything by a desire to remedy the perceived lack of local political legitimacy inherent in international administrations. In East Timor, for example, the UN has been under considerable pressure to localize its administration and hand over power to Xanana Gusmao's National Council for Timorese Resistance (CNRT) coalition, the unquestioned (but also unelected) source of legitimate domestic political authority in the territory. In such cases, there is ultimately no real alternative to some form of election – in East Timor's case, for a constituent assembly which will have the task of drawing up a new constitution for a new country.

But what the 'as quickly as possible' approach to the exercise of the democratic process simply fails to take account of is the reality that if held too early, elections in fragile situations can easily undermine the longer-term challenge of building a sustainable democracy.

There are three reasons for this. First, elections in conflictual situations act as catalysts for the development of parties and other organizations which are primarily (and often solely) vehicles to assist local elites gain access to governing power. These parties are not, in most cases, broad-based vehicles for presenting competing policy and ideological platforms, but rather narrowly based elite cartels. In other cases, exemplified by the transformation of liberation movements such as East Timor's Fretlin or the Kosovo Liberation Army, political parties are merely thinly disguised variants of the armies which fought in the original conflicts. Either way, holding elections too early in the transition period can have the perverse effect of stymieing the development of more aggregative and programmatic political parties – institutions which are now widely accepted to be important facilitating agents for successful democratization.

Second, because of the underdeveloped and deeply divided nature of most post-conflict societies, elections often have the effect of highlighting societal fault lines and hence laying bare very deep social divisions. In such circumstances, the easiest way to mobilize voter support at election time is often to appeal to the very same insecurities that generated the original conflict. This means that parties have a strong incentive to 'play the ethnic card' or to take hardline positions on key identity-related issues, with predictable consequences for the wider process of democratization. The 1993 elections in Burundi, for example, which were supposed to elect a power-sharing government, instead mobilized population groups along ethnic lines and served as a catalyst for ethnic genocide. Bosnia's 1996 and 1998 elections effectively served as ethnic censuses, with parties campaigning on ethnic lines and voters reacting to heightened perceptions of ethnic insecurity by re-electing hardline nationalists to power.[3]

The third reason for caution about elections in post-conflict situations is more economic than political. The key problem here is the distorted economic base that most societies emerging from a protracted period of armed struggle inherit. In almost all post-conflict situations, but particularly in developing countries, local economies have been shattered by the conflict. There is often an enormous and highly visible disparity between the financial and other resources of local actors compared to that of the international community. In addition, handsome international development aid commitments and other potential financial rewards await the new, localized government administration. Local elites therefore tend to conclude – rightly, in many cases – that access to the state itself is a primary means for gaining economic advancement. One consequence of this is that, as well as being highly charged *politically*, elections in such circumstances also function as highly contested forms of *economic* competition, in which access to the resources of the state is the real prize. It is no surprise that two of the most successful examples of conflict transformation in the 1990s – South Africa and Northern Ireland – took place in economically developed countries which offered many more lucrative alternatives to politics as a means of economic advancement for local elites.

Taken together, all of these factors have the effect, when an election is held, of heightening tensions and undermining broader prospects for the institutionalization of democratic politics. In addition, a more immediate problem often comes not from the domestic realm but from the approach taken by the international community itself. International policy-makers, not least at the UN, have typically viewed elections as a convenient punctuation point in a peacekeeping mission, which can usher in not just a new government but also provide a convenient exit point for international involvement. Thus Cambodia's exemplary 1993 election, the culmination of the biggest UN peacekeeping mission to date, was followed by a rapid departure of international forces – a departure which did little to translate results of an exemplary electoral process into solidifying a fragile new polity.

The wider obsession in the 1990s with elections as a form of conflict resolution is perhaps the most obvious manifestation of this 'quick-fix' mentality. The world is littered with elections, often conducted at the behest of the international community, which only served to inflame and politicize the root causes of conflict. Given this, it is not surprising that elections held too early in the process of state rebuilding (or 'premature elections', as they have become known) often have the opposite results to those intended. The December 1991 Algerian elections, which were aborted after the fundamentalist Islamic Salvation Front clearly won the first round of voting, and which led to the suspension of the Constitution and the strengthening of military rule, were one case in point. Another was the return to war in Angola by Jonas Savimbi after he too looked likely to lose the 1992 presidential elections. In both cases, early and ill thought-through elections appeared to undermine the broader path of democratic development.

There are, however, powerful pressures, both domestically and internationally, for early elections to occur as part of the process of rebuilding in post-conflict societies. For one thing, given the risk-averse nature of the international community when it comes to peacekeeping commitments, such elections can (as noted above) provide a clear 'exit strategy' for international involvement. But supporting the difficult process of transforming a poor, traumatized and war-ravaged society into a well-functioning democracy requires more than the presence of a few hundred UN officials for 18 months, with an election at the end. It means, quite simply, being prepared to invest substantial time and money in an open-ended process of social and political development. With the exception of the Balkans, which benefits from its location in Europe (and where informed observers are talking about an international presence in the region for *decades*), there are few post-conflict societies anywhere in the world where international actors have the inclination to pursue such an open-ended strategy. In most cases, the roving eye of the international media and the governments of major Western states moves on to other, more fashionable, issues.

A second-best alternative to this (admittedly, in most cases, unrealistic) kind of open-ended commitment is not to rush into immediate elections following a peace deal, but rather to encourage local involvement for a few years until some of the basic elements of a pluralistic party system and a functioning state have been established. This appears to be the approach being taken by the UN in both East Timor and Kosovo, where local-level democratization and security have taken precedence over the holding of a national poll, and where national consultative bodies of local leaders have been introduced *without* an electoral process. In East Timor, for example, the UN has developed the National Consultative Council, made up of representatives of East Timor's government-in-waiting, into a form of unelected legislature. In early 2001, in the lead-up to the August 2001 elections, its membership was increased from 15 to 33 representatives, with the new members representing districts, women, youth and the Church.

The problem, of course, is that this approach cannot be carried on indefinitely, and even with many years of international tutelage there are no guarantees that a democratic society will emerge. But the same can be said of too many opportunities for popular consultation as well. One criticism of the democratic principle of popular consent becoming a prerequisite for progress in a peace process, for example, is that it is open to abuse: every little step on the way can become an opportunity for procrastination or reworking by opponents. Thus in Northern Ireland, critics contend that the rolling process of elections in the lead-up to the Good Friday Agreement merely kept unresolved issues alive, giving losers the hope that they may achieve their aims 'next time', and that fundamental principles which had apparently been agreed upon were, in fact, open to revision indefinitely.

In addition, the above-cited problem in war-torn societies of political parties often being little more than thinly disguised former armies, who may view electoral politics as a vehicle for the continuation of their previous struggles, is difficult to wish away even over a longer-term period. Previous ethnic conflicts can be replicated in the form of new ethnically exclusive political parties. In such contexts, holding an election before the norms of civic, peacetime politics have taken hold almost inevitably results in increased support for extremist ethnically exclusive parties. This has been a recurring feature of elections in Bosnia, for example, and is one reason why the OSCE in Kosovo have devoted substantial resources to establishing a network of 'political party service centres' there, which are intended to support the territory's nascent political groupings and provide them with logistical and material assistance and, by implication, move them towards becoming functioning, policy-oriented political parties as well, rather than the narrow and personalized vehicles for ethnic extremists that were evident in Bosnia.

Lest all this be taken as a counsel of despair, it is important to emphasize that under some circumstances, well-timed and designed elections and other devices for public consultation in the midst of peace negotiations can do much good. The 1998 Northern Ireland Assembly elections, for example, ushered in a power-sharing executive of predominantly pro-peace members drawn from both sides of the communal divide. It succeeded not only because its timing capitalized on the weariness with the conflict and the moderate sentiment in a significant section of the Northern Irish community, but also because the 'rules of the game' were structured in such a way as to promote moderate voices over extremist ones, and to facilitate intra-group as well as inter-group competition. Similarly, the break-through 1994 elections in South Africa deserve to be viewed as crucial steps on the road to peace. In both cases, several years of bargaining and negotiation between rival elites preceded the electoral contests, meaning that they came to be viewed less as zero-sum, either/or choices than as devices by which the public could approve, or reject, a new multiethnic vision for the country that had been the subject of painstaking debate and many years of violent conflict.

Importantly, in both cases political leaders eschewed what is clearly the most damaging form of democratic legitimation – a yes or no vote on the peace deal in a plebiscite or referendum. Rather, in both South Africa and Northern Ireland, early referendums were rejected in favour of a patient, carefully calibrated series of negotiations that brought extremist elements from both sides together. In each case, only after a basic package of territorial and constitutional issues had been agreed to was a national vote held – not as a yes/no referendum, but in the form of a general election that asked voters to decide on a range of issues aimed at building peace, not just on self-determination. In both cases, the result was a victory for compromise, for the moderate forces in those societies and, in a wider sense, victory for the democratic process as well.

By contrast, one of the starkest lessons of all is the danger of using 'all-or-nothing' mechanisms such as plebiscites or referendums to solve conflicts over statehood. The terrible violence which followed the announcement of the results of the 1999 East Timor referendum, for example, gives a graphic illustration of the possible consequences of holding a ballot *before* basic issues of politics have been aired and discussed. In effect, such one-off plebiscites can serve to short-circuit any nascent routines of political dialogue that may be emerging, and funnel all issues down into a single for or against choice. Such an exercise represents not the triumph of democracy but, more often, the rejection of politics as a means for reconciling divergent views.

Because of this, many referendums have the effect of heightening tensions, forcing both voters and politicians to adopt fixed positions and pushing rhetoric towards extreme positions. This is compounded by the highly charged nature of plebiscites on territorial disputes or self-determination, in which those with the minority view tend to see the result as a threat to their security and, sometimes, their continued existence. With no other options, minority groups often see extra-constitutional avenues like violence as their only recourse. In certain circumstances, the logic of ordinary elections can work the same way. The slide into civil war in Sri Lanka, for example, was stimulated by the increasing inability of the Tamil population to achieve their objectives via constitutional and democratic means, as they always formed the parliamentary opposition to the Sinhalese major- ity. War became a more promising option for political change: exit, not voice.

Despite hollow claims that the 'will of the people' must prevail, it is only the most obtuse interpretation that would recommend building peace in this way. Majoritarian devices like plebiscites are typically blunt instruments that obscure as much as they reveal. As a device for resolving deep-rooted sociopolitical con- flicts, they are a particularly poor choice for one simple reason: *in a yes/no vote, one side will always lose.* Unlike in ordinary elections, in which an issue may be debated and reconsidered every few years, plebiscites – particularly on highly charged issues such as self-determination or statehood – tend to be one-offs. There are no second chances, no face-saving ways to sugar-coat the pill and no creative options such as power-sharing arrangements that build in some voice for the losers. Losers, in such circumstances, often perceive themselves to be losers for ever.

Despite all this, the 1990s have seen a plethora of plebiscites in sticky situations around the world. In the Balkans alone, a total of five referendums on autonomy or independence were held in 1990 and 1991 in Slovenia, Croatia and Bosnia. Each one pushed the region closer towards war. Votes for independence not only frag- mented Yugoslavia, they radicalized the anti-independence Serb minorities, partic- ularly in Croatia and Bosnia. More recently, the referendum on independence for Kosovo, which was proposed as part of the aborted peace talks in Rambouillet, France, in early 1999, was widely seen as a 'game breaker' that moved Serbia's strategic choices away from the negotiating table and towards ethnic cleansing.

In East Timor, what the UN referred to as a 'popular consultation' process was a choice between ongoing integration with Indonesia or independence. Yes or no. Under such circumstances, it was inevitable that the referendum itself would become the cause of intense conflict. Even the 'overwhelming' vote for East Timor's independence that followed the August 1999 plebiscite, with 78.5 per cent voting in favour of this option, left a significant proportion of the electorate – 21.5 per cent – who had rejected independence in favour of remaining part of Indonesia. Following the announcement of the election result, this group was a fissionable, angry and insecure minority that, with the active encouragement of the Indonesian military, acted accordingly.

Moreover, because they are usually based on the most simple interpretation of majority rule, referendums almost always disadvantage minorities. This is not just because they are majoritarian in terms of assessing victory, but also because they do not enable voters to express their strengths or gradations of opinion on an issue. Another reason is that, in ethnically divided societies, referendums have an alarm- ing tendency to turn into an ethnic census, a head count of rival groups, and to encourage the mobilization of voters around stark, all-or-nothing positions which are tailor-made for extremist voices and issues to gain circulation and currency.

Even previously non-divided societies can be polarized by the harsh logic of ref- erendums on contentious issues. Possibly the best example of this comes from the small Pacific island state of Palau, a former US Trust Territory which separated from the Federated States of Micronesia (FSM) in 1978 as a result of a referendum. Since then, Palau has held no less than eight subsequent referendums, as pro- and anti-independence forces became further divided over a 'non-nuclear' clause in the new country's Constitution, which was opposed by the USA, with which Palau, like other former members of the FSM, has a 'compact of association'. These eight referendums bitterly polarized the polity of a small and fragile new state, leading to the assassination of one president and the apparent suicide of another.[4]

Most national governments show much greater awareness of this dilemma than the international community. For example, successive Indian governments since 1947 have rejected UN resolutions which would allow a plebiscite on self-determination in Kashmir because of the likelihood that it would trigger a bloody war for independence.[5] Indeed, it is difficult to point to one successful use of referendums to resolve a deeply contentious issue such as self-determination. Even in relatively successful cases such as Eritrea, which voted overwhelmingly for independence in 1993, referendums typically serve to legitimize choices that have already been decided on the battlefield.

In the Western Sahara, successive attempts to hold a self-determination plebiscite in the Moroccan-claimed territory to determine whether the region should remain part of Morocco or become an independent state have been repeatedly postponed, with the Moroccan government accused by the pro-independence Polisario front of manipulating the voters' list. Most observers do not believe that Morocco will allow a referendum to take place until they are absolutely confident that the result will be in their favour. Such an exercise undermines the legitimating function of the democratic process, rendering the referendum itself an empty symbolic activity.

There are clear democratic alternatives to plebiscites in most cases, but they involve taking a longer-term approach to decision-making than most international actors are willing to consider. One that deserves greater attention is the French approach to dealing with democratization and decolonization in New Caledonia. In the 1980s, New Caledonia was brewing into a potentially very violent and irreconcilable conflict between the indigenous Kanak peoples and the French-origin *caldouch* settlers. The former wanted independence, the latter continued integration with France. Violence between these groups, which required the intervention of French armed forces, resulted in a 1988 peace agreement, the Matignon Accord, which guaranteed a referendum on sovereignty after ten years of increased educational and infrastructural aid to the marginalized Kanak peoples. This ten-year period gave the space for two things to occur: genuine economic and political development on the one hand; and increasing space for alternatives to full independence to be discussed on the other. By the time the date for the referendums had arrived, a consensual agreement had been negotiated between leaders of both sides (and of metropolitan France). The new agreement outlined a period of phased devolution of control from Paris, such that by 2015 only the overarching issues of security, defence and foreign affairs will still be in French hands. The agreement has received overwhelming support within New Caledonia and seems to have set the territory on a peaceful path which meets many of the basic needs and concerns of both communities. As in other successful peace processes, the issue was put to a vote only *after* fundamental agreement on most contentious issues had been reached.

The key issue here is one that is consistently overlooked by the international community: the temporal dimension of democracy and peacebuilding. By lengthening the process of negotiation in New Caledonia, the agreements provided the space for new political alliances to be forged, and for disputants to move away from fixed and artificial non-negotiable positions towards a more fluid and nuanced view of their conflict. The result was that an issue that could easily have degenerated into a nasty civil war has instead, by skilful political handling and creative institutional approaches, apparently led to a much more benign outcome instead.

Contrast this with East Timor, where a rushed all-or-nothing referendum inevitably became a focal point for conflict. Had Indonesia's leaders (and the international community) pursued the New Caledonia strategy of phased autonomy, devolution and development – as indeed some governments in the region were urging them to do – then perhaps a less bloody outcome would have been the result. For example, instead of an all-or-nothing vote, East Timorese could have been asked to elect a constituent assembly with responsibilities for a range of constitutional issues, including the nature and timing of self-determination. This would have brought both pro- and anti-independence forces into the same fold, and a power-sharing executive could have had responsibility for deciding upon key issues of governance in a more considered atmosphere than the heightened tension of a public plebiscite. A staggered autonomy process, such as the one France is currently using in New Caledonia, could have gradually developed East Timor while increasing self-government and postponing the ultimate question of independence. Indeed, this was the essence of the proposal from the Australian Prime Minister to then Indonesian President Habibie in early 1999, which many see as having precipitated Indonesia's changed approach to the East Timor question.

Critics respond that such a gradual approach would have been unrealistic for an oppressed people hungry for freedom, and that there was no alternative to the independence vote. But a clear indication of the danger of referendums is that, while the international community likes to encourage such devices to solve thorny issues in the developing world, they are used rarely and with great caution in most Western states. Major democracies such as the United States, Japan, India and Germany have never held a national referendum in the post-war period, even on contentious territorial issues such as the expansion of the union in the USA or the presence of American military bases in Japan. In Germany following the fall of the Berlin Wall, a national referendum on reintegration was rejected in favour of an early national election in which parties supporting rapid reunification triumphed. In Canada, since Quebec's divisive and inconclusive 1995 referendum which rejected independence by the barest of margins (50.6 to 49.4 per cent), and the earlier rejection of the Charlottetown Accords in 1992, the national government has avoided putting the issue to a nationwide vote and is now attempting to handle constitutional issues without recourse to yes-or-no referendums. Time will tell how the British government handles the similarly vexed issue of European monetary union.

While referendums are unavoidable in some cases, they should not be used in divided societies which are being asked to make stark choices about their future. In such cases, where a bare majority '50 per cent plus one' is the threshold for victory or defeat, the plebiscite is a zero-sum game that rarely defuses conflict. In fact a threat of a referendum in such circumstances will often play into the hands of hardliners, who know how easy it is to mobilize mass support around nationhood issues. Thus the promise by former Israeli Prime Minister Ehud Barak to hold a referendum on the final shape of the Israeli–Palestinian Peace Accords was part of a series of steps which played into the familiar cycle of escalating conflict and increasing polarization in both Israel and Palestine, with disastrous consequences for the peace process and the region.

The wider lesson is clear: in any transition from conflict to peace, elections and other types of ballot need to be viewed as the beginning of a long-term process of democratization, not the end point. Ill-considered polls are sometimes worse for long-term democratization than no elections at all. They need to be carefully designed to promote moderate sentiment, and carefully timed to avoid the perils of a too early stimulation of competitive politics. Most importantly, they need to be seen as just one step in a much more complex and lengthy process of civil-society building.

Notes

1. For a survey of these, see P. Harris & B. Reilly (eds), *Democracy and Deep-Rooted Conflict: Options for Negotiators* (Stockholm: International IDEA, 1998).
2. For the best discussion of the structural patterns of ethnic conflict, see D. Horowitz, *Ethnic Groups in Conflict* (Berkeley: University of California Press, 1985).
3. For more on such cases, see B. Reilly & A. Reynolds, 'Electoral Systems and Conflict in Divided Societies', in P. Stern & D. Druckman (eds), *International Conflict Resolution after the Cold War* (Washington, DC: National Academy Press, 2000).
4. See A. Leibowitz, *Embattled Island: Palau's Struggle for Independence* (Westport, Conn.: Praeger, 1996).
5. For a good discussion of this and related issues, see T. Sisk, *Power Sharing and International Mediation in Ethnic Conflicts* (Washington, DC: United States Institute of Peace Press, 1996).

16
Territorial Options

Yash Ghai

Introduction

A great deal of conflict, in ancient as well as modern times, has concerned territory. Most inter-state wars have been about territory and sovereignty over it. Today most internal conflicts are over the territorial organization or partition of the state. Land and territory are emotive subjects, revered as the cradle of history, legends and myths of communities. They are also the source of material wealth and physical security. Self-rule, jurisdiction, national security, rights of citizens, mobility, employment and resources hinge on territory and sovereignty. It is the artefact of sovereignty with its connotations of control that give territory its political and even emotional significance.

When territory is the source of conflict, various territorial options – none of them easy – may be available to solve it. In the mid-twentieth century, major reorganizations of territory took place with decolonization, with massive withdrawals of foreign sovereignty, and the redrawing of boundaries or the partition of former colonies. The redrawing of boundaries (as the securing of independence) is seldom easy. African colonies were carved out without any regard to geography or demography, and their emergence into statehood raised acute ethnic conflicts about boundaries, cutting as they did across indigenous communities, cultures and institutions. Such was the desire of minorities for territorial reconfiguration and such was the resistance of majorities, that Julius Nyerere urged the new states to learn to live with colonially endowed boundaries, precisely because they were so absurd – and this became the official policy of the Organization of African States. India has tried to solve its problems with China and Pakistan by redrawing boundaries – with little success. Solutions to the Israeli–Palestine conflict have foundered over precise boundaries that should separate their territories, compounded by Israeli claims to the sacredness to Jews of lands, in 'Judea and Samaria', which constitute also the heartland of the Palestinian West Bank. Boundaries, even when they are redrawn, frequently leave bitter legacies, as in Ireland and India/Pakistan/ Bangladesh. It is not therefore surprising that the redrawing of boundaries has usually taken place under the hegemony of a dominant power or by the victorious after a war.

Sometimes when the redrawing of boundaries cannot be achieved, sovereignty over the disputed territory may be shared. In history condominiums represent this sharing, as over the Sudan (between the British and the Egyptians) or the New Hebrides (between the British and the French). Sometimes sovereignty over disputed territory may be exercised by the international community – at least for temporary periods, as with the UN administrations of South West Africa (Namibia) and East Timor, or as has frequently been proposed for Jerusalem.

Solutions to today's problems frequently involve territory in some sense, even if it is to make territory and sovereignty less salient, as in the EU by diminishing the significance of borders among member states through mobility of their nationals, the provision of common currency, the direct access of groups to Brussels, resource transfers, common policies and institutions. This may be regarded as a species of merger of territory, more clear-cut cases of which lie in classical federations, or the integration of princely states in post-independence India, or the union of Eritrea with Ethiopia.

At other times the solution is seen to lie in making territory and sovereignty more salient, as in the disintegration of the Soviet Union and the former Yugoslavia or the dismemberment of Czechoslovakia along ethnic fault lines. Occasionally the normal consequences of territory are obliterated or minimized by quirks of sovereignty – denials of citizenship or franchise or exclusion from land or other economic rights negate in part or wholly the constitutional status of lawful residents, and thus, in an important sense, delink them from the territory. South Africa did this by stripping Africans of citizenship rights, and eventually of citizenship itself (with the establishment of Bantustans). Israel, by conferring limited, second-class citizenship on Israeli Arabs, has maintained itself essentially as an ethnic state. More drastic versions of this approach are represented by ethnic cleansing or forced expulsions or transfers of population, for which India/Pakistan, Cyprus, Israel and Yugoslavia provide contemporary examples. The converse of this approach is to flood territory inhabited by one group with members of another community, to dilute the claims of the original community, as with transmigration policies of Indonesia which have seen, for example, the Javanese become the majority community in West Irian, or white settlers in Australia and North and South Americas. In Sri Lanka, one cause of the resentment of Tamils against the Sinhala is that successive governments have established settlements of the Sinhala in Tamil 'homelands'.

Because most of the approaches above are fraught with difficulties (tending mostly to sharpen conflicts), and some may indeed be outdated in this age, today the solutions to territorial disputes are sought through the territorial reorganization of the state. The purpose of this chapter is to examine future prospects for some form of the spatial distribution of power, whether it is federation, devolution or autonomy. To achieve a federal state, with its clear understanding of divided sovereignty, through the disaggregation of a previously unitary state is the hardest of the three options, while devolution seems to assume the ultimate undivided sovereignty at the centre, the protection of self-government being the restraint of the central authorities (as with the Scottish devolution). Autonomy frequently refers to an asymmetrical relationship of a part of the state to the central authorities (such as Puerto Rico with Washington, Åland with Helsinki, or Hong Kong with Beijing), with legal guarantees that can span the range between federalism and devolution. Thus while there are legal and political differences between these terms, in practice the distinctions are not always clear-cut. As limitations of space do not permit explorations of differences, I use the term 'autonomy' throughout the chapter to refer to all three forms of spatial distribution of power.

The importance of autonomy in contemporary world

Autonomy has a special fascination for politicians and political movements. It serves as a device both to bring states together in regional associations (the EU being the most outstanding example) and to keep states intact by accommodating and diffusing secessionist claims. The latter issue is particularly acute in multiethnic states; in many states political stability, social peace and their very future as sovereign entities depend on a satisfactory resolution of ethnically based claims for autonomy (as in Indonesia, Sri Lanka, India, the Philippines, Russia, Papua New Guinea, Canada, Yugoslavia, etc.). Some states have fragmented due to failure to handle autonomy effectively (Pakistan with the loss of Bangladesh and Indonesia with the loss of East Timor). It is no exaggeration to say that today the very future of some states, like Russia and India, depends on how disputes about autonomy are resolved. Autonomy could be a staging post for full integration (Hong Kong–China) or for complete separation (Palestine–Israel or Cook Islands–New Zealand). But autonomy also serves other purposes, examples of which are provided by the EU concept of subsidiarity, to ensure efficiency and accountability, and China's strategy for the unification with Hong Kong, Macau and Taiwan through the policy of 'one country, two systems'.[1]

Autonomy has acquired new importance today, because of the value which is being placed on identity rooted in the culture and other traditions of a group. There are many ways in which identity can be nurtured (e.g. through recognition of linguistic, religious and cultural rights), but autonomy is the preferred choice of groups for the possibilities it offers also of political power or self-government to protect their culture and other interests, a particularly important consideration for groups with distinct but vulnerable cultures, such as indigenous peoples. There are currently three forms of self-government: territorial/regional autonomy, cultural/group autonomy and independence. The appeal of territorial autonomy is partly that it is an alternative to both, which for different reasons are deemed to be less acceptable than territorial autonomy. A particular advantage of autonomy, based on territory, is that it enables ethnic problems to be solved without 'entrenching' ethnicity, although some forms of autonomy may indeed entrench ethnicity, as with reservations where the cultural dimensions and the need to preserve the identity of the group, may serve to sharpen boundaries against outsiders, or the claims of the francophones in Quebec. Autonomy often provides a basis for a compromise as it is a mid-point of competing claims; that of a separate statehood/sovereignty and a unitary state (as in Kosovo's relationship with Serbia; devolution proposals in Sri Lanka; current negotiations between China and Taiwan; Russia and Chechnya; current negotiations in the Sudan). Autonomy can thus fudge the thorny issue of sovereignty, which has been so troublesome in several conflicts. Self-government and self-determination can be accommodated within the confines of autonomy (with substantial devolution of powers, and the paraphernalia of 'statehood' such as a flag, postage stamps and even an anthem) while retaining intact the boundaries of the state. Various forms of autonomy are also linked to consociationalism, which, as a political form of power-sharing, has been gaining popularity in recent years (Bosnia, Belgium).

Autonomy enables a region to exercise substantial self-government without assuming all functions of a state or losing the benefits of metropolitan nationality; it has been used as a form of decolonization (as with associated states such as the Cook Islands which opted for a link with New Zealand after decolonization, but assumed most functions of self-government; and as in the case with several British territories in the Caribbean). In a somewhat related way, autonomy has been used when a region of a state does not want to join a bigger union (e.g. Greenland and the Faeroes when Denmark joined the EU; and special provisions could be negotiated for Åland when Finland joined the EU because of its pre-existing autonomy). This observation illustrates the flexibility of autonomy, which can comprise a wide variety of arrangements regarding structure and powers. Consequently it allows considerable flexibility in negotiations and permits a gradual transfer of powers, giving time for adjustment to both sides.

While there is no consensus on the effect of autonomy on diffusing conflicts, the promise of autonomy (or the concession to renounce separation in favour of autonomy) can bring parties round a table and start the process of negotiations, even if the overall agenda is wider (Bougainville and Papua New Guinea; the Sudanese; Spain and Catalonia and the Basque Country, etc.). Sometimes merely the commitment to consider autonomy can serve to diffuse tensions, as in South Africa where the agreement to consider a 'white homeland' secured the participation of hardline Afrikaners to the Interim Constitution. Even if autonomy does not or cannot solve all problems, it can serve as a holding operation, allowing a 'cooling off' period and facilitating further negotiations (Palestine–Israel, New Caledonia–France).

Territorial autonomy can increase the political integration of ethnic groups with the rest of the country by accentuating intra-group differences and leading to the fragmentation of previously monolithic ethnic parties. The proliferation of parties enables coalitions of similarly situated ethnic parties (Nigeria, India) across the state. Local problems which might otherwise have created a national crisis are dealt with by the locality itself. Territorial asymmetrical arrangements encourage demands for similar arrangements by other groups (India, Nigeria, Papua New Guinea, China). The proliferation of these arrangements increases the prospects of national unity as it diffuses state power and enables central authorities to balance regional with national interests.

Autonomy arrangements, because they divide power, also contribute to constitutionalism. The guarantees for autonomy and the modalities for their enforcement emphasize the rule of law and the role of independent institutions. The operation of the arrangements, particularly those parts governing the relationship between the centre and the region, being dependent on discussions, mutual respect and compromise, frequently serve to strengthen these qualities.

The legal basis for autonomy

The presence or absence of an entitlement in either international or national law to autonomy, as well as provisions limiting its scope, can play an important role in the conduct of negotiations and the relative bargaining position of parties, especially when there is international or third-party mediation. While there is no general right to autonomy under domestic or international law, there is an increasing recognition internationally and regionally that in some circumstances there is at least a strong moral case for autonomy.[2] There is also growing political support for autonomy internationally and regionally, as well as in certain national constitutional laws. In various conflicts where the international community or foreign states have become involved, autonomy has been adopted as a solution (League of Nations in Finland and Åland; southern Philippines; Bosnia; Kosovo; Crimea).

General principles

For a long time the principal provision for minorities was art. 27 of the International Covenant of Civil and Political Rights (ICCPR). It was drafted to exclude collective rights, as it was addressed to the right of individual members of a minority, and it has been narrowly interpreted. However, in recent years the UN Human Rights Committee (which supervises the implementation of the ICCPR) has adopted some interpretations of art. 27 which recognize that a measure of autonomy and group rights may be necessary for the protection of cultural rights of minorities. This broader approach is reflected in a UN Declaration on the Rights of Minorities adopted by the General Assembly in 1992. Unlike the ICCPR, it places positive obligations on the state to protect the identity of minorities and encourage 'conditions for the promotion of that identity' (art. 1).

Regional instruments in Europe as well as policies towards ethnic groups place increasing importance on the identity of the minorities and consequently support a measure of self-government. The European Community used conformity with these norms as a precondition for the recognition of new states in Europe. The ability of existing states (which is relatively unregulated by international law) to confer recognition on entities, especially breakaway entities, can be a powerful weapon to influence their constitutional structure.

Indigenous peoples

Another source of support for autonomy are international instruments for the rights of indigenous peoples. The Convention on Indigenous Peoples adopted in 1991 and representing a reversal of the approach followed in the 1959 convention recognized the 'aspirations of these peoples to exercise control over their own institutions, ways of life and economic development and to maintain and develop their identities, languages and religions, within the framework of the States in which they live'. The Draft UN Declaration on the Rights of Indigenous Peoples (submitted by the UN Sub-Commission on Minorities, August 1994) goes even further and proclaims their right to self-determination, under which they may 'freely determine their political status and freely pursue their economic, social and cultural development' (art. 3). The principle of self-determination gives them the 'right to autonomy or self-government in matters relating to their internal and local affairs', which include social, cultural and economic activities, and the right to control the entry of non-members (art. 31).

Self-determination

The third and broadest basis is self-determination, in itself a difficult and controversial concept, but which is increasingly being analysed in terms of the internal, democratic organization of a state rather than in terms of secession or independence. The UN General Assembly resolved many years ago that autonomy is a manifestation of self-determination. The greater involvement of the UN or consortia of states in the settlement of internal conflicts has also helped to develop the concept of self-determination as implying autonomy in appropriate circumstances.

Such a view of self-determination has some support in certain national constitutions. Often constitutional provisions for autonomy are adopted during periods of social and political transformation, when an autocratic regime is overthrown (when there is considerable agitation and legitimacy for autonomy), or a crisis is reached in minority–majority conflicts, or there is intense international pressure (in which case autonomy is granted rather grudgingly). Propelled by these factors, a number of constitutions now recognize some entitlement to self-government.

The resistance to autonomy

Despite the theoretical advantages of autonomy and developing norms, there has been considerable resistance to it on part of governments. Even when granted, it may not survive, due to continuing questioning of its legitimacy by the state, or due to difficulties of managing it. In numerous cases, a settlement on autonomy has eluded negotiators, or one party has escalated its demands beyond autonomy (Sudan and Sri Lanka are obvious examples). Questions of territory can arouse deep emotions, motherland versus homeland, and other historical associations. There can also be disputes about the precise boundaries of the territory in question, as in Palestine, Sri Lanka, India (in relation to the division of the Punjab in the 1960s) and the Philippines.

Occasionally a minority may reject autonomy because it is seen as compromising the fundamental goal of separate statehood, such as Turks in Cyprus and Tamil Tigers in Sri Lanka. In such cases a solution may be to make autonomy a temporary expedience, pending further negotiations or a referendum after a specified period allowing for time to see if autonomy provides an acceptable measure of self-government (such as in the Israel–Palestine agreement or the agreement between France and the Kanaks in New Caledonia; a similar procedure was successfully adopted in the September 2001 agreement between Bougainvilleans and the national government in Papua New Guinea, which brought the civil war and the attempted secession to an end. The parties agreed on a high degree of autonomy for Bougainville now, but also agreed to hold a referendum 'no sooner than 10 years and no later than 15 years' which would include the option of full independence.

The establishment of autonomy involves a major or at least a significant reorganization of the state. For a long time autonomy was seen to clash with the project of 'nation' and 'state' building which underlay much modernization theory – and with the ambitions of 'nationalist' leaders. It upsets long-held views of the sacredness of territory and the unity of 'motherland'. It necessitates a significant reallocation of resources, including that of political power.

The leaders of the majority community may be reluctant to concede autonomy, fearing the loss of electoral support among its own community (a problem that has bedevilled Sri Lanka). Majority leaders, even if well disposed to autonomy, may not have the confidence that they would be able to implement the autonomy agreement, especially if it requires an amendment of the Constitution, a referendum or even merely fresh legislation. There may be fears that autonomy will be merely a springboard to secession. This is seen to be a serious problem when the group demanding autonomy is related, and contiguous, to a neighbouring kin state. Autonomy granted to a minority in its 'homeland' may in turn create new minorities (as with Muslims in the Eastern District of Sri Lanka which the Tamil Tigers want under their control, or Christians in Mindanao, the reorganization of states in Nigeria and India, or the fear that Malaysian Borneo states may get too close to Indonesia). This may trigger demands for autonomy by the 'new minorities' and lead to further fragmentation of the state. There are of course ways to deal with these new minorities through special representation in the region, special consultative councils, local government and by vesting special responsibilities in the central institutions for their welfare and protection (e.g. in Canada minorities in any province can appeal to the centre against provincial discrimination, or constitutions of states which emerged out of the former Yugoslavia, or in the 2000 constitutional proposals of the Sri Lanka government). But these methods have seldom been effective. Connected with the preceding point is the fear that if autonomy can be justified on ethnic grounds, the rationalization and rules justifying the grant of autonomy (identity, a sense of discrimination or injustice) may encourage the mobilization of other communities along ethnic lines, indeed to manufacture 'ethnic communities'. Autonomy may be resisted for another reason – the unpredictability of its consequences. The adoption of the federal device changes the context of ethnic relations. Territorial or corporate federal arrangements are not purely instrumental. Merely by providing a framework for inter-ethnic relations, they affect and shape these relations. They may fashion new forms of identity or reinforce old identities. They may enhance or decrease the capacity of particular groups to extract resources from the state. They may provide new forms of contention and dispute. Equally autonomy may break up the internal unity of a community, leading to intra-community conflicts (Mindanao, Sri Lanka, Bougainville), and jeopardize autonomy.

There may also be a concern with economic and administrative efficiency which is frequently seen to be jeopardized by complex autonomy arrangements, both upwards in relations to the centre, and downwards to local authorities. Because autonomy arrangements are frequently negotiated, involving different political parties, ministries, etc., rather than planned, there may be a mismatch between powers, institutions and resources. Autonomy inevitably adds to the costs of government (even if there are in fact efficiency gains, as much theory of decentralization claims). Autonomy also affects the operation of the economy, especially as there may be regional taxes and restrictions on the mobility of labour or preferences for local capital or labour. A related difficulty can arise from the unequal regional distribution of resources, giving a particularly sharp edge to ethnic differences. Autonomy may be interpreted merely as a way to ensure for the richer region (and community) the unequal share of that wealth; if it is a minority which resides in the rich region, it may produce resentment (and possible retaliation) by the majority group, and if it is the majority group which lives in the richer region, it may lead to the ghettoization of the other. Secessionist groups or those demanding internal autonomy are frequently accused of greed and unwillingness to share their resources with others, as in Katanga, Biafra, Bougainville, etc.

A further limitation, connected to the need for habits of tolerance and compromise, is that federalism may be unable to accommodate communities with very different ideas, beliefs and practices. There is sometimes fear that the fundamental values of the state may be compromised by the recognition through autonomy of different cultural or religious values. A classic, although simplified case of this, was the civil war in America (when Abraham Lincoln justified the stance of the northern states by saying that 'This country cannot endure permanently half slave and half free'). In more modern times, this was one (although not the fundamental) reason for the rejection of a federal solution to the Jewish–Arab problem in Palestine under the mandate or the UN schemes.[3] The Muslim League in colonial India rejected a federal solution for Muslims for the same reason, and the position of the French in Quebec is not dissimilar.

A specific objection to autonomy regimes comes from those who espouse an individual-oriented view of human rights. The notion of group rights that is the basis of some, even if a minority of autonomy regimes, is considered problematic from that point of view. But even those who are less committed to an individualist conception of rights have problems with some kinds of autonomy systems. Steiner, valuing the diversity and richness of ethnic groups, has cautioned against autonomy regimes which hermetically divide one community from another. He writes, 'Rights given ethnic minorities by human rights law to internal self-determination through autonomy regimes could amount to authorisation to them to exclude "others".'[4] 'Enforced ethnic separation both inhibits intercourse among groups, and creative development within the isolated communities themselves. It impoverishes cultures and peoples.'[5]

The reluctance about autonomy may be reinforced by a sense that autonomy arrangements for the purposes of ethnic coexistence have not worked; there are certainly many examples of failure, abandonment of autonomy, and attempted and even successful secession on the back of autonomy (as was demonstrated by the break-up of the former Yugoslavia). Even if such drastic consequences are not envisaged, there may be reluctance on the basis that the relevant political culture is alien to habits_of consultation and compromise necessary for success.

The future of autonomies: a framework

From the preceding analysis it would be clear that there is no easy way to forecast the future of autonomies. We have already noted some paradoxes of autonomy: it (a) seeks to solve problem of territory, and yet may aggravate it; (b) is intended to solve the problem of identity, yet it may accentuate identity and stimulate the 'manufacture' of new communities; (c) seeks to increase pluralism, yet depends for its own success on pre-existing traditions of pluralism; and (d) aims to resolve conflict, yet aggravates disputes. It is in part around the resolution of these contradictions that the future of autonomies will depend.

It seems certain that the claims for autonomy will continue and multiply. There is now strong support for autonomy, politically, morally and legally. These include new international norms, the concern with stability and the search for regional peace, regional and international interventions in disputes regarding autonomy, and the ability of groups to mobilize domestic and international support for autonomy or external involvement in internal affairs. There is also resistance to autonomy, from the international community, states or regional associations (as in ASEAN), arising from the commitment to integrity of states. More importantly, the majority community is usually opposed to autonomy of minorities. The future of autonomies will depend on how these competing forces are balanced.

In part it will depend on attitudes to, and the use of, violence. Since the birth of, or the struggle for, autonomy is so often tied to violence, the dialectics of violence will be a determining factor. Will the community seeking or defending autonomy be able to mobilize violence – certainly the purchase of arms, often with the financial and logistical support of the diaspora, is easy enough? Will the state retaliate in kind, and if it does, would the citizenry tolerate high levels of violence? If the Canadian Supreme Court's decision on the unilateral right of Quebec to secede is any guide, Canada has low tolerance for violence, and pressures will build for a political settlement, which would normally favour autonomy. In India too there are limits to the use of violence, although in the Punjab and Kashmir the scale of violence has been very high. Russia has shown propensity for high levels of violence, at least in Chechnya. Limits to the use of violence may also be dictated by economic costs; in some countries almost a third of the national budget is spent on armaments and armies, investments dry up, and there is a massive brain drain. Sri Lankan governments have repeatedly resorted to negotiations with the Tamil Tigers because the cost of violence and disruption is too high. Limits on the use of armed force may also emanate from foreign pressures, the effectiveness of which in turn depends on dependence on external funds. For example, Papua New Guinea has been under considerable pressure from Australia and New Zealand to moderate the use of arms in Bougainville and to consider instead the grant of autonomy.

The future of autonomy may depend on how compelling or fashionable the concept of 'identity' remains. The political recognition of identities involves asymmetries in the constitutional and political systems, and is hard to justify in the face of 'universalizing' values. There could be a swing back to a more 'ordered' and 'manageable' society. Identity has fewer resonances in Asia and Africa than in Europe and Canada.

Predictions about autonomies have also to be alert to other distinctions. We may need to distinguish between the fortunes of existing autonomies and the prospects of establishment of new autonomies. Established autonomies are likely to survive for the costs of dismantling are high, and known to be high. Even suspensions of autonomous governments can entail severe costs, as India has discovered in Kashmir or Uganda under Obote when he dismantled Buganda's autonomy or Milošović when he removed Kosovo's autonomy.

Another distinction that might be mentioned is the differences in political systems within which autonomy is located. The more democratic and pluralistic a state is, the better the chances that autonomy may be successfully negotiated and operated. It is thus not surprising that the more successful examples are to be found in Europe and Canada, even though more autonomies have been formed or agitated for in Asia and Africa. Relatively fewer autonomies have been withdrawn or suspended in Europe than in Africa. The Soviet Union and the former Yugoslavia had many formal provisions for autonomy, but in reality the communist party dominated all public institutions and allowed little autonomy, an observation which applies to China today. Post-colonial states in Asia and Africa, engaged on the project of modernization and 'nation-building', had little patience with autonomists, and even where formal provisions exist for autonomy, they are hedged with qualifications, and permit extensive central interventions.[6] With this complexity and diversity of political systems and traditions, and socio-economic circumstances, which have a fundamental effect on the future of autonomies, it is hard to make firm predictions. But one statement can be made with some certainty – questions of, and controversies on, autonomy will remain key political issues for the foreseeable future.

Notes

1. See Y. Ghai, *Hong Kong's New Constitutional Order: the Transfer of Sovereignty and the Basic Law* (Hong Long: HKU Press, 1997).
2. For more details and references see Y. Ghai, 'Autonomy as a Strategy for Diffusing Conflict', in P. Stern & D. Druckman (eds), *International Conflict Resolution after the Cold War* (Washington, DC: National Academy Press, 2000).
3. C. Cruise O'Brien, *The Siege: the Saga of Israel and Zionism* (New York: Simon & Schuster, 1986), p. 228.
4. H. Steiner, 'Ideals and Counter-ideals in the Struggle over Autonomy Regimes', *Notre Dame Law Review*, 66 (1991), 1539–68 at 1551.
5. Ibid., p. 1554.
6. Y. Ghai, 'Decentralisation and the Accommodation of Ethnic Diversity', in C. Young (ed.), *Ethnic Diversity and Public Policy: a Comparative Inquiry* (Basingstoke: Macmillan – now Palgrave Macmillan, 1998).

Part V
Peacebuilding

Peacebuilding is often associated with schemes to reinforce a peace after a peace accord has been reached. The term presupposes that there is a peace to build upon. In practice, peacebuilding can occur at almost any stage in a peace process and can, for example, take the form of confidence-building measures in advance of a ceasefire and negotiations. The implementation of any peace accord is highly dependent on political will and the ability of the accord to maintain a relevance to changing circumstances. In a sense, the post-accord dispensation needs to develop a life of its own. Ultimately, it needs to regularize the transfer of power and facilitate the transition from a peace agreement to a lasting peace settlement.

A key part of any process of institutionalization is the need to reform those institutions linked with security and the judiciary. These institutions may be powerful stakeholders in the 'old order', often necessitating a long and delicate reform process. Matters are often complicated by an increase in crime rates, which in turn are linked with the failure of the post-war economy to fulfil public expectations.

Barring partition, which is rarely the 'clean break' its proponents suggest, the former conflicting groups in an ethnonational conflict will be destined to share the same territory and polity. While power-sharing and other technical mechanisms can be used to ease certain functional relationships, the wider issue of reconciliation is dealt with less easily. Truth recovery schemes have been employed in various locations, and often encounter the same difficulties over amnesties, partial involvement of former combatants, and compensation. In approaching this and other problems of peacemaking, there has been an active search for parallels between peace processes, and substantial lending and borrowing between cases. Symbols and symbolism, often regarded as marginal in modern politics, can play a strong role in fostering and signifying reconciliation.

17

From Peace to Democratization: Lessons from Central America

Cynthia J. Arnson and Dinorah Azpuru

> The transition from war to peace does not come spontaneously or easily ... years of strife inevitably leave deep scars, bitter memories and rancour. Peace is won only by effort and resolve. There must therefore be a change in attitudes, a change in mentalities. Reconciliation must be the new challenge; social justice and the struggle against poverty, the new goals.
> (UN Secretary-General Boutros Boutros-Ghali, on the occasion of the final demobilization of El Salvador's FMLN, December 1992[1])

Introduction

In 1999, at a seminar on peacemaking and preventive diplomacy sponsored by the UN Institute for Training and Research, a participant identified two types of peace: the 'no more shooting type', and the 'no need for more shooting type'.[2] The remark captured an essential distinction governing the resolution of conflicts, between ensuring the minimal conditions for peace – ending the fighting between armed factions or between insurgents and the state – and building peace over the long term, by establishing stable polities that process and deal with conflict without recourse to violence. This latter effort involves an attempt to address at least some of the conditions that led to conflict in the first place.[3]

This chapter attempts to explore not only how the shooting stopped in two Central American republics, El Salvador and Guatemala, but also how and why peace has endured. El Salvador's 12-year war between 1980 and 1992 claimed some 75,000 lives; Guatemala's 36-year conflict ended in 1996, after 200,000 deaths. At the time of writing, El Salvador had traversed ten years since the signing of the peace accord and Guatemala five. In neither country had the ceasefire been breached. Our principal task in this chapter is to explain the durability of the settlements in Central America, in sharp contrast to other parts of the world where they have fallen apart in relatively short order. In other words, rather than focusing on the shortcomings of implementation – the part of the glass that is half-empty – we will focus on the part that is half-full.

In spite of their differences, both countries share several characteristics that make a comparison useful. These include: a history of exclusionary authoritarian rule involving many decades of direct rule by the military and marked by pervasive human rights abuse; socio-economic systems characterized by high levels of poverty and inequality; weak democratic institutions, persistent impunity and limited adherence to the rule of law. Decades of political exclusion fostered the development of guerrilla insurgencies of Marxist inspiration committed to the overthrow of the existing political and economic system. These insurgent/counter-insurgent wars evolved within the dominant framework of the Cold War.

While conditions that led to negotiated settlements in each country differed, as did the dynamics of the negotiations, the post-accord phase in El Salvador and Guatemala has also been marked by similarities: an extended UN presence, the successful demobilization of combatants (and their less successful reintegration into productive life), the transformation of guerrilla organizations into political parties, reform of greater or lesser degree of the armed forces, and the establishment of truth commissions to grapple with the legacy of human rights violations. Even if implementation has been highly uneven, there is general agreement that the peace accords represent significant milestones in the political evolution of each country.

El Salvador and Guatemala differ in many respects from other international experiences with peacemaking and peacebuilding in that the state, while institutionally weak, had not collapsed either before or during the conflict, and foreign troops played no central role in re-establishing the functions of a central government.[4] The distinction is important, as it focuses attention less on the role of the international community in preserving a settlement than on what states do or do not do to build a stable peace. To be sure, the international and domestic factors cannot be considered in isolation, and much of the story of peace consolidation in Central America lies in the creative tension between the two.

In explaining the durability of peace in El Salvador and Guatemala, we stress four elements. The first is that the stability of the peace is intimately related to those factors – internal and external – that led to the settlements in the first place. That is, the confluence of circumstances that made the conflicts in El Salvador and Guatemala 'ripe for resolution'[5] signified a fundamental realignment in the interests of major actors, such that military options appeared foreclosed and key goals came to be seen as more attainable through peace than through war.[6]

Second, peace as an absence of armed confrontation has been sustained over time to a great extent because the peace accords represented a conscious effort to address at least some of the root causes of conflict, even if implementation has been incomplete and highly problematic in some areas. Attention to root causes stemmed not only from the effort of the parties to the conflict to use the peace talks to advance their own core interests, but also from a recognition by the UN officials and the parties involved that a stable peace would have to address at least some of the issues that gave rise to conflict in the first place. We end this chapter by discussing the limitations of the accords in seriously impacting on poverty and inequality, factors that helped fuel conflict in both countries. While we do not argue that peace accords can or even should serve as alternative models for overcoming centuries of poverty and underdevelopment, we do note that the durability of peace is all the more remarkable in Central America given the shortcomings in the socio-economic arena.

Third, we explore the complex and at times contradictory relationship between peace processes and democratization: the liberalization of authoritarian regimes during the war provided an incipient institutional framework for transforming conflict from the military to the political sphere; the peace process furthered democratization by expanding the representativity of the political system and by channelling resources to institutional strengthening; at the same time the very existence of the peace process reflected the limitations of democratization, in that the process became a venue for discussing and attempting to resolve issues that the democratic transition had failed to address.[7]

Finally, we stress the critical role of the international community in settling the Central American wars, first in observing and mediating peace talks amid high levels of distrust, then in establishing human rights verification missions that began operations long before the armed conflict ended, in verifying the accords through sizeable missions, and finally, in renegotiating aspects of the accords through high-level diplomacy when implementation faltered. In both El Salvador and Guatemala, the principal outside role was played by the UN, although other countries from the region as well as the United States and countries of Western Europe provided important additional support. Furthermore, international financial institutions and foreign governments marshalled significant monetary resources to support the accords' various commitments. Third parties, particularly the UN, helped diminish (but did not eliminate) the elements of risk and uncertainty that are present in any post-conflict phase, and exerted significant although at times uneven political pressure in favour of accord compliance.[8]

Critical issues in the achievement and maintenance of peace

Changes in the international and domestic political context

Common to both conflicts was a changed international environment occasioned only in part by the end of the Cold War. Beginning in 1987, an agreement signed by the presidents of Central America known as Esquipulas II called for an end to outside intervention in the region's wars, favouring instead internal dialogues between governments and insurgent groups throughout the region. Under the umbrella of Esquipulas II, and before the fall of the Berlin Wall, the 'contra' war in Nicaragua ended, leftist exiles returned to El Salvador and Guatemala's small guerrilla movement had begun to breach its political isolation by a dialogue abroad with a Church-led National Reconciliation Commission.

The end of the Cold War removed the principal ideological underpinning of the insurgent movements (the Farabundo Marti National Liberation Front (FMLN) in El Salvador and the Guatemalan National Revolutionary Unity (URNG) in Guatemala), as well as removing an alternative socialist model of political and economic development. To the extent that the insurgent movements were partially financed by external sources, that, too, disappeared. Just as important, the end of the Cold War reduced the stakes that the dominant external actor – the United States – saw in the Central American conflicts.

The waning influence of the United States contributed to another change critical to the settlements in El Salvador and Guatemala: an expanded, and unprecedented, role for the UN. El Salvador's peace talks represented the first time the UN had attempted to mediate an internal armed conflict. And the launching of the human rights observer mission in El Salvador in 1991 marked the first time that the UN had monitored (as opposed to reported on) human rights in a member state, let alone the first time such an effort was undertaken during wartime.

Despite the common external environment that contributed to peace, internal conditions in El Salvador and Guatemala differed dramatically in one central aspect: in El Salvador, the FMLN by 1989 had fought the Salvadorean government to a battlefield stalemate; in Guatemala, the guerrillas, while retaining a minimal capacity for skirmishing, were basically a defeated military force. Thus, the stalemates that emerged from both situations were different, as were the insurgents' capacity to wrest concessions at the bargaining table. In El Salvador, there were classic manifestations of a 'hurting stalemate', in that both sides saw the impossibility of attaining their goals through military victory.[9] In Guatemala, by contrast, the stalemate was more political in nature. In both cases, however, the war prevented political, military and economic elites from realizing key goals, be they democratization, professionalization, international legitimacy or the ability to compete in a new globalized world.

The content of the settlement package

The scope of the issues addressed in the agreements contributed decisively to the maintenance of peace in Central America. We highlight four issues in this regard: demobilization of combatants, the creation of power-sharing mechanisms, institutional reform to the armed forces, and mechanisms to address accountability for, and knowledge of, human rights violations.

Demobilization

Quite apart from any structural change attempted through a peace agreement, the importance of properly addressing the needs of ex-combatants, both as they demobilize and then as they reintegrate into society, appears as minimum conditions of a peaceful transition. The laying down of arms signifies acceptance of the terms of the settlement package by insurgents, removes their principal source of pressure and bargaining power, and involves an assumption of risk that, once disarmed, ex-combatants will not be targeted for elimination by their former enemies. Demobilization and reintegration thus mean attending to the physical safety, food security, access to land and credit, employment and other needs of ex-combatants, even if none of these things can be guaranteed in the strictest sense.[10] Both El Salvador and Guatemala achieved much greater success with the process of demobilization than with the process of reintegration, because of the specificity of the agreements, the presence of the UN, and the financial support of the international community.[11]

In El Salvador, the phased demobilization of the FMLN was to last between February and October 1992, and the accord itself contained 'an intricately designed and carefully negotiated mechanism'[12] linking demobilization with the fulfilment of key government obligations.[13] UN officials interceded twice to reschedule the parties' mutual commitments, and the demobilization of the last of the FMLN's 12,362 troops took place on 15 December 1992.[14] The armed forces also underwent significant reductions, and by mid-1993, official estimates were that it had just over half (54.4 per cent) of its personnel during wartime. Civil defence and other paramilitary bodies such as the Territorial Service were also disbanded, bringing to approximately 66,000 the total number of demobilized combatants in the post-war period. Economic and social reintegration programmes, however, had only 'mixed results', according to the UN, and failure to address the needs of ex-combatants, particularly former government soldiers, led to several outbreaks of violence in the mid-1990s.[15]

The demobilization of insurgents in Guatemala was easier than in El Salvador, given the small number of URNG combatants; the official number came to 2950. The entire process of demobilization lasted between March and May 1997, ending only a few months after the signing of the peace accords. Supervised by the UN, the process took place without major incident.[16] The rocky process of political re-insertion of the URNG involved its conversion into a legal political party, a process that nonetheless took close to two years; meanwhile, the left remains fragmented and weak. Despite some initial success, the process of economic reinsertion has also been incomplete. A survey of ex-combatants carried out in 2000 revealed concerns over the lack of stable jobs, adequate housing and sufficient economic resources to sustain a family. These problems are common to the majority of the Guatemalan population, but appear to have been more acute for ex-combatants.[17]

Guatemala also faced violence from former members of government security forces dismantled by the peace accords. Early in the post-conflict period, the Ambulatory Military Police (PMA), for example, staged what one former government official called a 'near riot' in order to press demands for severance pay and assistance in returning to civilian life.[18] Former members of the PACs, civil defence patrols widely cited for human rights abuses during the conflict, also demanded compensation.[19]

The failure to adequately reabsorb ex-combatants has, by most accounts, contributed to a spiralling crime wave in both countries.[20] Even if demobilized fighters from both sides in El Salvador and Guatemala have not become 'spoilers' in the classic sense of the term, their apparent participation in violent crime does constitute a threat to the long-term viability of the democratic transition linked to the peace process.

Power-sharing

Fen Osler Hampson recalls that an agreement must create instruments for participation that allow for the parties to work as equal partners during both the negotiation and the implementation phases.[21] Overall, the peace accords in El Salvador and Guatemala were more successful in ensuring a role for former insurgents in verification and implementation mechanisms than they were in incorporating and sustaining the interest of other social actors. The according of special power and status to former guerrillas during an implementation phase, independent of and prior to any expression of popular will, was identified by UN negotiator for

Guatemala Jean Arnault as one of the undemocratic but necessary features of a peace settlement.[22]

In El Salvador, a supervisory body known as the National Commission for the Consolidation of Peace (COPAZ) was given responsibility 'for overseeing the implementation of all the political agreements reached by the Parties', and consisted of two members each of the FMLN and the government (including a military representative), as well as one representative from each political party or coalition in the Legislative Assembly.[23] (The archbishop of San Salvador and ONUSAL were designated as observers.) In practice, the formula allowed for the guerrillas as well as the political parties to have a voice in verification. Gridlock developed, however. This reflected divisions among the parties, the lack of technical expertise, and the relatively lower stake of the political parties in a successful outcome, given their virtual exclusion from the negotiations process.[24]

In Guatemala, an Accompaniment Commission (*Comisión de Acompañamiento*) consisted of equal numbers of government and URNG representatives (a proportion far outweighing the URNG's political strength), as well as four prominent citizens agreed to by the parties, one representative of Congress, and the chief of mission of MINUGUA (who had voice but no vote). Enhancing participation in the implementation of the accord in Guatemala was the establishment of 15 multisectoral commissions charged with making recommendations in several key areas. The consultative mechanisms in the Guatemalan peace agreement highlight one of its principal features: that it is an accord on *processes* for discussing change, rather than an accord on specific results.[25] These commissions have provided for an unprecedented debate over key social and political issues, although concrete results are less tangible. The lack of more active involvement of Guatemala's political parties in the implementation phase may have slowed the approval of key legislation related to the accords.

Security force reform

The settlement packages in Central America also gave priority to institutional, and especially military reform, given the armed forces' dominance in the political life of both countries and the military's role in extensive human rights violations during the war. The attention to military issues reflected not only the role of the armed forces as a key root cause of conflict, but also the practical necessity of moulding a security environment in which former combatants would not simply be murdered when they laid down their arms. The accords in Guatemala and El Salvador differed substantially, however, in the extent and specificity of measures aimed at armed forces reform, a difference rooted principally in the weakness or strength of the guerrillas' bargaining position.

The Salvadorean agreement was detailed and sweeping in its overhaul of the Salvadorean security apparatus. The accord redefined the armed forces' mission in terms of external, not internal security, abolished rapid-reaction counterinsurgency battalions that had participated in some of the worst atrocities of the war, established a civilian Ad Hoc Commission to purge the officer corps of corrupt and abusive members, abolished the National Intelligence Department and set up a new intelligence agency under civilian control, disbanded the National Guard and Treasury Police, two internal security bodies notorious for their abuses, and established a new National Civilian Police (PNC) open to former members of the FMLN as well as the National Police.

Despite numerous delays in implementing provisions regarding the military, five years after the peace agreement, the UN stated that 'the armed forces have been reduced and have respected the profound changes in their nature and role called for by the peace accords'.[26] The transformation of the police represented a significant achievement that nonetheless was subject to repeated political efforts to sabotage the reform process.[27] Problems involved the lack of experienced personnel and financial resources, weak mechanisms of internal discipline and accountability, and the creation of parallel security structures out of sync with the PNC's new and democratic doctrine.[28] The UN's five-year assessment of the peace process concluded that the PNC represented an 'unprecedented' and 'qualitative change in the institutional structure of the country', but one that had 'not been consolidated without the occurrence of distortions'.[29]

In the first five years of the peace accords, Guatemala witnessed a notable reduction in levels of militarization. Counter-insurgency campaigns beginning in the 1960s saw a proliferation of military bases throughout the country, as well as the creation of military and paramilitary structures especially in rural areas to combat and defeat the insurgency. Civilians armed by the military often acted autonomously from the army and were involved in numerous human rights violations.

Some security force reforms began taking place before the final peace agreement was signed, including the partial demobilization of civil defence forces, and the elimination of *fuero militar* (military court jurisdiction over common crimes committed by the military) and of tax privileges enjoyed by the armed forces. Ultimately, as a result of the Agreement on the Strengthening of Civilian Power and the Role of the Army, more than 275,000 mostly indigenous members of the civil defence patrols were completely demobilized. All 2421 members of the PMA, which performed police functions and also served as a para-state security company for banks and other companies, were also demobilized on schedule. Estimates vary as to the reduction of the army, but it claims to have reduced its forces from 45,000 to around 31,000.[30] Changes (via constitutional reform) limiting the armed forces' role to external and not internal defence, however, were compromised by the failure of a constitutional referendum that included military reform measures. Related changes such as the drafting of a new military doctrine, the elimination of military influence in intelligence matters, and the dismantling of the military-run Presidential Chief of Staff (*Estado Mayor Presidencial*) have also been slow to come about. In a report detailing advances and setbacks of the peace process, the UN verification mission asserted that the reform of the army had been uneven.[31]

As in El Salvador, the Guatemalan Peace Accords called for the establishment of a new National Civilian Police.[32] At the end of 1999, the Guatemalan government claimed to have a new police force that was almost 16,000 strong, with all agents formed in the new Police Academy established at the conflict's end.[33] MINUGUA reported that by June 2000, there was a police presence in most of Guatemala's municipalities, but serious problems remained in terms of infrastructure, equipment and administration. It also underscored the serious weakness in the investigative capacity of the new police.[34] As in El Salvador, the new police has been unable to successfully fight the post-war increase in common crime. In both countries, the army has been called in several times to assist in fighting crime, a contradiction of the peace accords.

Truth and justice

Intimately related to questions of military reform in both countries were issues of truth and justice, given the scale and intensity of human rights abuses during the conflict. Drawing on the examples of transitions from authoritarian to civilian rule in Latin America's Southern Cone, the peace accords in Guatemala and El Salvador established truth commissions, this time under UN auspices, to investigate and report on human rights abuses committed by both sides.[35] Although invested with different powers and mandates, the truth commissions in El Salvador and Guatemala produced comprehensive and detailed reports that stunned many observers. The issue of punishment for those responsible for violations has constituted a major setback in both countries because the peace accords were accompanied by amnesties. And it remains to be seen whether an official acknowledgment of the truth may over time help in the process of political healing at the societal level, especially if most recommendations of the commissions remain unfulfilled.

The UN Commission on the Truth for El Salvador, composed of international representatives, issued its report on 15 March 1993, ascribing 85 per cent of abuses to state agents, paramilitary groups or death squads allied with official forces, and 5 per cent of abuses to the FMLN. In a novel and controversial step, it named the names of over 40 military officers and 11 members of the FMLN responsible for ordering, committing or covering up abuses. Although the commission's findings were vehemently denounced by the Salvadorean government and armed forces, they contributed to a process by which senior military officers, including the Minister of Defence, were ultimately purged from the Salvadorean army, as previously recommended by the Ad Hoc Commission.

The mandate of Guatemala's Historical Clarification Commission (CEH) was weaker than El Salvador's, containing specific provisions that it have no 'judicial aim or effect' and that it not name individual names of perpetrators. Partly as a result of its limited powers and restrictions of the length of its investigation, the Catholic Archdiocese's Human Rights Office established a parallel, non-governmental effort (the Recovery of Historical Memory, or REMHI Project), to assist in gathering documentary evidence of abuses during the conflict.[36] The CEH issued its report in February 1999, attributing 93 per cent of violations to state or state-supported agents, and 3 per cent to guerrilla forces. The report accused agents of the state of 'acts of genocide' against the Mayan indigenous population during counter-insurgency operations in the early 1980s.[37]

In spite of unmistakable advances in the knowledge of human rights violations during the Central American conflicts, there has been no explicit acknowledgement of responsibility by the armed forces of either side, despite their involvement in the majority of abuses.

In both countries, those with the most to lose from a broader sense of accountability have defined post-war reconciliation in terms of forgetting the past and moving on, leaving unaddressed the material and psychological needs of thousands of civilian victims. Guatemala has made somewhat more progress than El Salvador regarding reparations to victims and their communities, and continual exhumations of massacre sites in rural areas have kept the issue of wartime atrocities before the public. But the task of a deeper reconciliation within society and between individuals remains unfinished and may never be accomplished.

The link between democratization and peace: the importance of political opening

Because political exclusion, direct military rule and fraudulent elections were key root causes of conflict in Central America, post-conflict political openings constitute another central element in the maintenance of peace.

Post-war elections in both El Salvador and Guatemala were heavily influenced by the limited democratic openings that began during the conflict, which constricted the political spectrum to the centre and right. In both countries, moderate, centrist parties held the formal reins of power in the mid-1980s, subsequently to be displaced by right-wing parties tied to the commercial elite. In El Salvador, the absence of institutional guarantees, particularly an independent and autonomous electoral tribunal and procedures for free registration and verification of election results, constituted an important flaw in the electoral regime which has only partially been overcome in the post-war period. In Guatemala, by contrast, the 1985 Constitution designed an autonomous electoral tribunal and established other political guarantees, such that international observers of elections held since 1985 largely upheld their transparency.

El Salvador's 'elections of the century' took place in June 1994, two and a half years after the signing of the peace accords. Despite what the UN deemed 'deficiencies' in the electoral system – and despite a troubling upsurge of political violence and targeted assassinations of former guerrillas – the FMLN emerged as the second strongest political force in the country. It consolidated that position in subsequent national and local elections: by 2000, the FMLN held two more seats than ARENA in the legislature, and also increased its share of mayoralties at ARENA's expense. Nationally, however, ARENA has remained dominant, in part because of bitter infighting and splits within the FMLN.[38]

In Guatemala, the first general election of the post-war era was held in October 1999, also two and a half years after the signing of the peace agreement. The URNG, allied with other left-wing parties, took third place in the elections, although its showing was far behind the two dominant parties on the right. Voter participation in 1999 increased over other years, but the outcome was not particularly promising for the peace process: the elections were won by the conservative Guatemalan Republican Front (FRG), which has been reluctant to accept the peace accords as a commitment of the state, rather than of one particular administration. Since

President Alfonso Portillo of the FRG took office in January 2000, implementation of the accords has notably slowed, although publicly the peace accords remained a central element of the President's discourse.

In both countries, less quantifiable but nonetheless appreciable is the impact of political openings on political discourse. In sharp contrast to the conflict era, it is now possible to openly debate a broad range of once taboo issues: the role of the military in national life, human rights, intelligence reform, the role of the state in the economy, etc. The forums for intersectoral dialogue have also multiplied. There are notable exceptions to the general aura of tolerance – increased threats against human rights workers in Guatemala among them – but measured against the past, the importance of the broadening of civil discourse should not be underestimated.

A related change involves greater freedom of association and growing participation by diverse groups in civil society, involving many that openly oppose government policy, including on military issues.

The key role of third parties and support from the international community

Most observers would agree that without international presence and pressure, the negotiation and maintenance of peace in Central America might have never been possible. Some have gone so far as to conclude that the international role in the Central American peace processes was *the* key ingredient of their success.[39] The processes of negotiation involved phases of observation, moderation and mediation and the final accords in both countries gave specific responsibilities to UN verification missions (ONUSAL and MINUGUA) to oversee the peacebuilding process over a period of years.

The accords gave wide latitude to the UN missions, including the capacity to identify, monitor, manage and resolve major conflicts, as well as the power to issue public reports and statements; this latter aspect enabled the missions, through criticism, to marshal international pressure in favour of compliance. Active verification included at times deploying senior UN officials from headquarters in New York in order to overcome crises in implementation.[40]

Once the agreements were in place, the efforts of the UN missions were complemented by the work and financial contributions of other UN agencies, foreign governments and non-governmental organizations in providing development assistance, repatriating refugees, monitoring elections and other activities. Bilateral and multilateral contributions in the hundreds of millions of dollars allowed both countries to finance commitments made in the accords, and constituted the international community's most important source of leverage in favour of accord compliance.

However critical the role of the international community in negotiating and maintaining peace, we underscore the UN's own recognition that durable peace, while it can be shaped by outsiders, can only be secured by the parties themselves.[41]

The need for deeper democratization and social development

Most analysts view as remote any resumption of civil war in El Salvador and Guatemala, at least the kind of civil war that took place in the late twentieth century. Yet many scholars note that both countries face the potential for future unrest if key problems are not addressed. These problems centre on the need for a deeper democratization that widens and makes more meaningful citizens' participation in political life, and the need for social development, to reduce the high levels of poverty and flagrant socio-economic inequality in both countries.[42]

To be fair, the political and social challenges faced by El Salvador and Guatemala mirror those faced by other countries in Latin America and the developing world. However, the legacy of war makes progress in these areas both more urgent and more difficult. As previously noted, major advances in political democratization have contributed significantly to the maintenance of peace. But achievements in the social arena have been modest and accompanied by dramatic rises in the rates of crime, dashing expectations that life would improve significantly in the post-conflict period.

Socio-economic issues

Despite improvements during the 1990s, for example, 47.5 per cent of Salvadorean households were classified in 1999 as poor (the rate in rural areas was 61.2 per cent), and per capita income in 1997 was 5 per cent *less* than it was in 1978, before the outbreak of war.[43] By the late 1990s, 43.8 per cent of Guatemalan households lived in poverty (the rate in rural areas was a staggering 74.5 per cent) and income inequality was the second highest in the hemisphere.[44]

The lack of specificity in the Salvadorean accord on social and economic issues led to the establishment of several commissions and forums. These initiatives – most of them undertaken in the first five years after the signing of the accord – failed to establish concrete goals, or to forge consensus over the direction of economic policy at the end of the twentieth century.[45]

The implementation of the sweeping goals established in Guatemala's socio-economic accord has been sluggish, and has faced numerous obstacles unforeseen by the parties. The government has increased social spending for education and health, but the cornerstone of the socio-economic accord, the tax issue, remains highly contentious.[46]

Political issues

Although progress on the political front has been more tangible than in the socio-economic arena, both Guatemala and El Salvador are far from consolidated democracies. State institutions in Central America, particularly legislatures and political parties, have low levels of legitimacy among the population.[47] Judicial systems constitute one of the weakest links in terms of democratic infrastructure; they remain inefficient, underfunded, antiquated, overly partisan and subject to corruption.[48]

The shortcomings of the justice system, combined with the inefficiency of law-enforcement institutions such as the National Police, are more acute given rampant common crime in the post-war period. El Salvador and Guatemala have some of the highest homicide rates in Latin America and some of the highest rates of crime victimization. Most significant for the long-term viability of the peace process is the high correlation between crime and diminished support for the democratic process overall.

Low rates of electoral turnout in both countries are also worrisome and threaten the legitimacy of electoral processes themselves. In addition, civil society remains highly fragmented, with little capacity to articulate interests and little connection to political parties that traditionally mediate demands.

An analysis of the post-settlement era in El Salvador and Guatemala leads us to reaffirm that peace accords are not panaceas, ushering in new golden eras of democracy, freedom and development. Rather, they are significant and unprecedented stages in both countries' transition from authoritarianism to democracy, creating, as conflict resolution specialist Robert Rothstein has put it, 'a new set of opportunities that can be grasped or thrown away'.[49] Peace accords in both countries resolved historic crises of political exclusion that had spawned decades of violence and war, and the settlements launched significant processes of institutional reform. That the societies emerging from peace processes are still highly imperfect should not detract from the accords' significance: the agreements should not be blamed for the limits of democratization or for the failure of market-oriented economies to overcome centuries of poverty and underdevelopment.

That being said, accords can be judged not only by degrees of compliance or non-compliance, but also by the extent to which they address root causes of war and satisfy short- and long-term post-war needs for demobilization, security, participation, recovery and justice. On all of these counts, the glass has been both half-empty and half-full, and the role of the international community in pushing the line upward cannot be underestimated. Peace in both countries reflected the establishment of a coalition of social forces that defined or fulfilled its interests along lines of compromise rather than conflict. An ongoing task of the post-war period in El Salvador and Guatemala is to solidify and expand that coalition, through the provision of concrete benefits and an ongoing commitment to democratic reform.

Acknowledgements

The authors would like to thank Woodrow Wilson Center Latin American Program interns Craig Fagan and Audrey Yao for their invaluable research assistance.

Notes

1. United Nations, *The United Nations and El Salvador 1990–1995*, Blue Book Series, Vol. IV (New York: United Nations Department of Public Information, 1995) (hereinafter cited as United Nations Blue Book), p. 283.
2. United Nations Institute for Training and Research, 'The Challenge of Democratic Transitions in Post Conflict Situations: Applying Lessons from the Past to Future UN Peacemaking and Peacebuilding', Final Report, seminar held 26–29 March 1999, mimeographed, p. 1.
3. See M. Doyle & N. Sambanis, 'International Peacebuilding: a Theoretical and Quantitative Analysis', *American Political Science Review*, 94, 4 (December 2000), 779–801; C. Arnson, 'Introduction', in C. Arnson (ed.), *Comparative Peace Processes in Latin America* (Stanford, Calif.: Woodrow Wilson Center Press and Stanford University Press, 1999), pp. 1–28; and Á. de Soto, 'Reflections' in Arnson (ed.), *Comparative Peace Processes in Latin America*, pp. 385–7.

4. B. Walter, 'Designing Transitions from Violent Civil War', University of California Institute on Global Conflict and Cooperation, Policy Paper No. 31, December 1997.

5. The phrase is from I. W. Zartman, 'Ripening Conflict, Ripe Moment, Formula, and Mediation', in D. Bendahmane & J. McDonald, Jr (eds), *Perspectives on Negotiation: Four Case Studies and Interpretations* (Washington, DC: Center for the Study of Foreign Affairs, Foreign Service Institute, 1986). Elisabeth Wood has emphasized that the structural basis of compromise is in place when the expected returns from conflict are less than the expected returns from compromise. See E. Wood, *Forging Democracy from Below: Insurgent Transitions in South Africa and El Salvador* (Cambridge, UK: Cambridge University Press, 2001), p. 205.

6. Authors' interview, former Deputy Secretary for Peace Ricardo Stein, Guatemala City, 24 October 2000; C. Call, 'Assessing El Salvador's Transition from Civil War to Peace', paper prepared for the International Peace Academy/Stanford University International Security and Cooperation Project on 'Implementing Peace Agreements after Civil Wars', mimeographed, August 1999, p. 2.

7. See D. Azpuru, 'Peace and Democratization in Guatemala: Two Parallel Processes', in Arnson (ed.), *Comparative Peace Processes in Latin America*, pp. 97–125; J. Arnault, 'The Case of Guatemala', paper presented to the seminar on Peace Settlement and Democratic Transition, Geneva, Switzerland, April 1999, mimeographed, pp. 1–2.

8. Walter, op. cit.; F. Osler Hampson, *Nurturing Peace: Why Peace Settlements Succeed or Fail* (Washington, DC: United States Institute of Peace, 1996); and W. Stanley & D. Holiday, 'Everyone Participates, No One is Responsible', paper prepared for the International Peace Academy/Stanford University International Security and Cooperation Project on 'Implementing Peace Agreements after Civil Wars', mimeographed, August 1999; and T. Whitfield, 'The Role of the United Nations in El Salvador and Guatemala: a Preliminary Comparison', in Arnson (ed.), *Comparative Peace Processes in Latin America*, pp. 257–90.

9. R. Córdova Macias, *El Salvador: Las negociaciones de paz y los retos de la postguerra* (San Salvador: IDELA, 1993); T. Lynn Karl, 'El Salvador's Negotiated Revolution', *Foreign Affairs*, 71, 2 (Spring 1992), 147–64.

10. See United Nations Institute for Training and Research, op. cit., p. 4.

11. For an evaluation of the programmes of reintegration of former guerrillas in Guatemala see ASIES, Union Europea and Cruz Roja Española, *El Programa de Incorporación para los Ex-combatientes, 1997–2001* (Guatemala: Artgrafic de Guatemala, 2001).

12. United Nations Blue Book, p. 245.

13. These included obligations regarding the FMLN's political status, the transfer of land to ex-combatants, and security reform.

14. The numbers included 8876 combatants and 3486 war-injured members. United Nations Blue Book, Annex II, p. 285. A major crisis in the peace process erupted when it was discovered in mid-1993 that one of the FMLN's constituent groups had maintained extensive and clandestine arms caches in Nicaragua as well as El Salvador. The weapons were ultimately destroyed, but not before the UN Security Council branded the discovery 'the most serious violation to date of the commitments assumed under the peace accords'. United Nations Blue Book, p. 456.

15. Ibid., p. 429; C. Call, 'Sustainable Development in Central America: the Challenges of Violence, Injustice and Insecurity', paper prepared for Florida International University et al., Proyecto Centroamérica 2020, mimeographed, January 2000, p. 5; and P. Williams & K. Walter, *Militarization and Demilitarization in El Salvador's Transition to Democracy* (Pittsburgh, Pa: University of Pittsburgh Press, 1997), pp. 151–63 and 180–1.

16. S. Jonas, *Of Centaurs and Doves, Guatemala's Peace Process* (Boulder, Colo.: Westview Press, 2000); and Stanley & Holiday, op. cit.

17. ASIES, Union Europea, Cruz Roja Española, op. cit.

18. Authors' interview, Ricardo Stein, Guatemala City, 24 October 2000. As in El Salvador, the episode revealed the danger of privileging the demobilization of those who had taken up arms against the state over the needs of ex-government forces, including some who participated in the repressive apparatus of the state.

19. In addition to the PACs and the PMA, the 'military commissioners', civilians under military supervision who were in charge of security in virtually every small town in Guatemala, were also demobilized.
20. Although data are difficult to come by, numerous studies of crime in the post-war period cite the failure to economically reintegrate ex-combatants, as well as general conditions of unemployment and the proliferation of weapons, as principal explanations for the rise in common crime. See D. Azpuru, 'The Political Impact of Crime: the Case of Guatemala', paper prepared for delivery at the 2000 meeting of the Latin American Studies Association, Miami, Florida, 16–18 March 2000; José Miguel Cruz, paper prepared for delivery at the 2000 meeting of the Latin American Studies Association, Miami, Florida, 16–18 March 2000.
21. See Olser Hampson, op. cit., p. 222.
22. Arnault, op. cit., p. 2.
23. COPAZ's composition and duties were spelled out in substantial detail in the September 1991 New York Agreement. See United Nations Blue Book, p. 159.
24. D. Holiday & W. Stanley, 'Building the Peace: Preliminary Lessons from El Salvador', *Journal of International Affairs*, 46, 2 (Winter 1993), 427–9.
25. J. Arnault, 'Visión General de Implementación', in Woodrow Wilson Center Latin American Program, *El Proceso de Paz en Guatemala: Logros y Desafíos*, Abril de 1999, pp. 19–20. In such an atmosphere, one former government official involved in implementation lamented that 'everyone participates, but no one takes responsibility'. Authors' interview, Ricardo Stein, op. cit.; this sentiment is reflected in the title of Stanley & Holiday, op. cit.
26. United Nations, A/51/917, 1 July 1997, p. 16. See also Ricardo Córdova Macias, *El Salvador: Reforma Military Relaciones Cívico-Militares* (San Salvador: FUNDAUNGO, 1999).
27. G. Costa, *La Policía Nacional Civil de El Salvador (1990–1997)* (San Salvador: UCA Editores, 1999).
28. W. Stanley, *Protectors or Perpetrators? The Institutional Crisis of the Salvadoran Civilian Police* (Washington, DC: Washington Office on Latin America and Hemisphere Initiatives, 1996).
29. United Nations, A/51/917, op. cit., p. 3.
30. Stanley & Holiday, op. cit.
31. MINUGUA, *Consideraciones sobre la situación actual del proceso de paz* (Guatemala: MINUGUA, June 2000).
32. In contrast to El Salvador, the participation of ex-guerrillas in the new police force was not specified.
33. By comparison, there were 9500 police when the peace accords were signed at the end of 1996. SEPAZ, *Balance del Cumplimiento de los Acuerdos de Paz, 1996–1999*, op. cit.
34. MINUGUA, *Informe del Secretario General de las Naciones Unidas sobre la Verificación de los Acuerdos de Paz en Guatemala, 1°. de noviembre 1999-30 de junio 2000* (Guatemala: Oficina de Información Pública y Capacitación de MINUGUA, September 2000), p. 4.
35. For a discussion of truth commissions worldwide, see P. Hayner, *Unspeakable Truths: Confronting State Terror and Atrocity* (New York: Routledge, 2001).
36. Authors' interview, Oficina de Derechos Humanos del Arzobizpado, 25 October 2000. In April 1998, REMHI's four-volume report on political violence, *Nunca Más*, was published. Two days later, the senior church official overseeing the project, Bishop Juan Gerardi, was murdered. In June 2001, a Guatemalan tribunal found three military men, including a former chief of intelligence, as well as a priest guilty of Gerardi's murder. The judicial process is still ongoing.
37. *Guatemala: Memoria del Silencio, Conclusiones y Recomendaciones de la Comisión para el Esclarecimiento Histórico* (Guatemala: Servigráficos, S.A., 1999, 2nd edition), p. 22.
38. See J. Spence, M. Lanchin & G. Thale, *From Elections to Earthquakes: Reform and Participation in Post-War El Salvador* (Cambridge, Mass.: Hemisphere Initiatives, 2001),

pp. 4–10. See also 'FMLN Becomes Largest Party in Legislature', in *Central America Report*, Vol. XXVII, No. 11, 17 March 2000, Inforpress Centroamericana, pp. 1–2.

39. According to Fen Osler Hampson, where there has been unified and sustained third-party involvement in both the negotiation and implementation of the agreement, settlements were more durable than in those cases where settlements were 'orphaned' and third-party intervention was sporadic.
40. In the autumn of 1992, for example, the FMLN refused to demobilize on schedule in response to the military's failure to carry out a purge mandated by the peace accords. UN Secretary-General Boutros-Ghali dispatched Under-Secretary-General for Peacekeeping Operations Marrack Goulding and Assistant Secretary-General for Political Affairs Álvaro de Soto to El Salvador to work out a compromise. Special envoys of the Secretary-General also visited Guatemala several times to monitor progress in implementation.
41. United Nations Institute for Training and Research, op. cit., p. 4.
42. See Ricardo Córdova Macías and Gunther Maihold, 'Democracia y ciudadanía en Centroamérica', in R. Córdova Macias, G. Maihold & S. Kurtenback (eds), *Pasos Hacia una Nueva Convivencia: Democracia y Participación en Centroamérica* (San Salvador: Imprenta Criterio, 2001).
43. Programa de las Naciones Unidas para el Desarrollo, *Informe sobre Desarrollo Humano, El Salvador 2001* (San Salvador: Algiers Empresores, 2001), p. 116; Consejo Nacional para el Desarrollo Sostenible, *Estado de la Nación en desarrollo humano 1999* (San Salvador, 1999), pp. 19–20.
44. Poverty data are from Instituto Nacional de Estadística de Guatemala, *Encuesta de Condiciones de Vida* (Guatemala: 2001); and J. Londoño & M. Szekely, 'Persistent Poverty and Excess Inequality: Latin America, 1970–1995', Office of the Chief Economist, Inter-American Development Bank, Working Paper 357, October 1997, mimeographed, p. 26.
45. See R. Córdova Macías, 'A Balance of the Process of Peace of El Salvador', paper presented at the conference *El Salvador: an Assessment of the Implementation of the 1992 Peace Accords*, organized by the United States Institute of Peace, Washington, DC, December 1999.
46. Despite these controversies, some reform measures have advanced, including most notably the creation of the Superintendency of Tax Administration (SAT) and increases in personal income tax. In August 2001, the Guatemalan Congress approved a new tax package, earmarking portions for peace accords implementation. The tax plan was opposed by most organized sectors in Guatemala, who allege high levels of corruption in the FRG government.
47. See M. Seligson, M. Young, D. Azpuru & M. Lucas, *La Cultura Democrática de los Guatemaltecos, Cuarto Estudio* (Guatemala: Development Associates, University of Pittsburgh, ASIES, 2000) and M. Seligson, J. Cruz and F. Córdova, *Auditoría de la Democracia: El Salvador, 1999* (San Salvador: IUDOP, University of Pittsburgh, FundaUngo, 2000).
48. See Call, 'Assessing El Salvador's Transition', pp. 33–4; M. Popkin, *Peace without Justice* (University Park, Pa: Pennsylvania State University Press, 2000); and H. Byrne, 'Trials and Tribulations of Justice Reform in Guatemala', *LASA Forum*, XXXI, 1 (Spring 2000), 10.
49. R. Rothstein, *After the Peace: Resistance and Reconciliation* (Boulder, Colo.: Lynne Rienner, 1999), p. 224.

18
Military and Police Reform after Civil Wars

Charles T. Call and William Stanley

Armed institutions and civil war settlements

A basic goal of any civil war settlement is to re-establish a legitimate state monopoly over the use of force in society, under terms agreeable to the parties to conflict. For all parties, the composition and control of state forces will shape post-war
security. Whatever party expects to gain control of the government must consider
whether post-war military and police will remain unitary and loyal to the new order.
Groups that expect minority representation or limited power-sharing within the
post-war order must consider their risk of persecution and violence at the hands
of the new government forces. In addition to the particular interests of the former
civil war adversaries, the long-term stability of post-civil war regimes, particularly
those based on liberal democratic models, depends on institutional arrangements
that minimize the likelihood that organized coercive forces of any kind will intervene in politics. .

To address these concerns, most peace settlements envision some degree of
reform of military and police forces. Although the type and extent of reforms differ dramatically from case to case, a common element in most settlements is the
creation of some kind of counterbalance of political and institutional forces that
makes it less likely that one group will be in a position to intervene forcefully
in politics.[1] Here we discuss two widely drawn upon models, which we will call
'military merger' and 'demilitarization and police reform'. These two paths are not
mutually exclusive in theory, but have generally proven so in practice. 'Military
merger' refers to the notion that integrating former enemy armies into one
another (usually into the government armed forces) is necessary to establish security guarantees (and overcome the domestic security dilemma) among parties to
conflict. This has been most common in African settlements, including Zimbabwe,
South Africa, Mozambique and Sierra Leone. Such power-sharing provides all sides
with, at a minimum, eyes and ears within the post-war armed institutions. Presence
in the military gives the parties early warning of any effort by their former adversaries to carry out repressive actions.

The second path, 'demilitarization and police reform', postulates that the
best means of establishing security guarantees among former enemies is to try to

Table 18.1 Security arrangements and peace plan implementation[3]

Security guarantees in peace accord	Accords implemented	Accords partially implemented	Accords collapsed/not implemented
Demilitarization and police reform	El Salvador Namibia	Guatemala	Haiti Kosovo
Integration of opposing forces within military	Mozambique South Africa Zimbabwe	Bosnia	Angola Liberia Rwanda Sierra Leone
Temporary external guarantees only	Nicaragua	Cambodia	

demobilize or reduce the power of combatant armies, shifting the bulk of interior security responsibilities to a reformed civilian police force. This option usually involves reducing the budget and size of armed forces, demobilizing rebel armies, and confining the military to external defence missions. Demilitarization is accompanied by significant institutional development and reform of the civilian police, which may include former enemies in its ranks. This model was followed in El Salvador, Guatemala and Namibia.[2] Other models exist, including the presence of international monitors or the complete elimination of the armed forces. Political conditions constrain what models are possible in any given case. The demilitarization and police reform model appears to be feasible only in cases where there is a low probability of renewed military conflict (see Table 18.1).

In this chapter, we argue that no single model for post-conflict security should be followed under all circumstances, as local conditions should be the departure point for developing effective and accountable security guarantees. However, we find that the path of demilitarization and police reform holds advantages over military merger. Strong civilian police can serve, among other things, as a counterweight to the military. Moreover, civilian police with appropriate training, doctrine, personnel selection, civilian oversight and mechanisms of internal control are likely to be more respectful of the rule of law and individual rights, and are likely to use force more selectively. At the same time, militaries that are less involved in internal security have fewer opportunities and pretexts for intervention, and are less likely to abuse or threaten members of the public.

Military reform

There is little consensus regarding the best approach to military institutional development after civil wars, and few peace processes provide detailed plans for redesign of military doctrine, conduct or organizational structure. Policy-makers associated with defence establishments in Western countries have tended to advocate efforts to develop new roles, missions, equipment and capabilities for post-civil war militaries.[4] They argue that militaries that are engaged in higher levels of professional development are less likely to get involved in politics. The historical record, particularly in Latin America, appears to contradict this argument, as the more highly institutionalized and 'professional' militaries in the region, especially in the Southern Cone, committed some of the worst atrocities during military authoritarian regimes of the 1970s and 1980s. Human rights advocates have generally argued for reduced military roles, force size and budgets, arguing that weaker militaries are less likely to threaten democracy.[5] Western powers and intergovernmental organizations such as the UN, NATO and the OSCE, have pursued a variety of strategies in different contexts – seeking demilitarization in some cases and supporting military development in others. Western powers deliberately took sides during some recent civil conflicts, bolstering one side militarily.[6]

Military mergers

In several cases, international actors have supported military mergers as part of peace processes. These efforts have usually entailed limited efforts to build smaller national militaries that integrate former civil war adversaries, while developing a somewhat higher level of professionalism. Mozambique's peace process required the demobilization of 70,000 government and rebel troops, combined with a simultaneous effort to form a new national army that would receive international training and general assistance. The new army was to include roughly equal representation (at the officer level) of the two opposing sides. In practice, it proved difficult to recruit troops for the new army, and as of early 2001, force levels remain at around 12,000, well below the 30,000 called for in the peace accord. Although there have been complaints from the Mozambican National Resistance (RENAMO) that its representatives in the new army have less influence than officers originally from the ruling Front for the Liberation of Mozambique (FRELIMO) party, the integration of the two sides into a single military force has generally been successful.[7] Peace processes in Zimbabwe and South Africa similarly involved successful integration of former adversaries, although Zimbabwe's successful military merger at independence in 1980 experienced serious problems in 2000.

While these successes show the potential feasibility of integrating former enemies, in Angola, Liberia, Rwanda and Sierra Leone, similar military merger schemes proved impossible to implement. These failures may reflect these particularly difficult contexts, rather than indicating an inherent flaw with the idea of sharing power within the military. All four of the failure cases were ones with determined spoilers, where very little confidence had been built between the adversaries.[8] Integration of opposing forces into the military is primarily a way of providing security guarantees for the more vulnerable parties in an accord. Determined spoilers such as Jonas Savimbi of the National Union for the Total Independence of Angola (UNITA), the Hutu-dominated government forces in Rwanda before 1994, Charles Taylor in Liberia, or the Revolutionary United Front in Sierra Leone proved to be more interested in relative gains than in security. Where spoilers do not win, but do not settle either (as in Angola and Sierra Leone), the government has no incentive to permit integration of national forces until such time as the spoiler makes a credible commitment to stop fighting. Where the spoiler wins, as did Taylor in

Liberia, the planned integration simply never happens, and former opponents are in no position to enforce the original agreement. Where the spoiler loses (Rwanda after the genocide), the winner has little incentive to permit extensive integration of forces.

Military reform deferred

In some cases, peace plans make no detailed provisions regarding post-war military institutional arrangements. In Cambodia, for example, the agreement authorized the UN mission (UNTAC) to help canton existing forces, oversee the demobilization of 70 per cent of each faction's forces, and fully disarm militia forces. What kind of military force would exist thereafter would depend on the outcome of the election and the preferences of the new government. In practice, demobilization did not take place, largely because the Khmer Rouge defected from the process. The May 1993 elections produced a victory for the Front for an Independent, Neutral, Peaceful and Cooperative Cambodia (FUNCINPEC), but the militarily more powerful State of Cambodia (SOC) faction rebelled and forced FUNCINPEC to accept a power-sharing agreement under which the heads of each faction would be co-prime ministers. UNTAC then brokered a hasty deal among the military leaders of the three factions (excluding Khmer Rouge) to form a unified military command.[9] In practice, the various factional forces were not integrated down to the unit level, and the dominant SOC units later backed SOC leader Hun Sen in seizing de facto power. The lack of institutional reforms to reduce the likely political use of military force clearly contributed to the overturn of the democratic process in Cambodia. This was one of several ways in which the formula for ending Cambodia's civil war lacked adequate planning for institutional reforms beyond the elections.

The unsuccessful experience of Cambodia and other cases illustrates the importance of institutional security reforms after wars. Cambodia's disappointing post-electoral democratic performance has unfolded with a security apparatus still firmly in the hands of only one party of the earlier conflict. In Angola, Rwanda and Sierra Leone, peace processes faltered before planned military mergers – or any effective security guarantees – could be put into place. Where military mergers have occurred, they appear to have helped prevent renewed conflict and found useful employment for thousands of combatants who might otherwise turn to illicit activities. In Zimbabwe, South Africa and Mozambique, the integration of enemy military officers and soldiers into a single armed force represented an important component of successful peace processes. We now turn to an alternative path, more prevalent in recent years.

Police reform and democratic consolidation

While successful military mergers and other military reforms can have an important impact on short-term stabilization of a peace process, police reforms and accompanying steps towards reduced military power and prerogatives arguably have more impact on the prospects for long-run consolidation of peaceful, democratic systems. Societies recovering from civil war often suffer high rates of violent crime due to such factors as the prevalence of military weaponry, the lack of employment opportunities for former combatants, and the ease with which clandestine military structures can be adapted to become self-sustaining criminal enterprises. Ironically, in places like El Salvador and South Africa, civilians faced greater risk of violent death or serious injury after the end of the conflict than during it.[10] Political violence may be concealed amid such generalized violence, and the public may perceive more political violence than is actually occurring. Overall public confidence in the post-war government can depend heavily on the government's ability to provide general public security. Moreover, in the absence of open combat, citizens are more likely on a daily basis to deal with police than with military forces. The tenor of those interactions, particularly the fairness of police conduct with respect to both individual and group rights, and the police's moderation in use of force, will have a significant effect on whether the public trusts and supports the new order. As police scholar David Bayley puts it, 'The police are to government as the edge is to the knife.'[11] Abusive, corrupt or neglectful police conduct can quickly undercut public commitment to a post-war order and can lead to a variety of damaging reactions such as reconstitution of ethnically or ideologically based militias.

Unfortunately, a huge gap exists between the importance of police reform and the international community's ability to deliver assistance to police institutional development. While donor states and international organizations have ample ability to provide military training and development, few resources are available to help post-civil war governments build efficient and humane police forces. Moreover, efforts to build civilian police institutions are beset by multiple dilemmas: peace-plan implementers must, for example, choose between incorporating personnel from old security forces and starting fresh with new people. Measures that may help new governments deal effectively with typical immediate post-war crime problems can be damaging to the long-term development of more democratic policing models. New policing models may be needed to replace inhumane, repressive or politicized policing traditions, yet foreign models may not be well adapted to local cultures and conditions.

Not only does the international community have limited capacity to implement police reform, but also it has not generally made a priority of security for the general public during peace negotiations. This chapter turns now to a more detailed discussion of the challenges of long-term police institution building after civil wars. We believe that the international community will need to devote substantially more resources to post-civil war policing issues if it hopes to deal effectively with the various dilemmas that arise regarding these crucial public services and institutions.

Police reform

Of 18 recent agreements to settle civil wars, 12 included some provisions for police reform. Table 18.2 categorizes peace implementation cases according to whether minimal police reforms were included in peace accords, and whether reforms have

Table 18.2 Post-civil war police reforms

Police reform included in peace accord?	Police reform implemented?	
	Yes	*No*
Yes	El Salvador, Namibia Guatemala, N. Ireland South Africa, Bosnia Eastern Slavonia Mozambique Haiti, Kosovo[12]	Angola (Lusaka) Rwanda Somalia Sierra Leone I (Abidjan)
No	Cambodia Nicaragua	Liberia Western Sahara Sri Lanka Sierra Leone II (Conakry)

been implemented to date. In many cases, agreed-upon police reforms were limited to brief references to incorporating former enemies into the police, to enhanced training or professionalization, and to conformity with international human rights standards. Croatia's Erdut Peace Agreement (1995), for example, provides only that a transitional administration in eastern Slavonia will 'help establish and train temporary police forces, to build professionalism among the police and confidence among all ethnic communities'.

In other cases, lengthy provisions called for not only incorporating former enemies, but also for fundamental reorientation of policing along new models emphasizing citizen service. Northern Ireland's Good Friday Agreement (1998) and Angola's Lusaka Protocol (1994) stipulated that post-war policing would be impartial, non-partisan, committed to the rule of law and human rights, representative of diverse communities, and professional. Peace agreements in El Salvador and Guatemala, as well as international interventions in the non-negotiated cases of Haiti and Kosovo, resulted in the replacement of old security forces with new police forces trained in new academies under new doctrines. In Bosnia, agreed-upon 'advisory' roles for the International Police Task Force opened the door to downsizing, retraining, purging, inclusion of ethnic minorities, and acceptance of 'democratic principles' among Federation and Republika Srpska police forces.

Significant police restructuring is rare in peace agreements, and rarer still in implementation. Of the 12 cases of police reforms in peace agreements, in only 8 cases was any reform really implemented.[13] Only in the cases of El Salvador, Namibia and South Africa were most of the provisions and international expectations regarding police reform realized in practice (it remains too early to draw conclusions about Northern Ireland). In two cases (Cambodia and Nicaragua) police reforms occurred although they were omitted from peace accords; however, these reform processes were less profound than those written into peace agreements.

These cases suggest three broad propositions: first, police reform matters for medium- and long-term public security and democratization. In more successful cases, police reforms helped improve human rights performance and the public's expectations for and understanding of how police should protect citizens. Second, far-reaching public security reforms are unlikely to be implemented if not written directly into peace agreements. Where authorities eventually implemented reforms without any prior agreement to do so, the outcome was more limited than in cases of agreement. Given the difficulties of getting civil war adversaries to focus on less pressing public interest issues during negotiations, international actors need to be prepared to provide agenda-setting leadership on this issue. In El Salvador, for instance, the UN drafted a new police law and insisted on the inclusion of non-combatants so that the new civilian police would benefit the public as a whole as well as helping to protect the disarming guerrillas.

Third, recent experiences with public security reforms point to a series of tensions or trade-offs that confront local and international decision-makers regarding longer-term public security issues. Coping with these tensions requires planning, realistic assessment of public security threats and available resources, and institutional engineering to minimize the costs to the public of implementing peace accords. Drawing mainly upon the cases where signatories both agreed to and implemented public security reforms, the following subsections address the choices and tensions encountered.

Transitional security

In most peace processes some kind of transitional arrangement is included, if for no other reason than that most peace plans require the various factions' armed forces to be separated from one another, cantoned and at least partially demobilized. Transitional arrangements may well shape subsequent institutional developments. Unfortunately, neither national nor current international capabilities are usually able to provide transitional security in a manner that is effective and acceptable to local populations. Existing public security forces are the most obvious resource for providing interim security. But these often include large numbers of individuals with histories of political violence, provocation and extensive human rights violations. Sometimes a degree of vetting is done to remove the most egregious offenders, but such screening is generally done hastily, superficially and without adequate information. Under these circumstances, existing forces can pose a threat to the security of disarmed rebels, their supporters, returning refugees or minority ethnic groups. They are also likely to violate human rights more generally, and may pose a threat to nascent democratic institutions.

The most common approach to dealing with these drawbacks of existing forces is for the UN or another international body to deploy civilian police observers (CIVPOL) to monitor the local police and attempt to prevent abuses. While CIVPOL can be quite effective in this monitoring role, they do face a number of limitations. CIVPOL officers do not always speak the local language, are cobbled together from disparate cultures and backgrounds, often with little international experience, are generally deployed for short tours (typically six months), and most important, are not available in the numbers required around the world. Donor countries can ill afford to lose their police officers, and thus international policemen cannot be counted upon to serve as the administrative and investigative police for entire countries.[14] Using international military troops as interim police is another option, as occurred in Somalia and Bosnia. However, many countries, especially the United States, are deeply reluctant to expose their troops to the potential dangers and costs of extended policing tasks. In addition, military forces are not appropriate for most public security tasks, since their training, equipment and doctrine emphasize use of overwhelming force, rather than the controlled application of force necessary for police work.[15]

Consequently, the provision of interim security remains a challenge for almost every peace process. The international community could do more to relieve the public security pressures on governments after civil wars by increased public safety training for military peacekeeping forces, increased use of military police capabilities already available, and wider use of gendarme-type support units. In addition, the UN should continue its efforts to improve the availability, quality, consistency and management of CIVPOL. Until these measures occur, however, transitional security dilemmas will persist.

Models of policing

Those peace agreements that do address public security reforms have often granted wide latitude to implementers, especially international actors, in designing, training and equipping new police forces. What model should be adopted? Adoption of foreign models means that policing may not respond to the realities of the society. In particular, foreign models may fail to address particular security problems that contributed to the conflict in the first place. Yet reliance upon local structural and doctrinal models may simply recreate exclusionary structures and recruitment patterns, reinforce doctrines that might sow the seeds of future conflict, or leave some sectors of the civilian population unprotected.

Perhaps the most important consideration for international technical assistance donors is that they make the effort to familiarize themselves with local conditions, and seek input, rather than attempting to transplant complete policing systems without adaptation.[16] In situations where several bilateral donors are involved in developing new or reformed police institutions, there is potential for confusion as different national contingents provide distinct, and sometimes contradictory, advice. This can be dealt with in part by having different nationalities focus on different specializations – one on general policing, another on investigations, etc. Where multiple nationalities participate in training, as has occurred where CIVPOL missions have provided training, confusion and contradictions can be minimized if the mission prepares a common field training syllabus. The development over the past decade of international norms regarding basic standards for police conduct, and especially for police use of force, helps provide guidance to different training contingents.[17]

Police force composition

A core interest of some armed opposition parties is that their combatants have the possibility of participating in state military or police forces. This participation is one guarantee that their members will not suffer persecution from state forces once they lay down arms. Even relatively small representation generates greater transparency and greater confidence on the part of former rebels or their support- ers. Thus, incorporation of previously disenfranchised political and social groups into the police can be both a means of political reconciliation as well as a source of legitimacy for the new police among some popular sectors.

Although some international peacekeeping personnel recognize the importance of including former enemies in new or reformed police forces, other international personnel (especially military and police) can equate attention to composition with politicization. CIVPOL missions and police advisors from bilateral donors have often pressed these issues only tentatively, even where failure to incorporate oppo- sition or distinct ethnic groups into the police represents a serious violation of a peace accord. In Bosnia, most international police officers were more comfortable enhancing police skills and capabilities than enforcing agreements to incorporate minority ethnic groups into cantonal police forces.[18] Similarly, in Guatemala an EU project implemented by the Spanish Civil Guard tended to accept the *ladino*- dominated government's low priority on recruiting Mayans into the police.[19]

Some peace agreements have established educational and other personnel stan- dards for admission to reformed police forces. Higher standards are likely to produce more effective police, as well as improved conduct vis-à-vis the public. But there are costs as well. High educational standards may exclude historically oppressed groups from participating in the police. Waiving some educational standards, or providing remedial training, may be needed to make a reformed police adequately inclusive. Other exclusionary standards, such as stature requirements, could often be low- ered to accommodate groups such as Mayan Guatemalans, without in any way compromising the future professionalism of the police.

Finding the right international police for the job

The international community is not well organized to deploy specialists in train- ing and developing police forces. Because CIVPOL are recruited mainly to moni- tor transitional public security forces, they are not well prepared to advise and support institutional development.[20] The tasks of creating new police academies, drafting doctrine, restructuring police forces and establishing specialized police units require experienced senior police managers and supervisors. Bilateral pro- grammes such as that of the US Justice Department may be properly structured to do this kind of work, but are few in number, and limited in capacity. Moreover, no bilateral effort possesses the capacity to deploy field trainers to supervise and build upon classroom training. The Spanish Civil Guard (GCE) has played a crucial role in countries such as Guatemala and Mozambique, but has sometimes made unfor- tunate choices of personnel and exhibited a tendency to transplant Spanish mod- els with little adaptation to local conditions.[21] Commonwealth countries have provided assistance in Sierra Leone and South Africa, but these programmes are rel- atively small. The EU, though increasingly supportive of police development pro- jects, depends on national agencies such as the GCE to implement projects.

The emergence of new multilateral programmes has done little to expand the pool of qualified technical assistance personnel, or improve the coherence and rationality of their deployment. It has also failed to contribute to improved continuity across missions. The OSCE, for example, took over police development efforts from the UN in the eastern Slavonia region of Croatia, and is responsible for training in Kosovo. Yet very few 'lessons learned' are retained from mission to mission, and fresh senior police officers, new to international police development, continue to dominate police missions, reinventing the wheel with each new operation. A key problem with many of the cases examined is that police development was an afterthought, not integrated into peace implementation. This reflects the absence of an institutional home for police development within the UN bureaucracy. CIVPOL, as already noted, is not organized to plan and implement police development. The UNDP, though it has growing experience in this area, lies outside the Department of Peacekeeping Operations and coordination has sometimes been poor between UNDP and peace missions.

Conclusions

Reconfiguration of military and police forces after civil wars is central to the stability of any negotiated settlement, as well as to the prospects for long-term consolidation of a democratic framework of government. Our review of cases showed marked differences in the success rates of different approaches to military reform. Reduction in the size and authority of militaries, combined with strengthened civilian police institutions, has enjoyed moderate success in all cases it was introduced, and seems to correlate with successful overall peace implementation. Military mergers have also been important components of successful peace processes, but are alone insufficient to prevent a reversion to war. These varied outcomes may reflect the political contexts shaping the overall peace process. The contexts where it was possible to negotiate total disarmament of opposition groups in exchange for partial demilitarization of the state were ones in which both parties were highly motivated to stop fighting, and fairly confident of their opponent's commitment to peace.[22] Contexts where the parties insisted on power-sharing agreements were more often ones where one or more parties were not fully committed to peace, where perceived risks of bolt-from-the-blue attacks were high, and where all sides insisted therefore on power-sharing within the military. From a normative point of view, we concur with Donald Rothchild that settlements that lock in group powers, rights and prerogatives (as is typically the case in military power-sharing approaches) are less likely in the long run to produce consolidated peace than are settlements that establish national institutions designed to protect individual rights across the board.[23]

In the absence of renewed combat, police are more likely to affect average citizens than are military troops. The effects of reconstituting police after civil war depend heavily on institutional features of the new or reformed police: who is allowed to join the police, who commands, how police are held accountable for their conduct, how they are trained, and what doctrines they follow. These qualities, in turn, are heavily affected by how peace implementers handle transitional security arrangements, as well as what resources they can bring to bear to

build new policing institutions

build new policing institutions. Unfortunately, despite the importance of police reform and public security issues, the international community has little capacity to assist in this area. The UN, regional organizations and member states need to undertake a major effort in institution building of their own, so as to have the capacity to provide or help provide transitional security, and to have the ability to assist in the construction of military and especially police forces that conform to democratic norms.

Acknowledgement

Parts of this chapter appeared in *Global Governance*, 7, 2, copyright 2001 by Lynne Rienner Publishers, used with permission.

Notes

1. See J. Frazer, 'Sustaining Civilian Control: Armed Counterweights in Regime Stability in Africa', PhD dissertation in political science, Stanford University (1994).
2. The Guatemalan military reforms have not been fully implemented. Military force levels and budget were cut substantially as required, but reforms to the constitutional and legal status of the military stalled following defeat in a public referendum. Nonetheless, there has been no overt breakdown of the process, rebel forces disarmed ahead of schedule, and there has been one successful cycle of legislative and presidential elections.
3. The categories in the table are simply characteristics that are really shades of grey. Tables 18.1 and 18.2 are included as heuristics. Categorizations are based heavily upon case chapters prepared for the Stanford University/International Peace Academy project on Implementing Peace Agreements after Civil Wars (August 2000).
4. S. P. Huntington, *The Third Wave: Democratization in the Late Twentieth Century* (Norman, Okla.: University of Oklahoma Press, 1991).
5. L. Diamond, 'Democracy in Latin America', in T. Farer (ed.), *Beyond Sovereignty: Collectively Defending Democracy in the Americas* (Baltimore, Md: Johns Hopkins University Press, 1996), p. 87.
6. Such intervention has occurred in the midst of faltering peace processes. After the apparent failure of peace processes, for instance, the US intervened in Haiti in 1994, NATO bombed Yugoslav forces in Kosovo in 1999 and the British backed the government in Sierra Leone in 2000.
7. P. Chabal, 'Mozambique: Prospects for Stability', London: King's College and UNHCR Center for Documentation and Research; WriteNet Paper No. 11/2000, online at http://www.unhcr.ch/refworld/country/writenet/wn11_00.pdf as of 22 May 2001.
8. S. J. Stedman, 'Spoiler Problems in Peace Processes', *International Security*, 22, 2 (Fall 1997), 5–53.
9. J. Shear, 'Riding the Tiger: the UN and Cambodia', in W. J. Durch (ed.), *UN Peacekeeping, American Policy, and the Uncivil Wars of the 1990s* (New York: St. Martin's Press – now Palgrave Macmillan, 1996), pp. 170–2.
10. C. T. Call, 'Why the World's Most Successful Peace Processes Produce the World's Most Violent Countries', paper delivered at International Studies Association Conference, Chicago (March 1999).
11. D. Bayley, *Patterns of Policing: a Comparative International Analysis* (New Brunswick, NJ: Rutgers University Press, 1985), p. 189.
12. Though not cases of civil war settlement, Haiti and Kosovo are included because of their importance in shaping international approaches to police reform and because prior

peace agreements (for Haiti the 1993 Governor's Island Accord, and for Kosovo the 1999 Rambouillet Accord) included significant police reform provisions. Although the Haitian government and the Yugoslav government, respectively, failed to observe (or sign) these agreements, in each case the accords served as roadmaps for subsequent international implementation of police reforms.

13. In the other four cases of agreed-upon reforms, renewed combat precluded implementation of institutional reforms.

14. For more on CIVPOL, see T. Tanke Holm & E. Barth Eide, *Peacekeeping and Police Reform* (Boulder, Colo.: Lynne Rienner, 2000); C. T. Call & W. D. Stanley, 'Protecting the People: Public Security Choices after Civil Wars', *Global Governance*, 7, 2 (Spring 2001); and C. Call & M. Barnett, 'Looking for a Few Good Cops: Peacekeeping, Peacebuilding and UN Civilian Police', *International Peacekeeping*, 6, 4 (Winter 1999).

15. Military reluctance to undertake public security tasks in a growing number of transitional settings has led to experiments in Bosnia and Kosovo with the use of constabulary or gendarme-type police units who combine police training and military capabilities, yet the need for gendarme-type forces in peace operations abroad outstrips the available supply.

16. One illustration of this problem is the work of the Spanish Civil Guard (GCE) in Guatemala, who wrote a disciplinary code for the new Guatemalan civilian police that is a near replica of the GCE code and, in practice, far too complex and cumbersome to work effectively given the low level of education of most Guatemalan police officers and commanders.

17. United Nations, *Compendium of United Nations Standards and Norms in Crime Prevention and Criminal Justice* (UN Document ST/CSDHA/16).

18. Author interviews with several UNCIVPOL officers, Sarajevo, March 1999.

19. The term 'ladino' is used in Guatemala to refer to people who identify themselves as belonging to the dominant Hispanic culture, as distinct from the various (mainly Mayan) indigenous cultures.

20. Call & Barnett, op. cit.

21. W. Stanley, 'Building New Police Forces in El Salvador and Guatemala: Learning and Counterlearning' and M. Malan, 'Peace-Building in Southern Africa: Police Reform in Mozambique and South Africa', both in *International Peacekeeping*, 6, 4 (Winter 1999).

22. See M. Peceny & W. Stanley, 'Liberal Social Reconstruction and the Resolution of Civil Wars in Central America', *International Organization*, 55, 1 (Winter 2001), 149–82.

23. Donald Rothchild, 'Implementation and Its Effects on Building and Sustaining Peace: the Effects of Changing Structures of Incentives', paper prepared for Stanford University/ International Peace Academy project on Implementing Peace Agreements after Civil Wars (October 1999).

19
Transformation and Reconciliation

Brandon Hamber

> The old is dying and the new cannot be born; in this interregnum there arises a great diversity of morbid symptoms.
>
> (Antonio Gramsci, *Prison Notebooks*)

Post-apartheid South Africa is a complicated place. In structural terms, a significant proportion of post-apartheid South Africa is the same as it was prior to 1994. Voters continue to cast their ballots largely, although not exclusively, along racial lines; the majority of the poor are still black and white-owned business continues to have the lion's share of economic control despite what are often simultaneous challenges from a rising black elite and the working class alike. However, political power has irreversibly changed hands in South Africa. Racism and discrimination have been outlawed, and large-scale socio-economic development is under way.

The freedoms enjoyed in most democratic countries flourish under – what is largely held – as one of the most liberal constitutions in the world. Individual rights are formally protected and a number of bodies have been set up to entrench human rights and provide an institutional frame for the new democracy. Such institutions include the Human Rights Commission, the Electoral Commission, the Commission on Gender Equality, the Public Protector's Office, the Auditor General, the Cultural Commission to protect minority rights, as well as the Independent Broadcasting Authority. The rights to strike and to collective bargaining are guaranteed, and a discourse of rights is increasingly becoming common currency for the average South African.

This chapter assesses the changes that have taken place in South Africa post-1994, with specific reference to the notions of transformation and reconciliation. The different balances of forces at the time of transition are considered and some of the implications of settlement outlined. The chapter focuses specifically on the impact of the negotiated settlement on transformation, i.e. the degree to which socio-economic change of the society has been facilitated, or not, by the negotiated settlement; and whether, in fact, the negotiated settlement through its complex set of compromises has, despite bringing peace, frustrated fundamental social transformation.

The chapter grapples with whether the concept of reconciliation and the much hailed inclusivist agenda of South Africa's negotiations have merely meant that reconciliation has become a euphemism for the compromises made during the political negotiations – compromises that papered over the fissures of the past in the interest of national unity but at the expense of the socially marginalized. The chapter also considers the degree to which the unifying spirit that came out of the negotiations provided South Africa with a window of opportunity to effect radical and lasting change.

The making of a new South Africa

Since the advent of democracy in 1994, South Africa, unlike some of its neighbours, has managed to avoid large-scale internal civil strife in the first few years of its new dispensation. Many would argue this is a direct product of the approach to nation-building which emerged from the 1990–94 negotiations, i.e. an approach to governance predicated on compromise, consensus and reconciliation. This is not to say that relative political stability came easily, or that it is guaranteed in the future. Peace in South Africa, at least in the first few years of democracy, was forged on the back of hard-won concessions made during the negotiations, as well as a bedrock of political violence resulting in the deaths of nearly 15,000 people between 1990 and 1994.

The compromises made, at least from the perspective of the African National Congress (ANC), included, among others, temporary power-sharing and job reservation for selected civil servants until 1999. Guarantees on what could be described loosely as aspects of federalism were also made. These gave regional power to some of the ANC's adversaries, such as the Inkatha Freedom Party (IFP), diluting, at least to some degree, the ANC's ability to carry out its national transformation agenda.

Furthermore, although not formally agreed at the negotiations, some guarantees on the nature of the economic model to be adopted by the new government were part of the broad spirit of agreement. This is typified by constitutional clauses that protect property rights and the 'independence' of the Reserve Bank. In essence, big business, despite being tied to necessary fairer employment practice and principles, such as those of equity and affirmative action, has been allowed to continue without large-scale governmental intervention or redistribution. This made the earlier policies (and rhetoric) of the liberation movement with regards to redistribution and nationalization slip from the agenda, while facilitating greater white 'buy-in' into the process.

A further agreement made at the negotiations was that amnesty would be granted to members of the old regime (and from the liberation forces) for crimes committed during the apartheid era. The ANC argued that the amnesty provisions were vital, in the words of Archbishop Desmond Tutu, in preventing the country going up in flames.[1] Amnesty was an inescapable cornerstone of stability that ensured (limited) right-wing cooperation with the peace process and prevented derailment of the process by conservative forces within the military, police and some IFP circles.

The balance of forces

As much as the concept of compromise brought with it a new spirit of inclusion, the making of the compromises themselves was rooted in fear. Indirectly agreeing that compromise is necessary is an acknowledgement that your rivals have a significant amount of power. In the South African case the settlement proved that white-dominated power, despite significant challenges from the majority, was firmly entrenched. The shadow of this tacit acknowledgement, as well as the real concrete concessions made by the ANC, has left a spectre across South Africa where power struggles – be they in the political arena or boardroom – still lurk below the surface and shape race relations and attitudes to the new democracy.

However, power not only rested with the apartheid regime; power existed and exists at multiple levels. Amnesty, as was finally facilitated by the Truth and Reconciliation Commission (TRC), provides a good case study in that regard.

The TRC process began in December 1995 and ended, technically at least, when the commission handed its 3500-page report to then President Mandela in October 1998. The TRC had the functions of granting amnesty, documenting victim cases and producing its final report, which was to outline the causes, nature and extent of political violence between 1960 and Mandela's inauguration in May 1995. About 20,000 people came forward and told how they had been victimized under apartheid. More than 7000 people applied for amnesty and, to date, nearly 800 have received amnesty for such crimes as murder and torture.

When considering amnesty in more detail though, it is important to note that it was criteria-driven and this differentiates South Africa from countries such as Chile, Zimbabwe or Argentina, where amnesty was blanket. Although a provision for amnesty was made in the post-amble to the Interim Constitution, it was vague enough to allow a rather liberal interpretation of it in the legislation that gave birth to the TRC. Essentially the approach adopted traded truth for justice, i.e. amnesty was conditional on perpetrators disclosing fully all the details of the act for which they sought amnesty.

However, this would not have been possible without the power balances at the time of the transition. Often the word 'compromise' is used to describe the South African transition, implying that the spread of power during the negotiations was equally weighted. This is not true and is demonstrated by the fact that although the ANC did not have sufficient power to demand prosecutions of former human rights abusers (and in reality the criminal justice system in South Africa probably did not have the resources or efficiency to prosecute large numbers of individuals anyway), it had sufficient power to prevent the National Party (NP) from granting itself blanket amnesty and ensure that amnesty was conditional on full disclosure to the TRC.

Thus, as much as the white-dominated parties at the negotiations had power at the negotiations through their monopolization of the security forces and their economic control, so too did the ANC. As obvious as it sounds, they had the majority force of the masses and certainly the international moral high ground. Guelke goes as far as arguing that the settlement in South Africa was not fundamentally different from the transfer of power to black majority rule in Kenya, Zimbabwe and Namibia.[2] He argues that there is a myth that South Africa came up with a political model new to Africa. He writes that the temporary power-sharing arrangements in South Africa were similar to those in other countries and that, in their day, the transitions in Kenya, Zimbabwe and Namibia were all hailed as a miracle of accommodation and reconciliation.

However, it is arguable that what differentiates South Africa from other African countries is the degree of acceptance of mutual dependence of former adversaries in an international context where formal democracy and economic sustainability have become intertwined; and specifically the extent to which, for better or worse, South Africa has become internationally synonymous with reconciliation. However, at the same time a level of suspicion and a mutual acknowledgement of differing levels of power are present and linger in the post-apartheid context. It could be argued that this fear – coupled with the balance of forces tipped in favour of the ANC which afforded them the space to make some compromises without threatening their inevitable rise to political dominance – resulted in a new inclusivist hegemony. Cooperation thus became central to the process, ensuring that it did not completely collapse or that division became insurmountable and cause more conflict and deaths – this process was embodied by Mandela as an icon of peacemaking and conciliation.

This conciliation, despite grumbling from the ultra-left and ultra-right, both sceptical of change for different reasons, managed to bring with it a level of political stability built on a platform of gruelling negotiations that went on in fits and starts for nearly four years. Some of the concessions and agreements made at the last minute were made from a point of exhaustion with the process and the fear of returning to the brutal days of old, but it would be mistaken not to acknowledge that despite all the mutual fear a profound change was effected in the psyche of a significant proportion of South Africa through the process. As a result the acceptance of the need for change by a critical mass of South Africa (even if they wanted different things from the change), and an overarching spirit of inclusion and compromise dominated the last days of negotiations and the early days of the new democracy. This is captured by Marais when he writes:

> The settlement and the launch of the transition depended on an activated awareness of 'common interest' between the old order and the popular movement – on an acknowledgement that friend and foe have to pass through the gateway of concessions and compromises in order to avert disaster for their respective agendas. This principle of inclusion became the central ideological tenet of the new South Africa....The transition proceeded on the basis of mechanisms and structures that attempt to 'reconcile' – even *transform* – conflicting interests into inclusive policies, projects and programmes.[3]

The new national project that resulted, at least in terms of its potential for the country as a whole, cannot be easily dismissed. From an ultra-right perspective, and given Mandela's relentless magnanimity, it would have been difficult to sustain an argument that there would be no place for a minority in the new South

Africa. Similarly, despite his own Marxist perspective, Marais feels that even the leftist impulse to immediately identify inclusion, conciliation and assimilation as the seeds of betrayal of the working classes was incorrect. For Marais the principles embodied in the new South Africa did not, in and of themselves, scuttle attempts to marshal a popular transformation project; rather, 'What mattered were the terms on which inclusion and assimilation occurred – specifically, which social classes' interests would become privileged in the resultant hegemonic project ... in the South Africa of 1994, the class content of that project was still undefined.'[4]

What is more, as was outlined above, the ANC had a sizeable majority (about 65 per cent electoral support) which was sufficient to seize political control and begin to push through substantial social reform, thus maintaining their legitimacy with their supporters despite the concessions made at the negotiating table. In Northern Ireland, for example, the situation is profoundly different. The balance of forces are more evenly weighted and in this sense are a far more accurate reflection of an attempt at a power-sharing relationship. The result is that there is little room for manoeuvre with all parties fearful that any compromise they make will swing power into the hands of their rivals.

The issue of a truth commission for Northern Ireland provides a good example of this. In Northern Ireland because power is more evenly weighted all sides are opting to leave *their* truths hidden for now. As has been argued elsewhere,[5] most political players demand truth from those they perceive as the other side or sides, but seem unwilling to offer the truth from their side, or acknowledge and take responsibility for their actions or inactions in the past. This is mostly due to fear that such acknowledgement (public or otherwise) will weaken their position as parties vie for power in the new dispensation and that the truth may be used against them within the context of the delicate peace that prevails.

Transformation and reconciliation

Reconciliation is a process and not an outcome and, in times of transition, a fraught and haphazard process at that. Transformation is a continuous aspirational progression – it cannot be said that a society is in a state of absolute or complete transformation, just as the boundaries of what is termed 'transition' are difficult, if not impossible, to define. Transformation is a multi-level phenomenon that is dependent on different levels of structural change, stability and equitable social delivery as well as the relationship that ordinary citizens have with structural changes.

To date, the ANC had fared fairly well in its attempts to try and usher in a range of social development programmes. For example, as early as August 1998, 1.4 million homes had been electrified and connected to the national grid[6] and an additional 3.5 million people were supplied with water by March 1999.[7] However, South Africa remains a profoundly unequal society. In terms of inequality, South Africa is behind 33 other developing countries including Brazil and Jamaica.[8] Although the blame for the inequality lies squarely with the legacy of apartheid, critics[9] have highlighted the fact that the ANC-dominated government's economic policies are unlikely to redress such imbalances in the short term given their focus on 'trickle-down' economics, privatization and deference to the market as the driving force of the economy.

However, although it is tempting, and sometimes necessary, to measure the amount of change in a society solely by delivery targets (e.g. the number of houses built, the level of inequity) and performance of the economy, such an approach can easily lose sight of the fact that other levels exist within society, i.e. individual subjectivity, identity and emotionality. In this sense, understanding whether change has occurred, whether what societies may call progress has taken place, and estimating the degree to which society is considered to have resolved its conflicts are psychological processes that rest on how citizens understand their relationships to others, themselves and institutions in that society. These understandings obviously need to be placed within the parameters of the socio-economic context, but at the same time they are not wholly dependent upon it and are influenced by the social memory of the past, culture and perceived (and real) levels of social power.

Given a legacy of political violence, delivery itself is not free from contested relationships (i.e. conflict between who benefits from change and who does not). Delivery has to take into account how those living in a new democracy understand the way their needs are being addressed, e.g. speedily, with care, with compassion, with acknowledgement of their previous suffering. Such factors determine how citizens will relate to the object of delivery. In this sense, a newly delivered house is more than the sum of its parts – it represents symbolically issues such as worth, citizenship and belonging. Such feelings of self-identity and dignity are the antithesis of inferiority embodied in oppression and the alienation of marginalization. Transcending such states of being, within the framework of new institutions that protect more ethereal rights and through structural change, is what helps entrench the value system of a new society.

New value systems are vital to societies that have experienced protracted political conflict, particularly if violence has been legitimated by different forces (be these paramilitary or state forces) in the conflict. A new moral regimen – along with structural change – prevents ongoing violence, which has the ability to mutate (e.g. from political violence to criminal violence) in societies where the conflict has damaged the social fabric. The legacy of the past in a country like South Africa continues to play itself out in the average citizen's views of the use of institutional violence.

South Africans of all races still overwhelmingly support the death penalty, feel it is the constitutional right to carry a firearm and advocate tougher dealings with criminals, while routinely calling for vigilante action if the police do not act in a timely fashion. The culture of violence of the past is alive and well. Ramphele, therefore, writes:

> The same process that degraded the morality of the oppressors has had an impact on the oppressed. We tend to justify the acts of those who are oppressed. The survival culture during the struggle spawned a particular approach to life and undermines the building of a culture of rights *and* responsibilities. Unless we acknowledge the extent to which that past continues to shape the future, we will not be able to address the issue.[10]

Thus, transformation at the level of citizenship and entrenchment of a human rights culture can be said to still be in its infancy in South Africa. Furthermore, although the negotiated settlement can be said to have set in place much of the democratic 'software',[11] i.e. the Human Rights Commission, Constitution, much work still remains to be done to root such instruments and bodies in the social fabric so as to effect social, psychological and economic transformation.

The language of potential

In deeply divided societies it is important to understand reconciliation (among other understandings) as an expression of potential, while acknowledging that much work will remain to be done in the post-settlement period. The work of sustaining peace will be as much about buying politicians into a more inclusivist form of governance, as it will be about ensuring that the issues which caused the conflict (racial and structural inequality in South Africa's case) are addressed. However, this process will need to take account of the so-called psychological dimension of citizenship and how the populace relates to new forms of social change.

All the while, or at least in the early days of the political change following protracted conflict, a new vision will need to be articulated to guide social policy-makers – the power of a new discourse cannot be underestimated; in this sense South Africa has laid a firm foundation. An unequivocal human rights discourse is essential in post-conflict societies. Each wavering of the new government (e.g. South Africa's new Minister of Security telling his police publicly to bring criminals in with bloody noses) will reinforce pre-existing justification for violence that is present in all conflict-ridden societies. The result can be that new forms of violence can manifest and change such as crime or ongoing police abuse of power will be the result – a reality borne out in the South African context.

Boraine supports Tutu's often criticized conceptualization of the 'rainbow nation' on the grounds of its 'potential' value.[12] Similar to the understanding of reconciliation as process, Boraine feels we should never make the mistake of talking about the rainbow nation of South Africa as if it is already present when, in fact, it represents the potential for social harmony. Similarly, healing can be understood as an aspiration rather than as a concrete reality. He writes:

> It may be that to speak of a nation being healed after deep wounds have existed for so long, or to speak of the uniting of a nation which has been so long divided, is to speak the language not of fact but faith. But that does not make it illegitimate.... But we must never make the mistake of assuming we are talking about something which is already present. That is the danger of talking about South Africa as the 'rainbow nation'. When Tutu does this, he understands this as a potential, the promise, the hope, but sometimes the term is misunderstood and misinterpreted as a claim that is where we are now and dismissed as cheap rhetoric.[13]

In this sense reconciliation (or even the concept of making or sustaining peace), if this is understood as an aspiration, can help a divided nation set a common goal, which is the polar opposite of the goal of political conflict. To use Boraine's term, 'the language of potential' can be instrumental in moving divided societies forward and should be understood as being complementary (and often the first step) towards the process of making concrete and structural change.

Furthermore, the symbolic value of acts of atonement cannot be underestimated in deeply divided societies; a good example of such an act was Mandela's donning of a rugby jersey at the World Cup. Leadership, both symbolic and real, can bolster the reconciliation capital in a new democracy, increasing the probability of producing a peace dividend that transcends old divisions and, in so doing, lays the groundwork for necessary structural change in the long term. Lodge writes:

> In new democracies the quality of political leadership matters more than in established political systems, however carefully scripted the constitutional safeguards may be against the abuse of power. Institutions are still fluid and susceptible to being shaped by dominant personalities.[14]

Thus, at the very least, the reconciliation project in South Africa, with the TRC at its helm, brought South Africa through the transition with relative political stability. The humanist approach of Mandela and Tutu brought compassion (even if only momentary) to an extremely brutalized country. Despite the horrors revealed by the TRC, glimmers of humanity shone through and provided some hope for the future – it made the vision of a new society, even if only fleeting, seem attainable. Such leadership, and the articulation of a new vision, can create windows of potential in situations where relations between political players seem immovable. This can help give momentum to the peace process or the consolidation of peace and the realpolitik taking place in the negotiations forums. In so doing a new potential can be fostered, although this is a potential that is not without its risks and tensions.

Ndebele captures this process of creating 'windows of opportunity' or in his words a 'working position', when he writes:

> ... the negotiated settlement appears to have unexpectedly delivered a will to live with unresolved tensions, while seeking to ensure that the painful wound of tension does not fester. Instead opposite poles can enter into controlled engagements in which fixed positions are gradually abandoned until a comfortable, if imperfect, solution is accepted as a *working position*. These working positions are crucial to ensuring that compromise is understood not as a manipulation, but as offering substantial opportunities to the negotiating parties.[15]

To return to the argument of Marais, the inclusivist South African settlement did not negate attempts to marshal a popular transformation project, but the outcome was dependent on the terms on which inclusion and assimilation occurred (although in retrospect Marais would probably feel that capitalism has won the day). Nonetheless, by understanding negotiations as a process loaded with opportunity, the idea that reconciliation has become a euphemism for the compromises made during the political negotiations – compromises that sustained white control of the economy at the expense of structural change – can be easily negated. Similarly, the more cynical view, that the rapprochement between the old and new regimes was a strategy to consolidate a new black elite under the banner of reconciliation, can also be rejected. The 'truth' lies somewhere between (and about) these polemics and is deeply embedded in an intricate web of relationships and interdependencies that are far more nuanced than such reductionist views convey.

The complexity of making and sustaining peace – and in South Africa's case ensuring economic transformation thereafter – requires political creativity and risk taking. It also demands a recognition that transformation is made up of more than the process of capitulation and delivery, and more than the exercise of making peace. As much as intricate relationships exist between the oppressed and the oppressor, or between warring parties, so too do more complex socio-economic, political and even psychological relationships embody the process of structural change and politician transformation in young democracies.

Looking to the future

> The achievement of democracy was the defining challenge – the long walk continues.[16]

In South Africa, although there were other institutions set up to facilitate the transition, the TRC played a pivotal role in political life for the first few years of transition. Importantly, with the TRC came a vision of a new society with new values. Beyond the specifics of the operations of the TRC – and the fact that many victims received poor administrative treatment,[17] and limited reparations and psychological support[18] – the commission embodied a restorative and conciliatory spirit. This spirit was consistent with the first term of office of the ANC and helped create a window of opportunity for the new South Africa. It was a period in which a new democratic ethos gripped the country and values such as reconciliation found their way into the body politic. This period in South Africa's recent history is captured by Lever and James when they write:

> More than anything else, these initiatives [*the TRC*] were the mark of Mandela's presidency, the creation and consolidation of what is sometimes called the democratic 'software'. These initiatives were doubly reinforced by Mandela's concern with reconciliation between the former enemies and the peaceful co-existence of South Africa's main population groups.[19]

However, in the second term, and under the presidency of Thabo Mbeki, the national agenda has taken a different, and perhaps necessary, turn. This may in part be about political leadership styles – but also highlights the fact that South Africa's democracy is maturing to some degree. Concerns of the general public have shifted from a focus on ending years of active political conflict through compromise towards concerns about delivery of services and changing the fundamental structure of the inequality in South Africa. In this sense, the TRC and other institutions helped create a bedrock of legitimacy for the future years of governance – albeit a foundation founded on a set of multifaceted compromises.

In the ANC's second term of office, President Mbeki has, perhaps inevitably, had to elevate delivery of social and public service over and above the creation of structures aimed at securing legitimacy for his government. Legitimacy is now dependent on delivery. Specifically, President Mbeki has linked black poverty to white wealth and stated his belief that social and political stability cannot be achieved without growth.[20] Correctly, he has continually emphasized the link between economic justice and reconciliation.[21] Compared to Mandela, Mbeki has placed less emphasis on placating white fear (at least in his rhetoric) and has shown more concern with transformation issues – a typical Mbeki argument is that social harmony is impossible in a context where poverty and prosperity continue to be defined in racial terms.[22] Mbeki has also berated the so-called new black elite for the 'abuse of freedom in the nature of entitlement' who attempt to satisfy their 'seemingly insatiable and morally unbounded greed'.[23]

Interestingly, however, a level of inconsistent 'confidence' in Mbeki's presidency has emerged – an inconsistency, it could be argued, that is a direct product of the negotiation. For example, President Mbeki emphasizes growth through the new economic policy that is 'business friendly', thus appeasing the largely white business community. However, his equally public emphasis on race and the need to transform the racial economic hierarchy creates a sense of suspicion within the selfsame community. Similarly, his promise of delivery, transformation and his so-called pragmatic approach have instilled some confidence in the majority. Nonetheless, his focus on the new economic policy has resulted in sharp criticism from the unions and leftists within the ANC, particularly its alliance partners (i.e. COSATU (Confederation of Trade Unions) and the South African Communist Party) – straining the relationship significantly and prompting industrial unrest.

It appears that the character of appeasement of the first term of the ANC government has slipped away and real issues and contradictions are now surfacing. In this sense, Mbeki's often confusing public approach to issues, at least in the early years of his presidency, can be seen to be mirroring – perhaps inescapably – the contradicting tensions and perspectives that were accommodated in the negotiations, i.e. a process laden with the opportunity of transformation, but founded in a so-called context of economic and political realism.

These tensions can be said to exist on a continuum with the overhaul of apartheid and its structures and societal transformation as a stated goal (certainly of the ANC) on one end and, on the other, the acceptance of the need to balance this against ensuring stability. Efforts have been made not to derail the economy, which is still largely white controlled, and to create an environment that will maintain international capital interest and ensure that the inclusionist project continues. This balancing act constantly slows down transformation.

This is not to say that the ANC-dominated government's radical agenda has been made impossible by an all-powerful economic force or even by the negotiations – the ANC too has made its choices and are active and powerful players in the new political and economic environment of South Africa. At this stage, it is more accurate to see the dominant forces of capital coexisting with the political ambivalence of the ruling elite whose perspectives and approaches to transformation have been tempered by the process of negotiations, the realism of governance and, for some government officials, their new class status. Whether this more moderate outcome, fraught as it is with almost irreconcilable tensions, will serve the interests of the country best in the long run remains to be seen.

Notes

1. Archbishop Desmond Tutu, interview with Michael Ignatieff, *Getting Away with Murder*, Special Correspondent Programme, BBC 2.
2. A. Guelke, 'Dissecting the South African Miracle: African Parallels', *Nationalism and Ethnic Politics*, 2, 1 (Spring 1996), 141–54.
3. H. Marais, *South African Limits to Change: the Political Economy of Transformation* (London: Zed Books and Cape Town: University of Cape Town Press, 2000), p. 94.
4. Ibid., p. 95.
5. B. Hamber (ed.), *Past Imperfect: Dealing with the Past in Northern Ireland and Societies in Transition* (Derry/Londonderry: University of Ulster/INCORE, 1998).
6. T. Lodge, *South African Politics since 1994* (Cape Town and Johannesburg: David Philip, 1999).
7. SAIRR, *South African Survey 1999/2000 – Millennium Edition* (Johannesburg: South African Institute of Race Relations, 1999).
8. M. McGrath & A. Whiteford, 'Disparate Circumstance', *Indicator SA*, 11, 3 (1994), 47–50.
9. See, for example, P. Bond, *Elite Transitions: from Apartheid to Neoliberalism in South Africa* (London: Pluto Press, 2000); COSATU Parliamentary Office, *Accelerating Transformation: COSATU's Engagement with Policy and Legislative Processes during South Africa's First Term of Democratic Governance* (Cape Town: COSATU Parliamentary Office, August 2000); and Marais, op. cit.
10. M. Ramphele, 'Law, Corruption and Morality' in W. James & L. Van de Vijvers (eds), *After the TRC: Reflections on Truth and Reconciliation in South Africa* (Cape Town: David Philip, 2000), p. 173.
11. J. Lever & W. James, 'The Second Republic' in James & Van de Vijver (eds), op. cit.
12. A. Boraine, *A Country Unmasked: South Africa's Truth and Reconciliation Commission* (New York: Oxford University Press, 2000).
13. Ibid., p. 378.
14. Lodge, op. cit., p. 110.
15. N. Ndebele, 'Of Lions and Rabbits: Thoughts on Democracy and Reconciliation', in James & Van de Vijver (eds), op. cit., p. 156.
16. Extract from President Mandela's farewell speech to Parliament, 29 March 1999.
17. Lever & James, op. cit.
18. See B. Hamber, 'Repairing the Irreparable: Dealing with the Double-binds of Making Reparations for Crimes of the Past', *Ethnicity and Health*, 5, 3/4 (2000), 215–26 and 'Does the Truth Heal: a Psychological Perspective on the Political Strategies for Dealing with the Legacy of Political Violence' in N. Biggar (ed.), *Burying the Past: Making Peace and Doing Justice after Civil Conflict* (Washington: Georgetown University Press, 2001).
19. Lever & James, op. cit., p. 198.
20. Ibid.
21. Boraine, op. cit., pp. 350–1.
22. Lodge, op. cit.
23. Mbeki, *The Star* (4 June 1998), cited in Lodge, op. cit.

20
The Role of Symbols in Peacemaking

Roger Mac Ginty

Introduction

Serious commentary on contemporary Western politics tends to be disdainful of the political use of symbols. In this view symbols are superficial crowd pleasers that are often restricted to electoral campaigns and offer a poor disguise for the real business of politics such as service delivery, good governance and policy transfer. More critically, symbols might be regarded as somehow irrational, appealing to primeval emotions and gross populism. If symbols are employed at all, they are often part of a rebranding exercise; market-tested and intended to modernize and reposition a political enterprise rather than hark back to historical myths or past glories.

Many current theories and practices of conflict resolution tend to reduce peace-making to a technical exercise. They borrow from the language of business management and emphasize legal mechanisms and definitions, and often squeeze out the more human factors of emotion and sentiment. This tendency to overlook symbols and ritual (and indeed human emotions and displays) in narrative and analysis of peacemaking processes risks missing vital evidence in explanations of why conflict persists and has a violent character. Jon Abbink provides the example of how traditional conciliation methods used by the warring Suri and Dizi groups in south-west Ethiopia were undermined by the Derg regime in the early 1990s. Traditionally, cycles of inter-group violence were brought to an end through a three-day reconciliation gathering of local elders that was marked by ritual and symbols such as the slaughter of two or more oxen and the washing of the community leaders in animal blood. The Derg government approach to peace-making was secular and technocratic, and developed from Western experience.[1] Crucially, it ignored the cultural expressions and expectations of the local groups, and without their active support it failed.

This chapter argues that symbols play key roles – both positive and negative – in contemporary peace processes and transitions. Moreover, it argues that most peace processes are based on two broad principles – separation or integration. Whichever of these categories that the peace process or transition fits into will play a significant role in the extent and nature of the symbols deployed.

Symbols in politics and conflict

A danger with any consideration of political symbols is a lack of definition in which the terms symbols, symbolic and symbolism become a catch-all for any ritual, sign, initiative or activity. This chapter's core concern is with definite and deliberately articulated symbols that can be connected with a particular group or cause. Although this definition is wide, encompassing everything from flags and statuary to language and ritual acts, the emphasis is on consciously employed symbols rather than events that are regarded as somehow symbolic of a broader trend. In other words, symbolism through allegory is not the primary concern of this piece.

There is an immense sociological and anthropological literature on the use and meanings of symbols.[2] It emphasizes the social and communicative nature of symbols, their sociocultural relativism and their inclusive and exclusive roles in the formation and maintenance of group identity. It also highlights the symbolic inventory of colours, flags or historical references that each group, community, political party or state is capable of appropriating and mobilizing for its own purposes.

A subdivision of this literature concentrates on the use of symbols in conflict situations.[3] It is important to note that contention over symbols is normally derivative of a deeper conflict and that symbols can be seen as a mobilization or expression of the conflict rather than a cause of the conflict. The point mirrors similar arguments on ethnicity and the causes of conflict. While ethnicity per se is rarely enough to cause a conflict, conflicts become 'ethnicized', with elites using claims based on ethnic difference and superiority to mobilize groups. The outward manifestation of such conflicts may lead observers to label them, somewhat erroneously, as 'ethnic conflicts'. Similarly, conflicts involving clashes over symbols may be labelled as 'symbolic conflicts', but a more prosaic conflict over power and resources usually lurks beneath. The peculiar nature of ethnonational conflicts often involves the mass mobilization of people, appeals to group history (whether spurious or real), and the creation of identity bonds. Symbols can play a key role in all of this, promoting a particular world-view, manipulating emotions, objectifying group insiders and outsiders, and creating boundaries between groups. John Armstrong notes how some symbols act as 'traffic lights' delineating the barriers that separate groups.[4] Symbols are also capable of condensing complicated and often contradictory messages into a single unifying image, slogan or movement.[5] As such, and when combined with other conflict conditions, they can be incredibly efficient and low-cost tools of popular mobilization and media management.

A key feature of political and group symbols is their ability to embody multiple meanings. Rarely possessing an intrinsic value, symbols rely on subjective interpretation and so any message associated with them risks distortion, inflation or complication. This ambiguity of symbols is often a key factor in their contribution to conflict, with antagonists holding varying perceptions of the same symbols. One group, for example, may regard a flag as a neutral and legitimate statement of identity, while another group regards it as offensive and inflammatory.

The multiplicity of meanings can also help explain the longevity of symbols across generations and groups, and their reinvention and reinterpretation.

Notably, symbols are often explicit targets in ethnic violence. The 1992 destruction of the Babri Masjid mosque by Hindu nationalists in India is just one example from a decade littered with cases of the deliberate targeting of religious sites and cultural heritage.[6] Many physical attacks on symbols can be explained by the peculiar nature of violence often associated with ethnonational conflicts. Violence in such conflicts is often informal, civilianized and intermittent. Sustained periods of tension are interrupted by inter-group rioting and attacks on local and specific targets. Combatants may be ill-disciplined, lacking in political control and not formally aligned with any military or political grouping. In such circumstances, attacks on symbols may take the form of low-level vandalism of a graveyard or place of worship. As such, they may be classed as intimidation rather than a sustained military campaign. They may also be marked by a gratuitous quality, lacking in any obvious strategic or military rationale. Instead, they are designed to broadcast wider messages of subordination and contempt. As such they can act as a warning of more serious violence to come.

Aside from direct attacks on the symbols associated with another group, opposing groups may compete in the promotion of their own symbols. Simultaneously, antagonists may seek to deny or delegitimize the symbols associated with others. Nationalist groups seeking statehood may employ and invent symbols to help convey the impression of quasi-statehood. To a certain extent, the Palestine Liberation Organization engaged in this activity prior to the establishment of the Palestinian National Authority and is currently pursuing this strategy with even more vigour in the hope of achieving actual statehood. It has, for example, recruited a diplomatic corps and adopted other trappings usually associated with formal statehood. The strategy can concurrently be regarded as a loyalty-building exercise for group members, and a signal of political and nationalist intent for group outsiders.

Symbols in peace processes

Peace processes are often tentative enterprises that operate in the face of continuing division and violence. Rather than marking an end to conflict, they endeavour to move the conflict towards a less costly mode. Antagonists do not automatically lose their mutual antipathy or exclusive goals. Instead the peace process may be regarded as conflict by other means, or an opportunity to intensify or diversify the conflict. In such circumstances, it is unsurprising that the conflicts over or via symbols outlined above retain their salience. Moreover, the group symbols themselves retain their purpose. Indeed, the peculiar nature of peace processes often means that conflict over symbols attracts greater significance and potency. Possible reasons for this are reviewed below.

First, antagonists have a tendency to regard a peace process as a 'zero-sum game' that will deliver either victory or defeat. Some peace processes reach a stage of reciprocal bargaining, in which a series of trade-offs pave the way for common agreement. Many peace processes, on the other hand, fail to reach a stage in which formal negotiations occur against a mutual understanding of the need to regulate the conflict and allow for the rational evaluation of each side's position. Instead, the nascent peace process is interpreted as a threat, or as an opportunity to press home an advantage. In such 'all or nothing' politics, all issues, even symbolic and seemingly of little intrinsic worth, must be contested or defended. Failure to defend a group symbol risks broadcasting a message of a more general weakness on key positions or articles of faith.

Second, and related to the above point, peace processes normally witness a vast increase in political activity. They often operate at multiple levels, with many participants engaging with many issues. This sheer bulk of activity, together with the sensitive nature of many of the issues raised, provides opportunities for politics with a high symbolic content. For example, first-time meetings between former antagonists (Gerry Adams and David Trimble in Northern Ireland), the emergence and identification of guerrilla leaders as political figures (Subcomandante Marcos in Chiapas, Mexico), and the intervention of significant third parties (Bill Clinton in the Oslo process) all provide the occasion and space for the employment of symbols for political purposes. Furthermore, the often drawn-out nature of peace processes, with sustained periods of political inactivity and interruptions due to violence, presents opportunities for symbolic politics.

Indeed, peace process participants may see certain attractions in engaging opponents on issues of symbols. Arguments over symbols may be seen as deflective, steering negotiations and engagements away from more substantive issues. In certain circumstances, such arguments may even be described as confidence-building measures, allowing time for judgements to be reached on the seriousness of the opposition on peacemaking initiatives. Contests and slippage on matters of symbols can aid in the acclimatization of a constituency to a need for movement on more substantive issues.

Third, group mobilization often plays a key role in peace processes. Groups shut out from negotiations, or perhaps unhappy with the course of negotiations, may seek to demonstrate their strength in numbers through mass demonstrations. Street politics is a phenomenon closely associated with many peace processes and it provides multiple opportunities for the deployment of political symbols. The transition to majority rule in South Africa, for example, was accompanied by a series of mass rallies and politicized funerals. The targets of such politics are often intra-group, as different organizations vie for the pre-eminent position as sole and legitimate representative of the group. Symbols are particularly effective at the intra-group level, making intuitive and instant connections with a common inventory of history, language and political iconography. They are often low cost and repetitive, requiring a minimum of articulation and intellectual defence. A 'flag war' in Belfast in summer 2000 saw every available lamp-post in certain districts of the city festooned with flags linked to militant organizations. It was very much an intra-loyalist affair and was a manifestation of intense competition between rival groups for pre-eminence. In some respects the 'flag war' offered the militants a non-violent means of competition and only after several months did it erupt into a violent feud.

While the sheer weight of numbers in mass demonstrations signifies popular will, it is often complemented by more expressive and televisual features in the form of slogans, banners or street theatre. The mass protests against ETA violence in the Basque Country from the late 1990s onwards were given added poignancy and impact because of the silence of the assembled crowds.[7] In pre-transition South Africa, the Inkatha Freedom Party (IFP) made the right to carry 'traditional weapons' a key feature of a series of mass marches. For the IFP the weapons held cultural value, but for their opponents, particularly the white minority, they contributed to the image of '... thousands of Zulu migrants, with red headbands and traditional and modern weapons, hacking their way into the country's political arenas'.[8]

A fourth reason for the salience of symbols in peace processes is the likelihood that a peace process will expose antagonists to unpalatable challenges, thus encouraging groups to make recourse to symbols as a form of comfort. For example, antagonists may be forced to recognize the legitimacy of a group or organization they have previously demonized, while simultaneously admitting to violence and contradictions associated with their own position. The proposed outcome of the peace process may also be unappealing, involving, for example, power-sharing or the ceding of territory. In such circumstances, symbols may offer a reassurance, certainty and comfort, and an escape from present dangers. They can reinforce social order and 'dull rather than awaken critical thought'.[9] This calming role operates primarily at the intra-community level but carries the risk, because of the multiple interpretations open to symbols, of offending other groups.

A final point worth making is that disputes concerning symbols are often much more difficult to resolve than material ones. Indeed, the 'business management' approach favoured in many peace initiatives is simply unable to come to terms with the sentiment and emotion that fuel claims over symbols. Issues such as the status of Jerusalem or the decommissioning of paramilitary weapons in Northern Ireland may risk becoming symbolic lines in the sand. As such they are peculiarly resistant to attempts to disaggregate them and negotiate over them as though they were concrete, tradable issues.

Symbols of accord

So far, the main focus of this chapter has been the role of symbols in the promotion of single group identity or their role in conflict. These may be classed as symbols of discord. But symbols can be harnessed to promote accord in the context of a peace process or transition. Neutral and inclusive symbols can be employed to help cement a new post-accord dispensation and promote multiculturalism or the acceptance of diversity. The crucial issue is the nature of the peace process or accord. At the macropolitical level, most peace accords can be divided into two broad, and admittedly oversimplified, categories: those based on separation and those based on integration. In the former case, the separation of antagonists means that the use of exclusive symbols will persist. In the latter, the proposed accommodation will be based on inclusion and the integration of formerly warring parties under a single political entity. In such cases, the invention and promotion of symbols of accord and unity may be beneficial. This argument is worthy of further explanation, beginning with the separation model.

Some peace processes are based on managed separation, or a recognition that the antagonists are mutually incompatible and attempts at integration would necessitate coercion and probably prolong and intensify the conflict. These processes manifest themselves in secessions and (re-)partitions and are built on a recognition that continued coexistence requires a new regulation of relations between the warring parties and independence from each other. But clean breaks are rarely possible. Populations are seldom as obedient as a political cartographer's pen might wish them to be, and vulnerable minorities may become separated from their preferred state. As a result, peace accords in such circumstances often involve a recognition that the antagonists will continue to share resources, boundaries and populations. Examples include the Oslo process, East Timor and Indonesia, and the former Yugoslavia. For the power holder, the essential driving force is the need to cut losses, regroup around the centre and secure against further separatist violence. For the power seeker, the aim is to secure independence from what is perceived as the alien and dominating power. For both, there is a common motive of security that cannot, it is judged, be achieved without a measure of ethnic separation.

Once a degree of separation and independence is achieved, the aims become the consolidation, institutionalization and reinforcement of that independence. In such circumstances, both those who sought to gain power and those who sought to hold onto power may engage in nation-building exercises that offer significant opportunities for the use of symbols. The leadership elite in the former power holder may attempt to mask or soften any loss of territory or prestige by recourse to nationalist certainties and symbols; a trend visible in the latter stages of the Milošović regime in rump Yugoslavia. Third parties and the international community often play a facilitation role in these ethnic separations. Symbols, in the form of white UN vehicles, blue helmets or the Red Crescent/Cross, play an intricate part in the provision of humanitarian services attendant with the separation.

'Power gainers' may make similar use of symbols. In Croatia, for example, the national flag is displayed with ubiquity; on car licence plates and government documentation but also on everything from hotel menus to artwork. East Timor also underwent a self-conscious process of 'Timorization' following the Indonesian departure in 2000. An East Timorese team was included in the Sydney Olympics, a diplomatic corps was trained, Portuguese was adopted as the national language, and the construction of a national museum was commissioned.[10] In both cases there was the conscious use of symbols as part of a state and nation-building programme. In the case of Croatia, the context was post-war independence, while in East Timor the state-building occurred in preparation for the withdrawal of the UN Transitional Administration in East Timor (UNTAET). Substantial minorities remained in both locations, and they may well have felt that the partisan nature of the symbolism was exclusionary. In the Croatian case at least, Article 15 of the Constitution noted that 'Members of all nations and minorities shall be guaranteed freedom to express their nationality, freedom to use their language and script, and cultural autonomy.'[11] The reality of a post-war environment, however, in which gains were jealously guarded and politics was often characterized by insecurity, meant that constitutional provisions alone were unable to counter the weight of monocultural symbols.

The post-Dayton Federation of Bosnia-Hercegovina represents an uneasy mix of the separation and integration models. Like Northern Ireland, it is a case of separation within integration, with a macro-level peace accord promoting a single political entity, but significant separation persisting within it. Separate Bosnian Muslim/Croat and Serb political entities coexist under a central government and rotating presidency. Following the failure of local politicians to agree on a new federation-wide flag, coat of arms, currency and passport, neutral designs were imposed by the international community.[12]

The significance of symbols can also be witnessed through the immense importance attached to the preservation and rebuilding of religious sites across Bosnia-Hercegovina. These buildings are often the first to be reconstructed following the cessation of hostilities and the resettlement of returnees. They act as symbols of religious and cultural identity to threatened communities and, more practically, as community focal points. Moreover, the fate of such reconstruction initiatives are often taken as indicators of the well-being of multiculturalism at a local level. The reconstruction of the sixteenth-century Ferhadija mosque in Banja Luka in the Serb-controlled part of the Federation sparked intense opposition from Serbian nationalists in 2000 and 2001. One of 15 mosques destroyed in the city during the war, its reconstruction was regarded by Muslim returnees as an indicator of their acceptance in the city. A government statement noted that the rebuilding would be '... a test of the capability of the republic's democratic forces and institutions'.[13] Significantly, sectarianism crystallized around this issue – the rebuilding of a symbol – rather than more overtly political issues. At one stage Serb demonstrators managed to halt the ceremony marking the start to the mosque rebuilding and even set a pig loose on the site.

The other main model of peace process and transition is based on an integrative framework. Antagonists agree to regulate the violent manifestations of the conflict and coexist under a single political dispensation. While the wider political entity (the state) retains its essential integrity, there may be a reordering of its constituent parts. This might involve a new constitution or the formulation of a power-sharing system of government calibrated to take account of diversity. Similarly, government bodies and policies may be reformed to make them more inclusive of minorities. In such circumstances, it is possible to identify two approaches to symbols. In the first, new, inclusive symbols are invented (or amalgamated from prior existing symbolic inventories) to signify a new beginning and a shared future. These symbols may be intended to be neutral and capable of connecting with all sections of the community. In the second approach, the essential differences and loyalties in society are acknowledged and so all symbols are afforded mutual respect. Again, it is worth emphasizing that the integrative framework is an ideal type conceptualization and that reality is often complex.

Post-apartheid South Africa represents a case in which new symbols were mobilized to promote national unity. The extent of the transition, the virtual invention of a new state, gave an opportunity for the wholesale replacement of an exclusionary nomenclature. The new symbols of statehood were based on a plural civic nationalism. A new flag with six colours represented diversity. Place names and national holidays that had been linked with the Afrikaans history and culture were replaced with more neutral forms. For example, the new currency was based on the 'big five' animals of the African bush. Notably the symbol of the rainbow was adopted to signify the new South Africa's multicultural inheritance. The changes in the official symbols of state took place in the context of radical constitutional and political change, and depended on sensitive judgements to avoid triumphalism and a sense that the Afrikaans legacy was being devalued and excluded. This was not always successful, and at local level there were attempts to exorcise settler history with the removal of statues and memorials from a number of town centres. The *Masakhane*, or programme of national unity, was elite-led and could not mask the broad political trend of black empowerment and white power loss, as well as the persistent economic divisions in South African society.

While symbols of discord are derivative of broader conflicts, symbols of accord are very much linked to the wider peace process or transition, and are unable, unaided, to promote reconciliation. Data from the *Northern Ireland Life and Times* survey shows that attitudes towards neutral symbols, such as a new flag for Northern Ireland or a single memorial for all of the victims of the conflict, are split along communal lines and that attachment to partisan symbols remains strong, despite macro-level political changes.[14] A physical memorial to the dead of a conflict is unlikely to prove cathartic unless reinforced by feelings of remorse and conciliation among a significant section of society. The great advantage of newly invented symbols of accord is that they do not represent the imposition of one group's symbols at the expense of those of another. Instead they are deliberately accessible and non-divisive, consciously avoiding the exclusive symbolic inventories of rival groups. The non-organic nature of these symbols carries the risk that they may be interpreted as artificial and contrived, making little connection with popularly held sentiments.

The growing corpus of peace accords, transitional agreements and new constitutions reached in the 1990s provides evidence that the multicultural approach has been gaining a more prominent place in peacemaking. The Guatemalan peace process was marked by a number of agreements, one of which addressed cultural inclusion. The 1995 'Agreement on Identity and Rights of Indigenous Peoples' noted that '. . . educational and cultural policy must be oriented to focus on recognition, respect and encouragement of indigenous cultural values'.[15] The agreement also reaffirmed a constitutional right to indigenous dress, a recognition of temples and holy places, and the right to names and place names. The 1996 peace agreement with the Moro National Liberation Front in the Philippines noted that, 'Muslim culture, mores, customs and traditions . . . as well as the cultures, mores, customs, and traditions of Christians and indigenous people, shall be preserved through the regular public and special schools in the Autonomous Region. . . .'

A 1996 joint agreement between the Zapatistas in Chiapas and the Mexican government noted that, 'It is necessary to enshrine, at the constitutional level, the right of all Mexicans to a multicultural education that recognizes, disseminates, and promotes the history, customs, traditions, and general culture of the indigenous peoples, who are the root of our national identity.'[16] The agreement was not implemented, but it does show a widening of peace processes and transitions away from purely territorial and security issues to encompass issues of social and cultural inclusion.

Conclusion

This chapter argued that peace processes and transitions could be placed in two broad categories: separation and integration. A variety of conditions determine whether any peace process is likely to fall into one or the other category. These conditions are not easily controlled and include the strength of the parties to resist pressures from the international community (often in favour of integrative measures or at least resistant to outright separation), the state of play on the military field, and changing international norms on state sovereignty and boundaries. Symbols deployed during a peace process or transition are very much a dependent variable, reflecting whether the integration or separation paths are followed.

The symbols most closely associated with the ending of ethnonational conflicts are memorials objectifying loss and signifying the ethos required for future cooperation and reconciliation. But 'end points' in conflicts are elusive and symbols are capable of playing both facilitating and complicating roles in the journey to find them. Symbols can be (re-)energized by the uncertainty surrounding peace processes and transitions, used to mobilize groups, objectify grievances, boost confidence between antagonists, and secure safe passage for third parties. A key problem relates to the multiplicity of meanings held by symbols. Agreement on contested symbols is often illusive precisely because of the difficulty in agreeing on the nature, significance and meaning of the symbols in contention. Instead, arguments over symbols may be interpreted as a mask for disagreement on more fundamental conflict issues, and can provide antagonists with issues that can be 'inflated' to have wider resonance and mobilization potential within their community.

Against such a background, the positive potential of symbols can be overlooked. This potential is very much dependent on the nature of the peace process or transition. Those based on ideas of, or containing elements of, accommodation, inclusion or integration can utilize symbols to positive effect. In such circumstances, the role of symbols of accord is very much complementary to wider peacemaking efforts, and the new symbols run the risk of rejection or failure to find resonance with their target communities. A more sensitive issue is also at play: what position is afforded to prior-existing symbols of group identity in a post-agreement period? Exclusive symbols of group loyalty are impossible to disinvent, as is the offence they may cause to others. It may be possible, however, to undermine the loyalty and emotion they are capable of generating. This is very much dependent on the wider peace process or transition, but the key seems to be the relevance of single group symbols in a post-accord dispensation. If individuals and groups feel genuinely included in a new political and cultural order then exclusive symbols will have little meaning. If the underlying causes of the conflict (for example, political and cultural exclusion) remain unaddressed, then it will remain entirely rational to adopt symbols in the struggle for redress.

Notes

1. J. Abbink, 'Violence and the Crisis of Conciliation: Suri, Dizi and the State in South West Ethiopia', *Africa*, 70, 4 (2000), 527–50.
2. Notable contributions to the literature include: P. Bourdieu, *Language and Symbolic Power* (Cambridge: Polity Press, 1991); C. Elder & R. Cobb, *The Political Uses of Symbols* (New York: Longman, 1983); R. Firth, *Symbols Public and Private* (London: Allen & Unwin, 1973) and D. Kertzer, *Ritual, Politics and Power* (New Haven: Yale University Press, 1988).
3. See S. Harrison, 'Four Types of Symbolic Conflict', *Journal of the Royal Anthropological Institution*, 1, 2 (1995), 255–72; D. Horowitz, *Ethnic Groups in Conflict* (Berkeley, Calif.: University of California Press, 1985), pp. 216–19; S. J. Kaufman, *Modern Hatreds: the Symbolic Politics of Ethnic War* (Ithaca, NY: Cornell University Press, 2001), pp. 15–47 and 203–21; and C. Krohn Hansen, 'The Anthropology of Violent Interaction', *Journal of Anthropological Research*, 50, 2 (1994), 367–82.
4. J. Armstrong, *Nations before Nationalism* (Chapel Hill, NC: University of North Carolina Press, 1982), p. 7.
5. B. Turner refers to 'compactness' in *Organisational Symbolism* (Berlin: Walter de Gruyter, 1990), p. 4.
6. P. Bacchetta, 'Sacred Space in Conflict in India: the Babri Masjid Affair', *Growth and Change*, 31, 2 (Spring 2000), 255–84.
7. 'Silent Protest at Basque Murder', BBC News website, 29 July 2000.
8. A. Sitas, 'The New Tribalism: Hostels and Violence', *Journal of Southern African Studies*, 22, 2 (June 1996), 235–48.
9. R. Klatch, 'Of Meanings and Masters: Political Symbolism and Symbolic Action', *Polity*, 21, 1 (Fall 1998), 137–54 at p. 145.
10. Details of these initiatives can be found on the UNTAET website: http://www.un.org/peace/etimor/etimor.htm (2001).
11. The text of the Croatian Constitution can be found at: http://www.vlada.hr/english/docs-constitution.html (2001).
12. 'Bosnian Coat of Arms Imposed by Outside Arbiter', BBC News website, 28 November 2000.
13. 'Violence at Bosnia Mosque Ceremony', BBC News website, 18 June 2001.
14. The survey results can be found at: http://www.ark.ac.uk/nilt/ (2002).
15. The full text of the 'Agreement on Identity and Rights of Indigenous Peoples' can be found at: http://www.incore.ulst.ac.uk/cds/agreements/index.html (1995).
16. 'Joint proposals that the Federal Government and the EZLN agree to remit to the national debating and decision-making bodies in accordance with paragraph 1.4 of the rules of procedure.'

21
Borrowing and Lending in Peace Processes

John Darby

In 1998 Herri Batasuna, the political party closest to ETA's aims, invited all the main Basque political parties and other movements to participate in an 'Ireland Forum' in order to explore the relevance of the Northern Ireland process to the Basque Country. The development was inspired by the 'pan-nationalist' front in Northern Ireland which brought together the main interests favouring a broad nationalist position – Sinn Fein, the SDLP, the government of the Irish Republic and Irish-American interests. The 'Ireland Forum' led directly to the Lizarra Agreement. Four days later ETA declared a ceasefire. Mees argues that the Basque peace process is almost unimaginable 'without the domino effect of the Northern Irish model'.[1] Herri Batasuna's leader Arnaldo Otegi confessed that 'Ireland was a mirror for us, and so was the republican movement'.[2]

The open adoption of the Northern Ireland model by the Basques was not exceptional, except in degree. There has been a high level of deliberate 'borrowing' between contemporary peace processes, inspired and stimulated by the proliferation and perceived success of other processes during the 1990s. 'If the Arabs and the Israelis can do it', the Irish Taoiseach Albert Reynolds wrote to John Major the UK Prime Minister in 1993, 'why can't we?'[3] Eight years later Senator George Mitchell, chairman of the Northern Ireland talks and leader of a fact-finding commission on the Israeli–Palestinian violence, reversed the advice: 'I regularly say to the political leaders in the Middle East ... if they can do it in Northern Ireland, you can do it in the Middle East.'[4] Some negotiators, notably the South Africans, were more proactive and became evangelists for peace. Nelson Mandela as an individual became a significant incentive for budding negotiations, particularly in Africa. The use of 'famous people' to lend support and advice in crisis areas was institutionalized by the Carter Center at Emory University. Visits between those engaged in peace negotiations in different countries became commonplace. A shared language evolved, referring to 'hurting stalemates', 'respect for cultural diversity', 'confidence-building measures', 'a conflict-resolution situation', even the term 'peace process' itself.

By the late 1990s the interdependence between peacemaking initiatives in different parts of the world was widely visible and acknowledged. In the midst of the mounting crisis in December 2000 the Israeli Prime Minister Ehud Barak had time to reflect that, 'if we don't make an agreement and drift, God forbid, into a situation of deterioration, there will be cracks in other peace deals'.[5]

Why so much borrowing?

The key to the rise in borrowing lies in changes in the ways in which contemporary peace processes are negotiated. Before the early 1990s many peace processes either depended on friendly external support[6] or followed on the heels of military intervention by the UN. Since the ending of the Cold War, not only has the number of negotiated accords risen steadily, but the proportion of them negotiated by the parties primarily engaged in the conflict has increased. The absence of an external custodian shifted the driving force from military sanctions to evolving joint procedures for talks. Consider the 38 formal peace agreements signed between 1988 and 1998. In the first five years, from 1988 to 1992, 6 of the 10 peace agreements (60 per cent) were brokered with the direct involvement of the UN. But the UN was involved in only 10 of the 28 agreements signed between 1993 and late 1998 (35.7 per cent). The change in pattern has been accelerating; of the 15 agreements reached between 1996 and 1998, only 2 (13.3 per cent) involved the UN.[7] While UN activity has increased somewhat since 1998, contemporary peace processes include a significant body of internally negotiated accords, with more or less assistance from external actors.

The cascade

The increasingly internal nature of peace processes has increased the search for new approaches and guidelines. Historical models, especially those preceding the end of the Cold War, were often dismissed as irrelevant. Instead guidance and support were sought from contemporary processes. As a consequence a cascade of borrowing developed during the 1990s. The fountainhead was South Africa, where a raft of innovative approaches to negotiations was developed: 'the channel'; sufficient consensus; bush summits; transitional institutions;[8] the imaginative use of symbols to encourage national unity; most of all, the fact that the process was accomplished through negotiation and compromise rather than force. These seemed to offer a new way forward to others, including Israel–Palestine and Northern Ireland, and a secondary set of models emerged.

The cascade effect might be best illustrated by following a specific flow path, from South Africa to Northern Ireland and thence to the Basque Country. The connection between South Africa and Northern Ireland pre-dated the Irish peace process, to links between Sinn Fein and the ANC during the years of violence, links strongly emphasized in republican rhetoric and iconography.[9] ANC leaders made a number of visits to Northern Ireland at strategic stages during the peace process, most notably in the week following the Good Friday Agreement when they met republican prisoners and advised a Sinn Fein gathering that 'the Belfast Agreement was a major step forward'.[10] The 'ideological sympathy'[11] between the two revolutionary organizations was a key factor in persuading recalcitrant members of

Sinn Fein to back the agreement. The influence of South Africa on Northern Ireland was not confined to militant parties. A number of cross-party groupings from Northern Ireland visited South Africa.[12] A conference in 1992 brought together leading political players in Northern Ireland and South Africa across a wide range of parties, and follow-up meetings were held in Boston (1995), Belfast (1997) and South Africa (1997).[13] The South African connection continued during the post-accord implementation stage. The South African human rights lawyer Brian Curran helped to oversee the early release of paramilitary prisoners, and in 2000 was appointed as independent mediator in the dispute over Orange marches at Drumcree. Cyril Ramaphosa of the ANC acted as an independent inspector of IRA arms dumps in order to overcome the decommissioning impasse. In addition to this comradely support, Northern Ireland adopted a number of negotiation approaches pioneered during the South African process, notably the use of 'sufficient consensus' to ensure the process overcame minority delays.

The Good Friday Agreement in April 1998 promoted Northern Ireland as another model of a successful peace process. The agreement was greeted with almost universal enthusiasm internationally. A survey of 30 reports from 20 countries was unanimously supportive, although some urged caution. A few pundits dwelt on perceived similarities and differences between Northern Ireland and their own regions. The Calcutta *Ananda Bazar Patrika* called for 'the same policy of peaceful dialogue' to be adopted in Kashmir. Israel's *Maariv*, under the headline 'The Irish Model', contrasted Irish peace with a peace that 'is increasingly becoming more remote in this region'.[14] The enthusiasm was greatest in the Basque Country. Interest there was partly rooted in ideological empathy. ETA/IRA contacts stretched back into the Troubles, and Sinn Fein had developed a close association with Herri Batasuna. A number of republican strategies were borrowed, most notably the use of strategic ceasefires and the determination to forge a broad alliance of constitutional nationalists. The 'pan-nationalist front' combining Sinn Fein, the SDLP, the Irish government and Irish America inspired the 'third space' which performed a similar function for Basque constitutional and revolutionary nationalists. Any shift within a militant revolutionary movement towards a broader accommodation including constitutional nationalists is a strong indicator of ripeness for negotiations. Indeed, the broad nationalist front in Northern Ireland influenced not only ETA, but also the Corsican independence group FLNC, who carried it a step further into dialogue with 'non- and even anti-nationalist groups such as elements within the French centre-right or sections of the socialist party'.[15]

The flow from South Africa through Northern Ireland to the Basque Country and beyond is, of course, merely illustrative of the cascade. Other examples can be cited. The South Africans 'studied with great deliberation the Latin American examples before setting up its own Truth and Reconciliation Commission'.[16] The South African TRC in turn was followed with great attention in Latin America, especially for its innovative public hearings, and for its power to grant amnesty to individuals. So far, despite considerable interest, and envy at the resources applied to the problem in South Africa, there has been little evidence that the South African model has been taken on board.[17]

What is borrowed?

Borrowing has taken a variety of forms since the early 1990s. Before considering these in more detail, it is important to emphasize that they operated within an international context conducive to peace processes. The great increase in the number of peace accords since the end of the Cold War in itself created an ambience which encouraged protagonists to imitate their example. During the early 1990s it sometimes appeared that delegations from the former Soviet Union and Yugoslavia were randomly scouring the world for models for democratic transformation. As time passed, the traffic became more specific and strategic, and began to fall into recognizable categories.

Constitutional models

In detailing 12 reasons for South Africa's success, Roelf Meyer, the National Party negotiator, began by highlighting two: first, that they 'made a fresh start in 1990 – a clean slate'; and second, that they dared to do it by themselves, without any 'formal external intervention'. The ANC present a similar view. 'We designed an individual process', claimed Pravin Gordhan. 'There is no model that I am aware of.'

Despite the indisputably innovative features of the South African agreement, few major decisions were taken without at least reviewing comparative alternatives. Gordhan continued: 'But at the same time we were very aware in designing our constitution that there were many models available to us in many parts of the world – Canada, United States, Nigeria, India, Australia, etc. We looked at all of them and chose what we thought was appropriate to our own situation.'[18] Germany became the main constitutional model, especially for the Upper house. The distinctiveness of the South African approach was its refusal to adopt constitutional and institutional structures en bloc, but its willingness to adopt specific elements from other constitutions and then to adapt them to local needs.

This sensitivity did not go unnoticed. Other constitution builders, notably the Fiji Constitution Reform Commission, launched a systematic search for constitutional models appropriate to Fiji's tense and stratified conflict between native Fijians and Indians, including solicited papers and hearings in London and Suva.[19] The resulting Constitution was a modified consociational democracy, which soon came under challenge during an attempted coup.

This selective approach to constitutional change was also a feature of the Northern Ireland accord. The joint role of the British and Irish governments as guardians of the process, with prime responsibility for agenda and deadline setting, drafting key papers and enforcing ground rules, was an innovative approach to reassure all negotiating parties that the proceedings would be even-handed.

Approaches to negotiations

Modern peace processes are more often multi-party than bilateral. This raises the problem that, if relatively small parties carry the same weight as major actors, they have a potential veto on progress. The South Africans came up with a device to forestall this eventuality.[20] The 'sufficient consensus' rule ensured that the process should continue, despite the dissent of smaller parties, if the two major parties agreed. 'Disagreement would be recorded; dissenters could remain in the process, await its outcome, and then decide whether to support it.'[21] The 'steamroller effect'[22] of this rule raised charges that the two largest parties had formed a conspiracy of bullies, but it emphasized the common commitment to a solution and the recognition that the maintenance of momentum was critical. The formula reached in South Africa has been widely adopted and adapted. It was interpreted in Northern Ireland as 'the requirement that substantive decisions should have the support of majorities of both unionist and nationalists',[23] and was incorporated into the agreement.

Borrowings from other negotiations were sometimes quite casual and serendipitous. In 1996 the introduction of proximity talks in Northern Ireland to deal with the Unionists' refusal to communicate directly with Sinn Fein was suggested by Irish Foreign Minister Dick Spring, who had apparently read about its use in the Dayton talks in a morning newspaper.[24]

Dealing with violence

As most peace processes follow periods of violence, they must deal with fears that ex-militants would seek to influence the negotiations by the use of tactical violence. In Northern Ireland the Mitchell Principles were introduced in 1996 to address these fears. Before participants were admitted to multi-party negotiations they were required to agree to six principles, including their commitment:

- to democratic and exclusively peaceful means of resolving political issues;
- to the total disarmament of all paramilitaries;
- that such disarmament must be verifiable by an independent commission;
- to renounce and oppose any effort to use force or the threat of force to influence the course of the outcome of all-party negotiations;
- to abide by the letter of any agreement reached in all-party negotiations and to resort to democratic and exclusively peaceful methods in trying to alter any aspect of that outcome with which they may disagree;
- 'to take effective steps' to end 'punishment' killings and beatings.[25]

The insistence that all participants in multi-party talks sign up to the Mitchell Principles was a useful device for regulating political violence. The suspension of Sinn Fein and the departure of the UDP for breaches of the principles, however temporary, were necessary to sustain credibility. Their acceptance of the suspension, however truculent, indicated their determination to remain within the peace process.[26]

A second threat posed by violence to the Northern Ireland peace process was the issue of decommissioning. 'No guns, no government' summarized unionist refusal to allow government to function until paramilitary weapons had been handed over. The IRA refusal to decommission led to the suspension of the power-sharing executive in February 2000. In the end the compromise which allowed the Ulster Unionists to return to government in May was an IRA declaration that they would 'initiate a process that will completely and verifiably put IRA guns beyond use'.[27]

The key move was the IRA's agreement to permit inspection of its arms dumps by two independent inspectors, Martti Ahtisaari, the former Finnish President, and Cyril Ramaphosa, the former ANC leader. After their first inspection in June the inspectors reported that the armaments they had seen could not be used 'without our detection'.[28] The device they installed was described as a dual-key system, similar to a bank deposit box with two keys held by the IRA and the inspectors. The dual-key system was borrowed from El Salvador, where the UN had successfully applied it in the early 1990s.

> UN inspectors held one of two keys that had to be turned simultaneously to open arms caches belonging to the left-wing FMLN guerrilla movement.... Tonnes of weapons and explosives belonging to the FMLN were locked in secure dumps as part of peace negotiations between the Marxist guerrillas and the pro-American government in San Salvador.[29]

This approach bypassed the decommissioning dispute and allowed the peace process to continue, although it did not resolve the issue.

Institutional modelling

New forms of peace processes require new institutions, so it is not surprising that the peace negotiations of the late 1990s should borrow heavily from each other. The 38 peace accords between 1988 and 1998 shared many similarities, partly from bilateral and multilateral influences, but also because they evolved within the same international context. Three themes will be outlined here: approaches to human rights, truth commissions and policing reform.

International law played an important part in shaping peace agreements, and in turn was influenced by them. The shaping was sometimes positive, as in setting minimum standards for compliance in Northern Ireland and South Africa, and sometimes negative, such as the failure to set or enforce such standards in Israel–Palestine and Bosnia-Hercegovina. In any case international law imposes at least 'a superficial similarity' on peace agreements, including reform of policing and the judicial system, human rights commissions and compliance with international standards of human rights.[30] The traffic was two-way. Peace agreements became an arena for the debate on self-determination. The fact that so many peace accords are 'neither entirely domestic nor entirely international documents' challenged traditional views of statehood. Christine Bell also suggests that international law has other lessons to learn from peace agreements in other fields, including ethnic balance, dealing with the past and the role of civic society.

The interrelationship between past and future practice is increasingly worked out through truth commissions. It is sometimes forgotten that truth commissions operated in Latin America before the South African model was established. Argentina, aware of the limitations of the case-by-case approach to past crimes, introduced a truth commission to address the broader political and moral reponsibility. This was later adopted by Chile, El Salvador, South Africa and many other countries. Although the approaches varied, the key innovation was that 'truth commissions are meant to function as moral panels, not legal courts'.[31] The South African TRC radically extended the model and by the late 1990s it was rare for a peace accord not to include the intention to establish some approach to addressing past grievances.

Policing reform and training are examples of practical borrowing. The need to reform the police to reflect a new dispensation, and the difficulty in implementing it, is a common feature of peace processes, including those in the Basque Country, South Africa and Northern Ireland. Since 1993 the RUC sought lessons on community policing from various forces in the United States, including the NYPD and the LAPD, and a close relationship had been established with the South African Police Services, including bilateral meetings. The Patten Commission on the future of policing in Northern Ireland, one of whose members was a South African, drew on examples from South Africa, the United States, Canada, Spain and the Netherlands. In Latin America the exemplars were different, but the approach not dissimilar. The UN was involved in guiding through radical reforms of the police in Guatemala and El Salvador, and so was Spain. The Spanish Civil Guard was involved, both as an implied model, but more directly in implementing the transition to a civilian force. They helped to establish training academies in both places; in El Salvador they helped to frame the curriculum and provided instructors, and in Guatemala 'the Spanish Civil Guard contingent was put in charge of overall restructuring, particularly in the operations of the new training academy'.[32]

Negative borrowings

It has been argued that some cases are unsuitable wells from which to draw lessons for other countries. Arend Lijphart has suggested that Northern Ireland, Cyprus and the Lebanon are all unsuitable models because of their 'complex international dimensions',[33] although this did not prevent him from drawing extensively from Northern Ireland's experience. Approaches from one peace process to another have sometimes been adopted with insufficient consideration of local concerns; Ben Reilly points out that the almost universal rush to hold early elections may merely count heads rather than reflect a deeply entrenched democracy. In another sense, too, borrowings may have negative as well as positive effects. Those opposed to agreement are as willing to learn by example as those in agreement. Northern Ireland had particular interest for Basque nationalists and there are parallels between the breakdown of the Basque ceasefires in 2000 and the IRA breakdown in 1996. In each case the militants became increasingly frustrated by the failure of the respective governments to advance towards inclusive negotiations after the declaration of a ceasefire. The renewal of tactical violence by the IRA ultimately led to their re-entry into a more accelerated process, and it is unlikely that the lessons escaped the attention of ETA.

The problems caused by decommissioning in Northern Ireland provide another example of the negative potential of borrowings. Although insistence that the IRA hand over its weapons did not feature as a major disagreement in the early negotiations, it became increasingly a line in the sand both for the IRA and for Unionists.

In the three years following the accord it was the most serious obstacle to progress. Why did it assume such negative force? International experience presents no clear answer. Decommissioning was rarely a major issue during the many peace processes in Latin America since the 1980s, although a number of Colombian guerrilla groups laid down their weapons in exchange for amnesties and other benefits.[34] In Israel, even after the transfer of power to the Palestinian Authority, Yasir Arafat was unable to persuade the leaders in Palestinian refugee camps to hand over their weapons.[35] The 1991 South African National Peace Accord did not ask the ANC to hand over their arms caches, but required that firearms should not be displayed at public meetings. The retention of weapons by militants was accepted as an unfortunate reality in many other agreements, including the Anglo-Irish war in 1921. In other settlements, however, weapons were decommissioned. As Mac Ginty has pointed out, 'over 850,000 ex-combatants have been disarmed in eight sub-Saharan states: Ethiopia, Angola, Eritrea, Liberia, Mali, Mozambique, Namibia and Uganda'.[36] In 1996 rebel groups in Niger laid down their weapons after the 1996 accord. Even the Kosovo Liberation Army (KLA) handed over its weapons to NATO peacekeepers within the 90-day deadline agreed under a post-war accord signed in June 1999, although some of the weapons were merely transferred to the Kosovo Corps, a defence force newly created from the KLA. 'We are not going to take off our uniforms and our weapons off', said one of their commanders. 'We are only changing to new uniforms and a new badge.'[37]

So recent peace processes include plenty of examples where weapons were decommissioned, and plenty where they were not. Northern Ireland's legacy to other peace processes is that decommissioning is likely to be a requirement in future peace processes.

Lessons learned and missed

The search for comparative models has become a boom industry in recent years for countries entering peace processes, sometimes without sufficient regard to local differences. Despite this caveat, three observations may be made.

À la carte, not table d'hôte

Since the early 1990s the tendency to seek complete constitutional templates for incipient peace processes has been replaced by a more nuanced search for guidelines that might instruct specific aspects of a peace process. This à la carte approach also carries its own dangers: it is sometimes too random, determined by casual and chance contacts; it may ignore important cultural differences. Despite these caveats, the more specific the borrowing between peace processes, the more likely it is to succeed. The adoption of proximity talks in Dayton and Belfast allowed talks to start despite deep distrust and distaste. The borrowing of approaches to policing reform, and of human rights clauses from other peace accords, have become commonplace, notably in Latin America. In each case the merits of the central idea were adopted, but were then adapted to local circumstances.

More trade-offs

Peace processes are typically conducted by a number of parallel negotiating teams, each dealing with a relatively discrete facet of the dispute, such as political structures, demilitarization and reforms of the police and army. The demands of negotiations probably make this inevitable, but it reduces the potential for trade-offs, even in cases where trade-offs seem natural: decommissioning in exchange for demilitarization; dealing with victims of violence in return for amnesties or the release of militant prisoners. There have been cases when such reciprocation greatly eased progress, as in Guatemala when the URNG agreed to suspend its 'war taxes' in return for the government's agreement to demobilize its civil defence patrols. It is natural, and proper, that the increased borrowing between peace processes is usually the result of a search for appropriate models and structures. One of the most striking lessons from recent peace processes, however, is the need to encourage borrowing across the entire spectrum of negotiations.

Lessons missed

Given the success of the South African process, it is perhaps surprising that some of its innovations were not more widely imitated. These include South Africa's constitutional court and transitional council, but also innovations in negotiations such as the *bosberade* (bush summits), where disputants left the plenary negotiations to resolve bilateral or inter-party disputes. Another useful South African device was the *channel*, a deadlock-breaking mechanism representing the main parties, that met daily in secret to review progress and encourage new initiatives. Nor were neglected innovations confined to South Africa. Despite the success of the joint British–Irish direction of the process, Northern Ireland provides the only contemporary example of its use. Many of these mechanisms would benefit from a dusting-off and reappraisal.

Notes

1. L. Mees, 'The Basque Peace Process, Nationalism and Political Violence' in J. Darby & R. Mac Ginty (eds), *The Management of Peace Processes* (London: Macmillan – now Palgrave Macmillan, 2000).
2. Ibid., p. 180.
3. A private letter quoted in E. Mallie & D. McKittrick, *The Fight for Peace: the Secret Story behind the Irish Peace Process* (London: Heinemann, 1996), p. 187. A similar point was made by the Sinn Fein leader Gerry Adams in his *Selected Writings* (Dingle: Brandon, 1997).
4. D. de Bréadún, 'If They Can Do It in Northern Ireland You Can Do It in the Middle East', *Irish Times*, 24 May 2001.
5. *The Independent* (London), 26 December 2000.
6. For example, the Spanish government convened the first meeting between the Guatemalan government and the URNG (Unidad Revolucionaria Nacional Guatemalteca), and was the only non-regional member of the four-nation innovative Friends of the Secretary-General, set up in 1990 to support negotiations in El Salvador.
7. J. Darby & J. Rae, 'Peace Processes from 1988–1998: Changing Patterns', *Ethnic Studies Report*, XVII, 1 (1999).

8. See P. du Toit, *South Africa's Brittle Peace: the Problem of Post-Settlement Violence* (London: Macmillan – now Palgrave Macmillan, 2001).
9. See A. Guelke, 'Comparatively Peaceful: South Africa, the Middle East and Northern Ireland', in M. Cox, A. Guelke & F. Stephen, *A Farewell to Arms? From 'Long War' to Long Peace in Northern Ireland* (Manchester: Manchester University Press, 2000).
10. 'ANC Applauds Participants in Agreement', *Irish Times*, 30 April 1998.
11. Guelke, op. cit., p. 228.
12. For a representative of one of the loyalist parties the main benefit of visiting South Africa was not his introduction to new approaches to negotiations, but observing 'civilised cooperation' between members of the ANC and National Party (author interview with UDP member, April 2000).
13. K. Cullen, 'Wise Lessons from South Africa Nurture Peace in North', *Irish Times*, 13 May 2000.
14. D. McCaffrey, 'Irish Referenda', *USIA Media Reaction Daily Digest*, 28 May 1998.
15. F. Letamendia & J. Loughlin, 'Peace in the Basque Country and Corsica', in Cox et al., op. cit., p. 246.
16. J. Zalaquett, 'Truth, Justice and Reconciliation: Lessons from the International Community', in C. Arnson (ed.), *Comparative Peace Processes in Latin America* (Washington, DC: Woodrow Wilson Center, 1999), p. 349.
17. See P. Hayner, 'In Pursuit of Justice and Reconciliation', in Arnson (ed.), op. cit., pp. 368–71.
18. P. Gordhan, 'Political Leadership in Divided Societies: the Case of South Africa', paper presented at Parliament Buildings, Stormont, 10 April 2000.
19. See Sir P. Reeves, T. R. Vakatora & B. V. Lal, 'The Fiji Islands – towards a United Future: Report of the Fiji Constitution Review Commission' (Fiji: Parliament of Fiji Paper No. 34, 1996). The commissioned papers were published in a separate volume, B. V. Lal and T. R. Vakatora (eds), *Fiji and the World* (Fiji: University of the South Pacific, 1997).
20. For a more detailed discussion of South Africa's innovative negotiating rules, see du Toit, op. cit., esp. pp. 94–7.
21. D. Atkinson, 'Brokering a Miracle? The Multiparty Negotiating Forum', in S. Friedman and D. Atkinson (eds), *South African Review 7: The Small Miracle* (Johannesburg: Ravan Press, 1994), p. 22.
22. Du Toit, op. cit., p. 96.
23. Guelke, op. cit., p. 230.
24. Mallie & McKittrick, op. cit., p. 363.
25. 'The Mitchell Principles' in Report of the International Body on Decommissioning, *Irish Times*, 18 February 1996.
26. K. Fearon pointed out that 'the degree of seriousness with which Sinn Féin treated the indictment indicated precisely how serious they were about the talks process and their desire to be part of it'. See K. Fearon, *Women's Work: the Story of the Northern Ireland Women's Coalition* (Belfast: Blackstaff Press, 1999), p. 100.
27. The IRA statement and the joint statement by the two governments in response are printed in the *Irish Times*, 8 May 2000.
28. 'Unionists Divided over Arms Dump Visit', *The Times*, 27 June 2000.
29. H. McDonald, 'Foolproof "Dual-keys" Used to Seal IRA Arsenals', *The Observer*, 2 July 2000.
30. C. Bell, *Peace Agreements and Human Rights* (Oxford: Oxford University Press, 2000), p. 313.
31. J. Zalaquett, 'Truth, Justice and Reconciliation', in Arnson (ed.), op. cit., p. 356.
32. G.Vickers, 'Renegotiating Internal Security: the Lessons of Central America', in Arnson (ed.), op. cit., p. 407.
33. A. Lijphart, 'The Framework Document on Northern Ireland and the Theory of Power-sharing', *Government and Opposition*, 31, 3 (Summer 1996), 267–74.

34. M. Chernick, 'Negotiating Peace amid Multiple Forms of Violence: the Protracted Search for Settlement to the Armed Conflicts in Colombia', in Arnson (ed.), op. cit., pp. 177–9.
35. *New York Times*, 29 September 1999.
36. R. Mac Ginty, 'Biting the Bullet: Decommissioning in the Transition from War to Peace in Northern Ireland', *Irish Studies in International Affairs*, 10 (1999), 238.
37. *New York Times*, 20 September 1999.

Conclusion: Peace Processes, Present and Future

John Darby and Roger Mac Ginty

Sequencing peace processes

The term 'peace process' has become increasingly popular since the 1990s. It arose primarily from the growing recognition that the cycle of activities necessary to produce just and lasting agreement stretches both backward and forward from the actual period of negotiations.

The origins of any agreement are always controversial, but often unrecognized at the time – changes in the international climate, initiatives from civil society, secret meetings, chance encounters between significant actors. It is even more difficult to determine when a peace process has succeeded, but it is clearly not the final full stop on a peace accord. The function of an accord is to identify general principles and parameters of agreement. Their implementation may prolong the peace process cycle for many years, during which institutions must be established and reforms carried through. The difficulty of achieving this, and the emergence of new divisive issues, often lead to a rejection of the accord. Hence the growing popularity of 'peace process' as the most accurate expression of this protracted business.

Peace processes are not strictly linear, and different societies sometimes tackle problems outside the normal sequence. If every peace process had to wait for a complete ending to violence, few would get off the ground. The individual histories peculiar to each country account for the distinctive sequencing of each process. Indeed, not only is it possible to tackle traditional 'post-settlement' tasks such as decommissioning and disarmament early in the process, but the momentum created by this may assist the move towards negotiations. It is the deviations from the normal model which sometimes provide the most instructive insights into the business of making peace.

This chapter will follow the cycle of peace processes through four phases: (a) pre-negotiation; (b) the management of the process, including negotiations and violence; (c) peace acccords; and (d) post-accord reconstruction. These follow the structure of the book, and will draw from the chapters, all written by leading experts within their research fields. It is not suggested that these phases are sequential. Violence in particular is a feature of all phases of all processes, as are distrust and fear, but the challenges they present alter as the context changes during the evolving process. These challenges are universal, common to all peace processes. The chapter will conclude by presenting ten propositions about the nature and problems of contemporary peace processes.

(a)   Getting into talks: pre-negotiation

Conflicting parties rarely want to reach a settlement at the same time. During the war in Bosnia during 1993 and 1994, for example, the willingness of Muslims, Serbs or Croats to engage in negotiation was determined primarily by their fortunes on the field of war and the resulting territorial gains or losses. By definition, these conditions never coincide for all parties. The result is a pendulum-like swing, with ethnic rivals proposing talks in turn, but rarely at the same time. Windows of opportunity, when all parties are simultaneously prepared to negotiate, are rare, and of limited duration. Yet it is only during such relatively infrequent opportunities that a settlement may be reached.

The central metaphor in determining these opportunities is Zartman's concept of a 'ripe moment', when the parties reach a mutually hurting stalemate and 'find themselves locked in a conflict from which they cannot escalate to victory and this deadlock is painful to both of them'. The concept has been criticized by some as too passive, although Zartman insists that 'unripeness should not constitute an excuse for second or third parties' inaction'.

When compromise is in the air, other metaphors may be applied. Imagine the set of factors required to end ethnic violence – 'track-two' approaches (non-governmental contact by such mediators as the business community, academics or churches), secret talks, a ceasefire, agreement to negotiate, mediation, demilitarization, decommissioning – as a circle of dominoes standing like the stones at Stonehenge. The ending of violent conflict requires all the dominoes to topple. The process can be triggered by moving any one of the dominoes forward, creating a momentum which collapses its neighbour, and so on to the next one, and the next. If one domino stands out of place, of course, it can affect the sequence of changes. The dominoes are more numerous, and more entrenched, in some conflicts than in others.

Most often the process requires a combination of more than one of these triggers to create momentum. Then the momentum itself, by providing the opportunity for opponents to work together, can become an agent in the process. The peace processes in South Africa, Northern Ireland and Israel–Palestine all began with secret talks. These have certain advantages over traditional diplomacy as a preliminary to substantive talks: the formal barriers imposed by protocol are dropped; the temperature of the water and the temper of one's opponents may be tested with limited risk; 'what-if' scenarios can be floated without commitment. Secret talks can be a useful transition process for those who rose to leadership as security or insurgent leaders, and who often have little or no experience of the art of compromise. The exclusion of the media helped to keep the talks in Oslo and Northern Ireland secret. Secret talks are attractive to negotiators because, in du Toit's words, they have 'low exit costs'.[1]

It is not uncommon for the constitutional and paramilitary opponents of the existing government to form a temporary alliance in advance of negotiation. As John Loughlin demonstrates, the 'pan-nationalist front' in Northern Ireland, the 'third space' in the Basque Country and similar developments in Corsica, forged temporary alliances between constitutional and revolutionary nationalists. Even the Tamil United Liberation Front (TULF) in Sri Lanka insisted that talks could not be confined to constitutional parties but must include the Tamil Tigers. When a militant revolutionary movement shifts towards a broader approach which includes constitutional nationalist parties, it is a strong indicator of ripeness for negotiations. These alliances help to compensate for the asymmetrical nature of negotiations, where the initial advantage leans towards the government side, but they carry a price. The long-term cost may be increased bitterness between ethnic protagonists during negotiations and in post-settlement peacebuilding.

Occasionally the move from secret to open negotiations is managed by the protagonists themselves. Far more often, as Christopher Mitchell points out, a third party becomes involved. Intermediaries such as the business community, the churches and academics were active in South Africa and Northern Ireland. Mediators, such as the Norwegian academics who were critical in starting the Oslo talks, often play a more effective role during the preliminaries of a peace process than later.

In the suspicious climate that accompanies the early stages of pre-negotiation, confidence-building measures can reassure opponents, but they carry high risks. Confidence-building measures are concessions by one side to encourage movement from the other – the declaration of a ceasefire, the inclusion of militants in talks, decommissioning of weapons. The symbolic gestures by Mandela to white South Africans greatly eased the first stages of negotiations. The danger is that premature concessions may be banked rather than reciprocated by the recipients, as was the case with Andrés Pastrana's territorial concessions to the Revolutionary Armed Forces of Colombia (FARC). The general lesson is that unilateral confidence-building gestures should only be conceded rarely. It is better to negotiate reciprocal gestures, as when significant demobilization by Guatemala's armed forces and by the FMLN were carried out, with UN supervision, by 1993. Thus each side can point to mutual concessions to demonstrate momentum towards agreement.

The preliminaries to peace processes are not subject to standard formulae. Chance can play a critical role. Changes of government in the UK, Israel, Sri Lanka and Colombia were the triggers for negotiations or for suppression. Even when they led to negotiations, however, a breakthrough was unlikely if the ground had not been prepared in advance. A combination of preparation and opportunism is needed for a successful peace process.

(b)   Managing the process: dealing with negotiations and violence

During the years of violence preceding peace negotiations, cross-ethnic communications diminish and hostile stereotypes become entrenched. Opposing aspirations are expressed in mutually exclusive terms. The belief grows that one's opponents are cohesive, devious and successful, while one's own side is divided and frustrated. These are not ideal conditions for negotiations.

How can confidence be built at this stage in the fledgling process, and rules and procedures established to move it forward? Israel's recognition of the PLO as legitimate representatives of the Palestinian people in Oslo A, coupled with acceptance of the Palestinian right to self-determination, had immense symbolic significance. There and elsewhere the fact that negotiations are taking place at all presumes an acceptance, often implicit, that the representatives of militants have been admitted to negotiations in return for giving up violence. Their inclusion, whatever pressures it imposes on the process, admits militants to the common enterprise and applies a moral pressure on them to preserve the process in the face of violence from dissidents or spoiler groups.

The decision to include militants does not presume that the mechanics of their admission had been agreed. They are often required to surmount a tortuous series of 'good behaviour' tests. Probation periods were set before Sinn Fein was admitted to talks in Northern Ireland, and Sharon's insistence in 2002 that negotiations with Palestinians could not start until violence had ended for two clear weeks created an effective stalemate. Nevertheless it is necessary to agree to rules which regulate the resumption of violence. The South African process, while not requiring arms decommissioning, insisted that arms should be banned from public meetings. In Northern Ireland the Mitchell Principles were devised, and imposed, as conditions for entry to talks and for punishing breaches by paramilitaries associated with negotiating parties.[2]

As a general rule, secrecy diminishes in importance as negotiations proceed. The need to involve the community in the forthcoming compromises increases. An excess of early publicity entrenches differences before an agreement can be reached. An excess of secrecy not only encourages conspiracy interpretations but also fails to prepare public opinion for the necessary compromises. Of course, secrecy and transparency are not so easily controlled. Gadi Wolfsfeld concludes, in his comparison of the media's role in Israel and Northern Ireland, that the news media are more interested in conflict than in peace and 'are best thought of as fair weather friends'.

The prime responsibility for preparing discussion papers on procedures for negotiation usually falls to government, especially if the talks involve a number of competing parties; the talks in Northern Ireland were eased considerably by the central involvement of two governments. Shuttle diplomacy may be needed to establish the preconditions and ground rules for participants. If these can be agreed, proximity talks are often necessary before the participants are willing to meet in plenary sessions, although ad hoc meetings on specific aspects of the negotiation process provided a useful middle way in Northern Ireland. As Pierre du Toit shows, these ground rules can be made by insiders, as in South Africa, or by outsiders, as in Namibia. In the former case, progress is sometimes more readily achieved by hardline than by moderate leaders, because concessions by the former are more convincing to their community. F.W. de Klerk, Nelson Mandela, Gerry Adams and David Trimble all had previous associations with intransigent positions, but were able to lead their respective followers into peace agreements.

The key role in managing the process does not always belong to local actors, especially in the early stages of negotiations. External actors are often essential. The involvement of the British and Irish governments as joint custodians of the talks in Northern Ireland reassured both communities during negotiations and greatly facilitated progress. Neighbouring states and the UN continue to play key parts in certain settings. In both El Salvador and Guatemala, Cynthia Arnson and Dinorah Azpuru point out,

> the principal outside role was played by the United Nations, although other countries from the region as well as the United States and countries of Western Europe provided important additional support. Furthermore, international financial institutions and foreign governments marshalled significant monetary resources to support the accords' various commitments.

The issues under negotiation are distinctive to each conflict, but some themes are constant. The early release of prisoners is almost always a sine qua non for paramilitaries engaged in talks; it is also a highly emotive reminder to victims of violence that their sensibilities have been pushed into the background in the interests of securing peace. Reforms in policing, security and the administration of justice are also constant features if an accord is agreed. Protection for human rights, and aspirations towards economic reform, are more common in Latin American accords than elsewhere. No clear pattern is discernible on decommissioning; it emerged as a major threat to the process in Northern Ireland, but hardly rated as a problem in South Africa.

Pierre du Toit shows how 'rules and procedures provide structure to the process of negotiating for peace'. He describes a number of innovative negotiation devices developed to cope when the South African process stalled: the *bosberade* or 'bush summits' designed to smooth out bilateral disagreements; the 'channel', a sub-committee of three which met daily to maintain momentum; and the creation of new institutions such as the Transitional Executive Council and the Independent Electoral Commission to counter the asymmetrical nature of power structures in South Africa. Some of these have been consciously imitated in other places. The concept of 'sufficient consensus', for example, designed to keep dissenters in the process if they were outvoted on a specific issue, was effectively applied in Northern Ireland. Northern Ireland itself developed distinctive procedures, notably the development of the Mitchell Principles as a device to enable parties previously associated with violence to enter talks under specific conditions.

Thereafter time frames and deadlines are essential to maintain momentum, and deserve greater research attention. The 1994 ceasefires in Northern Ireland were followed by a fatal lack of urgency which eventually led to the ending of the IRA ceasefire. In Israel–Palestine the 1993 Oslo A Accord set a specific date (May 1999), five years from the start of its implementation, for the transfer of authority and land. The deadlines were not always met, but they imposed an obligation on parties which carried substantial weight. It is less important that a deadline is met than that negotiators conform to the concept and demands of a deadline.

One by-product of establishing deadlines is that negotiations sometimes advance in surges rather than by gradual increments. This encourages the emergence of a brinkmanship style of negotiation, conspicuous in Northern Ireland, when all-night sittings became de rigueur for signpost agreements along the path to settlement. Sometimes the deadlines were missed by a few days. The deadline for the 1998 agreement was Thursday April 9th. In fact the accord was finalized on the following day, presenting it with a more memorable name, the Good Friday Agreement. This approach carries obvious risks, but has some incidental benefits. It demonstrates how a deadline focuses attention. It confirms to a divided community that its leaders are fighting a tough fight, thus helping to prepare them for the compromises to come. The help is often necessary, for the interests of leaders and their supporters may diverge as a deal is completed. By that time it is as difficult for the negotiators to leave the process as to stay in it. By the more optimistic reading, their engagement in a common enterprise creates a common bonding; more cynically, the failure of the peace process and a return to war places those who initiated the strategy in personal danger from militants within their own community, and under electoral challenge.

The process of making an accord is always played out to a background of violence. Even when political violence is ended by the declaration of a ceasefire, it mutates into other interrelated forms to threaten the evolving peace process: violence by the state; violence by militants; violence in the community; and the emergence of new violence-related issues in the negotiations.[3]

Violence by the state, including the use of 'dirty tricks' by governments and the threat presented by reform of the security apparatus, has attracted less academic attention than violence by militants. Recent years have seen an increase in the use of illegal force by national governments. A UN report in 2001 found evidence of systematic terror in East Timor 'planned and carried out' by the Indonesian army.[4] The Israeli government has openly admitted using torture since 1999,[5] and has been in breach of international agreements over settlements in the Palestinian Authority. There is little new about governments adopting covert force during wars. More worrying is the apparent willingness to acknowledge this openly, thus undermining international norms of behaviour. There is also a danger that the post-September 11 'war on terror' could legitimize overly robust state action.

Violence by militants and violence in the community have attracted much greater research attention, a situation unlikely to change. The willingness to commit suicide in the interests of a cause fundamentally undermines the premise of all security policies, and tilts the equation from those with greater power to those with less. The current debate about spoilers is well treated in chapters by Stephen Stedman and Marie-Joëlle Zahar. It is an important debate, both in helping to clarify terminology, and for its policy implications. The common ground is the evidence that, as Stedman expresses it, 'the presence of spoilers, spoils and hostile neighbours pose the greatest threats to fledgling peace processes'. The greatest short-term threat comes from spoilers. The 'documented increases in violent crime' identified by Charles Call and William Stanley in their chapter, usually emerges later.

The declaration of a ceasefire alters the context of conflict at a stroke. Issues that cannot even be discussed during wars – release of prisoners, amnesties, policing and army reforms – not only become part of the new agenda, but demand immediate attention. Demobilization and disarmament are among the most serious of these. As Virginia Gamba points out, arms not surrendered during peace processes more often than not end up fuelling other conflicts or armed crime. Alongside Gamba's plea for a greater priority for these issues, it is hard to avoid the conclusion that demobilization and decommissioning, which presented Northern Ireland with its most serious post-accord problem, might be more systematically handled in tandem during negotiations, with simultaneous and reciprocal reduction of the state's and militants' ability to resume hostilities.

All of the forms of violence detailed above are separate threads in a single weave. The pattern that unites them is the central role of violence both before and after the declaration of a ceasefire.

(c) Peace acccords

One of the main aims of this book is to stimulate more study into peace accords, as well as the process that precedes and follows them. Christine Bell describes the 1990s as 'the decade of the peace agreement'. Her review of peace accords found 'over 300 peace agreements of one description or another', signed in more than 60 situations, during the 1990s. Despite this, it has been a strangely neglected subject until recently. The most obvious need for more research is the accelerating and understandable tendency by peacemakers to borrow the text, frameworks and approach adopted in earlier peace accords, demonstrated by the similar language of many Latin American peace agreements.

Before the point is reached when a peace accord is being negotiated, a fundamental question needs to be addressed. Can the central grievances be resolved within the existing national framework, or do they require secession and autonomy? Yash Ghai underlines the paradoxes of autonomy:

It (a) seeks to solve problem of territory, and yet may aggravate it; (b) is intended to solve the problem of identity, yet it may accentuate identity and stimulate the 'manufacture' of new communities; (c) seeks to increase pluralism, yet depends for its own success on pre-existing traditions of pluralism; and (d) aims to resolve conflict, yet aggravates disputes.

Given these tensions, many contemporary peace processes concentrate on the constitutional options that occupy the space between secession and conceded reforms. Most of them demand an element of power-sharing. As Timothy Sisk points out,

it is difficult to envisage a post-war political settlement that does not, or would need to, include guarantees to all the major antagonists that they will be assured some permanent political representation, decision-making power, and often autonomous territory in the post-war peace. Indeed, the gist of international mediation in such conflicts is to encourage parties to adopt powersharing in exchange for waging war.

Although this is the central deal in most peace processes, power-sharing arrangements rarely survive in the long term. It is best to regard them as a transitional process. 'Ideally', Sisk continues, 'power-sharing will work best when it can, over time, wither away.'

Peace accords have broader aims than political agreement. Bell suggests that most peace accords involve three elements: a central deal on democratic access to power; the establishment of human rights institutions; and some mechanisms to address past human rights violations. Most interest focuses on the first of these, and 'human rights mechanisms can be conceded as the universally recognized chic language in which to write peace agreements'. Future research attention needs to be applied to the substance of the human rights and reconstruction dimensions of peace accords.

Peace accords are not only concerned with the clauses in the agreement. If the peace accord reached through negotiations between elites is to become a settlement accepted by their followers, it must be subjected to democratic validation through referenda or the discipline of elections. The choice is important – the hurried referendum in East Timor increased the level of violence instead of easing it. Ben Reilly's view is that 'the consent of the electorate, and the legitimacy of a new, post-conflict dispensation is the key – and underappreciated – variable in determining whether a peace deal will succeed or fail'.

(d)   Cementing the peace: post-accord reconstruction

As peace accords are negotiated, it is tempting to defer sensitive issues to post-settlement negotiation, running the risk of laying minefields for the future in the interests of short-term gain. During the Oslo negotiations, for example, five critical issues, including Jerusalem, settlements and refugee return, were 'blackboxed' to enable the two sides to move forward on other less inflexible issues. In Northern Ireland the deferred issues included some very divisive matters – reforms in policing and the administration of justice, arms decommissioning, and the sharing of executive power. The South African agreement also transferred potentially deadlocking issues, including affirmative action and the integration of the armed forces, to the agenda of the first elected government. The transfer of ex-paramilitary activists into the police and security forces in the Palestinian Territories and South Africa were tangible acknowledgements of past abuses and an effective way to convert a potentially destabilizing armed threat into support for the new structures. It is also a tangible demonstration of commitment to fair employment practices. The integration of ex-militants into the security forces, of course, is not always possible or even desirable. William Stanley and Charles Call warn that 'the path of demilitarization and police reform holds advantages over military merger'.

Brandon Hamber adds a warning about the dangers in the desperate rush to seize the historic moment, either by fudging or deferring contentious issues.

'Reconciliation has become a euphemism for the compromises made during the political negotiations – compromises that papered over the fissures of the past in the interest of national unity but at the expense of the socially marginalized.' The need to move smoothly from an elite-driven political settlement towards a more fair and democratic society cannot be exaggerated. In South Africa the inability to deliver either economic regeneration or greater social equality led to a growing sense of disillusion with peace itself. Similarly in El Salvador and Guatemala, both relatively successful peace processes, 'achievements in the social arena have been modest and accompanied by dramatic rises in the rates of crime'. The post-settlement task, as Arnson and Azpuru demonstrate, is to solidify past achievements 'through the provision of concrete benefits and an ongoing commitment to democratic reform'. Approval of a settlement through referenda or elections is certainly an exercise in democracy but, in Reilly's words, they should be regarded as 'the beginning of a long-term process of democratization, not the endpoint'. They provide a licence to encourage a strengthened and energized civil society. Civil society has been rediscovered, or at least redirected, through recent peace processes, playing a vital role in the reconstruction of South Africa, Guatemala and El Salvador, and generating energy into the campaigns to endorse the Good Friday Agreement in Northern Ireland.

Apart from having to confront these continuing disputes, post-settlement administrations also inherit the problems left by years of violence and confrontation. Truth commissions have become a common but far from universal approach to these problems, with mixed records of success. Is it possible that, in certain circumstances, they demonstrate an unwillingness to let go of past injuries and may prolong tensions? The Latin American truth commissions and the Truth and Reconciliation Commission in South Africa were certainly attempts to address the hurts of victims as a basis for reconciliation. The controversy surrounding these bodies demonstrates the cliché that it may take as long to repair community dysfunction as it took to create it, and that means decades rather than years.

Ten propositions

In 2000 we presented a series of eight propositions, as conclusions to our book *The Management of Peace Processes*.[6] They were based on studies conducted between 1996 and 2000 of the peace processes in South Africa, Northern Ireland, Israel–Palestine, the Basque Country and Sri Lanka, and were carried out in collaboration with colleagues living in those five places. They were drawn up at a time when there was optimism, if not about all the processes themselves, about the new approaches to peacemaking evolving during them. Research carried out in the short intervening period, much of it reflected in this book, indicates the need for a review of the propositions. Most of them have been reinforced. Three additional propositions have been added. One proposition – the increasing search for comparative models – has been removed and treated more fully as Chapter 21 of this book. Two others have been amalgamated. The resulting ten propositions are presented here in a revised and modified form.

Proposition 1   Most ceasefires collapse in the first few months. The survivors are likely to deliver some level of success

A successful peace process is organic and cumulative. The public euphoria following the ending of violence contrasts with the mutual suspicion of the early negotiations. Constitutional politicians are forced to negotiate with people they regard as criminals, often at the risk of alienating their voting support. They overlook the risks facing the militants who have entered negotiations, and whose position is severely undermined if the talks collapse. Tests were imposed in Israel, in Northern Ireland and in the Basque Country before militants were admitted into talks. These delays may be understandable but can be dangerous, as the breakdown of the IRA and ETA ceasefires demonstrates.

If the process survives the first nervous contacts, it tends to strengthen. Sometimes it is reinforced by internal pressure from public opinion, as happened in South Africa when the process faltered in 1992. In the Middle East, too, support for violence among Palestinians declined from 57 to 21 per cent between 1994 and 1996, in tandem with suicide bombs by Islamic Jihad and Hamas. This dynamic does not mean that the negotiators have become friends; from the start of the Northern Ireland process in 1994 until well after the Good Friday Agreement in 1998 Unionists refused even to speak directly to members of Sinn Fein. It is sufficient that they can define a common problem and attempt to negotiate an accommodation.

The dynamic of achieving this position locks those involved in negotiation in an uncomfortable embrace. The participants become more attracted to the positive rewards of a historic breakthrough. It becomes increasingly difficult for any of them to contemplate a return to the earlier violence. Failure to make progress would rule out another initiative for the foreseeable future. It would also probably mean the end of their political careers and, sometimes, threaten their lives.

In addition, working relationships develop between the negotiators as they concentrate on the practical minutiae of negotiations and become better acquainted with the boundaries within which their opponents operate. These benefits depend on maintaining forward momentum. Persistent stalemates may confirm initial suspicions and lead to a strengthening of the internal cohesion of competing parties, and an erosion of the common ground identified during negotiations, as happened within both the Israeli and Palestinian communities in late 2000.[7]

Developments in the Middle East present a test for this proposition. Has anything been delivered there during the peace process? An immediate reaction is pessimistic: the post-2000 violence of the al-Aqsa intifada; the suicide bombings; Israel's incursions into the Palestinian Authority; the economic collapse in both territories; the unsuccessful attempts to renegotiate the Oslo Accords. Against this, the Palestinian Authority has been established; acceptance that there should be a Palestinian state, a distant prospect in 1991, is almost universal, even in Israel and the United States. The agenda has changed in both concept and reality. The Saudi Arabian and US peace initiatives in 2002 illustrate one fundamental truth: whether or not they succeed, the concept of a peace process has been remarkably resilient amid the most unpromising circumstances.

Generally speaking, the further the process develops, the stronger its shock-absorbent facility and the more capable its ability to withstand the inevitable atrocities designed to undermine it. The policy implication is to focus economic and political support on the initial stages of the process.

Proposition 2 A lasting agreement is impossible unless it actively involves those with the power to bring it down by violence

Is it possible to make a settlement without including parties with militant associations? The greatest initial obstacle to an inclusive peace process is the unwillingness of constitutional politicians to deal with parties associated with violence. This has altered somewhat during the last decade, and the involvement of the 'veto holders' – those who were in a position to prevent a settlement – has become more common, almost a trend. The vehicle for their involvement is invariably secret negotiations through mediators or with political parties representing the gunmen. The unwillingness of the Spanish government to treat directly with Basque separatists, however understandable, prevented the development of a peace process during the 1990s. The absence of a political front for the Kosovo paramilitaries in early 1998 ruled out any possibility of negotiations with the Serbs.

Other peace processes were sparked off by the decision to include militants. The settlement in South Africa started with the release of Nelson Mandela and ANC prisoners in 1990. In Northern Ireland there were seven unsuccessful attempts to reach agreement through negotiation between constitutional politicians, until the inclusion of Sinn Fein and the loyalist parties led to the Good Friday Agreement. Contemporary developments in peace processes reinforce this conclusion. It is difficult to think of a situation where serious ethnic violence was terminated without either unacceptable repression or the involvement of those perpetrating the violence. The failure of the Colombian government's approach to FARC in 1998 is a warning that the involvement of militants in talks is a necessary condition, but not a sufficient one, for success.

Even when the political representatives of militants are included in negotiations, the question then arises about how to respond when more extreme groups continue or resume campaigns of violence. The relationship between governments and militants presents an uncomfortable moral ambiguity. Having accepted the principle of amnesties for earlier terrorists in order to attract them into negotiation, the negotiators then assume a stern approach to the use of terror in the future. At the same time they must also keep the door open to the inclusion of late converts. At this point the creation of a mechanism is necessary to regulate the process – criteria for admission to talks, the conditions for expulsion and the future inclusion of spoilers. The Mitchell Principles proved to be a useful model in Northern Ireland.

The reality is that total inclusion is never possible. There are always zealots who will not compromise. The more numerous and compromising the moderates, the greater the likelihood that the extremes can be marginalized. So the demand for inclusive talks is always a qualified one. Just as the principle of 'sufficient consensus'[8] was adopted in South Africa in recognition of the impossibility of progress if all participants had veto powers, it is necessary to apply a principle of 'sufficient inclusion' in relation to militant organizations. This does not mean the inclusion of all parties using or threatening to use violence. The principle of 'sufficient inclusion' is that a peace process includes both all actors who represent a significant proportion of their community, and all actors who have the ability to destroy an agreement. The two groups are often coterminous.

Proposition 3   Spoiler groups can only be neutralized with the active involvement of ex-militants

Agreement by violent groups to negotiate is never unanimous. It often leads to the formation of splinter groups determined to continue the armed struggle. If they in turn enter the process, further breakaway spoilers emerge. The actions of spoilers move increasingly towards the margins during and after the process of peace negotiations. This traffic raises the question of how spoiler violence will be tackled by a coalition government which includes former militants.

At some point during the process, when all the splinter groups likely to join the process have done so, two rumps may remain – mavericks who are engaged in crime for personal advantage, and ideological zealots. They pose different problems. It is relatively straightforward to criminalize the former and to confront them through a reformed police force and justice system acceptable across the community. It is much more difficult for ex-militants to turn against groups who share their general orientation but have refused to buy the peace process.

One key aspect is the size of the spoiler group and the seriousness of its threat to the peace process. If the spoilers carry significant popular support, as Hamas does, the authority of negotiators such as the PLO is seriously circumscribed. The ANC's dominance of political protest in South Africa, on the other hand, made condemnation a lot easier. Condemnation of militants from within one's own broader political family usually indicates either a growth in confidence or external pressure. The acquiescence of ex-militants in stronger security action against zealots may be the ultimate test of a peace process.

Proposition 4   During peace negotiations the primary function of leaders is to deliver their own people. Assisting their opponents in the process is secondary

Despite the continuing emphasis on 'bottom-up' approaches among major funding bodies, NGOs and some international organizations, peace movements have a poor record in stimulating peace talks. In South Africa there were 75 meetings between the Democratic Alternative for South Africa (IDASA) and the ANC, but the triggers for negotiations eventually came from other sources. The ability of the peace movement in the Basque Country to organize peace demonstrations involving hundreds of thousands of Basques has had little influence on ending ETA's campaign. On the other hand, the role of civil society organizations in Northern Ireland – the business community, churches, media – was substantial, and offers promising research possibilities; but this came into serious play only after the negotiations had been completed. So how can such peacemaking efforts be connected to peace processes, which are invariably conducted between elites?

In any internal peace process there are power holders and power seekers. Power holders represent those – usually, but not always, the state – who have traditionally controlled the reins of government. The power seekers want to alter the prevailing political, economic, legal and cultural arrangements, often by force.

Peace accords are negotiated by the elites of both power holders and seekers, who must then persuade their followers to endorse it through an election or referendum. Power seekers who abandon violence and enter talks are always vulnerable to accusations of betrayal; in the emotional atmosphere it is a powerful challenge to their leaders. There are similar constraints on power holders. 'Political leaders', as Bercovitch observed, 'cannot lead where their followers are unwilling to go.'[9] The work needed to prepare their followers for the shift usually starts many years before it becomes public.

The transitional problems facing both power holders and seekers are superficially similar. In both cases extremists rather than moderate leaders are more likely to deliver suspicious followers. Reluctant converts, like Buthelezi and Viljoen in South Africa, are more convincing, and more trusted by the extremes. At that point the similarity ends. The power holders – usually the state – enter negotiation because they recognize the inevitability of change before their followers do; their main difficulty is to convince their supporters that the resulting changes are minimal. The power seekers – usually militant leaders – get into negotiation because they recognize the advantages of negotiation before their followers do; their main difficulty is to convince their supporters that the negotiations are achieving major concessions. If the process moves too slowly, it hurts the power seekers. If it moves too speedily, it hurts the power holders.

In navigating this complex journey the primary function of leaders is to deliver their own followers. It is true that both sets of leaders are more likely to recognize the difficulties of their opponents as negotiations evolve. They also come to realize that a peace process cannot be completed unless their opponents also have enough to satisfy their followers. This mutual dependency is in tension with the risk that assisting their opponents may alienate their own supporters. The reality is that the loss of their followers is a greater threat to party leaders than the collapse of the process.

Propositions 5 and 6   Members of the security forces and paramilitary groups must be integrated into normal society if a peace agreement is to stick. A corollary is that peace accords need to address the needs of victims of violence

The problem of reintegrating ex-militants into society is sharpened by their ability to undermine the peace process. In Gaza and Jericho, South Africa and elsewhere the problem was partially addressed by transferring ex-guerrillas into the regular army and police force.

There are other options. Prudence demands that those who were engaged in the war must be provided with jobs and training. The ending of violence leaves an inheritance of high risk. The shrinkage of the security industry – army, police, prison officers, private security guards – brings onto the unemployment register people skilled in the use of arms. A similar risk of redundancy faces the militants whose lives have been devoted to armed resistance. Their speedy return to civil society is essential, less because they deserve a reward than because they have the means to destabilize the peace process.

Historically, two distinct approaches have been applied to the victims of violence – what John Groom has called the Nuremberg Tribunal way and the South African way.[10] The punishment of war crimes continues today through the UN's war crimes tribunal in the former Yugoslavia. In South Africa, as in Chile after Pinochet's fall, a new model was created in a Truth and Reconciliation Commission. Northern Ireland's Victims' Commission approached the problem from a rather different angle. All these approaches focused on individual victims, but violence also leaves a collective heritage.

If there is need to reintegrate ex-militants and members of the security forces into society, there is also need to anticipate society's response to the provision of preferential treatment for people convicted of murder, bombings and mutilations. When the Argentine military declared a self-amnesty after the Falklands-Malvinas defeat, the newly elected Argentine Parliament, reflecting public outrage, declared it null. In Uruguay the public reaction to an Impunity law led to a petition by 25 per cent of all registered voters for a plebiscite to repeal it, although the resulting plebiscite was defeated. The early release of prisoners reminds the relatives and friends of their victims – police, soldiers, security staff and, most of all, civilians – of the hurt they have suffered.

In the interests of equity, but also in order to manage the peace process successfully, any moves to reintegrate militants into society must be balanced by recognition of the needs of the bereaved and the wounded. These needs demand a delicate touch, and reach beyond monetary compensation. War memorials, for example, need careful treatment in divided societies if they are to avoid becoming shrines to division rather than to common suffering. Reparations, too, can provoke rather than ease tensions if the amounts are low or they are unaccompanied by investigations of atrocities. Even after reparations were instituted by law in Chile, and accepted by the victims' relatives, there were few prosecutions against the military because they were protected by the 1978 Amnesty law. In general the efficacy of truth and reconciliation commissions is heavily determined by timing and local sensitivities. It may have been appropriate to the needs of Chile and South Africa, but each society must find a form appropriate to its traditions and circumstances.

Proposition 7   A peace process does not end with a peace accord

There are no rules about the best time to reach formal agreement during a peace process. The agreements in Northern Ireland and Israel were only made possible by postponing some contentious issues for later resolution, leaving enormous minefields to traverse in the post-accord period. Even in South Africa, where a remarkably broad range of agreements had been agreed before the 1994 elections, the issues of truth and reconciliation lingered well into the future.

If negotiators wait until all major issues have been agreed, the process may collapse from mutual distrust or violence before they reach a conclusion. If they defer complex and divisive issues for later resolution, it will be more difficult to contain negotiations as mutual fears and suspicions flourish among the uncertainty. In either case post-settlement euphoria may be followed by post-agreement *tristesse*, and the all-important momentum lost. As the terms of the 1998 Good Friday Agreement were implemented, Northern Ireland unionist disillusion has grown steadily, raising the possibility that a majority within Northern Ireland's majority may seek to overthrow the agreement, while a majority of the minority support it. In the Middle East, despite Israeli withdrawals from Palestinian territories and the creation of the Palestinian National Authority following the 1993 Israeli–Palestinian Declaration of Principles, the peace process has become bogged down over issues of implementation – full Israeli withdrawal, agreement over Jerusalem and the settlements, and ceasefires.

It is becoming increasingly undeniable that many peace processes fail after apparent political agreement has been reached through an accord. The causes and dynamics are varied and under-studied, but some guidelines are evident. Parties may wish to renegotiate some provisions in an agreement which they find unpalatable or cannot sell to their supporters. Public expectations, initially raised by any agreement, are often dashed by inability to implement them, compounding the problems during negotiations with added distrust. The problems and challenges which emerge after an accord has been agreed are new, so there are fewer guidelines available for tackling them. They are likely to assume a more urgent research priority in coming years.

Proposition 8 Peace processes are deals: they require trade-offs

Peace negotiations are complex and multifaceted, involving a range of teams negotiating across a range of constitutional, political, economic and cultural issues. This 'disaggregation' – the conduct of negotiations through plenaries and subgroups, each dealing with a different issue and reporting according to a different time frame – is perhaps unavoidable.[11] In retrospect, however, a greater willingness to broaden the negotiation frame, and to encourage reciprocation between and within different issues in dispute is needed. In some cases, of course, this happens. In Northern Ireland, for example, a British–Irish Council was created to provide a balance for the North–South bodies demanded by nationalists, and concessions to encourage use of the Irish language were, somewhat awkwardly at times, balanced by similar advantage to those advocating the use of Ulster Scots. Other parts of the Good Friday Agreement, and other peace accords, might also have benefited from similar reciprocation.

Consider two cases. First, the early release of political prisoners might be more closely associated with the needs of their victims. Early prisoner release is usually a precondition to ceasefires, and is often regarded as one of the earliest tasks to be resolved in a peace process. Victims are often regarded as a post-accord problem. In practice the two are closely related. The early release of prisoners often infuriates the families of victims and the community at large. This is, of course, a moral issue, but it is also a pragmatic one. Peace accords require democratic approval, through an election or referendum. The creation of an initial injustice may undermine the agreement by alienating voters, as evidenced in Israel and Northern Ireland. The needs of victims should be confronted at a much earlier stage than has been customary. At its most emotive level this includes the problem of the disappeared, when family members are still ignorant of where the bodies of victims have been disposed.

Second, if a peace accord has terminated a period of political violence, there is a clear reciprocation between the need to demobilize the state security apparatus and the need to decommission paramilitary weapons. In 1992 an impasse in El Salvador, where the government distrusted the FMLN's compliance on demobilization, and the FMLN believed the government was reneging on the purification of the armed forces called for in the Chapultepec Accords, was resolved by UN mediation establishing that 'compliance with specific undertakings by one side would be contingent upon compliance with specific undertakings by the other side'.[12] Nevertheless, many peace accords, while indicating the need for both, does not address decommissioning by militants and demilitarization by the state as related. A peace accord does not banish suspicion and fear within either the security branches or ex-militants, and many will wish to hold their weapons as guarantees against its collapse. A predetermined agreement to phase in decommissioning and demilitarization in parallel offers a way to approach the problem, and to anticipate either issue becoming a serious obstacle to post-settlement reconstruction.

Proposition 9   Peace is a development issue

A formal peace process, negotiated between elites and focused on constitutional and legal issues, can only go so far. The issues that have the most chance of making an impact on people's lives inhabit the social and economic realm. These issues require serious attention during mainstream political negotiations lest the gap between public expectation and reality remain unfulfilled in the fragile post-accord years. Failure to address these 'bread and butter' issues may lead to a public disenchantment that overshadows political or constitutional compromises. In sum, peace processes must embrace development issues.

According to a popular story, King William of Orange crossed the river Boyne by boat during a famous Irish battle in 1690. The boatman asked him how the battle was progressing. 'What is it to you?' replied the King, 'You'll still be boatman whoever wins.' The lesson for those involved in contemporary peace processes is that poverty, inequality and social exclusion require serious attention (as part of any peace initiative). Uneven development is a major contributory cause of conflict. If a peace accord replicates serious inequality and provides few routes of economic opportunity then the accord itself may become the first step towards a new cycle of violence.

Notwithstanding complex constitutional transformations, the main problems facing many people in the Balkans, South Africa and elsewhere are economic. To speak of 'haves' and 'have nots' may be unfashionable, but when having nothing threatens peace, it becomes salient. *The Economist* summed up the persistent racial division in South Africa thus: 'Black children still die of tuberculosis, and increasingly of AIDS; white children are more likely to drown in the swimming pool.'[13]

Just as war affects different sections of society in different ways, peace has a differential impact. Peace will often impact upon men and women, young people and the elderly, urban and rural dwellers in different ways. It is no coincidence that wartime population displacement usually has the greatest impact on the most vulnerable, usually the elderly, infirm and dependent. Peace processes need to focus on the variations within society and not necessarily minister to those who can shout the loudest; often those who retain their arms. On top of structural inequalities within societies, the international economic system has the capacity to undermine peace. While the international community may promise a peace dividend, the reality of currency flows, uneven trade relationships and competition can hamper post-accord development.

Proposition 10   Peace processes: a record of failure?

In 2000 we compared peace processes to an expedition through a mountain range by 'a team of people who have previously been at each others' throats, often literally, and who are now roped together'. The first peak is a ceasefire, but this is followed by new mountains: negotiating a settlement; dealing with spoiler violence; the decommissioning of weapons; reforms in policing.

If one applies a business management audit to this metaphor, a number of processes can point to substantial progress. The agreements in Guatemala and El Salvador have stood for more than six years. South Africa has completed its transition from apartheid to majority rule with remarkable efficiency. The Northern Ireland process has achieved the implementation of historical political and administrative changes. In each case it is possible to draw up a list of objectives identified during peace negotiations, and to tick off a substantial proportion of them as accomplished.

There is also a debit side to the audit. Conventional crime rates have spiralled following the accords in South Africa and Guatemala, and relationships between Northern Ireland's divided communities have deteriorated since 1998. It may be necessary to confront unpalatable changes in order to create a fair society, but it raises a key theoretical question. Is it possible that a schematic approach to a peace process, with a specific agenda of tasks to be completed, may complete its agenda but that the peace process will fail? To put it another way, a peace process may reach a settlement, but fail to address the root causes of conflict and underrate the human costs of violence. Recently Edward Said has gone beyond this proposition and characterized the peace process in the Middle East as a method of reconstructing Israeli control over discontented minorities, implying that only a more radical approach will produce the necessary realignment of society.[14]

The implicit premise of any peace process is that a cycle must be followed, from violence through the various stages of negotiations, to a conclusion. It is difficult to identify many cases where the cycle has been successfully completed. Is a new approach and a new metaphor required? If so, what are the necessary characteristics of a new generation of peace processes?

Two developments are likely. First, there is need for a reassessment of the role of external actors in peace processes. In cases such as the Middle East, Sri Lanka and Ethiopia, peace cannot be delivered exclusively by local actors. Consequently pressure will grow for the UN and the United States, and some regional organizations, to find new approaches to intervention. These will not exclude the use of force to create conditions for negotiations and to help with the implementation of agreements. The second development will be a broadening of the remit for peace accords, with a new emphasis on human rights, economic reconstruction and democratization, as well as the traditional concern with political and constitutional matters. The business of making peace will continue, but will change.

Notes

1. P. du Toit, 'South Africa: in Search of Post-Settlement Peace', in J. Darby & R. Mac Ginty (eds), *The Management of Peace Processes* (London, Macmillan – now Palgrave Macmillan, 2000), p. 19.
2. The 1996 Mitchell Report, named after US Senator George Mitchell, chair of the International Body on Arms Decommissioning, laid down conditions for all negotiators. Before participants were admitted to all-party negotiations they were required to agree to six principles, including their commitment: to democratic and exclusively peaceful means of resolving political issues; to the total disarmament of all paramilitaries; that such disarmament must be verifiable by an independent commission; to renounce and oppose any effort to use force or the threat of force to influence the course of the outcome of all-party negotiations; to abide by the letter of any agreement reached in all-party negotiations and to resort to democratic and exclusively peaceful methods in trying to alter any aspect of that outcome with which they may disagree; and 'to take effective steps' to end 'punishment' killings and beatings.
3. For a more detailed discussion of these categories see J. Darby, *The Effects of Violence on Peace Processes* (Washington, DC: United States Institute of Peace, 2001).
4. The UN report was leaked by the *Sydney Morning Herald*: 'East Timor Massacre Work of Indonesia's Army', 20 April 2001.
5. See, as examples, reports in the *New York Times*, 14 September 1999 and *Los Angeles Times*, 4 December 1999.
6. This book was based on research during the 'Coming out of Violence' project, and was carried out between 1995 and 1998 as a collaborative and comparative study by John Darby and Roger Mac Ginty in Northern Ireland, Pierre du Toit in South Africa, Tamar Hermann and David Newman in Israel, Paikiasothy Saravanamuttu in Sri Lanka and Ludger Mees in the Basque Country. The research concentrated on six main themes: violence and security issues; progress towards political/constitutional agreement; economic factors; the role of external actors; the role of symbols; and responses within the community. Palgrave Macmillan are publishing the findings as a series of books.
7. The return to 'us against them' attitudes is described by Deborah Sontag in 'Eye for Eye Once Again', *New York Times*, 9 October 2000, and by Vivienne Walt, 'Poverty, Lack of Change Add to Anger in the Street', *USA Today*, 9 October 2000.

8. The condition of 'sufficient consensus' is defined by Friedman thus: '... consensus was sufficient if the process could move on the backing of only those who supported a proposal. Disagreement would be recorded; dissenters could remain in the process, await its outcome, and then decide whether to support it', in S. Friedman, 'Afterword: the Brief Miracle', in S. Friedman & D. Atkinson (eds), *South Africa Review*, 7 (Johannesburg: Raven Press, 1994), p. 22.

9. Ibid.

10. J. Groom, 'Coming out of Violence: Ten Troubling Questions', Proceedings of the International Peace Studies Symposium, *Coming out of War and Ethnic Violence* (Okinawa: Okinawa International University, 1996).

11. D. Bloomfield, C. Nupen & P. Harris, 'Negotiation Process', in P. Harris & B. Reilly (eds), *Democracy and Deep-rooted Conflict: Options for Negotiators* (Sweden: Institute for Democracy and Electoral Assistance, 1998).

12. F. Osler Hampson, *Nurturing Peace: Why Peace Settlements Succeed or Fail* (Washington, DC: United States Institute of Peace Press, 1996), p. 153.

13. Survey of South Africa', *The Economist*, 20 May 1995.

14. E.W. Said, *The End of the Peace Process* (New York: Pantheon, 2000).

Bibliography

Reports

Adibe, C. *Managing Arms in Peace Processes: Somalia* (UNIDIR's Disarmament and Conflict Resolution Project Series, Geneva; United Nations, 1995).

Adibe, C. *Managing Arms in Peace Processes: Liberia* (UNIDIR's Disarmament and Conflict Resolution Project Series, Geneva; United Nations, 1996).

Berman, E. *Managing Arms in Peace Processes: Mozambique* (UNIDIR's Disarmament and Conflict Resolution Project Series, Geneva; United Nations, 1996).

Constitutional Review Commission, *The Fiji Islands: Toward a United Future* (Suva, 1996).

Eide, A. *New Approaches to Minority Protection*, Minority Rights Group International Report 93/4 (London: MRG International, 1995).

Goulding, M. *Enhancing the United Nations' Effectiveness in Peace and Security* (United Nations: Report to the Secretary General, 30 June 1997).

Managing Arms in Peace Processes: the Issues (UNIDIR's Disarmament and Conflict Resolution Project Series, Geneva; United Nations, 1996).

Ohlson, T. *Power Politics and Peace Politics* (Uppsala: University of Uppsala, Department of Peace and Conflict Research), Report 50.

Raevsky, A. & B. Ekwall-Uebelhardt, *Managing Arms in Peace Processes: Croatia and Bosnia-Hercegovina* (UNIDIR's Disarmament and Conflict Resolution Project Series, Geneva; United Nations, 1996).

'Turning Strife to Advantage: a Blueprint to Integrate the Croats in Bosnia and Herzegovina', an International Crisis Group Report (15 March 2001).

Varennes, F. de, 'Minority Rights and the Prevention of Ethnic Conflicts', Working Paper, United Nations Working Group on the Rights of Minorities, E/CN.4/Sub.2/AC.5/2000/CRP.3 (Geneva, 2000).

Wang, J. *Managing Arms in Peace Processes: Cambodia* (UNIDIR's Disarmament and Conflict Resolution Project Series, Geneva; United Nations, 1996).

Conference proceedings, conference papers and occasional papers

Berman, E.G. 'Re-armament in Sierra Leone: One Year after the Lomé Peace Agreement', Small Arms Survey, Occasional Paper 1, Geneva (December 2000).

Call, C.T. 'Why the World's Most Successful Peace Processes Produce the World's Most Violent Countries', Paper delivered at International Studies Association conference, Chicago (March 1999).

Cetinyan, R. & A. Stein, 'Assassins of Peace?: Spoilers and the Peace Process in the Middle East', paper presented at the Annual Meeting of the American Political Science Association, 3 September 1999, Atlanta, Georgia.

Chesterman, S., T. Farer & T. Sisk, 'Competing Claims: Self-Determination and Security at the United Nations', an International Peace Academy Policy Brief (May 2001).

Downs, G. & S.J. Stedman, 'Evaluation Issues in Peace Implementation', paper presented at the annual meetings of the American Political Science Association, Washington DC, 30 August 2000.

Gordhan, P. 'Political Leadership in Divided Societies: the Case of South Africa', paper presented at Parliament Buildings, Stormont (10 April 2000).

Groom, J. 'Coming out of Violence: Ten Troubling Questions', *Proceedings of the International Peace Studies Symposium* (Okinawa: Okinawa International University, 1996).

Kane, A. 'The United Nations and the Maintenance of Peace and Security: Challenges and Choices', in *Proceedings of the Forty-Third Pugwash Conference on Science and World Affairs – A World at the Crossroads: New Conflicts, New Solutions*, Hasseludden, Sweden, 9–15 June 1993 (London: World Scientific, 1994).

Reilly, B. & A. Reynolds, 'Electoral Systems and Conflict in Divided Societies', Papers on International Conflict Resolution (Washington, DC: National Academy Press, 1999).

Sambanis, N. 'Conflict Resolution Ripeness and Spoiler Problems in Cyprus: from the Intercommunal Talks (1968–1974) to the Present', Paper presented to the American Political Science Association (25 September 1998).

Schneckener, U. 'Making Power Sharing Work: Lessons from Successes and Failures in Ethnic Conflict Regulation', *Institut für Interkulutrelle und Internationale Studien*, University of Bremen (Working Paper No. 19/2000).

Stedman, S.J. 'Implementing Peace Agreements in Civil Wars: Lessons and Recommendations for Policymakers', IPA Policy Paper on Peace Implementation (New York: International Peace Academy, May 2001).

Sutterlin, J.S. 'Military Force in the Service of Peace', *Aurora Papers*, 18 (1993).

Walter, B.F. *Designing Transitions from Violent Civil War*, IGCC Policy Paper 31 (San Diego: UC Institute on Global Conflict and Cooperation, 1998).

Wood, E.J. 'Civil War Settlement: Modeling the Bases of Compromise', paper presented at the 1999 Annual Meeting of the American Political Science Association, 2–5 September 1999.

Zahar, M. 'The Problem of Commitment to Peace: Actors, Incentives and Choice in Peace Implementation', paper presented to the Annual Meeting of the American Political Science Association, Washington, DC, 31 August–3 September 2000.

Zartman, I.W. 'Ripeness: the Hurting Stalemate and Beyond', paper presented to the International Political Science World Congress, Quebec City (August 2000).

Journal articles

Abbink, J. 'Violence and the Crisis of Conciliation: Suri, Dizi and the State in South West Ethiopia', *Africa*, 70, 4 (2000), 527–50.

Aggestram, K. & C. Jönson, '(Un)ending conflict', *Millennium*, XXXVI, 3 (1997), 771–94.

Al-Azm, S. 'The View from Damascus . . . Continued', *New York Review of Books*, XLVII, 13 (10 August 2000).

Anonymous, 'Human Rights in Peace Negotiations', *Human Rights Quarterly*, 18 (1995), 249–58.

Ayres, R.W. 'Mediating International Conflicts: Is Image Change Necessary?', *Journal of Peace Research*, 34 (1997), 431–47.

Bacchetta, P. 'Sacred Space in Conflict in India: the Babri Masjid Affair', *Growth and Change*, 31, 2 (Spring 2000), 255–84.

Bennett, W.L. 'Towards a Theory of Press–State Relations in the United States', *Journal of Communications*, 10 (1990), 103–25.

Berdal, M. & D. Keen, 'Violence and Economic Agendas in Civil Wars: Some Policy Implications', *Millennium*, 26, 3 (1988), 795–821.

Breytenbach, B. 'Cuito Cuanavale Revisited: Same Outcomes, Different Consequences', *Africa Insight*, 27, 1 (1999), 54–62.

Brosius, H. & P. Epp, 'Prototyping through Key Events: News Selection in the Case of Violence against Aliens and Asylum Seekers in Germany', *European Journal of Communications*, 10 (1995), 391–412.

Burton, M. & J. Higley, 'Elite Settlements', *American Sociological Review*, LII, 2 (1994), 295–307.

Darby, J. & J. Rae, 'Peace Processes from 1988–1998: Changing Patterns', *Ethnic Studies Report*, XVII, 1 (1999).

Doyle, M. & N. Sambanis, 'International Peacebuilding: a Theoretical and Quantitative Analysis', *American Political Science Review*, 94, 4 (December 2000), 779–802.

Du Toit, T. 'Bargaining about Bargaining: Inducing the Self-negating Prediction in Deeply Divided Societies: the Case of South Africa', *Journal of Conflict Resolution*, 33 (1989), 210–33.

Fearon, J. 'Domestic Political Audiences and the Escalation of International Disputes', *American Political Science Review*, 88, 3 (September 1994), 579–81.

Fisher, R.J. & L. Keashley, 'The Potential Complimentarity of Mediation and Consultation within a Contingency Model of Third Party Consultation', *Journal of Peace Research*, 28, 1 (1991), 21–42.

Galtung, J. 'High Road, Low Road: Charting the Course of Peace Journalism', *Track Two*, 7 (1998), 7–10.

Ghee-Son Lim S. & J. Keith Murnighan, 'Phases, Deadlines and the Bargaining Process', *Organizational Behaviour and Human Decision Processes*, 58 (1994), 153–71.

Goodby, J. 'When War Won out: Bosnian Peace Plans before Dayton', *International Negotiation*, 3 (1996), 501–23.

Guelke, A. 'Dissecting the South African Miracle: African Parallels', *Nationalism and Ethnic Politics*, 2, 1 (Spring 1996), 141–54.

Gurr, T.R. 'Ethnic Warfare on the Wane', *Foreign Affairs*, 79, 3 (May/June 2000), 52–64.

Hamber, B. 'Repairing the Irreparable: Dealing with the Double-binds of Making Reparations for Crimes of the Past', *Ethnicity and Health*, 5, 3/4 (2000), 215–26.

Harrison, S. 'Four Types of Symbolic Conflict', *Journal of the Royal Anthropologica Institution*, 1, 2 (1995), 255–72.

Hartzell, C. & D. Rothchild, 'Political Pacts as Negotiated Agreements: Comparing Ethnic and Non-ethnic Cases', *International Negotiation*, 2 (1997), 147–71.

Himmelfarb, S. 'Impact is the Mantra: the "Common Ground" Approach to the Media', *Track Two*, 7 (1998), 38–40.

Holiday, D. & W. Stanley, 'Building the Peace: Preliminary Lessons from El Salvador', *Journal of International Affairs*, 46, 2 (Winter 1993), 427–9.

Kahnerman, D. & A. Tversky, 'Prospect Theory: an Analysis of Decisions under Risk', *Econometrica*, IIIL, 3 (1979), 263–91.

Kaufman, C. 'Possible and Impossible Solutions to Ethnic Civil Wars', *International Security*, 20, 4 (1996), 136–75.

Kepplinger H.M. & J. Habermeir, 'The Impact of Key Events on the Presentation of Reality', *European Journal of Communications*, 10 (1995), 371–90.

Klatch, R. 'Of Meanings and Masters: Political Symbolism and Symbolic Action', *Polity*, 21, 1 (Fall 1998), 137–54.

Kleibor, M. & P. t'Hart, 'Time to Talk? Multiple Perspectives on Timing of International Mediation', *Cooperation and Conflict*, 30 (1995), 307–48.

Krohn Hansen, C. 'The Anthropology of Violent Interaction', *Journal of Anthropological Research*, 50, 2 (1994), 367–82.

Lieberfeld, D. 'Conflict "Ripeness" Revisited: the South African and Israeli/Palestinian Cases', *Negotiation Journal*, 15, 1 (1999), 63–82.

Lijphart, A. 'The Framework Document on Northern Ireland and the Theory of Power-sharing', *Government and Opposition*, 31, 3 (Summer 1996), 267–74.

Loder, K. 'The Peace Process in Mali', *Security Dialogue*, 28, 4 (1997), 409–24.

Loughlin, J. 'The Europe of the Regions and the Federalization of Europe', *Publius: the Journal of Federalism* (Fall 1996), 141–62.

Loughlin, J. 'Regional Autonomy and State Paradigm Shift in Western Europe', *Regional and Federal Studies*, 10, 2 (2000), 10–34.

Loughlin, J. & D.L. Seiler, 'Le comité des Régions et la supranationalité en Europe', *Etudes Internationales* (Décembre 1999).

McCrudden, C. 'Mainstreaming Equality in the Governance of Northern Ireland', *Fordham International Law Journal*, 22 (1999), 1696–775.

Mac Ginty, R. 'Biting the Bullet: Decommissioning in the Transition from War to Peace in Northern Ireland', *Irish Studies in International Affairs*, 10 (1999), 237–47.

McGrath, M. & A. Whiteford, 'Disparate Circumstance', *Indicator SA*, 11, 3 (1994), 47–50.

Mitchell, C. 'The Right Moments: Notes on Four Models of "Ripeness"', *Paradigms*, 9, 2 (Winter 1995), 38–52.

Mooradian, M. & D. Druckman, 'Hurting Stalemate or Mediation? The Conflict over Nagorno-Karabakh, 1990–95', *Journal of Peace Research*, XXXVI, 6 (1999), 709–27.

Power, S. 'Bystanders to Genocide', *Atlantic Monthly*, 288, 2 (September 2001), 84–108.

Putnam, R. 'Diplomacy and Domestic Politics: the Logic of Two-level Games', *International Organization*, 42, 3 (Summer 1998), 427–60.

Richardson Jr, J.M. & S.W.R. de Samarasinghe, 'Costs and Benefits of Violent Political Conflict: the Case of Sri Lanka', *World Development*, 21 (1995).

Roth, A.E., J. Keith Murnighan & Francoise Schoumaker, 'The Deadline Effect in Bargaining: Some Experimental Evidence', *The American Economic Review*, 78 (September 1988), 806–23.

Sala, M. 'Creating the "Ripe Moment" in the East Timor Conflict', *Journal of Peace Research*, XXXIV, 4 (1997), 449–66.

Saunders, C. 'Of Treks, Transitions and Transitology', *South African Historical Journal*, 40 (May 1999).

Saunders, H.H. 'We Need a Larger Theory of Negotiation: the Importance of the Pre-negotiation Phase', *Negotiation Journal*, 1, 1 (July 1985), 249–62.

Shinar, D. 'Media Diplomacy and "Peace Talk": the Middle East and Northern Ireland', *Gazette*, 62 (2000), 83–97.

Sitas, A. 'The New Tribalism: Hostels and Violence', *Journal of Southern African Studies*, 22, 2 (June 1996), 235–48.

Stedman, S.J. 'Spoiler Problems in Peace Processes', *International Security*, 22, 2 (Fall 1997), 5–53.

Steiner, H. 'Ideals and Counter-ideals in the Struggle over Autonomy Regimes', *Notre Dame Law Review*, 66 (1991), 1539–68.

Teitel, R. 'Transitional Jurisprudence: the Role of Law in Political Transformation', *Yale Law Journal*, 106 (1997), 2009–80.

Touval, S. 'Coercive Mediation on the Road to Geneva', *International Negotiation*, 3 (1996), 547–70.

Wall, J.A. 'Mediation: an Analysis, Review and Proposed Research', *Journal of Conflict Studies*, 25, 1 (March 1981), 157–80.

Wall, J.A. & A. Lynn, 'Mediation: a Current Review', *Journal of Conflict Resolution*, 37, 1 (March 1993), 160–94.

Wallensteen, P. & M. Sollenberg, 'Armed Conflict 1989–1998', *Journal of Peace Research*, 36, 5 (1999), 593–606.

Walter, B. 'The Critical Barrier to Civil War Settlement', *International Organization* (Summer 1997), 335–65.

Wehr, P. & J.P. Lederach, 'Mediating Conflict in Central America', *Journal of Peace Research* 28, 1 (1991), 85–98.

Wolfsfeld, G. 'Fair Weather Friends: the Varying Role of the Media in the Arab–Israeli Peace Process', *Political Communication*, 14 (1997), 29–48.

Wolfsfeld, G. 'Promoting Peace through the News Media: Some Initial Lessons from the Oslo Peace Process', *Harvard International Journal of Press/Politics*, 2 (1997), 52–70.

Woodward, S. 'Avoiding Another Cyprus or Israel', *Brookings Review* (Winter 1998), 45–8.

Wright, Q. 'The Escalation of Conflicts', *Journal of Conflict Resolution*, IX, 4 (1965), 434–49.

Books and chapters in books

Adams, G. *Selected Writings* (Dingle: Brandon Press, 1997).

Age, A. *et al.*, *Fighting for Hope in Somalia* (Oslo: NUPI, 1995).

Allen-Nan, S. 'Complimentarity and Coordination of Conflict Resolution Efforts in the Conflicts in Abkhazia, South Ossetia and TransDniestria', PhD diss, George Mason University (1999).

Alter, P. *Nationalism*, 2nd edn (London: Edward Arnold, 1994).

Anderson, B. *Imagined Communities: Reflections on the Origin and Spread of Nationalism* (Cambridge: Cambridge University Press, 1983).

Armstrong, J. *Nations before Nationalism* (Chapel Hill, NC: University of North Carolina Press, 1982).

Arnson, C. (ed.), *Comparative Peace Processes in Latin America* (Washington, DC: Woodrow Wilson Center, 1999).

Arrow, K. *Social Change and Individual Values* (Yale: Yale University Press, 1963).

Azar, E.E. *The Management of Protracted Social Conflict* (Aldershot: Dartmouth Publishing, 1990).

Baker, J. & T. deFrank, *The Politics of Diplomacy* (New York: Putnam, 1995).

Barber, J. & John Barratt, *South Africa's Foreign Policy – the Search for Status and Security 1945–1988* (Johannesburg: Southern, 1990).

Barth, F. (ed.), *Ethnic Groups and Boundaries* (Boston: Little, Brown and Company, 1976).

Bayley, D. *Patterns of Policing: a Comparative International Analysis* (New Brunswick, NJ: Rutgers University Press, 1985).

Bell, C. *Peace Agreements and Human Rights* (Oxford: Oxford University Press, 2000).

Benvenisti, M. 'The Peace Process and Intercommunal Strife', in H. Giliomee & J. Gagiano (eds), *The Elusive Search for Peace: South Africa, Israel and Northern Ireland* (Cape Town: Oxford University Press, 1990).

Bercovitch, J. & J.Z. Rubin (eds), *Mediation in International Relations* (New York: St. Martin's Press – now Palgrave Macmillan, 1992).

Biggar N. (ed.), *Burying the Past: Making Peace and Doing Justice after Civil Conflict* (Washington: Georgetown University Press, 2001).

Bloomfield, D., C. Nupen & P. Harris, 'Negotiation Process', in P. Harris & B. Reilly (eds), *Democracy and Deep-rooted Conflict: Options for Negotiators* (Stockholm: Institute for Democracy and Electoral Assistance, 1998).

Bond, P. *Elite Transitions: From Apartheid to Neoliberalism in South Africa* (London: Pluto Press, 2000).

Boraine, A. *A Country Unmasked: South Africa's Truth and Reconciliation Commission* (New York: Oxford University Press, 2000).

Bourdieu, P. *Language and Symbolic Power* (Cambridge: Polity Press, 1991).

Brams, S. *Negotiation Games* (New York: Routledge, 1990).

Brams, S. *Theory of Moves* (Cambridge: Cambridge University Press, 1994).

Brass, P.R. *Theft of an Idol: Text and Context in the Representation of Collective Violence* (Princeton: Princeton University Press, 1997).

Brown, M.E. (ed.), 'Internal Conflict and International Action', in M.E. Brown, *The International Dimensions of Internal Conflict* (Cambridge, Mass.: MIT Press, 1996), pp. 235–64.

Brynen, R. *A Very Political Economy. Peacebuilding and Foreign Aid in the West Bank and Gaza* (Boulder: Lynne Rienner, 2000).

Burton, J. *Deviance, Terrorism and War: the Process of Solving Unsolved Social and Political Problems* (New York: St. Martin's Press – now Palgrave Macmillan, 1979).

Campbell, J. *Successful Negotiation: Trieste* (Princeton: Princeton University Press, 1976).

Cassese, A. *Self Determination of Peoples: a Legal Reappraisal* (Cambridge: Cambridge University Press, 1998).

Chirot, D. & M.E.P. Seligman (eds), *Ethnopolitical Warfare: Causes, Consequences, and Possible Solutions* (Washington: American Psychological Association, 2001).

Cilliers, J. & C. Dietrich (eds), *Angola's War Economy: the Role of Oil and Diamonds* (South Africa: ISS, 2000).

Cliffe, L. *et al. The Transition to Independence in Namibia* (Boulder, Colo.: Lynne Rienner, 1994).

Coakley, J. (ed.), *The Territorial Management of Ethnic Conflict* (London: Frank Cass, 1993).

Cohen, R. *Theatre of Power: the Art of Diplomatic Signaling* (London: Longman, 1987).

Cohen, Y. *Media Diplomacy: the Foreign Office in the Mass Communications Age* (London: Frank Cass, 1986).

Cooper, C. et al. *Race Relations Survey 1992/93* (Johannesburg: South African Institute of Race Relations, 1993).

Conversi, D. *The Basques, the Catalans and Spain: Alternative Routes to Nationalist Mobilisation* (London: Hurst, 1997).

Corbin, J. *The Norway Channel* (New York: Atlantic Monthly Press, 1994).

Cornell, S. & D. Hartmann, *Ethnicity and Race: Making Identities in a Changing World* (Thousand Oaks: Pine Forge Press, 1998).

Costa, G. *La Policía Nacional Civil de El Salvador (1990–1997)* (San Salvador: UCA Editores, 1999).

Crocker, C.A. *High Noon in Southern Africa – Making Peace in a Rough Neighborhood* (Johannesburg: Jonathan Ball, 1992).

Crocker, C. et al. (eds), *Herding Cats: the Management of Complex International Mediation* (Washington, DC: USIP, 1999).

Cruise O'Brien, C. *The Siege: the Saga of Israel and Zionism* (New York: Simon and Schuster, 1986).

Darby, J. *The Effects of Violence on Peace Processes* (Washington, DC: United States Institute of Peace, 2001).

Darby, J. & R. Mac Ginty (eds), *The Management of Peace Processes* (New York: St. Martin's Press – now Palgrave Macmillan, 2000).

Diamond, L. 'Democracy in Latin America', in T. Farer (ed.), *Beyond Sovereignty: Collectively Defending Democracy in the Americas* (Baltimore, Md: Johns Hopkins University Press, 1996).

Du Toit, P. *South Africa's Brittle Peace: the Problem of Post-settlement Violence* (London: Macmillan–now Palgrave Macmillan, 2001).

Eide, A. *A Democratic South Africa? Constitutional Engineering in a Divided Society* (Berkeley: University of California Press, 1991).

Elder C. & R. Cobb, *The Political Uses of Symbols* (New York: Longman, 1983).

Esman, M.J. *Ethnic Politics* (Ithaca, NY: Cornell University Press, 1994).

Fearon, K. *Women's Work: the Story of the Northern Ireland Women's Coalition* (Belfast: Blackstaff Press, 1999).

Firth, R. *Symbols Public and Private* (London: Allen & Unwin, 1973).

Fisher, R. *Inter-Active Conflict Resolution* (New York: Syracuse University Press, 1997).

Fisher, R. & W. Ury, *Getting to Yes* (New York: Bantam, 1991).

Frazer, J. 'Sustaining Civilian Control: Armed Counterweights in Regime Stability in Africa', PhD dissertation in political science, Stanford University (1994).

Friedman, S. (ed.), *The Long Journey – South Africa's Quest for a Negotiated Settlement* (Johannesburg: Ravan Press, 1993).

Friedman S. & D. Atkinson (eds), *South African Review: 7 The Small Miracle – South Africa's Negotiated Settlement* (1994).

Gamba, V. (ed.), *Society under Siege: Crime, Violence and Illegal Weapons* (Johannesburg: Institute for Security Studies, the Towards Collaborative Peace Series, Vol. I, 1997).

Gatti, M. *The Secret Conversations of Henry Kissinger* (New York: Bantham, 1976).

Geldenhuys, D. *Foreign Political Engagement – Remaking States in the Post-Cold War World* (London: Macmillan – now Palgrave Macmillan, 1998).

Geldenhuys, J. *A General's Story – from an Era of War and Peace* (Johannesburg: Jonathan Ball, 1995).

Ghai, Y. *Hong Kong's New Constitutional Order: the Transfer of Sovereignty and the Basic Law* (Hong Kong: HKU Press, 1997).

Ghai, Y. 'Decentralisation and the Accommodation of Ethnic Diversity', in C. Young (ed.), *Ethnic Diversity and Public Policy: a Comparative Inquiry* (Basingstoke: Macmillan – now Palgrave Macmillan, 1998).

Ghai, Y. 'Autonomy as a Strategy for Diffusing Conflict', in P. Stern & D. Druckman (eds), *International Conflict Resolution after the Cold War* (Washington, DC: National Academy Press, 2000).

Ghai, Y. (ed.), *Autonomy and Ethnicity: Negotiating Claims in Multi-ethnic States* (Cambridge: Cambridge University Press, 2000).

Ghai, Y. 'Autonomy Regimes and Conflict Resolution' (Washington, DC: National Research Council, Committee on International Conflict Resolution, forthcoming).

Giddens, A. *The Third Way: a Renewal of Social Democracy* (Malden, Mass.: Polity Press, 1998).

Glazer, D. & P. Moynihan (eds), *Ethnicity: Theory and Experience* (Cambridge: Harvard University Press, 1975).

Gowing, N. *Media Coverage: Help or Hindrance in Conflict Prevention?* (New York: Carnegie Commission on Preventing Deadly Conflicts, 1996).

Greenfeld, L. *Nationalism: Five Roads to Modernity* (Cambridge: Harvard University Press, 1992).

Guelke, A. 'Comparatively Peaceful: South Africa, the Middle East and Northern Ireland', in M. Cox, A. Guelke & F. Stephen, *A Farewell to Arms? From 'Long War' to Long Peace in Northern Ireland* (Manchester: Manchester University Press, 2000).

Gurr, T.R., M.G. Marshall & D. Khosla, *Peace and Conflict 2001: a Global Survey of Armed Conflicts, Self-Determination Movements, and Democracy* (Integrated Network for Societal Conflict Research (INSCR) Program, Center for International Development and Conflict Management, University of Maryland, 2001).

Haas, R. *Conflicts Unending* (Yale: Yale University Press, 1990).

Hackett, R. *News and Dissent: the Press and Politics of Peace in Canada* (Norwood, NJ: Ablex, 1991).

Hallin, D. *The Uncensored War* (New York: Oxford University Press, 1986).

Hamber, B. (ed.), *Past Imperfect: Dealing with the Past in Northern Ireland and Societies in Transition* (Derry/Londonderry: University of Ulster/INCORE, 1998).

Hampson, F.O. *Nurturing Peace: Why Peace Settlements Succeed or Fail* (Washington, DC: United States Institute of Peace Press, 1996).

Hannum, H. *Autonomy, Sovereignty and Self-determination: the Accommodation of Conflicting Rights* (Philapdelphia: University of Philadelphia Press, 1990).

Hardin, R. *One for All: the Logic of Group Conflict* (Princeton: Princeton University Press).

Harris, P. & B. Reilly (eds), *Democracy and Deep-rooted Conflict: Options for Negotiators* (Stockholm: International IDEA (Institute for Democracy and Electoral Assistance, 1998).

Hayner, P. *Unspeakable Truths: Confronting State Terror and Atrocity* (New York: Routledge, 2001).

Hirshfeld, L.A. *Race in the Making: Cognition, Culture, and the Child's Construction of Human Kinds* (Cambridge: MIT Press, 1996).

Hobsbawm, E.J. *Nations and Nationalism since 1780* (Cambridge: Cambridge University Press, 1990).

Hoffman, M. 'Third Party Mediation and Conflict Resolution in the Post-Cold War World', in J. Baylis & N.J. Rengger (eds), *Dilemmas of World Politics* (Oxford: Clarendon Press, 1992).

Holbrooke, R. *To End a War* (New York: Random House, 1998).

Horowitz, D.L. *Ethnic Groups in Conflict* (Berkeley: University of California Press, 1985).

Horowitz, D.L. *The Deadly Ethnic Riot* (Berkeley: University of California Press, 2001).

Human Rights Watch, *Playing the Communal Card: Communal Violence and Human Rights* (New York City: Human Rights Watch, 1995).

Hume, C. *Mozambique's War: the Role of Mediation and Good Offices* (Washington, DC: USIP Press, 1994).

Huntington, S.P. *The Third Wave: Democratization in the Late Twentieth Century* (Norman, Okla.: University of Oklahoma Press, 1991).

Ikle, F. *How Nations Negotiate* (Harper & Row, 1964).

International Crisis Group, *Is Dayton Failing? Bosnia Four Years after the Peace Agreement* (Sarajevo: International Crisis Group, 1999).

Isaacs, H.R. *Idols of the Tribe: Group Identity and Political Change* (New York: Harper & Row, 1975).

Jabri, V. *Mediating Conflict – Decision-making and Western intervention in Namibia* (Manchester: Manchester University Press, 1990).

Jonas, S. *Of Centaurs and Doves, Guatemala's Peace Process* (Boulder, Colo.: Westview Press, 2000).

Kaufman, S.J. *Modern Hatreds: the Symbolic Politics of Ethnic War* (Ithaca, NY: Cornell University Press, 2001).

Kecskemeti, P. 'Political Rationality in Ending War', in W.T.R. Fox (ed.), *How Wars End* (Philadelphia: The Annals of the American Academy of Political and Social Science, 1970), pp. 105–15.

Kertzer, D. *Ritual, Politics and Power* (New Haven: Yale University Press, 1988).

Kissinger, H. *The White House Years* (London: Weidenfeld & Nicolson, 1979).

Kleibor, M. *International Mediation: the Multiple Realities of Third Party Intervention* (Boulder: Lynne Rienner, 1997).

Kriesberg, L. & S.J. Thornson (eds), *Timing the De-escalation of International Conflicts* (New York: Syracuse University Press, 1991).

Kruger, B.W. 'Prenegotiation in South Africa (1985–1993) – a Phaseological Analysis of the Transitional Negotiations', unpublished MA thesis, University of Stellenbosch, 1998.

Kymlicka, W. *Multicultural Citizenship: a Liberal Theory of Minority Rights* (Oxford: Oxford University Press, 1995).

Lal, B.V. & T. R. Vakatora (eds) *Fiji and the World* (Suva: University of the South Pacific, 1997).

Lapidoth, R. *Autonomy: Flexible Solutions to Ethnic Conflicts* (Washington, DC: United States Institute of Peace, 1997).

Lederach, J.P. *Building Peace: Sustainable Reconciliation in Divided Societies* (Washington, DC: United States Institute of Peace, 1997).

Lederach, J.P. 'Qualities of Practice for Reconciliation', in R. Helmick (ed.), *Reconciliation* (New York: Templeton Press, 2001).

Lederman, J. *Battle Lines: the American Media and the Intifada* (New York: Henry Holt, 1992).

Lemarchand, R. *Burundi: Ethnocide as Discourse and Practice* (Washington, DC: Woodrow Wilson Center Press, 1994).

Letamendia, F. & J. Loughlin, 'Peace in the Basque Country and Corsica', in M. Cox, A. Guelke & F. Stephen, *A Farewell to Arms? From 'Long War' to Long Peace in Northern Ireland* (Manchester: Manchester University Press, 2000).

Leys, C. & J. S. Saul (eds) *Namibia's Liberation Struggle – the Two-Edged Sword* (London: James Currey, 1995).

Lieberfield, D. *Talking with the Enemy: Negotiation and Threat Perception in South Africa and Israel/Palestine* (New York: Praeger, 1999).

Lijphart, A. *Democracy in Plural Societies* (New Haven, Conn.: Yale University Press, 1977).

Lodge, T. *South African Politics since 1994* (Cape Town and Johannesburg: David Philip, 1999).

Loughlin, J. *Regionalism and Ethnic Nationalism in France: a Case Study of Corsica* (Florence: European University Institute, 1989).

Loughlin, J. *Subnational Democracy in the European Union: Challenges and Opportunities* (Oxford: Oxford University Press, 2001).

Loughlin, J., C. Olivesi & F. Daftary (eds) *Autonomies Insulaires: vers une politique de différence pour la Corse?* (Ajaccio: Editions Albiana, 1999).

McGarry, J. & B. O'Leary, *The Politics of Ethnic Conflict Regulation* (New York: Routledge, 1993).

McGarry, J. & B. O'Leary, *Explaining Northern Ireland: Broken Images* (Oxford: Blackwell, 1995).

Mac Ginty, R. & J. Darby, *Guns and Government: the Management of the Northern Ireland Peace Process* (London: Palgrave – now Palgrave Macmillan, 2002).

Makovsky, D. *Making Peace with the PLO: the Rabin Government's Road to the Oslo Process* (Boulder, Colo.: Westview Press, 1995).

Mallie, E. & D. McKittrick, *The Fight for Peace: the Secret Story behind the Irish Peace Process* (London: Heinemann, 1996).

Manlow, R. *The Mass Media and Social Violence: Is There a Role for the Media in Preventing and Moderating Ethnic, National, and Religious Conflict?* (New York: Center for War, Peace, and the News Media, New York University, 1996).

Marais, H. *South African Limits to Change: the Political Economy of Transformation* (London: Zed Books and Cape Town: University of Cape Town Press, 2000).

Marx, A.W. *Making Race and Nation: a Comparison of South Africa, the United States and Brazil* (Cambridge: Cambridge University Press, 1998).

Mees, L. 'The Basque Peace Process, Nationalism and Political Violence', in J. Darby & R. Mac Ginty (eds), *The Management of Peace Processes* (London: Macmillan – now Palgrave Macmillan, 2000).

Mitchell, C. *The Structure of International Conflict* (London: Macmillan – now Palgrave Macmillan, 1981).

Mitchell, C. 'External Peace-making Initiatives and Intranational Conflict', in M.I. Midlarsky (ed.), *The Internationalization of Communal Strife* (New York: Routledge, 1992).

Mitchell, C. *Gestures of Reconciliation* (London: Macmillan – now Palgrave Macmillan, 2000).

Mitchell, G. *Making Peace* (New York: Knopf, 1999).

Moreno, L. *Federalizing the Spanish State* (London: Frank Cass, 2000).

Moses, R.L. *Freeing the Hostages* (Pittsburgh: University of Pittsburgh Press, 1996).

Nordquist, K.J. 'Boundary Disputes: Drawing the Line', in I.W. Zartman (ed.), *Preventive Diplomacy: Avoiding Conflict Escalation* (Lanham: Rowman & Littlefield, 2000).

Norlen, T. *A Study of the Ripe Moment for Conflict Resolution and its Applicability to Two Periods in the Israeli–Palestinian Conflict* (Uppsala: Uppsala University Conflict Resolution Program, 1995).

Ohlson, T. & S. Stedman, *The New Is Not Yet Born* (Washington, DC: Brookings, 1994).

Olson, M. *The Logical of Collective Action* (Schocken, 1965).

Olzack, S. & J. Nagel (eds) *Competitive Ethnic Relations* (Orlando: Academic Press, 1986).

Omi, M. & H. Winant, *Racial Formation in the United States from the 1960s to the 1990s* (New York: Routledge, 1994).

Posen, B. 'The Security Dilemma and Ethnic Conflict', in Michael Brown (ed.), *Ethnic Conflict and International Security* (Princeton, NJ: Princeton University Press, 1993).

Pruitt, D. & P. Olczak, 'Approaching to Resolving Seemingly Intractable Conflict', in B. Bunker & J. Rubin (eds), *Conflict, Cooperation and Justice* (New York: Jossey-Bass, 1995).

Prunier, G. *The Rwanda Crisis: History of a Genocide* (New York: Columbia University Press, 1995).

Przeworski, A. *Democracy and the Market* (Cambridge: Cambridge University Press, 1991).

Quandt, W. *Camp David* (Washington, DC: Brookings, 1986).

Rabinovich, I. *The Brink of Peace: the Israeli–Syrian Negotiations* (Princeton: Princeton University Press, 1998).

Rabushka, A. & K.A. Shepsle, *Politics in Plural Society: a Theory of Political Instability* (Columbus: Charles E. Merrill Publishing Company, 1972).

Ramphele, M. 'Law, Corruption and Morality', in W. James & L. Van de Vijvers (eds), *After the TRC: Reflections on Truth and Reconciliation in South Africa* (Cape Town: David Philip, 2000).

Reilly, B. & A. Reynolds, 'Electoral Systems and Conflict in Divided Societies', in Paul C. Stern & Daniel Druckman (eds), *International Conflict Resolution after the Cold War* (Washington, DC: National Academy Press, 2000).

Roach, C. 'Information and Culture in War and Peace: Overview', in C. Roach (ed.), *Communication and Culture in War and Peace* (Newbury Park: Sage, 1993).

Rothchild, D. *Managing Ethnic Conflict in Africa* (Washington, DC: Brookings, 1997).

Rothstein, R. *After the Peace: Resistance and Reconciliation* (Boulder, Colo.: Lynne Rienner, 1999).

Said, E.W. *Peace and its Discontents* (London: Vintage, 1995).

Said, E.W. *The End of the Peace Process* (New York: Pantheon, 2000).

Samuels, R. *et al.*, *Political Generations and Political Development* (Boston: Lexington, 1977).

Savir, U. *The Process* (New York: Randon House, 1998).

Seegers, A. *The Military in the Making of Modern South Africa* (London: I. B. Tauris, 1996).

Sen, A. *Collective Choice and Social Welfare* (San Francisco: Holden-Day, 1970).

Shaw, R.P. & Y. Wong, *Genetic Seeds of Warfare: Evolution, Nationalism, and Patriotism* (Boston: Unwin Hyman, 1989).

Shear, J. 'Riding the Tiger: the UN and Cambodia', in W.J. Durch (ed.), *UN Peacekeeping, American Policy, and the Uncivil Wars of the 1990s* (New York: Saint Martin's Press – now Palgrave Macmillan, 1996), pp. 170–2.

Sisk, T.D. *Democratization in South Africa – the Elusive Social Contract* (Princeton, NJ: Princeton University Press, 1995).

Sisk, T. *Power Sharing and International Mediation in Ethnic Conflicts* (Washington, DC: United States Institute of Peace Press, 1995).

Smith, A.D. *The Ethnic Origin of Nations* (Oxford: Basil Blackwell, 1986).

Smock, D.R. (ed.), *Making War and Waging Peace* (Washington, DC: USIP Press, 1993).

Spence, S., M. Lanchin & G. Thale, *From Elections to Earthquakes: Reform and Participation in Post-War El Salvador* (Cambridge, Mass.: Hemisphere Initiatives, 2001).

Stedman, S.J. *Peacemaking in Civil Wars: International Mediation in Zimbabwe, 1974–1980* (Boulder: Lynne Rienner, 1991).

Stein, J. & L. Pauly (eds) *Choosing to Cooperate: How States Avoid Loss* (Baltimore: The Johns Hopkins University Press, 1992).

Strobel, S. *Late Breaking Foreign Policy: the News Media's Influence on Peace Operations* (Washington, DC: United States Institute of Peace Press, 1997).

Tamir, Y. *Liberal Nationalism* (Princeton: Princeton University Press, 1995).

Teitel, R. *Transitional Justice* (New York: Oxford University Press, 2000).

Touval, S. *The Peace Brokers* (Princeton: Princeton University Press, 1982).

Touval, S. & I.W. Zartman (eds) *International Mediation in Theory and Practice* (Boulder, Colo.: Westview, 1985).

Turner, B. *Organisational Symbolism* (Berlin: Walter de Gruyter, 1990).

United Nations, *The United Nations and El Salvador 1990–1995*, Blue Book Series, Vol. IV (New York: United Nations Department of Public Information, 1995) (also known as the 'United Nations Blue Book').

Urwin, D. 'Territorial Structures and Political Developments in the United Kingdom', in S. Rokkan & D. Urwin (eds), *The Politics of Territorial Identity* (London: Sage Publications, 1982).

Wagner, R.H. 'The Causes of Peace', in R. Licklider (ed.), *Stopping the Killing: How Civil Wars End* (New York: New York University Press, 1993).

Waters, M. *Ethnic Options: Choosing Identities in America* (Cambridge: Harvard University Press, 1990).

Wolfsfeld, G. *Media and Political Conflict: News from the Middle East* (Cambridge: Cambridge University Press, 1997).

Wolfsfeld, G. *News about the Other in Jordan and Israel: Does Peace Make a Difference?* (forthcoming).

Wood, E. *Forging Democracy from Below: Insurgent Transitions in South Africa and El Salvador* (Cambridge, UK: Cambridge University Press, 2001).

Yack, B. 'The Myth of the Civic Nation', in Ronald Beiner (ed.), *Theorizing Nationalism* (Albany: State University of New York Press, 1999), pp. 103–18.

Young, C. *The Politics of Cultural Pluralism* (Madison: University of Wisconsin Press, 1976).

Young, C. (ed.), *The Rising Tide of Cultural Pluralism* (Madison: University of Wisconsin Press, 1993).

Young, C. *The African Colonial State in Comparative Perspective* (New Haven: Yale University Press, 1994).

Young, C. (ed.), *The Accommodation of Cultural Diversity: Case Studies* (Basingstoke: Macmillan – now Palgrave Macmillan, 1999).

Young, C. (ed.), *Ethnic diversity and Public Policy: a Comparative Inquiry* (Basingstoke: Macmillan – now Palgrave Macmillan, 1999).

Zahar, M. 'Fanatics, Mercenaries, Brigands ... and Politicians: Militia Decision-Making and Civil Conflict Resolution', PhD dissertation, McGill University, Canada, 2000.

Zartman, I.W. 'The Strategy of Preventive Diplomacy in Third World Conflicts', in A. George (ed.), *Managing US–Soviet Rivalry* (Boulder, Colo.: Westview, 1983).

Zartman, I.W. *Ripe for Resolution: Conflict and Intervention in Africa* (New York: Oxford University Press, 1985).

Zartman, I.W. 'Ripening Conflict, Ripe Moment, Formula and Mediation', in D. BenDahmane & J. McDonald (eds), *Perspectives on Negotiation* (Washington, DC: Government Printing Office, 1986).

Zartman, I.W. 'Ripeness: the Hurting Stalemate and Beyond', in P.C. Stern & D. Druckman (eds), *International Conflict Resolution after the Cold War* (Washington, DC: National Academy Press, 2000), pp. 225–50.

Zartman. I.W. & J. Aurik, 'Power Strategies in De-escalation', in L. Kriesberg & J. Thornson (eds), *Timing the De-escalation of International Conflicts* (Syracuse: Syracuse University Press, 1991).

Zartman, I.W. & M.R. Berman, *The Practical Negotiator* (New Haven: Yale University Press, 1982).

Index

Printed in the United States
20115LVS00001B/275